YOU CAN END ABUSE AND
TAKE BACK YOUR LIFE

GINNY NICARTHY, M.S.W.

seal press

Getting Free
You Can End Abuse and Take Back Your Life

The activity lists "Warning Signs Your Partner Is Not Changing" and "Signs He May Be Changing" have been adapted and reproduced with permission of EMERGE Counseling and Education to Stop Domestic Violence.

The activity list "Steps for Safety Planning at Home" and the sections "Children's Visits with Their Father" and "Helping Children Who Have Witnessed Violence" have been adapted and reproduced with permission of authors Meg Crager and Lily Anderson from "Helping Children Who Witness Domestic Violence: A Guide for Parents."

The checklist "Danger Assessment" is reproduced with permission of author Jacquelyn Campbell.

The "Know Your Rights" tip sheet has been reproduced with permission of the Northwest Immigration Rights Project.

"Technology Safety Planning with Survivors: Tips to Discuss if Someone You Know Is in Danger" by Cindy Southworth, Shawndell Dawson, and Cynthia Fraser of the Safety Net Project at the National Network to End Domestic Violence Fund has been reproduced with their permission.

Wheels on pages xxvi, 406, 407, 410, and 411 (Power and Control Wheel, Poder y Control Wheel, Equality Wheel, and Igualidad Wheel) developed by the Domestic Abuse Intervention Project, 202 East Superior Street, Duluth, MN 55802, 218-722-4134; downloaded from the web site (www.ncdsv.org) of the National Center on Domestic and Sexual Violence, Austin TX.
Wheels on pages 408 and 409 (Teen Power and Control Wheel and Igualidad Para Los Jovenes) adapted from the Power and Control Wheel, developed by the Domestic Abuse Intervention Project, Duluth, MN; downloaded from the web site (www.ncdsv.org) of the National Center on Domestic and Sexual Violence, Austin TX.
Wheel on pages 412 (Lesbian and Gay Power and Control Wheel), developed by Roe and Jagodinksy, inspired and adapted from the Domestic Abuse Intervention Project, Duluth, MN; downloaded from the web site (www.ncdsv.org) of the National Center on Domestic and Sexual Violence, Austin TX.

Some photos and illustrations are used by permission and are the property of the original copyright owners.

Published by Seal Press
An Imprint of Avalon Publishing Group, Inc.
1400 65th Street, Suite 250
AVALON
Emeryville, CA 94608

Cataloging-in-publication data has been applied for.

ISBN 1-58005-122-7

Fourth edition
9 8 7 6 5 4 3 2 1

Cover and interior designed by Justin Marler
Printed in the United States of America by Edward Bros.
Distributed by Publishers Group West

ა

In memory of Susan Schechter.

With clarity and honesty, Susan documented the early days of our movement and then pointed the way to our future. Her great heart, discriminating mind, and spirited commitment will continue to inform the movement against abuse of women and children for many years to come.

ა

CONTENTS

SECTION VI ➳ SPECIAL CHALLENGES 253

How to Assess Your Danger
Understanding the Power and Control Wheels

INTRODUCTION TO THE NEW EDITION

If you have been emotionally abused or physically battered by an intimate partner and you want to change your life, then *Getting Free* is for you. You may have picked up this book because you need answers to the problems you are facing. *Getting Free* will not make decisions for you; only you can do that. But reading it will help you decide what you can do to protect yourself and find a safer, more satisfying life.

If you are in immediate crisis, call the free hot line of the National Domestic Violence Coalition (tel. 800/799-7233) to speak with a trained advocate who can find you the help you need. Then you might turn to Who This Book Is For and How to Use It, which will guide you in selecting the material to read first.

A GUIDE TO THE NEW EDITION

In 1982, when Seal Press first published *Getting Free,* the movement against the abuse of women had already made great strides. Successes included the formation of many shelters for women who were battered and the establishment of phone hot lines. Advocates for abused women joined in state and national coalitions to educate professionals and the public about the seriousness of the problem and to change laws. By the mid-nineties, these actions had many important effects, including passage of an important piece of congressional legislation, the 1994 Violence Against Women Act (VAWA). VAWA provided funds for resources for women, including the establishment of a National Domestic Violence Hotline (tel. 800/799-7233), available twenty-four hours a day, and the website www.ndvd.org. Now almost every community in the country— and many throughout the world—have at least one emergency phone line or shelter dedicated to helping abused women.

For all the achievements of the domestic-violence movement through the years, much remains to be done. In 1982 I addressed some issues only partially, based on the research available; the other issues were not part of the public discussion at the time. In a second edition of *Getting Free* in 1987, I added several chapters that addressed the crucial subjects of emotional abuse, teen abuse, and lesbian abuse. Since the publication of earlier editions of *Getting Free,* a great deal of research has enlarged our knowledge about topics discussed in the book. Yet much of the problem has remained essentially the same, and I have, with a few exceptions, let the chapters stand as originally written. For up-to-date information available on the Internet and for relevant books, you may want to check out the Resources section at the end of *Getting Free*. In this edition I've added five chapters. The first two, Immigrant Women: Challenges and Solutions and Religious Challenges, address often-invisible populations. The last three chapters form a new section titled Stopping the Cycle of Abuse. Based on recent research, they offer new perspectives: Men Who Batter: Can He Change?; Nurturing Your Children: Safety and Resilience; and Looking Forward.

In addition to the new chapters, this edition of *Getting Free* incorporates some important visual aids for understanding your situation. Three of the most important, with explanations on how to use them, are the Power and Control Wheel; the Safety Plan for You and Your Family; and the Danger Assessment list. They are found in Who This Book Is For and How to Use It. Because of their importance, these three are repeated in the Resources section in the back of the book for easy reference, along with other lists and "wheels."

In recent decades, advocates for abused women, the women themselves, and researchers have enhanced their knowledge about how men who batter use power tactics to control intimate partners. In this new edition, I've emphasized some of that new learning about evaluating danger and maximizing protection. I encourage you to look closely at the ways your spouse may have gradually stripped you of control over major aspects of your life. Paradoxically, facing that truth can steer you toward safety. The next chapter will set you on that path.

Ginny NiCarthy
Seattle
July 2004

WHO THIS BOOK IS FOR AND HOW TO USE IT

If you're a woman who has been physically or emotionally abused by a man you were intimately involved with, this book is for you. If you're still involved with the man, it may help you leave him. If you've already left him, or if you're abused by a child, parent, or a lover of the same sex, you'll also find parts of it useful. It may also help you if you're a professional counselor, a friend to a woman who's abused, or if you want to guard against becoming involved in such a relationship yourself.

Many of the ideas and activities in the book are directed to women who have been subjected to frequent and dangerous beatings for a long time and who are married or have children. Many are directed to women who have numerous fears, low self-esteem, little money, and few contacts with anyone other than the violent man. All of those women are likely to need a lot of help to change their lives. But most of the book applies to any woman who's been physically, sexually, or emotionally abused by anyone she's in an intimate relationship with. If you've been abused "only" once, the book will give you an idea of how hard it is to separate from the man when the abuse grows worse and the relationship lasts longer. Some questions may help you understand whether you've been abused or not.

PHYSICAL ABUSE

Since the problem has come to public attention, many women have asked themselves, "Am I abused?" "Am I a battered woman?" In this book I use "battered" to refer to physical assault. "Abuse" includes physical, sexual, or emotional attacks, from mild to lethal. The word you use to describe your situation is not important. It is important to recognize what's being done to you and to know you don't have to take it. Has your intimate partner done any of these things to you?

- pushed or shoved you
- held you to keep you from leaving
- slapped or bit you
- kicked or choked you
- hit or punched you
- thrown objects at you
- locked you out of the house
- abandoned you in dangerous places
- refused you help when you were sick, injured, or pregnant

- subjected you to reckless driving
- forced you off the road or kept you from driving
- raped you
- threatened or hurt you with a weapon

Which of those acts happened repetitively? Which of them resulted in bruises, cuts, or broken bones? Which of them were aimed at specific parts of your body, indicating the man was in control of his actions? Which required medical treatment, hospitalization, or resulted in permanent injury or disfigurement?

How many times or how often have you been assaulted one way or another? How many of them could have resulted in serious injury if the man had miscalculated? Have the assaults stayed about the same in frequency, or are they changing? If changing, how?

Perhaps by the time you answered the last question you became convinced you're battered. Or maybe the more dangerous assaults at the end of the questions caused you to think you're not so bad off, since you haven't had any broken bones or had a gun held to your head, yet.

Although some of these actions are clearly more dangerous than others, almost all of them are potentially dangerous and all show a lack of respect and an effort to intimidate and control you. Many men and women occasionally push, hold, or slap each other, but that doesn't necessarily make it right. If everyone in your neighborhood or family has always done those things, that doesn't mean you have to continue the pattern. One problem with accepting a certain level of abuse is that there's a tendency for the abusive man to interpret it as permission to escalate the assaults into more dangerous and more frequent acts. You're the only one who can decide how much is too much and what you're ready to do about it.

SEXUAL ABUSE

Sexual abuse is so common that it too is beginning to seem almost normal to some people. Women have historically had so little to say about their sexuality that it's a very confusing area for many of us. Ask yourself whether your partner has done any of these things to you:

- told anti-woman jokes or made demeaning remarks about women
- treated women as sex objects
- been jealously angry, assuming you would have sex with any available man
- insisted you dress in a more sexual way than you wanted
- minimized the importance of your feelings about sex

- criticized you sexually
- insisted on unwanted and uncomfortable touching
- withheld sex and affection
- called you sexual names such as "whore" or "frigid"
- forced you to strip when you didn't want to
- publicly showed sexual interest in other women
- had affairs with other women after agreeing to a monogamous relationship
- forced sex with him or others or forced you to watch others
- forced particular unwanted sexual acts
- forced sex after beating
- forced sex when you were sick or when it was a danger to your health
- forced sex for the purpose of hurting you with objects or weapons
- committed sadistic sexual acts

Have you been less interested in sex since you became involved with your partner or since he made particular demands? Do you feel less physically attractive than you did before? Do you feel sexually humiliated or ashamed, or do you believe no one else would want you sexually? Are you afraid to initiate what you want sexually?

You might give in to your partner's wish because you truly want to, and you know he'll do the same for you. But if you give in because you're afraid not to, or because you know he'll keep at you until he wears you down, it will be an important step to admit that he's really forcing you.

EMOTIONAL ABUSE

Emotional abuse is sometimes even harder than sexual abuse to define and recognize. Almost everyone does it at some time or other and many couples develop a habit of hurling insults at each other. It's often hard to determine who did what to whom first, especially if the injury is delivered in a subtle way. How many of these things has your partner done to you?

- ignored your feelings
- ridiculed or insulted women as a group
- ridiculed or insulted your most valued beliefs, your religion, race, heritage, or class
- withheld approval, appreciation, or affection as punishment
- continually criticized you, called you names, shouted at you
- insulted or drove away your friends or family
- humiliated you in private or public

- refused to socialize with you
- kept you from working, controlled your money, made all decisions
- refused to work or share money
- took car keys or money away
- regularly threatened to leave or told you to leave
- threatened to hurt you or your family
- punished or deprived the children when he was angry at you
- threatened to kidnap the children if you left him
- abused pets to hurt you
- told you about his affairs
- harassed you about affairs he imagined you were having
- manipulated you with lies and contradictions

The list could extend to countless pages and is more difficult to put in order of less damaging to more damaging behavior because the subtleties and frequency can make them mere slights or devastating humiliations. If there are things you were subjected to that don't fit into any of the items above, write them down.

If you did some of those things to your partner, the picture might be confusing. If you want to assign blame, it could make a difference who started it, who did what, most, and worst. But the first thing to recognize is whether you were abused. Once you see that, you can evaluate the consequences. If you're still in the relationship or have only recently left it, you might not be able to tell yet what the long-range damage is, but answering the following questions may give you some ideas about it.

- Did you often doubt your judgment or wonder if you were "crazy"?
- Were you often afraid of your partner and did you express your opinion less and less freely?
- Did you develop fears of other people and tend to see others less often?
- Did you spend a lot of time watching for his bad, and not so bad, moods before bringing up a subject?
- Did you ask permission to spend money, take classes, or socialize with friends, and have fears of doing the wrong thing or getting in trouble?
- Did you lose confidence in your abilities, become increasingly depressed, and feel trapped and powerless?

If you answered "Yes" to many of those questions, it's probable you changed as a result of being abused. If you think you deserved to be abused because you also abused your partner, consider that your actions don't negate the problem. Rather, they indicate you have two problems:

your abuse and his. If you make a commitment to respect and protect yourself, you may find yourself being less abusive as well.

IMPORTANT TOOLS TO HELP YOU UNDERSTAND YOUR SITUATION

Power and Control Wheels

Turn to the Power and Control Wheel (see page xxvi; it is repeated in the back of the book for easy reference, along with other important tools to help you understand your situation). Intimidation, isolation, insults, economic and other types of control—the "spokes" of the wheel—can wear away your confidence, your sense of independence, and your will to resist. Most abused women say emotional abuse or tactics of power and control are more difficult to deal with than physical assaults. If you have been subjected to them you may have begun to believe there is something wrong with *you.*

When you feel beaten down by "spokes" of insults, intimidation, and control of your life, you can lose sight of the extreme physical danger hovering on the "rim."

If you are physically attacked—and even if you are seriously injured—you might feel relieved, knowing it is the perpetrator's fault. Clearly it is not something you did or something you imagined or exaggerated. It is right there in black and blue. Or in a bone fracture. Like the rim of the wheel, physical assault and the threat of it hold the system together. Each tactic can cause serious damage on its own. But each form of control reinforces the others and eventually you feel their combined demoralizing effect.

To leave or to stay—each option is frightening and that fear is one reason most abused women both stay *and* leave. They leave and return an average of seven times before a final separation. Maybe every time you are physically attacked you tell yourself you will leave—tomorrow. But when tomorrow comes your will is stifled by exhaustion, pain, fear, or your partner's apology. Or the worst is over, so you sigh in relief. Your partner's daily control tactics might fade in importance. In *Getting Free,* I try not to lose sight of either the "spokes" or the "rim." But to clarify the hazards of each, it is sometimes necessary temporarily to separate them.

When you look at the spokes of the Power and Control Wheel, you might think "Oh, that's not such a big deal. It's not as if I'm getting beat up all the time." It can be humiliating to admit that you have been deeply affected by what the abusive person has done to you. But your

VIOLENCE

physical · **sexual**

COERCION AND THREATS:
Making and/or carrying out threats to do something to hurt her. Threatening to leave her, commit suicide, or report her to welfare. Making her drop charges. Making her do illegal things.

INTIMIDATION:
Making her afraid by using looks, actions, and gestures. Smashing things. Destroying her property. Abusing pets. Displaying weapons.

MALE PRIVILEGE:
Treating her like a servant: making all the big decisions, acting like the "master of the castle," being the one to define men's and women's roles.

EMOTIONAL ABUSE:
Putting her down. Making her feel bad about herself. Calling her names. Making her think she's crazy. Playing mind games. Humiliating her. Making her feel guilty.

POWER AND CONTROL

ECONOMIC ABUSE:
Preventing her from getting or keeping a job. Making her ask for money. Giving her an allowance. Taking her money. Not letting her know about or have access to family income.

ISOLATION:
Controlling what she does, who she sees and talks to, what she reads, and where she goes. Limiting her outside involvement. Using jealousy to justify actions.

USING CHILDREN:
Making her feel guilty about the children. Using the children to relay messages. Using visitation to harass her. Threatening to take the children away.

MINIMIZING, DENYING, AND BLAMING:
Making light of the abuse and not taking her concerns about it seriously. Saying the abuse didn't happen. Shifting responsibility for abusive behavior. Saying she caused it.

physical · **sexual**

VIOLENCE

psychological makeup and even your sense of identity may be getting "beat up." Emotional abuse *is* a big deal and it can damage the strongest of people. The techniques have been used successfully by experts to break the will of prisoners of war and other captive peoples. See the chapter Emotional Abuse for ways to cope with the impact of those tactics. Your first step is to admit what has been done to you. The second step is to recognize that even if you are badly bent, you are not broken, or you wouldn't be reading this book.

Safety Plan

Even if you have not been hit or injured, if your partner emotionally abuses or tries to control you, it is important to plan for an emergency escape. *Many abusive people eventually escalate their mistreatment from emotional abuse to violence.* If you have recovered a couple of times from a black eye or even from a broken jaw, you might feel as if you can take whatever comes your way. But over time, if you have been assaulted, restrained, or threatened, those tactics will probably be used against you more often and your injuries will be more severe. That might happen gradually through a number of years or suddenly without warning. If it is gradual, you might not notice how much more psychological or physical danger you are facing.

To escape either type of threat, you might have to get away from the batterer quickly. Some emotionally abusive controlling men do not use violent tactics at all *until they are threatened by the loss of an intimate relationship.* Then everything can change overnight. The power and control tactics your partner uses to keep you under close watch can make it difficult to get away safely. You need to plan so that if it becomes necessary, you can leave as safely as possible. If it turns out that you never have to try to get away, the plan can still help you feel secure.

Take a look at Safety Plan for You and Your Family on the next page (this safety plan, like the Power and Control Wheel, is repeated in the back of the book for ease of reference, along with other important tools). Put a check mark next to each action you have already taken. Maybe you have called a domestic-violence hot line or shelter, or you have taught your children how to dial 911. Circle the dot beside each one that you can do right away. If you are not in immediate danger, give yourself a little time for those tasks. Packing a bag with essentials in case you have to leave in a hurry or providing your children's school with information might take a little while. But put a date next to each of the items that will take time as a reminder to take care of them—within the week if possible.

SAFETY PLAN FOR YOU AND YOUR FAMILY

Make a safety plan before you are in immediate danger.

If you are being assaulted or are threatened with assault call 911.

If you need help drafting a safety plan, call the Domestic Violence Hotline at 800/799-SAFE (800/787-3224 TTY).

Think of a safe place you can go to in an emergency and plan how you would get there:

• Practice the route, whether it is running to a neighbor's, driving your car to a police station, or getting to a safe place that is open 24 hours and where you can use a phone and be picked up by a friend.

• Talk to a neighbor about what kind of signal you can give that will serve as an alert for help, such as turning a light on and off, yelling a particular word, or banging on a wall in a specific way. Ask the neighbor to call 911 if you use the signal.

• Pack a bag with important papers (protection order, extra checks, and other documents listed in "Safety Plan for Staying or Leaving" in Chapter 25 Immigrant Women: Challenges and Solutions), money or a credit card for a cab or motel, an extra set of clothing, favorite toys for your children, and any medications. Leave the bag with a reliable friend.

• If you plan to use your car to get away keep an extra key with you at all times. Keep an extra key to your house with you as well.

• Memorize telephone numbers of the national hotline and your local shelter or hotline.

AT HOME

• Go to a room that has a way to get out.

• Go to a room that has a phone and a door that can be locked if you cannot get to a room with a way out.

• Stay out of the kitchen and bathroom (where there are things that can be used as weapons).

• Use the plan you have made to escape the house and/or to get help from a neighbor.

• Teach your children how to use your safety plan.

AT WORK

• Let a trusted coworker know about any danger you are in. Let him or her know about any phone harassment on the job.

• If it seems safe, talk to your boss about your safety.

• If you are or might be harassed by phone at work, ask for help in making your phone secure. If there are security guards, let them know that you are in danger, especially if you are being stalked. Show the guards a picture of the person to look out for.

• If you drive to and from work, ask to be escorted to your car. If the parking lot is not well lighted, ask to have it made safer.

• Vary your route each day, in case you are being followed.

• If you walk to a bus stop, try to be accompanied by coworkers.

SAFETY FOR YOUR CHILDREN

• Teach your children how and when to dial 911.

• See the "Safety Plan if You Leave" in Chapter 28 Nurturing Your Children, and Chapter 15 Protecting Yourself and the Children ("Making the Decision; Planning for the Emergency").

The best plan will incorporate most of these suggestions, but will also take into account your particular situation. An advocate at the national hotline can help you make a plan that is best for you. She can also give you a number for a local shelter or hotline where you can get similar advice from someone who knows your community.

It can be harrowing to face reality, especially the first time. It takes courage to focus mentally and emotionally on how to run from violence or to teach your children how to live with the threat of it. But as you complete the exercise, keep in mind that in the long run it will lower your anxiety. As you read this book you can fine-tune the plan, depending on your circumstances. Meanwhile, you have concrete ways to keep yourself as safe as possible. This should reassure you as you look at the Danger Assessment questions that are coming up.

Danger Assessment

There are two parts to using this questionnaire (like the Power and Control Wheel and the safety plan, the Danger Assessment questionnaire is repeated in the back of the book for easy reference). First, have a calendar handy. One that shows the entire year is best. Look at the items on the Danger Assessment list numbered 1 to 5; start with "Slapping." On your calendar put an X on the date of each violent incident you experienced. Then add a number that corresponds to the degree of danger you experienced or the seriousness of the injuries: Number 1, slapping, for instance, without lasting pain or injuries, through Number 5, for wounds or use of a weapon.

If you have been abused frequently you may feel overwhelmed by this task. If that is a problem begin by filling out the calendar just for this month. Then turn to three months ago and mark those dates. Next add information for six months earlier and then for one year ago. Later, for a more accurate picture of trends, fill in the missing months. Maybe you have been telling yourself, "It isn't that bad," or "So long as it doesn't get worse I can stand it." The Xs on your calendar and the numbers after them indicating severity give you an idea of what to expect in the future. Again, you can't be sure, but consider the possible implications of these questions: Have the incidents of abuse become more frequent during the course of the year? Is the severity increasing? Either one is a sign of danger. You should now be able to answer Question 1 pretty accurately.

Next put a check mark on the line next to each question to which your answer is "yes." The more items you check, the more likely you are to be in serious danger. But it is important to keep in mind that the questions are based on the collective responses of many women and won't all apply precisely to you. We're looking at what is *likely*. This exercise is similar to going through your house and noting that a wire is loose or there are oil-soaked rags in the garage. Those danger signs may have been present for the last ten years without the house burning down. But statistically, the more fire hazards there are, the more likely it is that a fire will start. If you couldn't replace the faulty wiring right away, you would at least want to have a plan to get out of the house in case of fire.

The Danger Assessment questionnaire was designed to discover what events or situations tend to place battered women at the most risk of being killed by partners. Researchers asked women whose partners had tried to kill them, and friends and relatives of women who had actually been killed, about their situations before the attempted or actual homicide. Then they compiled their answers to come up with a list of items that were most commonly present when abusers tried, successfully or not, to kill their spouses.[1]

The questions are not perfect indicators of the worst form of danger. Statistics about groups of people make no guarantees about what will happen to an individual. A small sample of the women who were killed, or nearly so, had no warning of what was coming. The Danger Assessment questionnaire would not have predicted serious danger. If you have not experienced many of the types of abuse listed and if your partner doesn't fit into the categories listed, that *might* indicate you are not likely to be in danger. You just can't be sure. But if you checked many items on the list, you almost certainly *are* in danger. And as every schoolchild knows, even if your wiring seems safe and there are no oily rags in the garage, the family should still have a plan to escape unpredictable fire.

The Danger Assessment studies did not address two important questions. How many of those women made safety plans and how many were able to follow them? A different study found that of women who were raped, physically abused, or stalked by partners, only 20 percent had protection orders to keep the abuser away.[2] Contrast that fact with this one: Of women who *did* obtain a permanent civil protection order, 80 percent experienced a reduction in the risk of police-reported physical violence.[3] If you have separated from your partner, your safety plan probably includes an order of protection. Many men who batter ignore such orders, but the statistics above suggest they have saved women's lives.

This is a good time to review your marked calendar once more. Your responses to the Danger Assessment questionnaire might have triggered memories of abuse you had put out of your mind. If you remember still more abusive events, revise the assessment accordingly. The assessment should inspire you to put more of your safety plan into effect. A realistic assessment of danger and a realistic safety plan go together.

DANGER ASSESSMENT

Jacquelyn C. Campbell, Ph.D., R.N.

Copyright, 2003

Several risk factors have been associated with increased risk of homicides (murders) of women and men in violent relationships. We cannot predict what will happen in your case, but we would like you to be aware of the danger of homicide in situations of abuse and for you to see how many of the risk factors apply to your situation.

Using the calendar, please mark the approximate dates during the past year when you were abused by your partner or ex-partner. Write on that date how bad the incident was according to the following scale:

1. Slapping, pushing; no injuries and/or lasting pain
2. Punching, kicking; bruises, cuts, and/or continuing pain
3. "Beating up"; severe contusions, burns, broken bones
4. Threat to use weapon; head injury, internal injury, permanent injury
5. Use of weapon; wounds from weapon

(If any of the descriptions for the higher number apply, use the higher number.)

Mark "Yes" or "No" for each of the following. ("He" refers to your husband, partner, ex-husband, ex-partner, or whoever is currently physically hurting you.)

_____ 1. Has the physical violence increased in severity or frequency over the past year?

_____ 2. Does he own a gun?

_____ 3. Have you left him after living together during the past year?

3a. (If you have never lived with him, check here. _____)

_____ 4. Is he unemployed?

_____ 5. Has he ever used a weapon against you or threatened you with a lethal weapon? (If yes, was the weapon a gun? _____)

_____ 6. Does he threaten to kill you?

_____ 7. Has he avoided being arrested for domestic violence?

_____ 8. Do you have a child who is not his?

_____ 9. Has he ever forced you to have sex when you did not wish to do so?

_____ 10. Does he ever try to choke you?

_____ 11. Does he use illegal drugs? By drugs, I mean "uppers" or amphetamines, speed, angel dust, cocaine, "crack," street drugs, or mixtures.

_____ 12. Is he an alcoholic or problem drinker?

_____ 13. Does he control most or all of your daily activities? For instance: Does he tell you who you can be friends with, when you can see your family, how much money you can use, or when you can take the car? (If he tries, but you do not let him, check here. _____)

_____ 14. Is he violently and constantly jealous of you? (For instance, does he say "If I can't have you, no one can."?)

_____ 15. Have you ever been beaten by him while you were pregnant? (If you have never been pregnant by him, check here. _____)

_____ 16. Have you ever threatened or tried to commit suicide?

_____ 17. Has he ever threatened or tried to commit suicide?

_____ 18. Does he threaten to harm your children?

_____ 19. Do you believe he is capable of killing you?

_____ 20. Does he follow or spy on you, leave threatening notes or messages on your answering machine, destroy your property, or call you when you don't want him to?

_____ Total "Yes" Answers

Thank you. Please talk to your nurse, advocate, or counselor about what the Danger Assessment means in terms of your situation.

As you read the rest of *Getting Free*, try to keep each of these exercises in mind. I refer to them in other chapters and I urge you to go back to them whenever you have questions about the degree of your danger or whether you have done all you can to be safe. The basic Power and Control Wheel is meant to provide an at-a-glance summary of what you face every day or every week. Special wheels for the new chapters on children and immigrants and for the established chapters on teens and lesbians all appear in the Resources section at the back of the book. You may want to copy wheels that capture your situation and keep them where they are easily accessible. If you are living with an abuser, store them in a place where he can't find them.

Each of the tools described above can be crucial aids in helping you make the decision to leave or stay and in carrying out the choice you make in the safest way you can. Appreciating the power of control tactics that are not violent, staying aware of the hazards you face, and following a well-designed safety plan can mean the difference between life and death for you and your children.

HOW TO READ THIS BOOK

If Your Situation Is Urgent

If you are in crisis, I strongly urge you to start with the tools above. If you are an immigrant, you may want to turn directly to Chapter 25, Immigrant Women: Challenges and Solutions, and begin with the specific part of the Safety Plan section that suggests how you can secure important documents and what to expect if you call the police. Then you might read the rest of the chapter, which gives you ideas about how to find help tailored to your situation and how to handle immigration status questions.

If you have children, first you can read Chapter 28, Nurturing Your Children: Safety and Resilience. You might start with the safety section, which tells you how to protect your children whether you stay or leave. If your crisis is related to custody, read that section so that you can protect yourself from courts that don't yet understand the ramifications of battering on children. You might then continue reading about how to help your kids be resilient.

When an abusive partner has used your religious beliefs to control you, a spiritual crisis might seem worse than a life-threatening event. In that case, you might begin with Chapter 26, Religious Challenges. You can read about eminent leaders from several religions and the ideas they have about the intersection of religion and abuse. A section in Chapter 9 deals with how to choose and evaluate professional helpers, but Chapter 26 adds to that by helping you evaluate religious advisers. If you have begun to doubt your own religious judgment, the ideas here should help restore your confidence.

Maybe you have to act soon on a decision to leave or stay. That might take you to Chapter 6, Making the Decision, or to Chapter 14, The First Week. Chapter 14 discusses the pros and cons of moving into a shelter or staying with relatives.

If You Are Not in Immediate Danger

If you are not in immediate danger, you may want to continue through the chapters on social aspects of abuse and historical changes in marriage and the family. With those ideas as background, you'll be encouraged to weigh your obligations to yourself and to the relationship, so that by the last chapter of Section I (Making the Decision to Leave or Stay), you'll be better prepared to decide whether to leave your abusive partner or to stay. The next sections give advice on how to choose and evaluate professional helpers and how to be your own counselor. Section IV (After You Leave) discusses various practical and emotional problems you'll encounter if you decide to leave the man. Section V (The Ones Who Got Away) relates experiences of women who were battered and who left their partners, and it includes advice from them based on their experiences.

When You Are Not Sure What to Do

You might be afraid you can never change your life. If you are sure you will be in a worse situation if you leave the man, you might want to begin with Chapter 21, The Ones Who Got Away. When you see that others, not so different from you, have gotten free and radically changed their lives, you might turn to Chapter 1 and read the rest of the book straight through. If you are so depressed or filled with self-hatred that you're nearly immobilized, you can start with Chapter 10, You Can Be Your Own Counselor.

You might think you should leave, but you hold out hope that your husband or partner will change. Chapter 27—Men Who Batter: Can They Change?—gives you an opportunity to learn about programs and groups for violent men. It gives you tools to evaluate whether it is a likelihood that your partner will change.

If you are a lesbian or a teenager (or a friend of one), turn to the chapters on those topics to see how abuse is different or the same for you as for others that this book addresses. In the Resources section in the back of the book, you will find a Power and Control Wheel specifically designed to help you recognize the techniques used against you. It will help you find your way out of your situation if that is what you want. In other chapters of the book, you will find that many solutions to your problems are the same as for the others. Some will be different for you because of your age or sexual orientation.

Chapter 22, Emotional Abuse, is for everyone. The Chart of Coercion is in some ways similar to the Power and Control tactics shown on the wheels, but it is different in other respects. You may want to pay special attention to the "crazy-making" examples. The questionnaires in that chapter are additional tools to help you recognize your situation.

Begin with the part of the book that looks most useful to you. You might reread some chapters, and they will have different meanings to you at different times. How they strike you will depend on your situation and what changes you've made in how you think about yourself, your partner, and your life.

If there is a concern that isn't covered in a single chapter, look in the table of contents for the parts of chapters that will tell you what you want to know. If you have a (personal) rule that says you must read a book from beginning to end without "skipping," please consider breaking it now. This could be an opportunity to take the first step toward doing what's good for you rather than following other people's outmoded rules. Feel free also to break that old rule about never writing in a book. This one is meant to be written in. Just be sure you keep it in a safe place.

When *Getting Free* was first published, not many books on the subject were available. Now there are so many that it is difficult to choose among them. In the Resources section at the back of the book, I have listed a few of the classics in the field and the most important new ones that speak directly to women who are abused or to their children. Much of the most up-to-date information is to be found on websites, and they are even more daunting to choose from because there are so many. Most of those listed in the Resources section have many links so you can just click a few times and you will find a wealth of information. You may be disabled, an immigrant, speak a language other than English, or you are a lesbian or a woman of color. You might live in a rural area or perhaps you are without a home. Something on the Internet can help you, regardless of your situation. In the Internet section of Resources, you will find an Internet safety plan, called Technology Safety Planning with Survivors: Tips to Discuss if Someone You Know Is in Danger.

A Note to Advocates, Friends, and Relatives of a Woman Who Is Battered

If you are a professional counselor or a friend of an abused woman, read *Getting Free* yourself and then pass it on to your client or friend, suggesting that she read whatever parts seem most appropriate for her situation. She may be able to focus on only one small part at a time, depending on how great a crisis she is in. Encourage her to write in the book and to do the activities. Offer to keep the book in a safe place for her if it is likely to be found by her partner. If some of the activities are not appropriate for her special situation, the two of you can make whatever modifications are useful.

In the first edition of *Getting Free* I said, "There remains a great deal to be learned about abuse." That is still true in spite of the great advances we have made in understanding domestic violence and what to do about it. It is still my hope, as I wrote then, that whoever reads this book will view it not so much as the answer but as a few more steps toward understanding a problem that affects us all. Professionals and victims—women and men—need to teach each other so that we can put an end to violence.

MAKING THE DECISION TO LEAVE OR STAY

CHAPTER 1

SOCIAL AND POLITICAL ASPECTS OF ABUSE

One of the most painful aspects of being abused by a man you love is a feeling of being alone with the problem. That emotional isolation often leads to a feeling of "I must be crazy." Fortunately, this situation is changing as more people are learning that abuse of women by their male partners is widespread. Somewhere between 25 percent and 50 percent of women who have intimate relationships with men will be physically abused by them at least once. Emotional abuse is even more prevalent.

Although individual women can be helped to foresee, prevent, and leave violent relationships, the problem won't disappear until there are basic changes in the society as a whole. All of us, including those in positions of authority, will have to revise the widely held idea that violence is an acceptable way to solve problems. In addition, we'll have to reexamine and restructure the quality of women's and men's lives and the ways they relate to each other. In this chapter I'll give an overview of woman abuse in society, present theories about why it happens, and suggest possibilities for change.

THE HISTORY OF BATTERING

Increased awareness of violence against women causes some of us to wonder if it's getting worse. Documentation of the problem is uncertain, incomplete, and recent. It's impossible to tell for sure whether battering was more common in the past, but there are some indications it was. The British philosopher, John Stuart Mill, commented on the subject in 1869: "From the earliest twilight of human society, every woman . . . was found in a state of bondage to some man. . . . How vast is the number of men in any great country, who are little higher than brutes, and . . . this never prevents them from being able, through the laws of marriage, to obtain a victim. . . . The vilest malefactor has some wretched woman tied to him, against whom he can commit any atrocity except killing her . . . and even that he can do without too much danger of legal penalty."

Until very recently women were considered the property of men. They

1

belonged to their fathers until marriage and then became the property of their husbands. And men had the right to treat their property as they wished. In British common law, husbands were authorized to "chastise" their wives with "any reasonable instrument." Later the law was modified so that men could beat their wives so long as the weapon was no thicker than a man's thumb.

United States laws were greatly influenced by British common law and the right and obligation of a husband to discipline his wife was retained in this country. In the last quarter of the nineteenth century a few states took that right away, yet those who continued to exercise it were still pro-tected from prosecution. A North Carolina judge stated, "If no perma-nent injury has been inflicted nor malice nor dangerous violence shown by the husband, it is better to draw the curtain, shut out the public gaze, and leave the parties to forget and forgive." We may imagine that many wives did forgive over and over again, just as they do today.

As recently as 1962, a woman who wanted to sue her husband for assault damages was turned down by a California Supreme Court judge because to hear the case "would destroy the peace and harmony of the home, and thus would be contrary to the policy of the law."

Proverbs and poetry illustrate the historical acceptance of the idea that it's natural for men to control women and for male violence to support the concept of male superiority. For example:

Old English proverb: "A spaniel, a woman, and a hickory tree, the more ye beat them, the better they be";

Alfred Lord Tennyson: "Man is the hunter, woman his game";

Russian proverb: "A wife may love a husband who never beats her, but she doesn't respect him."

Paradoxically, while most societies have assumed that men must use violence to control women, the prevalence of these violent actions has been systematically denied and hidden.

Minimizing the Problem

The nineteenth-century judge's instruction to "draw the curtain" is still followed by many members of the medical and counseling professions as well as by the judiciary. Doctors and nurses typically avoid asking bat-tered women for details about injuries or pretend to believe patients' fab-ricated stories of falling down stairs or running into doors. Therapists often fail to recognize abuse and accept a couple's denial or minimization of the violence. Police are trained to defuse the situation and to dissuade women from filing charges; prosecutors typically are reluctant to prosecute and judges to convict or sentence.

Small wonder that the abused women feels isolated and "crazy" when it appears that doctors, lawyers, and police are conspiring to deny the existence or seriousness of her condition or to assign the blame to her. Relatives and friends may also play into the woman's self-doubt by refusing to believe her. Many violent men insist that their women end relationships with everyone else. When an abused woman is the only person who knows of or admits to what's going on and the violent man defines the situation as not dangerous, not his fault, and not important, she begins to think there's something wrong with her.

Changing Attitudes

Alongside these persistent attitudes, new ones have begun to develop. Major changes began in the 1970s. We began to recognize the problem and to talk about it out loud; to understand that the victim neither asks for it, nor wants it, nor deserves it; to assign responsibility to the person who is violent; to support a woman who wants to prosecute and who chooses to leave a violent man.

Now that the curtain has been opened to expose the danger and the pain of violent relationships, it's possible to work on changing laws, retraining police, and educating prosecutors, judges, therapists, and medical personnel as well as the general public. All of this is being done. And we can seriously address the questions, "Why does he batter?" "Why does she stay?" and "Why does he stay?"

THE MASCULINE ROLE

What does it mean to be a man? Therapists questioned in a 1968 survey said that the healthy mature man is very aggressive, dominant, self-confident, independent, active, competitive, decisive, knows the ways of the world, is not easily influenced nor excitable in minor crises, and when he is emotional he almost always hides it.[1] Some therapists have changed their attitudes since the survey was made, but many have not.

Imagine for a moment what it's like for a man to try to live up to that image. The definition of masculinity is fostered directly and indirectly by all of our institutions: The church and the government assume the man to be the authoritative and financial head of the household; schools picture males as adventurous, strong, and brave in primary readers and high school history textbooks; television shows depict men as violent and powerful.

Family members support the notion that even newborn male infants are better coordinated, more alert, hardier, and stronger than female infants. It's ironic that even though most people believe males are born with certain traits, all institutions put pressure on males to develop those same traits and punish those who don't conform. No one explains why the social pressure is necessary if that's the way males naturally are. It's considered appropriate and necessary for even very young boys to be active, brave, competitive, and strong, and to hide their emotions. Parents are proud when their male toddler holds back his tears and picks himself up from a fall, and they're pleased when their son persists in sticking out a game without tears or complaint, even though he's hurt by a ball or another player. He's rewarded for his bravery and physical toughness and punished if he acts "like a sissy" or "like a girl" or a coward.

Boys may be given a general message not to fight, but they're also taught, as a matter of pride, never to let another boy get away with hitting them. "Don't fight, but if you're hit first, fight back."

Boys dream of being famous race-car drivers, boxers, or football heroes but as they grow older it becomes more and more difficult to live up to the image of the dominant, worldly, self-confident, aggressive, decisive male. How does a person pull that off if he's sixteen years old—or twenty-three or forty-five—and he's rarely left the town where he grew up, he's never had a permanent job, or if he knows he's stuck in the tedious job he's held for twenty years? What does he do when he feels weak, vulnerable, or dependent? Or when he doesn't know how to do what needs to be done—whether it's fixing the stopped-up kitchen sink, finding his way in a strange city, or handling a financial problem?

Many men, faced with a threat to their masculine image, try to hide their fears in bluff and bluster. They act as if they're confident and strong, independent, and competent, regardless of how they feel. Sometimes this bravado helps them learn to perform tasks well. But when they can't perform to their standards of masculinity, they may lash out verbally or physically, blaming whoever is handy, to save face. In either case the unacceptable feelings of helplessness, weakness, dependence, or incompetency are buried in a seemingly safe place, beneath conscious awareness. A great deal of pain is buried with them.

These feelings of failure or inadequacy are experienced by many men who have both low- and high-status jobs and include some who give the impression of self-confidence. Often it is only his wife who knows how vulnerable such a man feels and how fearful he is of being found out to be less than the ideal of masculinity.

A few men are fortunate enough to have been allowed and even encouraged as youngsters to express the "nonmasculine" traits of dependency, vulnerability, and emotionality. Others learn to do that as adults, through hard work and the courage to risk feeling vulnerable. In either case they'll be able to face problems with a realistic assessment of the challenge and to accept their fears and hopes about their capacity to meet it.

WHY DO MEN BATTER?

Why would a man use the person he loves as a punching bag? It's a cliche that there's a fine line between love and hate and that "You always hurt the one you love." Intimate relationships cause some people to feel vulnerable and dependent. If one person loves or seems to love more than the other, those feelings will be exaggerated in the one who loves most and will contribute to his or her giving the partner power. Many of us feel hostility toward those who have power over us. For men, who aren't supposed to be either dependent or powerless, love sometimes produces feelings of resentment, even rage, especially when the loved one who holds that power is "merely" a female, a person who's supposed to be inferior. It can be experienced as intolerable humiliation, though it may seldom be expressed or even recognized as such. The more vulnerable the man feels, and the more important invulnerability is to his idea of masculinity, the more he may hate the one he also loves.

Permission to Batter

Another important contributing factor is that men have society's implied permission to hit their wives or girlfriends. It's probably true that most people would say men shouldn't hit the women they love (or anyone else who they care for or who is smaller and weaker than themselves). But we've seen that historically this idea exists side by side with the traditional assumption that men should be able to control their wives by whatever means necessary. Traditional ideas die hard.

In one study, more than half of a sample of husbands indicated they would be jealous if their wives were unfaithful and that they would probably respond with some form of violence.[2] The response of strangers to male violence against women supports the idea that such a reaction is acceptable. Both experimental and real-life situations indicate that a woman assaulted by a man in public will not be helped by passersby.

Friends may blame the victim for being in the situation at all, family members may not believe that it's happening, and therapists are likely to ask what the woman did to provoke it. Although none of these people state in so many words that they approve of the violence, denial of the battering or the implication that the victim is at fault has the effect of giving the man a "hitting license," especially if the batterer is the victim's husband. He can be quite confident that his friends and family—and perhaps even hers—will stick by him; he probably won't go to jail or even be questioned by police. The social sanctions that keep most of us from acting on violent impulses don't operate in the arena of marriage.

Interpersonal Conflicts and Stresses

The question of why men batter is often confused with why men become angry at the women they love. A relationship between lovers or family members involves a continual chain of action and reaction, so that it's easy for a man who hits to say it's the woman's sarcasm (or coldness, drinking, poor housekeeping, extravagance) that caused it. Therapists have often taken this view and focused on what the women can do differently to cause change in the men.

Certainly couples trigger feelings in each other, and often they are related simply to expectations, needs, and wants at the moment the exchange takes place. They're just as likely to be the result of a history of exchanges between the couple. A man who's had several extramarital affairs will get a different response from his wife when he says he has to work late at the office than will a hard worker whose wife feels confident he's faithful to her.

An angry response can also be displaced from a relationship with another person. "You're reacting just like my mother/father/third-grade teacher." Or it can be a result of stress. Real-world problems such as job loss or a sick child can cause tension that easily explodes in anger, given the slightest opportunity. Yet one person's stress is another's challenge; one becomes angry, another depressed, and still another works it out in therapy.

Any of these situations can help explain why one person becomes explosively angry and another merely irritated or hurt or worried. None of them explain why one angry person hits his wife, another his child, why one goes out and gets drunk, another verbally lashes out, and still another cries or becomes silent and cold or covers up his feelings with jokes. None gives us the answer to why men batter.

Research indicates somewhere around 60 percent of men who batter grew up in homes where they were beaten or they witnessed one parent battering another. However, this is not an explanation, either. What about the other 40 percent? And what about those who grew up in abusive homes who didn't batter anyone? R. Emerson and Russell Dobash found in a study in Scotland that only 12 percent of the siblings of batterers were violent to anyone.[3] Children model parents' behavior, but they also interpret what they see and connect it with other events, ideas, and feelings. It's unpredictable how they'll use what they see and which parts of it they'll mimic. (This means that if your children have seen their father batter, there is a possibility of helping them interpret the battering in such a way that they won't want to imitate it.)

What makes a man hit the woman he loves is a varied and complicated mix: internal stress; society's permission to hit interpreted as an individual right; mimicking of violent parents or other role models; interpersonal struggles with the woman and others; feelings of anger, vulnerability, powerlessness, and inadequacy; and very few clear actions by the woman, the justice system, or others that unequivocally state that violence is not allowed.

THE FEMALE ROLE

Women have their image to live up to just as men do. According to the same group of therapists mentioned above, the healthy, mature woman's characteristics are the opposite of the man's: She's very emotional, easily influenced, submissive, excitable, passive, home-oriented, unworldly, indecisive, and dependent and not at all competitive, adventurous, aggressive, independent, or self-confident.

For some women, these characteristics are easier to live up to than those roles men must master. Yet most of us are not easily turned into the marshmallows these traits imply. To the extent we're able to be that kind of woman, we can thank the same institutions that mold the male character: the churches that have traditionally tried to suppress women's sexual power and their independence; the school readers that picture girls as hopelessly frightened of spiders and lizards and the dark; the television and magazine ads that show ninety-pound females who do little other than wash and curl their hair, paint their faces and nails, and douse themselves with good smells.

The messages, both subtle and direct, inundate us from infancy on ("Isn't she sweet, pretty, tiny, adorable?"). Gradually, we succumb to the idea that we're incapable of making decisions or of acting independently, and that we need protection from major responsibilities as well as from dangerous men. The protector, of course, is that special man in our lives. Many of us are fearful of venturing out at night without male protection and are afraid to live alone. Those of us who work for minimum wage find it burdensome and depressing to take the entire financial responsibility for ourselves and our children, though many of us must.

As young women we learn that when we are sexually open, we're subject to severe criticism from parents, men, churches, and schools. When we assert our independence, show our competence, and take responsibility in social interactions, men often become angry or hurt and may assume that we're expressing doubts about their ability to handle situations adequately. So when we're at our best—that is, acting openly, independently, competently, and responsibly—we face judgments from ourselves and others that are disturbing: "Maybe I'm not a 'real' woman, and maybe my man isn't a 'real' man unless he objects to my independence." Each time we subject ourselves to such a judgment we become less confident and open the door a little bit more to dependency, submissiveness, and eventual helplessness.

WHY DO WOMEN STAY?

Those of us who manage to rise above the most damaging aspects of sex-role socialization to become strong, adventurous, competent people would like to think we're free of male control and violence. But it isn't necessarily so. Although women who have been abused sometimes fit the stereotype of the submissive, dependent, helpless woman, many are the opposite—strong, independent people. They sometimes hold important, demanding, professional positions as doctors, media performers, or teachers, or they may work in traditionally male trades. These women have broken out of the restrictive traditional roles, yet they are still capable of falling in love, feeling responsible for what happens in an intimate relationship, and committed to going beyond the last mile to make it work.

Every woman learns as she grows up that to be a "whole person" she must have a male partner. Although divorced, single, and widowed women constitute more than 42 percent of the workforce, and though more than 16 percent of the whole female population never marries at all, the myth persists that every woman must have a man. A single woman may still feel like a freak who accidentally landed on Noah's Ark. Even though men who are widowed or divorced tend to be more depressed and remarry more quickly than women in similar circumstances, most women believe men get along very well without them. This contributes to their placing a low value on themselves and to the fear of never attracting and keeping another man.

Fear of Poverty

The belief that she will be provided for by a man may discourage a woman from taking seriously the need to earn an adequate income. If she does plan a career, discrimination in the job market is likely to make it hard to make a good living. If she leaves paid work for a few years to have children, she's likely to lose both income and self-confidence.

Even a woman who has a good job will suffer a big loss in income when she leaves a man, especially if she has custody of children. The man she's left probably earns much more than she; child support is almost never enough to cover expenses and it's often not paid at all. The fear of poverty or a greatly lowered standard of living is a major reason women stay in abusive situations, hoping year after year it will change and that they won't have to risk making it on their own.

In addition, women still usually take major responsibility for the children, are closer to them, and want custody of them, which adds to the financial burden. It may seem impossible to cope with all the children's emotional needs, including the loss of a father figure as well as working full time or more. Although many women do manage to do all that, the reality is that it's a very hard life. Until a woman has done it, and learned firsthand that it's still much less painful than depending on a man who can't be depended on, she'll be too afraid to risk leaving.

Love and Guilt

When an abused woman overcomes her fear of poverty and the pervasive ideas about woman's role and prepares to leave, she may be faced with the abusive man at his most irresistible: "I know I'm a brute, but I'm on my knees asking forgiveness. . . . How could you turn away from me when I most need you? . . . If you really loved me, you'd forgive and trust me. . . . Look how I'm hurting and how hard I'm trying. . . . I'm afraid I'll fall apart without you. . . . You're all I have, all I care about."

In a few sentences he can trigger the woman's addictive love (see Chapter 5), her guilt, her concern for him, her feeling that she's responsible for his life and feelings, her hopefulness, her idea that she should be a trusting, nurturing, forgiving woman, and that it would be wrong not to give him another chance, wrong to turn her back on him just as he's finally really ready to change.

She unpacks her bags. The cycle begins again.

WHY DO MEN STAY?

If a man feels so hostile to his chosen woman that he regularly hits her, why doesn't he leave? If pressed for an explanation, he too might say that it's love that has him locked helplessly in its grip, though he's more likely to mask his feelings with indignant complaints about the woman. He's unlikely to confess that he feels the need of a woman, and that life without an intimate partner would be intolerable. He may not even be willing to admit to himself the importance of the relationship, because emotional dependence runs counter to the accepted image of masculinity.

Often the man is as dependent on his woman as she is on him, though he may rarely admit it. In their mutual addiction they tend to shut out the rest of the world, she because she's ashamed of her bruises and because he demands that she cut off other relationships; he because he doesn't know how to form relationships and is jealous and fearful of her involvement with others. The more isolated they become, the more dependent they grow, and the more addicted to a relationship they expect to fulfill all their needs. Since no one can fulfill all of another's needs, the continued disappointment leads to increased stress, depression, and hostility.

Many men who batter are immature and emotionally dependent, though some successfully hide it in their work and social lives outside the home. They're often addicted to the women they abuse, and they batter in hopes of frightening the women so much that they won't dare "abandon" them. The fear of abandonment often leads to extreme jealousy and to suspicion that a woman will betray her husband with other men, a jealousy often interpreted by both partners as "love."

The batterer believes he can force change by frightening the woman into submission and fidelity, and he, like the woman he victimizes, perpetually renews his hope for change.

WHAT CAN BE DONE?

Since woman abuse is a problem that seems to have been with us since the dawn of history and it's tolerated by all of our institutions, it may seem impossible for you to break out of it.

But that isn't so. For the first time in history, women as a group are saying "No!" to battering, are helping each other get free of dangerous men, and are working together to create better lives with and without men. So far, they have changed laws and police procedures and attitudes of medical and counseling professionals, as well as maintaining shelters. There is a lot more to be done, but it's easier for a woman who wants to get out of an abusive situation to get help than at any time in history.

Individual women, with the help of each other, are finding their own ways to protect themselves from violence, usually by separating from dangerous men. The decision—whether to leave or to stay but to make a plan to be relatively safe—is the first hard step in the process of change.

CHAPTER 2

MARRIAGE AND THE FAMILY: NEW AND TRADITIONAL VALUES

The concepts of family, marriage, and loyalty to the man you love each have different meanings to individuals and to religious, cultural, and ethnic groups. These ideas don't always keep up with changing customs, so it will be helpful to take a fresh look at what you believe makes sense, whether others agree or not. In this chapter you'll have an opportunity to clarify what you value about marriage and the family.

WHAT IS A FAMILY?

In an age of rapid social change it's hard to know what our obligations are. You said the words "till death do us part," or if you're not married you may have just assumed you'd grow old with your partner, staying by his side through bad times as well as good. You may have grown up believing that unquestioning devotion and loyalty are necessary in marriage and that marriage is the central relationship of everyone's family. Leaving the man, even talking to someone about your relationship problems, may seem unacceptable. When you look back at the family you grew up in, you may remember that there were all kinds of flaws, even dangers, and damaging relationships. But perhaps it's comforting to you that at least the family was together.

When you think of leaving your man and try to imagine yourself as a single person, it seems everywhere you look there are either couples or "complete" family units—a mother and a father and two or more children. You see the couples at movies and restaurants. You see the families at the zoo. You see them—mother, father, athletic-looking boy, slightly younger, pretty little girl—on ads for washing machines, breakfast cereals, and living-room rugs. So, of course, that must be what a family is. Oddly, this picture of the two-parent, nuclear, "normal" family persists even among people who have seen or experienced many different kinds of families.

The picture is in stark contrast to the current reality that four and a half million families in the United States are headed by women, and, of these, almost half are single mothers with children under eighteen. The nuclear family has been shrinking in both size and number for a generation, and some marriage ceremonies no longer even include the words "till death do us part." To gain a new perspective on being a single person, you need to begin thinking of it as a different lifestyle rather than focusing on negative phrases such as "fifth wheel," "broken home," and "fatherless family." Being single doesn't mean you'll have a family organism with a permanent gaping hole where the father/husband has been amputated. Like almost 25 percent of the families in the nation, yours may be a woman-headed full household or a complete family that has one resident and one nonresident parent.

THE FAMILY IN PERSPECTIVE

Historically the husband was the protector of the wife and children. A woman constantly giving birth couldn't manage economically without a man's support. Nor could he manage without her. A man not only needed a woman to take major responsibility for the children and household tasks, but he also needed her help economically to supply the food, clothing, and other items that are now usually manufactured outside the home. They both needed the children to help out on the farm, in the store, or in the home.

Families traditionally have been urged to stay together on moral and religious grounds, and more recently for psychological reasons. However, the stability of the family—still sometimes defined as a gainfully employed father, a mother at home, and 2.5 children—has also served the interests of political and economic institutions. As long as women take primary responsibility for the care and training of the next generation and of most household tasks, men are free to work long hours in factories, business, and government. Thus, in a sluggish economy, when there is a surplus of workers, women may be encouraged to stay in the home and have more children through government bonuses and highly restrictive abortion laws.

In the United States it was considered wrong for mothers to leave their children in the hands of other caretakers. During World Wars I and II, however, this practice became acceptable as national priorities made it necessary to employ women in great numbers to promote "the war effort." Thousands of mothers were recruited into factories, and their children were presumed to be cared for adequately. In many cases childcare was provided at the workplace. But in the postwar years, as soon as the men came home to reclaim those jobs, it was generally agreed upon by heads of industry and government that a woman's place was in the home after all and that the children needed her constant presence. Today, when we have a scarcity of jobs, neither government nor industry see it as important or valuable to provide childcare for working mothers. And once again a movement is afoot to persuade women that their full-time services are needed in the home.

Government decisions and industrial needs are passed on to us in various ways in addition to the obvious ones of laws and company announcements. In a period of just a few years, new messages about social values are transmitted through television news and drama, movies, and popular magazines. Depending upon the historical period, it may seem that suddenly "everyone" is talking about having babies, or that all the previously contented homemakers on the block are planning to get paid jobs. Since most of us are uncomfortable with ideas that are different, we begin to change our thinking, too, without analyzing exactly who is promoting these new ideas and what their reasons are. We can easily lose sight of what we really want for ourselves.

WHO ARE YOU LISTENING TO?

It's a good idea to ask whose voice it is—besides your own—that gives you messages about your obligations:

"A woman's place is by her husband's side."

"No real woman leaves just because of a few family fights."

"It is the woman's responsibility to see that the family functions harmoniously."

"It must be her fault if he is being violent."

"She should learn to be a better wife."

"You can't run away from your problems."

"The family should stay together through thick and thin and work things out together."

Is it your mother's voice? Your husband's? Your minister's? Counselor's? Your father's? Shut your eyes for a minute and listen to the words that are most familiar to you, whichever words ring true about staying with your man. Who is it that says them?

Once you know where they come from, you can begin to analyze them. Are they what you really believe, or are they just words you've been repeating without thinking about what they mean or why they might be true? What are the reasons that a wife should stick by her husband regardless of how he treats her?

WHAT IS IMPORTANT TO YOU?

Now it's time for you to give some thought to what "family" means to you. What are your values and which of them are most important? What kind of family would best promote those values? Even if you're not married and not a parent now, it's a good idea to examine your values, since your involvement with an abusive partner is likely to include a dream of, or a plan to create, a family unit.

Many people believe that marriage, and even more certainly the family, provide and nourish the development of valued traits and situations: warmth, security (both emotional and financial), peace of mind, stability, companionship, loving and satisfying sex, someone to grow old with, children to carry on the family name and traditions, interdependence, affection, loyalty, and the sharing of responsibilities, worries, work, rewards, and pride in children and accomplishments.

Other people claim that not only do marriage and the family fail to promote these values, but they inhibit the development of freedom, adventure, social and intellectual stimulation, growth, flexibility, independence, and individuality. They assert that spouse battering, child abuse, and incest are indications that families are too often centers of stress that result in serious physical and emotional damage to family members.

Whether you view your own situation as relatively satisfying or not depends upon your relationship with your partner and your interpretation of that relationship—what values it provides you with, and how important they are. Being married to a gambler will not be so bad if financial security is not of great value to you. You won't be troubled by a "swinging" husband if fidelity isn't important to you. One person's emotional security may be another's boredom.

It's easy to lose sight of what's important when it seems impossible to ever have it. This first exercise will help you focus on the things that were once important to you and that still might be if you let them be. *Fill in the blanks as honestly as you can.*

Activity 1 ⤳ What's Important to You?

1. If I had twenty-four hours to live, I would try to be with_____

_____and to do_____

_____

I would not want to be with_____I would try not to

_____

_____

2. If I were to die, I would like people to say these things about me:

_____

_____

3. I hope my children and/or grandchildren won't ever have to_____

_____

_____

4. If I had plenty of money, I would_____

_____

_____

5. When the children grow up, I will_____

_____

_____

6. If I were younger, I would_____

_____

_____

7. If it didn't take so long, I would_____

_____

_____

8. Some of the things I wish I had done are_____

_____

_____

9. If I felt better or had more courage, I would_____

_____

_____

Perhaps you filled in the blanks with things that are only the most vaguely felt dreams or wishes, things you'd like to have or do, but don't really expect, and certainly haven't a plan to make happen. Many of us drift along, making the best of a hard life and losing sight of goals and values that were once important to us. If that's what you've done, this is a good time to get them back in your sight again. The next exercise will take you a step further in recognizing your goals. Without considering how likely you are to achieve them, *circle* each of the following values that's important to you.

Activity 2 ✌ What Are Your Values?

predictable relationship

security

enough money for comfort

wealth

peace of mind

flexibility

freedom

friends

fun

work

creativity

love

sex

close family

time for family

travel

education

independence

power

fame

glory

respect

achievement

service

leadership

control

being nurtured

nurturing

feeling useful

being well-liked

self-expression

participation in the arts

participation in sports

adventure

excitement

variety

being entertained

leisure time

close relationship

honesty

humor

order

rituals and tradition

shared childcare

integrity

time to read

country living

learning

privacy

meeting new people

To get a clearer view of how you're most likely to achieve your values, make a list of all the potential advantages and disadvantages of both married and single life. Use the items you put in the blanks and the circled values from the last two exercises to help you fill in the "Advantages" columns below the examples I've given in the next exercise.

Activity 3 ⁓ Advantages and Disadvantages of Marriage and Single Life

Marriage		Single Life	
Advantages	Disadvantages	Advantages	Disadvantages
1. Financial security	Financial dependence	1. Financial security	Poverty
2. Companion-ship	Lack of companionship	2. Choice of being alone	Loneliness
3. Reliable sex	Boring Sex	3. Better sex	Sexual hassles
4. Share childcare	Total care of kids	4. Total responsibility for kids	No help with kids
5. _____		5. _____	
6. _____		6. _____	
7. _____		7. _____	
8. _____		8. _____	
9. _____		9. _____	
10. _____		10. _____	

WEIGHING THE PROS AND CONS

Notice the seeming contradictions. Whether a particular condition occurs in marriage or as a single person depends upon individual experiences with certain people. If your man has a steady job in an expanding field, good health, and is willing to share the money equally, then you have some financial security. But if he's an alcoholic, gets laid off, leaves you for a younger woman, has a heart attack, or provides you only the bare essentials, you have no security. In the latter case you might feel more secure as a single person, providing for yourself.

See how many disadvantages of the single life can also be viewed as advantages. The purpose of doing that is not to make you decide to leave the man, but to help you realize that you have a real choice. "Having to make decisions by myself" can be viewed positively as an opportunity to become more independent.

This is a good time to stop saying: "I can't," "Maybe when the children are older," "I couldn't support the children," "I couldn't take the children from him," "I couldn't leave the children." Try substituting, "If I decided to leave . . . to support the children . . . to leave the children . . . how could I make the best of it?" The problems of single parenting are many, but the solutions are beginning to develop, and being a single parent— even under stress and in poverty—might be a relief and easier in some ways than trying to protect the children from an abusive man.

To clarify what values might be achieved in various kinds of relationships, consider what values were prevalent in your original family, as well as in each of the intimate relationships you've had. Compare those values with the ones that typified your life when you weren't in an intimate relationship. Include living alone, in a dormitory, or with friends. Note which situations enabled you to achieve your most important values.

How do your particular experiences square with your ideas about advantages and disadvantages of marriage and the single life? If you said an advantage of marriage is companionship, a father for your children, or sexual satisfaction, but during two marriages you haven't experienced any of those benefits, you'll need to decide whether your expectations of a husband are unrealistically high or whether you should make some changes in your choice of men.

If you're used to thinking of yourself only as a daughter, wife, or mother, you may find these questions bewildering at first. You can expect to take some time evaluating your life as an individual as well as a family member. Whenever you feel you're getting a slightly different slant on your life, return to these questions and change or expand your answers. Some of them will become clearer as you read the rest of the book and gain more understanding of your obligations and your options.

CHAPTER 3

IS IT EVER RIGHT TO BREAK UP THE FAMILY?

The family, meaning that nuclear family discussed in the previous chapter, represents to many people all that is good and the best hope for a better world. You may have gotten a message like that from many sources as you were growing up—and with it, the message that it's the woman's role to hold marriage and family together, certainly not to destroy the marriage or break up the family.

If you've decided that what you really want is to end your relationship with the man who abuses you, you may still feel guilty for taking a stand or feel responsible for other people's reactions. This chapter will focus on the question of your obligations to the man, and to children or other family members who may be involved.

WHERE DO YOUR GUILT FEELINGS COME FROM?

"He needs me."

"He'll fall apart."

"He'll kill himself."

"He has nothing else."

"I can't deprive him of the kids."

If you're worrying yourself with those kinds of warnings, it's especially important to determine whether they stem from your own reasonable fear based on past experience, or from an attempt by the man, his friends, or relatives to induce guilt and to "make" you stay with him. The situation becomes difficult to sort out when a man not only is manipulating your guilt feelings but additionally may be in real danger of "cracking up" or killing himself. Friends, relatives, and professionals may tell you it will be on your conscience if your man becomes self-destructive after you leave. Before assessing the value of those judgments, you need to consider several questions. The first is, "Who said it?"

If you're the only person explicitly stating these fears, you should ask yourself whether you've gotten the idea from other people's hints or from their indirectly stated fears. Perhaps those ideas are disguised as innocent questions: "Do you think he'll be able to manage without you?" Or as offhand comments: "He really doesn't have much to live for aside from you and the kids."

If these remarks come from people closer to him than to you, ask yourself further questions before deciding their judgments are right. "Does this person care about me at all? Has she only been hearing the man's interpretation of the relationship? Does she understand what kind of fear I live with every day? Have I ever told her, rather than hinting, or talking in vague generalities, exactly what he does to me?" Unless the person cares for you at least as much as for the man, and unless she thoroughly understands what it is you want to escape, her advice should be taken with a grain of salt. If the advising person is a professional who doesn't really know either of you, there are other questions to ask. (See Section II on Getting Professional Help.)

The people who are generous about advising you have experienced the same social conditioning you have, including the idea that you're responsible for the welfare and happiness of your man. Though they may have good intentions, the advice may not be the best thing for you. After listening to the ideas of the caring people in your life, you'll be the one to make the decision and to live with its consequences. It's a big responsibility, and there are no easy answers. You won't be able to hold anyone else responsible for the results of your decisions, no matter how free she or he was in handing out advice.

SUICIDE AND "CRACKING UP"

The two most frightening possibilities are that the man will kill himself or "go crazy." A question about suicide appears on the Danger Assessment list because many men who kill their wives also kill themselves. Please take attempts and threats of it seriously.

Has he done it before? If he's tried suicide or had a mental breakdown in the past, that's an indication that he has a poorly developed capacity to handle stress; if you leave him he may repeat his old patterns. But that doesn't mean he'll crack up completely just because you're not there. There may be other factors that will help him handle this situation more constructively than he's handled problems in the past. If he's had emotional problems before he met you, you're not the cause of them.

Has he talked about it? If he threatens self-destructive behavior, it doesn't mean he'll necessarily follow through, nor is silence a certain indication that he won't. Nevertheless, threats of suicide should be taken seriously. There's a commonly held belief that those who talk about suicide don't do it, which is definitely not true.

What Can He Do for Himself?

Even if your man has few friends and isn't close to his family, in an emergency friends may come through and family may become close. Try to find out from them whether they will be supportive if you leave, and if they seem to care, find a way to let them know you're leaving when you make the decision.

The more isolated the man is, the more likely he'll feel he can't handle being "deserted" or "abandoned" by you, and the more self-destructive he's likely to be. Many men who batter have no friends or close relatives and are entirely dependent on one special woman for emotional sustenance. It's as if their emotional survival depends upon a mutually suffocating relationship that fosters mutual helplessness. If you tell the man you're leaving, and especially if there are children who will go with you, he may feel he has nothing to live for. The man could solve his problem of dependence by developing friendships, by becoming involved in work or hobbies, or by enlisting the help of a professional person. You can try to urge, plead, beg, demand, threaten, and manipulate him into broadening his horizons, but it's ultimately his choice whether to make use of the opportunities available. If he refuses to provide himself the option of being less dependent on you, you'll need to decide where your responsibility to him will stop.

How Much Can You Help Him?

To clarify the limits of your obligations to your man, *make a list* of all the things you could do that might keep him from killing himself or cracking up. To broaden your perspective on what you can expect to accomplish, consider everything possible. If you stay with him day and night there's a good chance you can prevent his suicide. (Even then, he can probably do it if he's determined.) If you promise you'll never leave him, regardless of what he does, and that you won't become involved with any friends or activities that don't include or center around him, will that prevent him from going crazy? Perhaps you're close to living that way now. If so, is his stability improving or deteriorating? What about yours?

What other less demanding, less dramatic action could you take to prevent him from self-destructive acts? Some, such as helping him to find a counselor or make new friends, may require his cooperation. Being available whenever he feels emotionally shaky or trying to build his self-esteem may necessitate lots of time and emotional involvement. If you decide to leave him, perhaps a daily phone call will be enough to help him stay in a fairly stable condition.

Activity 4 ᘒ What Can You Do to Help Him?

1. _____

2. _____

3. _____

4. _____

5. _____

6. _____

7. _____

8. _____

9. _____

10. _____

When you've made your list of possibilities, *underline* the ones you could do without danger to yourself. Allow for accidental, as well as intentional, violence, especially if he abuses alcohol or drugs. Consider both psychological and physical danger. If being in regular contact with him saps your energy, lowers your self-esteem, and increases your depression, that's a serious danger to your mental health.

If you're going to do something that requires his cooperation, *write down* how long you're willing to help, and what amount of cooperation you want from him. If after three months he hasn't made a serious effort to make the change you agreed was important, it will be clear that no matter how helpful you are, he's not going to accept your assistance. And if you do decide to leave him, you'll have a record of all the things you tried. It should minimize your guilt feelings and lessen the probability of your taking unfair blame for something you couldn't control. You'll be clear about the low probability of your being able to save him from suicide or a breakdown. You'll know that even had you been able to do it, it would have meant risking your own sanity or your life on the slim chance you might have saved his. That is beyond any reasonable expectation.

WHAT ABOUT THE CHILDREN?

If you decide to leave and take the children, their father will very likely be hurt and angry. He may draw a dramatically bleak picture of total separation from his children from this day forth, even describing how they will gradually lose interest in him, or claiming you'll turn them against him.

At this point, your guilt feelings can do you in, especially if you're hoping the children *will* forget about him and won't want to see him. But there's no reason to buy the picture he's drawn. Neither of you can predict what it's going to be like, since each of you will change. The maturing process will have a great effect not only on the children, but on you two adults. In addition, as your individual lives develop in different ways and as you form new relationships with other people, your feelings toward each other will be modified.

Most of us find it hard to imagine feeling differently about anyone from the way we feel right now. When we love, we can't remember how it was to hate. When we're angry, we can't imagine how we could have been calm. But people do change. What you do today is important and will set the stage for future events, but it won't permanently set in concrete future relationships. There are many, many ways a father and his children can relate to each other whether they live in the same house or not.

A partial exception to this statement occurs when you think your life or that of the children is so threatened that you have to sever the relationship entirely and disappear to a place where the man can't find you. Even in that extreme situation, you may choose to resume contact in a year or two, or the children may exercise their right to spend time with their father when they're older. If you make the decision to cut all ties, it certainly shouldn't be done lightly. You're right to be concerned about its effect on the children. You'll probably want to consult not only a lawyer but also some friends or a counselor before you make the final decision. But be sure your consultants understand that both you and the children may be in very real danger if you maintain contact with the man.

Although it's your decision to take the children, the relationship the father maintains after the separation depends largely upon whether he's reliable and nonthreatening. In other words, he'll play a large part in whether he deprives himself of them.

What Does It Mean to Deprive the Man of His Children?

To evaluate just what "depriving" the father of his children means, ask yourself what he gets from them: Affection? Respect? Status? Attachment? A sense of continuity from one generation to another? An opportunity to nurture?

Pin down precisely what he gains now and how he gets it. Is there a way he can still get it, even if you separate? Status and continuity can exist whether he's a full-time father or not. Perhaps he limits his affection and nurturing to a few minutes before the children's bedtime each night, or to a half day on weekends when he feels good. If so, separation may mean the routine will change, but not necessarily that the children will be with their father less than before. Some divorced fathers become more fully involved with their children after a separation, because to have twenty-four-hour responsibility for them on a regular basis requires a more complex relationship.

It may be that the children's "respect" for their father is composed mainly of fear, and the more intimate relationship that develops from twenty-four-hour care (even for short periods) will result in a deeper or different kind of respect. The father may be surprised to find that what he loses in fearful respect is compensated for by an increase of trust and love.

Ways He Can Maintain Contact with the Children

If their father isn't abusive to the children, and if his expressed concern over losing a close connection with them is sincere, you can arrange for him to spend as much time as usual with them. However, it may take some time before you're able to work this out in a way that will guarantee your safety, both from his violence and from your own vulnerability to his persuasiveness. (See Chapter 15 Protecting Yourself and the Children and Chapter 28 Nurturing Your Children.)

If the father spends a good deal of time with his children in the evening and on weekends, then you may eventually consider shared custody. That is, if you leave and take the children with you, you might want to live close to his house so the children can have dinner with him several evenings a week, and spend half the weekends with him. But emphasize "eventually."

Shared custody will probably be much too dangerous to undertake until he's demonstrated for a full year that he's reliable in keeping appointments with the children, that he's not jealous of your new relationships, and that he fully understands your lifestyle is not his legitimate concern. He should demonstrate that he's neither violent nor emotionally abusive toward you or the children.

If you think you may want to consider such a plan later, let the man know it's a possibility. Discuss it with him one time, or write it out, and be sure he understands you won't even discuss it for a year. The reason for talking about it one time is so it will be clear to both of you that it's up to *him* whether he deprives himself of the children's company and affection. And that should help you keep in mind that he deprived himself of spending time with them; you didn't. If it's really important to him to spend time with the children he'll act in ways to make that happen.

Meanwhile, be clear about what you will and will not put up with during this interim period. It's your job to preserve your mental and physical health this first year by playing it safe. At the end of a year, you'll be in a better position to assess change and to distinguish progress from promises.

If your thinking becomes circular and repetitive, it's probably because you're determined to arrive at some solution that won't hurt anyone. You can't do it. Whether you go or stay, someone will be hurt, at least in the short run. The question is how to minimize it.

CHILD ABUSE

Children present special problems, since they haven't the power to control their own lives and may be more vulnerable to rejection and feelings of abandonment than the adults involved. On the other hand, they're sometimes much more flexible and resilient than adults.

If their father is brutal to the children as well as to you, your decision should be easier to make because of your obligation to protect them from physical or psychological abuse. You may be the only person very young children can count on to protect them from a violent father's dangerous miscalculations of his strength, which can easily result in permanent damage or even death.

Child abuse takes many forms. It's easy to gloss over or not even recognize it, because there's such a fine line between the physical punishment of children that's acceptable to most adults and the abuse that's out of control.

We're horrified when we hear about an adult beating, burning, or throwing a child. We wonder how an adult could do that to a small person. Yet many of us who've been confined for any period with a young child who continually cries or whines or who won't obey and is "into everything" can at least understand the urge.

When social isolation, poverty, feelings of inadequacy, or worry are added to the ordinary stresses of life, it's easy to lash out at the least powerful creature available. For a man, that's often a woman and sometimes children. For a woman it's often the children, and for a child it may be other younger children or the dog or cat.

Violence against children, like violence against adults, is initially unthinkable. The first time a person allows himself or herself to lose control, there may be immediate horror, remorse, and promises that it will never happen again. Yet that first violation of the inhibition has made the act "thinkable" and therefore likely to occur again. Eventually it may begin to seem normal.

To get a perspective on child abuse, imagine for a moment you're in the sole care of an eight hundred pound giant who insists you do things that you don't like and don't understand, and who smacks you with a fifty-pound hand or huge board when you don't do as you're told or when you cry or complain. It's so acceptable for adult parents and teachers to physically assault little children that we easily lose the perspective that we are, comparatively, all-powerful giants. We also have more resources to use to solve problems since our intellect is more highly developed. We have more information and we're supposed to have a better handle on our emotions.

Even though violence against children is understandable, it's not acceptable. If it's the father who's violent to them, it's your responsibility to keep the children safely away from him. If he's also violent toward you, the only way you'll be able to protect your children is to get them away from him.

If you're afraid he'll get custody even though he abuses the children, be sure to take them to a doctor any time it happens, whether you believe they need treatment or not. If you ask the doctor to document the injuries, you'll be able to use the record if later there's a custody dispute. The doctor may report the injuries to child protection authorities, which may make your life more difficult in the short run, but it will help you to protect your children in the long run. (See Chapter 8 and Chapter 28 for more details on custody.)

If you're the one who's violent to the children, admitting that you have a problem is the first step in solving it. You may need help to stop the violence, and asking for it is the second step. Call Parents Anonymous, or the children's protection division of your state department of health or welfare services, a counselor, or a crisis line. It will be hard to do, but once you have the support of people who understand your problem, and who can give practical help, you'll probably be very relieved to have your secret out. Not only can you learn to restrain your temper, but you can find better ways to discipline, play with, and enjoy your children. You can also get help in reducing your stress.

Each day that your child is in a household where violence occurs is a day that the child learns that physical brutality is acceptable. The child is learning from you—much more than from others—how to be an adult. If you want to improve the chances of the child's avoiding a violent relationship later, you can set the example of saying "No more" now.

Sexual Abuse of Children

Until recently, incest has been a taboo subject, and even those of us who now understand how widespread it is find it hard to imagine that anyone we know could do such a thing. Yet it happens in families of all classes, races, and lifestyles. It's not unusual for men who batter to sexually molest the woman's children, whether or not they're also his children. Don't shut your eyes to the possibility and don't depend on the child to tell you. If the man has molested your child, he very likely has also threatened her or him (yes, it happens to boys too) with dire consequences if they tell. The child may feel guilty and ashamed or afraid you'll blame her. This is likely to be so even though you've given no indication you would blame her, and even though she has no reason to feel guilty.

There are those who blame the "provocative" child for her own victimization. Some adults still cling to the mistaken idea that children even as young as five or six "asked for it" by their "sexy" behavior. But even a teenager feels powerless—with considerable justification—when faced with an adult's sexual demands. The authority of the adult, plus the teen's emotional turmoil about her sexuality, may cause a confused reaction. It's the adult who must take responsibility even if the teenager walks around the house half dressed. Rather than take advantage of her, the adult, whether he's her father, stepfather, or your boyfriend, should tell her to put a robe on.

If you have even the slightest suspicion that any adult in your household has made sexual overtures to your child, find a quiet place where the two of you can be alone and won't be rushed. Bring up the topic, explain that you're concerned about it, and that you won't blame the child for whatever has happened. Then ask.

If the child says, "No, nothing has happened," explain that even though it seems shocking, it's something that does happen, and she has the right to say "No" to sex anytime she wants to, no matter who the person is who wants it. Tell her also that if she ever has anything she wants to talk over with an adult besides yourself, you'll arrange to have her see a counselor.

To be used as a sexual object by a trusted adult is a betrayal that produces in the victim a disturbing mix of anger, guilt, and confusion and often results in sexual dysfunction when the child grows up. This doesn't mean the child will never recover, but that she'll need some help sorting out her feelings and rebuilding her self-esteem.

If you have reason to believe your abusive spouse has molested your child, it is important to get the child to a safe place as soon as you can safely manage it. Tell your child you are going to protect her or him, but don't explain just yet how you will do that. First make a careful plan to leave. If you have not already made a safety plan, do it now. Turn to Who This Book Is For and How to Use It for suggestions on how to do that. When you first discover the sexual abuse, you might be tempted to burst out in anger and let your partner know you are leaving. But if he knows about that ahead of time, he could increase the danger to you and your child. *So do not tell your child about the plan.* She or he has been keeping one secret and should not be burdened with another.

An advocate at a domestic-violence shelter can help you find safe temporary housing and refer you to professionals who can advise you how to handle any court procedures that your partner may initiate after you leave. Your husband might use the courts to harass you, which could include accusations of lying about the sexual abuse and claims that you are an unfit mother. A court social worker or child-protective worker might become involved, and the more you know about what to expect the better you will be able to protect yourself and your child. Ask the advocate to tell you what she knows about local social workers. In the section on Children's Visits with Their Father in Chapter 28, Nurturing Your Children: Safety and Resilience, you will find suggestions on how to handle a social worker's concerns.

Emotional Abuse

By now, you may be used to humiliation, severe ego damage, and unprovoked insults to the children as well as to yourself. You've lost the ability to distinguish them from kidding and minor incidents of rudeness. If you've given up hope of stopping the verbal abuse, you may try to persuade the children to simply tune it out. If the father bullies everyone, you may tell yourself the children understand and don't take his emotional abuse personally. The children may, in fact, claim it doesn't bother them, either because they believe they're to blame or because they want to ease the family tension. Yet, while they silently nurse hurts and grievances their self-esteem is being chipped away with each insult, sarcastic verbal assault, or outburst of temper.

Even if the man isn't cruel to the children, their witness of his brutal treatment of you is likely to damage their abilities to form satisfying intimate relationships as adults. This too is a kind of child abuse. Many women feel a deep sense of regret that they remained with the violent man because they had wanted to keep the family together for the children's sake. Some of them observe their grown sons beating their wives or their grown daughters being beaten, each following the most familiar pattern of an intimate relationship. "Why didn't somebody warn me about this?" they ask in despair.

Their father may threaten to abandon the children altogether if you leave with them: "I'm certainly not going to be a weekend father. They won't even know who I am after awhile. If you take them, I'll never see them again." If he makes such a threat, you're confronted not only with your self-blame for his "forced" abandonment of the children, but your own fears of having to care for them alone, which may be more than you bargained for. (Single parenting is discussed in Chapter 15.)

Kidnapping is usually an empty threat, born of the desperation of the moment. But it does happen, so it can't lightly be dismissed. If kidnapping seems to be a realistic possibility, you need legal advice and perhaps a counselor to help you cope with your anxiety.

WHAT DO THE CHILDREN DESERVE?

What positive things do the children gain from their father? Love? Security? Affection? Respect? Money? Stability? Fun?

How much would they lose if they moved away with you? You can only guess, of course, but at least you shouldn't assume they'll lose it all. They might lose a good deal of security, stability, and money, though not absolutely. As for affection, respect, love, and fun, there's no reason to assume those qualities will disappear. They'll just be available in different ways or at different times. Those times needn't be just every Sunday. There are many custody arrangements.

If you've had several intimate relationships with men, you may feel guilty about your children's attachments to them being broken when you separated. It *is* hard for children to separate from father figures, but it may not be nearly as hard in the long run as staying with an abusive man.

It's never enough to say "Children need a father." Consider what else they deserve, as well as your own rights. Do they deserve the right to be free of humiliating remarks? Free of physical abuse? Free of fear? Have they the right to an environment that promotes cooperation, mutual respect, and protection? The right to nonviolent adult models? If you've rarely exercised those rights for yourself, you may need the help of a friend or counselor to gain a reasonable perspective on those questions.

A child who's reluctant to leave the father may present you a difficult problem. This may happen even if the father is abusive to the child, and it will be particularly difficult if a child old enough to decide for him- or herself makes that choice.

It may be tempting to stay with the man, either because you're unwilling to separate from the child, or because you hope you can protect him or her. You probably won't be able to provide adequate protection. In addition, you'll be continuing the example of an adult woman who's helpless in the face of violence. The message is, "When people brutalize you, there's nothing you can do but take it."

It may be extremely difficult to leave your child with the father, but if you do, at least you're saying—in the most powerful way possible—"I don't have to take it. I *can* get away." You're providing a choice for the child, if he or she decides in a few months, or a few years, to leave the father and go to a safe home. In any case, don't make assumptions about who will get child custody. Get some legal advice about what is most likely in your particular circumstances.

You don't owe your children a two-parent family. Although claims are made to the contrary, there's no persuasive evidence that children are happier or healthier in a two-parent than a one-parent home. There is no evidence that children whose fathers don't live with them suffer from lack of a male image. There *is* some evidence that males who have violent fathers tend to be violent men. You owe your children the safest environment you can provide and the best opportunity to grow up to be responsible healthy adults.

CHAPTER 4

WHAT DO YOU OWE YOURSELF?

Try to read this section as if you felt free to make your own decisions. There will be a temptation to say to yourself, "That's all very well, but I'd be beaten to a pulp," or "That sounds great for two reasonable people, but he would kill me if I even suggested negotiation." Later, you'll want to consider whether it's safe to act on these ideas, and you might very well decide it would be too dangerous if you're going to continue to live with the man. But for the moment, consider only whether these ideas are just and reasonable. This chapter will help you to realize what rights you have and to remember that life wasn't always a kind of prison. If you're getting very few of the things that everyone has a right to, then you have no obligation to stay in the relationship.

Suggestions for asserting your rights are made to help you remember that it's possible to ask for what you want. Sometimes even unreasonable spouses surprise you when you act as if you really believe in your rights.

ARE YOU SOMEBODY BESIDES WIFE, MOTHER, OR GIRLFRIEND?

It's extremely easy for many women to fuse their identities with those of their children or their husbands—that is, to be unable to tell where the family leaves off and they themselves begin. When you lose sight of who you are, separate from your man and your children, it's easy to become confused about what you deserve and what you owe yourself.

Activity 5 ᘯ Who Are You?

In a sentence or two *write* the answers to these questions:

1. What do you want?_____

_____

2. What do you want to do now?_____

_____

3. What do you like to do?_____

4. Who do you like to spend time with?_____

_____

5. What do you like to wear?_____

_____

6. Where do you like to go?_____

_____

7. Where would you like to live?_____

_____

8. What do you want to be doing in five years?_____

_____

9. Ten years?_____

_____

10. Twenty?_____

_____

How many answers were something such as, "I don't know, I haven't thought about it," or, "I want to live here because I wouldn't want to disrupt the kids' schooling," "My husband likes me to wear . . . ," or, "There's not much point in thinking about it, because the kids are too young," "My husband wouldn't hear of it," "It costs too much," or, "I don't much care. I'm easy to please."

If you answered half or more along these lines, you've probably forgotten who you are. You stopped, somewhere along the line, being an individual person, separate from your family or your man. You either stopped considering what you wanted a long time ago, or you developed the habit of foreseeing obstacles almost before realizing what you wanted. Those obstacles are usually the things that others need or want. Or perhaps you've persuaded yourself that you have what you want to avoid facing the reality that your husband and children wouldn't hear you even if you did ask for something.

Try answering the questions again, without regard to how anyone besides yourself would be affected. You may be reluctant to do it, because it seems selfish and wrong. Selfish means devoted to, or caring for, only yourself. That's not what I'm suggesting here. What I'm urging is that you become aware of what you want and like, so that—along with the other people you're close to—you can find your share of satisfaction and happi-

ness. You have to know what each person wants before you can make decisions about what's good for a couple or a family as a whole and before you
can arrive at reasonable compromises. You are a person, and your desires
should be considered on their own merits, as much as anyone else's.

READING HIS FEELINGS, READING YOURS

Women are taught to anticipate the needs of others as part of their role,
especially as mother and wife. Because young children are unable to articulate their needs, their caretakers—mostly women—develop the ability
to interpret. Sometimes mothers forget that older children can speak for
themselves. Those children learn that their mothers will know what they
want sometimes even before they know it themselves.

But husbands, one might suppose, are quite able to articulate their
needs and wants, so why does a wife expend psychic energy figuring out
what they might be?

When we say that a man isn't supposed to be helpless or dependent,
that's not meant to include his emotional life. It's considered appropriate
for a man to be incapable of expressing certain emotions—tenderness,
love, vulnerability, inadequacy, loneliness, dependence, fear—and yet, he
must be given solace, somehow, when these feelings surface. Helpless in
the face of these emotions, he's dependent on the woman he's close to to
interpret them for him, and often to provide comfort, even when he
doesn't know he needs it.

It is often essential to a wife's safety and health to be able to meet her
husband's needs—even when he doesn't know what they are. If she isn't
able to do that, his feelings of vulnerability, dependence, or fear may
emerge as enraged demands for sex, a meal, or some other form of attention. The woman who's busy with another task or sound asleep at 2 a.m.
or lulled into inattention by the man's earlier good mood will pay a high
price for not being attuned to his wishes, whether he expressed them or
not. (This doesn't mean even a perfect mind reader will be safe. Some violent men explode whether all their desires are being attended to or not.)
You'll have to decide how much energy you're willing to put into mind
reading and whether it's really keeping you safe. However, even if you
continue to do a great deal of it, it's time you start "reading" your own
feelings as well. You may be such a stranger to them that you'll have to
begin by making careful note of when you're tired, sad, or feeling hurt,
rejected, or used. Begin by noticing physical signs or overt behavior.
When you're overly tired and sleepy, look for signs of hurt, rejection, sadness, or depression. When you snap at the kids for no apparent reason,

ask yourself if you're feeling unappreciated and used, or if you're angry at your spouse. When you can't eat, or when you stuff down sweets, or drink too much, what are you trying to compensate for? Loneliness? Lack of affection? When you become overly restrictive with the children, or resent other people's obvious good times, could it be that you're feeling your own confinement and lack of pleasure in life?

As you begin to recognize how you feel, you'll be able to explore what you want, and that's the beginning of a separate identity. Then you'll be on your way to answering the question: "What do I owe myself?" But there's another question that comes first.

"WHAT IF IT'S REALLY MY FAULT?"

If you believe you're responsible for the destructive aspects of the relationship, your awareness of your faults may keep you from even considering that you have a right to end it. This is an especially dangerous trap for you if you've lashed out at him verbally or physically at times. Perhaps you hit him back sometimes, or lost your temper and threw something at him, or even started the violence yourself. You may badger yourself with thoughts such as, "Maybe I brought it on myself," "I shouldn't be so sloppy at housekeeping . . . cold in bed . . . selfish . . . demanding . . . bad-tempered," "He put up with a lot from me."

Think of the things you did, or failed to do, that may have "brought it on yourself." How did you know they did? Did you get hit every time you did those things? *Only* then? Be scrupulously honest. Often a woman is beaten for "reasons" she doesn't understand at all. In a desperate attempt to create order out of chaos, she reconstructs events and decides her own shortcomings "caused" the beatings. For awhile that may be a useful survival technique as it seems to place some responsibility and control in her hands if she can actually change herself, or cause the man to react differently. But with a man who batters, such control over behavior rarely exists.

To make a sound decision, different questions and more precise answers are in order. If there's someone you've confided in all along, you should ask her help now. She may have a more objective memory than yours about the certainty of cause and effect.

If some of your actions or attitudes are always followed by beatings, look at them closely and decide whether it's reasonable for the man to object to them. Suppose he becomes violent every time you spend time with a woman friend, or whenever you aren't home to answer his calls from work, or when you complain, or when dinner is late.

Which of these "flaws" should you correct? Which do you want to change? It might well be worth your while to put time and effort into changing because you want to, and because it might please your man. But regardless of whether these are flaws that you both want changed, *your imperfections do not give your partner the right to "discipline" you with physical violence.*

Questions to Ask Yourself

Let's look at his objection to your spending time with women friends. If that always occasions his hitting or beating you, and if you're determined to stay with him, you might either stop seeing friends to protect yourself from his violence or you might decide to continue those relationships, but to keep them secret.

If one day you give in to your loneliness and go off with a woman friend hoping to get away with it but he learns this and beats you, you may feel you asked for it. A friend or relative may tell you the same thing. "After all, you knew he would beat you if he found out, didn't you?"

The phrase implies you deserved it, which means either you behaved badly, so you deserve to be punished, or that you behaved stupidly, since you should have known the consequences that would follow your action.

Ask yourself whether meeting your friend was wrong, whether any adult has the right to punish another, and whether people who behave stupidly deserve bad things to happen to them.

Was meeting a friend wrong? Do you deserve to have friends, to be with people who give you some of the warmth and concern you seldom get from your husband? Isn't that a minimum of what every person deserves? If you agree, ask yourself again whether you really "brought it on yourself." At worst you may find that you didn't act in the safest way. But you were protecting another equally important aspect of yourself, that seed of independence and individuality, hungering to grow and needing warmth and nurturance in which to do it. You risked your physical being on the chance you could nourish your spirit. It's impossible to make a really good decision if the alternatives are either risking a beating or resigning yourself to isolation.

Does one adult have the right to punish another? If your man beats you, he's likely to explain that it was a last resort, a reminder that he's the authority over all aspects of your life. Whether he has that right has nothing to do with whether you have faults. He certainly has the right to point them out and to ask you to change, just as you have a similar right in regard to his flaws. But you're not his child, not his employee, not his property. He doesn't have the right to control your life. (For that matter, it's now recognized that even the rights of employers to discipline their employees and of parents to punish children are severely limited by law.)

No position of authority brings with it the power of judge, jailer, and batterer. Certainly the institution of marriage, which is said to be based on love, respect, and companionship, should not foster such power. Nor should it grant the partner who has the most economic power and the greater physical strength the right to punish his spouse for either imagined or real faults.

Do people who behave stupidly deserve to have bad things happen to them? As discussed above, you took a calculated risk to get something you badly wanted. Just because you could have predicted you'd be beaten if caught doesn't mean either that you behaved stupidly or that you deserve a beating.

If you and your man each have serious faults, that doesn't necessarily mean you deserve each other. To the extent that you bring out the worst in each other, at least a temporary separation is indicated. This is especially true if you're both violent, alcoholic, or addicted to drugs, which make you dangerous to each other. It can give you some space so that you can each learn more kind and constructive ways of treating each other. Then you can either come back together, or you might form new relationships that will be constructive and mutually supportive.

If you really do believe that you're very difficult to live with, you can start changing your ways now by practicing the exercises in the Helping Yourself to Survival section, especially Chapter 11, A Courageous Act a Day.

WHAT DO YOU DESERVE?

For many people, to deserve something implies that it has been earned through work or suffering. Yet there are some things that everyone deserves, earned or not.

Freedom of speech is a fundamental right. Many a wife gives up this right soon after marriage, as she becomes aware of more and more things that upset or anger her husband. Perhaps the first statement to be eliminated is a comment about her past relationships, especially with men. Then she stops talking about her desires for the future, when he interprets that as a criticism of his ability to provide for the family. Next goes the expression of any negative feelings: depression, frustration, loneliness. She may no longer ask him questions about his work, where he's been, or how he feels, lest she be accused of prying or nagging. Finally she may give up stating her own opinions, to avoid being called stupid.

A woman will often do this, at first out of consideration for her man's feelings, later to protect herself from his temper. He may directly demand her silence on many subjects and before long, she persuades herself she has no right to speak up. She thinks there's something wrong with her for even wanting to express herself.

The right to have some aspects of life remain private ought to be recognized by both partners. Many men who are violent toward their wives call them several times every day to check on whether they're home, insist on accompanying them to the grocery store, and won't let them out of their sight unless it's absolutely necessary, which usually means when they're at work. They may closely question the woman about the smallest activities of her day and physically punish her if she refuses to respond to the cross-examination. Yet, if the woman asks questions related to their mutual concerns, such as whether they'll be going out Saturday night, or how much money is in the bank, she will be accused of invading male territory.

You may gradually have given up your rights without thinking much about them. How about the right to choose your friends? To decide how to spend money? How to use your time? What to eat, wear, and how to look?

Take the matter of your appearance. Most of us like to look attractive to the people we're close to, but it's your right to dress and arrange your hair and makeup to please your family or to please yourself. If your husband thinks you look too flashy or wants you to look too obviously sexy, or your daughter accuses you of looking "old" or dowdy, you don't have to accommodate them by changing your appearance. One way to begin establishing your separate identity is to dress in the style that's comfortable for you, that feels like the real you.

As for money and time, some of it belongs to the family and is subject to family decisions. But there are two important qualifications. Only some of it belongs to the family; you have a right to use some money and some time just to please yourself, no questions asked. Second, what does belong to the family should not be distributed or decided upon only by the male, but at least by the two adults in the household.

Perhaps by now you're ready to consider what basic rights everyone is entitled to. *Place a check mark* in the first column, indicating each item that you believe everyone deserves.

Activity 6 ⌇ Rights List

	Everyone has the right.	I exercise my right.
1. The right to privacy	_____	_____
2. The right to express ideas, including unpopular ones	_____	_____
3. The right to express feelings, even "negative" ones	_____	_____
4. The right to choose work, religion, lifestyle	_____	_____
5. The right to be free of fear	_____	_____
6. The right to have some time for yourself	_____	_____
7. The right to spend some money as you please	_____	_____
8. The right to emotional support from family and friends	_____	_____
9. The right to be listened to by family and friends	_____	_____
10. The right to cultivate friendships of your choice	_____	_____
11. The right to do creative, challenging, absorbing, worthwhile work	_____	_____
12. The right to decide whether to have sex or not	_____	_____

All but two of the above are rights you can exercise now. (These exceptions are the right to satisfying work and the right to choose one's work. Most people are not fortunate enough to do that without careful planning, training, and perhaps sacrifice of some immediate satisfactions.)

Put a check in the second column for each right you actually exercise.

If there are differences between columns 1 and 2, look closely at what's happened to your exercise of rights. Maybe you believe everyone except you has certain rights. Does that mean you're not quite a person? Does it mean that civil and human rights are suspended for women, or for wives—or for mothers until their children are grown?

In looking at these questions it's easy to be distracted by "Yes, but . . . " games. "Yes, but he's taking me out so I don't have any right to say where I'd like to go, or to refuse sex." "Yes, but I can't choose what to buy because he earns the money." "Yes, but none of us really has time or money to spare, so there aren't free choices to be made." "Yes, but he didn't choose his job and it's not satisfying at all, so I don't have any right. . . ."

Money

Let's look at money. It can certainly seem as if there is nothing to decide, especially if it all goes for necessities. However, even when there's not enough to pay basic bills, some of it is always spent on discretionary items. If your grocery bag includes beer, sweets, packaged gravy, pop, frozen foods, magazines, or cigarettes, you've already made some decisions about "nonessentials." It's difficult to make mutual decisions about these matters because one person's necessity is another's luxury.

Even if it's a small amount, each person should exercise the right to have funds to spend with no questions asked. If you spend money that way already, that's a start. But perhaps you manage it by slipping a magazine into the groceries, or stashing small amounts of cash away until you have enough to take the kids to the circus, buy your teenage son new jeans, or buy something you want for yourself. Or maybe you charge what you want, and then wait nervously for the blows when the bills come in.

In these ways you may get the things you want, but you pay a high price and you don't establish any rights. If you have to be sneaky to get away with it, or risk punishment, you're cast into the role of the irresponsible child who can't make her own decisions—a person who may have only what another person arbitrarily decides she deserves. A dangerous byproduct is an increase of your guilt feelings and lowering of your self-esteem.

Time

The same principle applies to time of your own. How much time you can arrange to have to yourself depends upon your lifestyle: your housekeeping standards, the size of your garden, how much of your spouse's time is available for childcare (i.e., how much time he's not working at an outside job, how old your children are, etc.). At a minimum, each of you should have one half day and one evening a week to do as you please.

A problem may be that one or both of you doesn't want to take that time. Suppose you don't want the time, or you like the idea but you don't know what to do with it. It will be good for you to take it anyway. Use it to take a class, to shop, to walk in the park, to see a movie that doesn't interest your partner, to cultivate a friendship to begin reestablishing your separate identity. You may spend a few hours being either bored or nervous until you get used to making decisions and participating in new activities, but it will be worth it in the long run.

It's good for your relationship if you each take some time for yourself, but if he insists that he doesn't need or want such time, you have little power to do anything about it. He might use the fact that he doesn't take his time to try to make you feel guilty for taking yours. In that case, you'll need to keep in mind that it's his choice. He's not making a sacrifice for you. He's doing what he wants, and you have the right to do what you want.

GETTING RESPECT IN THE WORKPLACE (AT HOME AND ON THE JOB)

Often both husbands and wives consider the wife's earned income to be merely "pocket money." Both men and women want to believe the man is supporting the family, because that's part of the traditional myth of masculinity. However, as inflation spirals, more people are admitting that it takes two incomes for most families to live well. A woman's income is buying goods and services that are important to the family and it's no less important than her partner's income. Women can no longer afford to accept these traditional propositions:

- Women deserve less money in the marketplace, because their work is less important than men's.
- Since they're earning only "extras," their work isn't very important.
- Since their work outside the home isn't of much value, and women really should be at home anyway, they should still do the housework and childcare.

Those statements should be replaced with these:

- Work is of equal value, regardless of the worker's gender.
- Women need work and adequate pay as much as men do.
- If two people parent children, both should be responsible for home and childcare.

This doesn't necessarily mean that each partner must do precisely half of each job, but that the number of hours worked in and outside the home is near equal and is acceptable to the person doing the work. When this idea prevails in society, we will no longer find women doing the three unpaid jobs of wife, housekeeper, and parent plus one underpaid job of waitress, secretary, or nurse. Men and women will share and appreciate each other's contributions both in and out of the home.

If your role is that of the traditional wife or mother and your tasks of housekeeping and childcare are rarely finished for more than a short time, the lack of a sense of accomplishment may also contribute to the idea that you haven't done anything of value. This feeling is one of the aspects of homemaking that makes the job hard. According to recent surveys, women who have no children spend about five and a half hours a day on housework. So don't sell your labor short.

If your children are in school or grown, you may not do much work at home. Some of us take housekeeping more seriously than others, and if you really want to make homemaking a full-time job even when your children are older, perhaps that's what you should do. But if you can take care of it in two or three hours a day, consider getting a part-time or full-time job outside the home. Knowledge that you're pulling your share of the weight will help you make a better decision about leaving or staying with the man. Before you decide whether to take a job, make a careful count of the hours you spend at homemaking and childcare, being sure to include trips to the zoo and other child-centered activities on weekends and in the evening. Also consider your volunteer activities in the community and the church. They are work too. If your man wants you to stay home, yet he looks down on the work you do at home, you need to change something. If you've begun to agree with him about the low value of what you do at home, you'll need to relearn respect for your work or to start looking for employment outside. In other words, start respecting what you do or start doing what you respect.

Look again at your responses to the second column in Activity 6 and decide which rights you're going to begin claiming. Decide whether it's going to be safe to do it while you're still living with the man. Just in case, plan to tell him about it when you're someplace you'll be safe or where you can get away quickly if he becomes violent.

UNDERSTANDING WHAT YOU BOTH DESERVE

Perhaps you'd like to make changes in your life but are thinking to yourself, "He deserves things that he's not getting, either," or, "There isn't any way I can get what I deserve." Let's consider both responses.

He's not getting what he deserves, either. A good place to start with this one is simply to ask him what he believes he deserves, and what he's not getting. He may refuse to participate in such a conversation. He may think it's useless to think about such things since no one gets much in life anyway. Or he might react with suspicion, in which case you should be honest and tell him you have your own list that you want to share.

If he's willing to participate, you can begin to make some tradeoffs so that each of you can get something you want and deserve. Tradeoffs won't work, though, unless there's at least a semblance of equality. If he believes he deserves peace and quiet when he gets home from work, does he recognize a time when you deserve peace and quiet? If he deserves not to be "nagged" about doing household chores on the weekend, will he agree not to nag you to sew buttons, serve meals, and so on during weekends? If not, you don't have grounds for negotiation.

If he flatly refuses to participate, there won't be much you can do. Maybe that will give you one more item for your own Rights List (Activity 6): "When I want to negotiate fair treatment for each of us, I deserve a response and some effort to work it out."

There isn't any way I can get what I deserve. If you've decided there isn't any way to get what you deserve, ask yourself why not, why won't it happen? It does to lots of people. It isn't always because they're lucky or smart, either. Most people who get what they deserve have realized that it's up to them to make it happen. You can't control some parts of your life, but you can focus on those parts you can do something about.

You can lay the groundwork to leave your husband or to acquire work skills. You can make plans to overcome whatever obstacles stand in the way of getting what you deserve.

This is not to say it's easy—all the more reason to get started planning now. Remember that the hardships and failures and disasters you envision if you get a job, go to school, or live without a man are frightening mainly because these choices are new to you. Your current way of life (having almost no freedom, being physically beaten and emotionally abused, feeling trapped and worthless) is probably much more dangerous and would be far more frightening to you if you weren't used to it. You can get used to the difficult aspects of a new way of life and the rewards will more than balance the hardship. Just give yourself a little time.

You owe it to yourself to begin getting the things you and every person deserve. No one is likely to give them to you unless you realize that it's your right to have them. You owe it to yourself to decide, to choose, and to make of your life what you want it to be.

CHAPTER 5

"BUT I STILL LOVE HIM"

Friends and relatives may despair, hearing you say you still love the man who abused you, especially if the abuse was physical and seriously damaging. Perhaps you're bewildered yourself, or humiliated by the awareness that you still love the man who acts in a hateful way toward you.

WHAT DOES BEING IN LOVE MEAN?

Though we can't explain the condition of being in love, we recognize it when it happens to us, and usually we accept it on faith when someone tells us it has happened to her. Note that it "happens" to someone, like "a bolt from the blue." One helplessly "falls in love." These phrases indicate the passivity of Cupid's victim. Love, according to song and story and poem, is out of your control, not something you choose to do or work at doing. It causes symptoms that are similar to illness: palpitations, trembling, loss of appetite, weakness.

These symptoms, reflecting both the pain and exhilaration of being in love, probably originated with the Greeks, who invented the concept of Western love that—with important modifications—we cling to today. But, in contrast to modern Americans, the ancient Greeks considered love an amusing pastime, or a distraction from more serious and important matters. They didn't view it as necessary to being a good person, nor as a lifetime commitment, nor did they associate it with the union of marriage.

Each age tends to view its concept of love as both the only way it could be and the way it's supposed to be. Patterns of love from past periods seem either comical or tragic. Morton Hunt, in *The Natural History of Love,* provides a useful modern perspective: "At no time in history has so large a proportion of humanity rated love so highly, thought about it so much, or displayed such an insatiable appetite for words about it."[1]

Most of us are appalled at the outmoded idea of loveless, unromantic, arranged marriages, but Hunt points out the absurdity of the contemporary idea that "the romantic attraction is considered to be adequate and indeed the only basis for choosing one's lifelong partner." He questions the commonly held idea that "sex drives . . . must be completely and permanently satisfied within marriage . . . and that tenderness, mystery, and excitement are expected to coexist with household care, child-raising problems, and the routine 15,000 nights together."[2]

To some extent we are stuck with these ideas, absurd or not, an impossible burden on marriage or not. We're all shaped by films, novels and songs, law, economics, and religion to believe that love properly takes only certain forms—and that all others are immoral, crazy, immature, or just infatuation.

Romantic as this twenty-first-century age is, there are variations on the theme of love, and you can analyze your feelings (and his) to determine whether you're involved in a dangerously romantic or addictive relationship or whether you share a healthy, nurturing love that might even withstand 15,000 nights of routine.

To get a clearer perspective on the particular kind of love you and your man share, *put a check mark* in front of each of the following that seems true:

Activity 7 ✌ How Do You Love Each Other?

1. I could never find another man to love the way I love him.
2. Without him, I have nothing to live for.
3. I know exactly what it is about him I love.
4. No one could ever understand him the way I do.
5. I suppose I should be interested in other people and activities, but I just want to be with him.
6. We help each other to explore new possibilities in life.
7. The idea of making love to another man is unthinkable.
8. Whenever I'm a few minutes late, or want to be alone, he thinks I'm with another man.
9. Loving him makes me feel more loving toward other people.
10. I try to keep on my "rose-colored glasses" and see only the best in him.
11. I love him so much, I can't stand the thought of his being with anyone else.
12. I hope he never leaves me, but if it comes to that I'll be okay.
13. He would never love another woman the way he loves me.
14. Often, I feel better when I'm away from him, yet I find myself calling him against my better judgment.
15. I feel good about myself when I'm with him.
16. I never let him see me without makeup, or with curlers in my hair. I want him always to see me at my best.

17. I feel that I'm nothing without him.
18. He brings out the best in me.
19. I don't know why I love him, I just do.
20. When things are going well with us, I don't need anyone but him.
21. He has many of the qualities I value and that I'm trying to develop in myself.
22. He's so much smarter and more capable than I am; he seems to know everything about everything.
23. When I try to imagine never seeing him again, I feel empty.
24. It's wonderful to spend time with him at sports, work, or having fun together with other people, and I enjoy being by myself or with women friends, too.
25. He's so special, I don't know why he's interested in an ordinary person like me.
26. Without me, he has nothing to live for.
27. He wants me to feel good whether I'm with him or not.
28. This time he means it. He's really going to change.
29. I know he loves me because he wants to know where I am every minute.
30. I like to hear about the good times he's had when he's been with other people.

As part of your analysis of your responses, look at three kinds of conjugal love that are common today. Romantic, addictive, and nurturing love all have some overlapping characteristics, but they can also be looked at separately.

ROMANTIC LOVE

Romantic love grows out of the courtly tradition of the eleventh- and twelfth-century "knights in shining armor." It was noble, pure, sacrificial, often tragically destined to be unconsummated, yet the lovers might be faithful to death, enduring years of tragic suffering because the fates refused to allow them to come together. These lovers were often able to maintain their enchantment because they loved from afar, rarely coming into close enough contact to distinguish the real character flaws (and virtues) of the beloved. These romantic adventures were definitely not to be contaminated by the lustful sexuality of the marriage bed.

Today, of course, romantic love is supposed to lead to sexuality, married love, and happiness ever after. The lovers are by no means distant from each other. There are no long nights of sonnet writing or years of anonymous serenading under balconies today. Contemporary love relationships are likely to begin with the question, "What's your name?" on Monday, followed by "How about a date?" on Tuesday, and a few Saturday nights later "Let's go to bed," which may or may not be accompanied by promises to love faithfully, forever.

But the poetry remains, in however altered a form. Popular songs envelop the romantic couple with the magic, the madness, the otherworldliness, and sometimes the delicious tragedy of sexual love.

The "magic" aspect of love implies powerlessness in the face of an overwhelming force, insists that the feeling is not subject to rational analysis. Nor need there be any nameable qualities that cause you to love the specific person. It's "the touch of his hand," "the very thought of you," or other vaguely felt responses to the idea of him more than to his tangible qualities.

To see how romantic your relationship is, take another look at your responses to the statements about love in Activity 7. Note how many checks you had for numbers 1, 4, 7, 10, 13, 16, 19, 22, 25. The more checks, the more romantic your relationship is.

Questions 1, 4, 7, and 13 reflect the feeling that there's only one man for each woman in the world. Perhaps you reject that notion when it's stated so obviously, but check marks for those statements give away your lingering belief in it.

If you responded positively to questions 19, 22, 25, and 28, you're a victim of the romantic beliefs that your man is someone out of the ordinary realm of humans. Yet you can't even say which of his characteristics you value. You believe he'll turn from beast to beauty, from frog to prince. Regardless of the evidence to the contrary, he'll stop his cruelty and become tender and loving. Positive responses to statements 10 and 16 indicate you love your own idea of the person, rather than who he really is, and you want him to perceive you only at your best. This fosters illusions and psychological distance. If you don't allow yourself to see your lover's flaws, you'll be able to maintain the idea that he's not an ordinary human being at all, but a superperson, who for some mysterious reason chooses to love you. By virtue of his love, you're raised a bit closer to the world of superpeople. If you risk displeasing him, he may leave you, thrusting you squarely back in the world of ordinary people— where you secretly fear you belong anyway. So it's easy to persuade yourself you'll fall apart without him.

This romantic relationship can be fun, exciting, all-absorbing, erotic, entertaining. It can keep you in a state of "delirious" happiness and plunge you into despair. It's a peak experience, a "high" unmatched by any other.

ADDICTIVE LOVE

There is a remarkable similarity between the effects of romantic love and of certain drugs, not only in the "high" state and the "low" of withdrawal, but in the potential for addiction. We've all been taught that certain drugs are dangerously addictive and that everyone should stay safely away from them, but there is a growing body of evidence that addiction lies as much in the person as in the substance.[3]

Many people have used cocaine, alcohol, cigarettes, sugar, or other allegedly addictive substances with no difficulty. Others have become hooked, either quickly or slowly. At first, they're high—their minds and feelings are expanding. But addicts eventually find that they've become dull and that their worlds have shrunk. As with drugs, this might happen with an overdose of television, running, crafts, reading, housework—or love.

Addiction is often learned. The effects of drugs are often the result of what the user *expects* to happen. If the beginning cocaine, marijuana, or alcohol user is coached to expect a "rush," or physical sensation, she is likely to experience what has been predicted to happen.

Having learned to anticipate it from an early age, a woman can experience romantic love as a special kind of high, in which the "oneness" of being a couple instantly banishes loneliness and the sense of alienation many of us suffer. If the woman has a good feeling about herself and some other solid connections through work or friends, she may realize she's in love with the idea of love rather than the actual person. If the man stops loving her, she will go through a period of mourning, but she won't let the breakup destroy her perceptions of herself. Nor will she imagine her lost love is the only man in the world for her.

But a woman who values herself less or needs love more will go a step beyond that romantic love into addiction. In addition to believing in the characteristics of romantic love, she'll be certain she can't survive without the man's love and that she wouldn't even want to, because there wouldn't be anything to live for. Her world has shrunk, and if the man stops loving her, she will feel abandoned and desolate. If he periodically neglects or abuses her, she'll allow herself to be persuaded each time that it didn't really happen, it was her fault, or it was a one-time aberration that will never happen again.

The degree to which she's vulnerable to this script depends upon how suggestible she is and the extent to which society—her friends, family, advertisements, songs, and movies—have coached her into expecting that being in love will bring ecstasy and that being abandoned by her lover must be a tragedy.

The man who believes he can't survive without love often fears that his woman will become involved with someone else if she goes to the grocery store alone or may work himself into a jealous rage if she happens to be away from the telephone when he calls. He wants to exercise total control over her life; if she refuses it, or seems to refuse it, his fear of being abandoned may lead to psychological or physical abuse of the woman he loves, and to the extent she's addicted to him, she'll be unable or unwilling to escape that abuse.

When this happens, the woman becomes helpless and dependent. Her life may be reduced to the addictive cycle: the overpowering need for him, the "high" of momentary fulfillment, and then the "downer" when the "supply" is removed. If he removes himself—emotionally or physically—often, or for long periods, she'll become absorbed in her loneliness and grief. Paradoxically, if he's always available, her dependence on him will only grow.

The more her world becomes centered on the addiction, the more narrow it becomes, and the more narrow her world, the more it centers on her addiction. When members of a couple are mutually addicted, they can sometimes work out a tolerable relationship, though it makes for very confined lives. When one person is a batterer, it is a deadly, dangerous relationship and often more difficult to break away from than other forms of addiction.

You can tell whether you're involved in addictive love by reviewing your answers to questions 2, 5, 8, 11, 14, 17, 20, 23, 26, 28, and 29. Positive responses to numbers 8, 26, and 29 indicate that the man is addicted to you. Check marks for numbers 2, 5, 11, 14, 17, 20, 23, and 28 reflect your addiction to him. In a two-way "habit" you both believe that without each other you have nothing to live for. When you're addicted you're sure you can fulfill all of the other's needs and that your demand for total, exclusive possession of each other proves your love. If there's some specific quality you value in him, it may be something you believe you lack. If you've convinced yourself you're not very smart or capable, you may feel a need to associate with a man who seems to have those qualities. If your self-esteem is very low, your need to be associated with a man who seems competent may be so great that you grossly overestimate his desirable qualities. You depend on him to be capable for both of you so that you don't have to develop your own capabilities. Meanwhile, your inflated view of his abilities may help him from moment to moment to deny his feelings of inadequacy and the need to overcome them. He won't grow, either, and you'll each become helpless and dependent on each other.

NURTURING LOVE

Nurturing love is the opposite of addictive love. It sustains life, promotes growth, and increases energy. It is not possessive, and it grows out of a realistic appreciation of the loved one's attractive qualities without a need to minimize his flaws.

Nurturing love is based on what each partner *wants* rather than needs. If the loved one has important qualities that the lover lacks, she'll want to develop them in herself rather than simply basking in the reflected light of the loved one's admired characteristics. This type of love allows for the expansion of abilities, knowledge, and experience rather than the shrinkage of relationships and activities. To find out if this is the kind of love you feel for the man in your relationship, check the number of your responses to questions 3, 6, 9, 12, 15, 18, 21, 24, 27, and 30. The more checks you have, the more nurturing your love is likely to be. If you have a healthy, mutually respectful relationship, one partner may lose his or her temper from time to time, but the result will not be battering. The man in a nurturing relationship can be expected not to hit his spouse but if he does lose control, he will immediately find a way to regain it, or will find professional help, and at the very least will arrange for the woman's safety if a similar situation is likely to occur.

REASONS FOR LEAVING SOMEONE YOU LOVE

When abused women say "I know I should leave, but I love him," they suggest "Because I love him, I can't leave him." But that doesn't necessarily follow. Loving an abusive man will make it hard to leave, but not impossible. Loving him may make you want to stay with him, but in the long run the most loving thing you can do for each other is to separate, at least temporarily. No one wants his or her loved one to continue a round of violence and remorse. If you separate, you'll at least interrupt that pattern. If you're involved in an addictive relationship that's abusive, you'll have to cut the relationship off immediately and totally. In either case, you'll have to get rid of the romantic ideas that he is the only one who can provide you what you need, that you'll never find another man to love, and that life isn't worth living without love.

By now you should have a pretty clear idea of what kind of love you're involved in and the extent of the problem you'll be faced with if you decide that for your safety you must leave. But for many women, it's a long step between that realization and taking action on it.

CHAPTER 6

MAKING THE DECISION

So here you are, thinking about separating from your man and dreading the thought of no one's voice to fill the silence when you come home from work. Perhaps you'll have one or more children to support and discipline, teach and love on your own. You may be thinking about a job you'll have to keep for many years, whether you like it or not, or worrying about responsibility for all decisions: where to live, what to buy, who to get to fix the toilet, how to do the income tax yourself. In short, whenever there's a question about what is to be done, you'll have to make the decision.

If you've been going around and around on a mental treadmill for some time, unable to decide whether to leave or stay, now is the time to take your first decisive step. It's time for action.

HOW SERIOUS ARE YOU?

Some people use self-help books to clarify their thoughts or to start changing their lives. Others read one after the other without ever helping themselves. They use the books as a way to avoid making changes while persuading themselves that they're "trying." Similarly, some abused women read everything that's published about women in their situation in hopes of finding a solution that will neither require them to leave the man nor take risks nor endure pain. That isn't going to happen. If you decide to change your life, it may be challenging, exciting, and rewarding, but it will also probably be difficult, lonely, and frightening at first.

As a check on how seriously you've been considering the content of this book, look back and see how many of the questionnaires you answered with pen or pencil rather than simply reading through them. The more active a reader you've been, the more serious you probably are about making a decision that you can live with and stick to.

If you've been just a passive reader, go back now and complete the questionnaires. They're designed to help you clarify your thoughts and feelings. Your participation is a message to yourself that you're taking your survival seriously.

WHAT'S THE WORST THAT CAN HAPPEN IF YOU LEAVE?

Do you imagine that if you're totally responsible for yourself or for the family, the day might come when you're faced with someone's judgment that you've been a colossal failure? One of society's rejects? Incapable of making it on your own or of being a competent single parent? Perhaps your fears take the form of vaguely felt apprehensions or maybe they're clearly visualized tragedies. You become so depressed you take an overdose of pills. You lose custody of the children because you can't support them and take care of them at the same time; your son becomes an alcoholic; child-protective services are called in because your children are reported to be neglected.

Your concerns may not be as acutely dramatic as that. Maybe they're along the lines of the children's daily discipline problems or the constant colds and years of runny noses that seem to be ahead. Or you imagine years of boring factory or office work, poverty and sameness with little hope of either romance or security. Or the continual emptiness of knowing there's no one special who cares, no one to understand in-jokes or to share responsibility, blame, and triumphs with you. The thought of starting over with someone else seems impossibly burdensome.

Perhaps your greatest fears are of boredom, lack of excitement, romance, and companionship. Try to make the frightening notion of being alone specific. Is it sex you'll miss? Or companionship? Someone to go places with, or to share the worries and pleasures of child-raising? All of the above, plus someone to lean on and be needed by?

Activity 8 ᢆ Worst Fears List

Worst Fear: Losing the home and garden that I've worked for for twenty-two years.

Reasons It's Likely	Reasons It's Unlikely
I can't afford the payments	I'll probably get the house, because I'll probably get custody
Bob probably won't pay house maintenence	Child support might include enough for payments
I'm too old to get a better job	Could have kids double up and rent two rooms
	Might be able to refinance

Do this exercise for yourself now.

Worst Fear: _____

Reasons It's Likely	Reasons It's Unlikely
_____	_____
_____	_____
_____	_____
_____	_____
_____	_____

You may be able to fill in some of the blanks with certainty. But other tentative answers may simply raise more questions. This is important. In some situations you may be able only to make guesses, and you'll need to find specialists in certain fields to answer your concerns. The questions may be about property settlement, custody, employment, or public assistance, and the people you turn to may be lawyers, job counselors, battered women's shelter staff, or social workers.

Getting expert advice can be costly. Call a shelter or women's center, legal services or the American Bar Association, or a crisis-line information and referral service to find out if there are any low-cost services for people in your circumstances. Be sure to say that you've been battered in case there are special services for battered women. (If you haven't talked about it, this may be hard to do, but it's a good time to start. Saying out loud that you've been battered is a good way to remind yourself that you have nothing to be ashamed of.)

If there are no special services for battered women in your community, you may have to travel to find them. If you have to pay high fees, it will probably be worthwhile in the long run, but first ask several people for referrals so you have a better chance of finding someone worth all that money. (See the next section for ideas on how to deal with doctors, lawyers. and counselors.) Your alternative is to spend more years worrying about events that may be extremely unlikely, and possibly to make some bad decisions on the basis of your miscalculations.

When you've gathered as much information as possible, modify your answers to the questions about the likelihood of your fears coming true. Share your new information with friends or relatives who you're sure understand you and have your best interests at heart. Be wary of advice that's too easy. ("Oh, you won't have any trouble getting a good job just because you're fifty years old.") But if most people you trust believe your fears aren't justified—and if they're standing by to help—you may want to reconsider your negative judgments.

WHAT'S THE WORST THAT CAN HAPPEN IF YOU STAY WITH THE MAN?

Many a woman who is involved with an abusive man describes herself as fearful, unwilling to take risks, or even cowardly. But those of us on the outside looking in see that such a woman takes enormous risks every day of her life. People have a remarkable ability to get used to almost anything and then to define their way of life as normal or even rewarding.

If you consider yourself a generally fearful person, you probably don't realize how many risks you take every day. *Make a list* of all the chances you took during the last few days, including risks of succeeding or failing, being hurt or being safe, of feeling accepted or rejected, or making your life better or worse.

Activity 9 ✢ Risk List

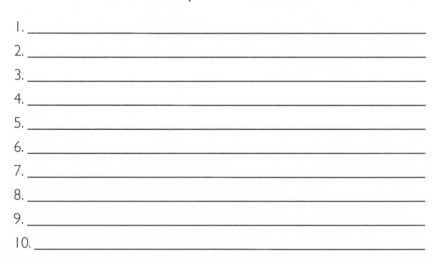

1. _____
2. _____
3. _____
4. _____
5. _____
6. _____
7. _____
8. _____
9. _____
10. _____

What's the most *likely* bad thing to happen if you stay? Consider the physical and psychological damage, both long-range and short-range, to you and your children. *List the things* you're afraid of. If they don't seem so bad, think back to the last time you were abused. Remember what you were afraid of then, and *write down everything* you were afraid would happen to you during the few minutes or few hours after the crisis. Do it even if it's very painful, and *compare that list* with the list of of things you're afraid of now. If there's a big difference, the chances are that you're letting the memory of the real dangers of your situation fade away so you won't have to think about leaving—and facing the unknown experience of being alone. Ask yourself, "If I stay, what are the odds of each danger happening?" Ninety percent likely? Seventy-five percent? If you're afraid of being killed, even a 20 percent or a 5 percent chance is too high.

Activity 10 ✐ Comparing the Dangers

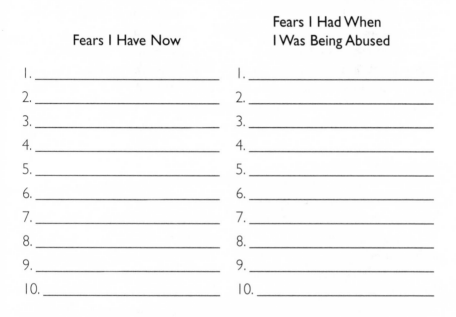

Fears I Have Now	Fears I Had When I Was Being Abused
1. _____	1. _____
2. _____	2. _____
3. _____	3. _____
4. _____	4. _____
5. _____	5. _____
6. _____	6. _____
7. _____	7. _____
8. _____	8. _____
9. _____	9. _____
10. _____	10. _____

Try to make yourself imagine what it would be like to die. Then force yourself to imagine what it would be like to kill the man, as some women have done after years of abuse. Think about what it would be like to be paralyzed or deaf from his brutal injury. Don't just shudder and shrug it away. Stay with the thought. Visualize yourself, your man, your family, the police, your relatives. Feel what you would feel if each of these actions were really happening.

Do you get enough from the relationship to risk all that?

If you do decide to separate from the man, you'll probably look back with amazement at the dangerous situation you lived in and at your low level of awareness of the danger. It's shocking how many women are able to endure such situations. Yet it's not altogether surprising that a woman in seemingly inescapable danger will use whatever psychological means she can to keep fear at a tolerable level. Denial is one of those methods, and it's quite useful at certain times. But if you want to get out of the situation, you'll have to break through that denial and admit just how much risk you face every day.

BALANCING THE SCALES

If you did Activity 3 in Chapter 2, you have a list of disadvantages of marriage in general and of the relationship with the man who abuses you in particular. Look at the lists again and add to them if you can think of other disadvantages. Now list the disadvantages of *leaving* this relationship.

Even though it's a bit repetitious, it will probably turn up new information. You might find that items you normally think of as disadvantages of leaving show up also on the "Disadvantages of Staying" list. "Fear of inability to cope" may appear on both lists, even though you normally focus on it only when you think of leaving.

Without, perhaps, stating it in so many words, you've probably been assuming or hoping or wishing that you could overcome the disadvantages of staying—that you would somehow eventually find a way to please your man so that he won't become violent. Now is the time to make your last serious attempt to do anything that might overcome a disadvantage of staying.

The same can be said for your hopes and dreams about overcoming the disadvantages of leaving. If you haven't been able to overcome them by this time, it won't change unless you make some very specific plans to deal with those obstacles and start carrying them out now.

Loneliness and financial insecurity often loom as very important disadvantages of leaving, because there's an assumption that you can't tolerate either situation and that you won't find love or security with anyone else, nor as a single person. List the ways you might overcome these disadvantages. Solutions may vary from methods of accepting the lack of love or security in your life, developing other satisfactions so that they're not missed so much, or finding people, places, or activities that will meet those needs in different ways.

Once you've listed the possible methods of overcoming the disadvantages, *underline* the ones you're seriously interested in trying soon. Then put down your "Plan of Action," the time when you'll start it and a time for completion of it. Your paper might look something like this:

Activity 11 ✎ Plan of Action

Disadvantages of Leaving	Plan of Action	Start	Complete Plan
Loneliness	Make new friends	This week	Two friends, three months
	Learn to like my own company	Today	One year?
	Enroll in class	Next quarter	Four months
No sex life	Be sensual by myself	Today	Three months to get used to it
	Talk to myself about not needing sex	Today	Six months to convince myself?
	Eventually meet a new man	One year?	Two years to be sure
Not enough money	Take computer course	Next quarter	Two years

Disadvantages of Staying	Plan of Action	Start	Complete Plan
Broken bones, internal injuries	Hide money and keys for escape	Today	Today
Bad example to kids	Talk to kids about how wrong it is	Today	Continue indefinitely
Depression	Talk to old friend 2X week on phone	Tomorrow	Three months to form habit
	Talk to self more positively	Today	Three months to form habit
No friends	Call Sally	Tomorrow	Three months
	Talk to neighbors	Next week	Three months to form habit

Disadvantages of Leaving	Plan of Action	Start	Complete Plan

Disadvantages of Staying	Plan of Action	Start	Complete Plan

Trying Out Your Plans

It's important to stick to the plan for a particular period of time so that you'll know you've tried hard to make things change. You may not succeed in making those changes, but it's important for you to know you made a serious, well-thought-out effort.

If you realize some time before your deadline for completing the plan that you're not following it, try not to feel guilty. Instead, figure out what's wrong with the plan and revise it, so that it becomes something you can really do. If you get to the deadline and find that you haven't really tried, don't immediately assume there's something wrong with you and that you have to keep pretending to yourself that you're going to follow the plan eventually. Accept the fact that it's not a plan you're ready to follow and that you haven't a way to overcome that particular disadvantage right now.

When you've made a reasonable attempt to change for a specified amount of time, *list* the advantages and disadvantages of leaving and staying one more time. If you still can't decide what to do, score each item on a scale from one to ten, with ten indicating the most important item. Make your decision on the basis of the highest score. If it makes you feel better, decide to do one thing or the other, not forever, but for a specific trial period. That period shouldn't be less than six months, though, because you'll need at least that much time to test the results. And just because it's a trial doesn't mean there is no commitment.

Activity 12 ↬ Leaving and Staying: Advantages and Disadvantages

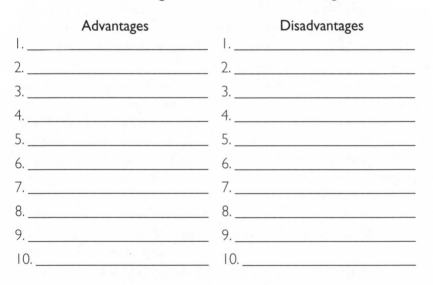

Advantages	Disadvantages
1. _____	1. _____
2. _____	2. _____
3. _____	3. _____
4. _____	4. _____
5. _____	5. _____
6. _____	6. _____
7. _____	7. _____
8. _____	8. _____
9. _____	9. _____
10. _____	10. _____

MAKING A COMMITMENT TO STAY

It's not enough to say, "Well, I guess I can't leave, so I'll just have to stay with him for now." That isn't a real commitment. The next time you're hurt or scared or angry, you'll probably begin the fantasies of leaving again. A commitment goes more like this: "The disadvantages of staying are not as bad as the disadvantages of leaving, so I'll stay with Tom for six months and carry out my plans to make changes in a very serious way. I won't even consider leaving until I've done all that I can think of for six months." If your man has made some concessions to you, a variation might be: "I'll stay with him and be serious about carrying out my plan of action, as long as he goes to AA . . . or to counseling . . . or as long as he doesn't humiliate me."

If you indulge yourself in fantasies of leaving the man even though you know you're not really going to, you're encouraging a dangerous self-delusion. But that doesn't mean you shouldn't have a plan to leave as a temporary emergency measure to protect yourself when you sense he is building up to violence.

What Can You Do if You Stay?

It may be possible to gain some freedom if you stay. Sometimes women think their husbands won't "let" them go to work, make friends, or hire a babysitter, but if they just go ahead and do it, they're surprised to find that the men either don't notice, don't mind, or grudgingly put up with it. Many women who get beaten are those who ask for nothing and are extremely compliant. If you're beaten for no apparent reason or punished even when you do your best to please, it may be worth the risk to assert your rights. Some men bully only those who are afraid of them. However, it's still a big risk to take, so it's a good idea to plan an escape to a safe place before you take any new chances.

Another alternative is to start changing your life secretly. Save money out of the grocery fund; don't tell the man you're going to a daytime class or support group. This too is potentially dangerous. An involvement with a violent man is always a very high risk, no matter what you try to change—or even if you don't change. (The same can be said for a psychologically abusive man, only the danger is to your self-concept and your ability to make decisions.)

Nevertheless, if you've been involved with the man for a long time, if you're unskilled for the job market, unemployed outside the home, have small children, have no real friends or supportive people, you may decide to stay with a violent man until you can change your life in such a way that you'll be more committed to permanent escape when you do leave and better able to stick to your commitment. Acquiring job skills, getting your children into school, making friends, joining a support group—all will help, though all of them can be begun after you leave too, and in some respects will be easier to do then.

If you don't succeed in averting his violence and after he beats you he's remorseful, take advantage of that phase to begin going out with women friends, to join a support group or enroll in community college, or to otherwise branch out and begin a life for yourself. By the time he's recovered from his guilt, he may be used to your new habits. It will be difficult to go out and meet new people if you have a black eye or a missing tooth. Try to make yourself do it anyway, because if you let too much time go by he may be into the violent part of the cycle again. As soon as your wounds become invisible it's easy for both of you to act as if it never happened.

Learning the Signs of Coming Violence

If you pay careful attention you may be able to see the man's rage building at quite an early stage. Perhaps you already know the signs. Does he drink more, find many petty things to complain about, want to go out every night, or sit morosely in front of the TV more than usual? If you feel it coming on but can't name the actual changes in him, work on sharpening your observations. It's important for your own self-confidence to be able to state clearly that his tone of voice, what he says, his habits, his behavior toward you and the children change before he goes into a violent rage. It's important to be as certain as you can, whether these changes take place weeks or merely hours or minutes before he becomes violent. Writing them down will help you get a clearer sense of the pattern and make you more self-confident of what you observe.

If yours is the sort of violent man who is terribly sorry after he abuses you and who promises never to raise a hand again, or who says he'll do anything you ask if you'll just stay and help him lick his problem, you may have a chance of developing an escape plan. It's during this "honeymoon" phase that you should point out that there are certain things he does that let you know he's building toward violence. If you can get him to agree with you that you should temporarily leave, or that he will leave at those times, so much the better. Probably, though, he will try to persuade you that it won't be necessary because he won't let those things happen next time.

Whether he agrees or not, you can tell him you're going to go to a safe place the next time you see the signs of violence beginning.

LEAVING TO PROTECT YOURSELF

When he gets into another violent phase, he probably won't remember or care that he's agreed you should find safety. But you will, and that will make it easier for you to take action. Once you've said out loud to him that a particular set of actions usually leads to violence, when you see it happen again it won't be so easy to say to yourself, "Maybe this time it won't happen," or "I must be imagining it after all."

The important question is what you can do to protect yourself. The best choice is to go to a good friend's or relative's house—a place where there's plenty of room for you with people who care about you. A danger is that in order not to impose on others you'll wait until it's too late. If you've gone to them or to other people after you've been beaten in the past, try to keep in mind that most people would rather help you protect yourself than to mop up after the damage is done.

You should stay in that safe place until the man's rage is spent. The trouble, of course, is that you might find it hard to know when that time has come. If you can get a third party to speak to him periodically, you might get more reliable information, and you'll avoid the possibility of being talked into going home too soon. There are two problems with this plan. The man may be so used to releasing tension by using you as a punching bag that he has no other outlet and will hang on until you return. The other is that—even though he is about to lose control—he may be adept at persuading you or your intermediary that his rage is all over and that he's prepared to be both loving and calm. And then, when you get home, you'll find that he's determined to punish you for leaving. You can probably remember times when he's manipulated you by temporarily controlling his violence so that you have believed the danger was over.

Planning for the Emergency

At the very least you should have enough money to pay a cab to take you to a safe place, and if you're in a strange community, enough to pay one or more nights' rent in a motel. You should also have an extra key to your car and the house and a list of telephone numbers to call in case of emergency. You may also want to stash a change of clothes for yourself and/or your children. Ideally, you'll keep these items at a neighbor's house, at your job, or someplace else away from your home. If you need to leave in a hurry, you may not have time to take them from the house. See the Safety Plan in the back of this book.

Even if you have no place to go except a motel, you should know which one and how to get there, and you should go from your house to it several times so that in a time of high stress you'll realize it's a non-threatening and familiar alternative to staying with a dangerous man. Your fear can very easily paralyze you, but that's not so likely to happen if you've rehearsed an escape plan ahead of time.

Rehearsing for Departure

Be sure not to tell the man that you're leaving to protect yourself. He'll almost certainly become even more enraged and controlling and will try to stop you. Try to anticipate his violence early enough so that you can slip away when he's at work, but if that's not possible, say you have to go get some milk for the baby, or offer to get beer for him, or say you promised a neighbor to bring her a recipe. Rehearse this ahead of time also. Have several plausible reasons to leave for different times of day or night. For example, if his rages build late at night, plan to have a reason to go outside. Develop a habit of forgetting to take part of the laundry in until late at night or walking the dog or throwing out the garbage at midnight. Once outside the door, just keep going. Get into the car and drive as quickly and quietly as possible or keep walking until you get to a telephone.

How and Why to Take the Children

You may want to leave by yourself in order not to upset the children, especially if you imagine them sleeping blissfully in the middle of the night. Chances are, however, they're lying awake terrified by the current of coming violence. They may be less frightened at getting up and being rushed away from a threatening father than finding out in the morning that you've disappeared without saying goodbye. Another thing to remember is that even if the father has never battered the children, you can't be sure he won't start now, especially when he discovers you've left the house.

Making your escape with children is more complicated than making it alone, but it can also be prepared for. Talk to them periodically about the importance of safety. Teach older children to call a relative, a friend, or the police when they hear or see violence. If a child or neighbor that the child runs to can call the police, officers may help you leave with the children.

If it's a baby you're concerned about, tell the man you hear her crying, take her out of her crib, and go out a back door or window before your partner realizes what's happening. Keep going until you're in a safe place.

When events happen so fast that you do have to leave without the children, arrange to go back for them as soon as possible. Either pick them up at school or return to the house with a police officer. You'll need to ensure the children's physical safety, let them know you haven't abandoned them, and protect your right to custody.

In custody cases there's a strong tendency to leave children with the parent who has them at the time the court becomes involved. If they're with you, your chances of gaining permanent custody are far better than if you leave them with their father, regardless of the reasons.

PREPARING TO LEAVE PERMANENTLY

Sometimes women who have left their partners suddenly or with a minimum of emergency planning never go back. Sometimes they follow a pattern of leaving and returning when the man's violence is spent. And sometimes they stay with him forever.

You may not be willing to make a decision to leave until you are physically injured. You'll have all the problems then of sudden escape and the crisis feeling that accompanies instant change. If you weigh the advantages and disadvantages of leaving in a calmer moment, your decision will probably be more reliable and less emotionally disturbing to you and your children. At the very least, planning will give you some financial security.

Although it's unusual, difficult, and often dangerous, some abused women stay with a man for months or years while planning a separation. For some it means going to school or getting a job or job training so they have an independent income when they finally do leave. For others it entails saving small amounts of money for a ticket across the country— or waiting another painful and high-risk year or two until the children are in school or old enough to take care of themselves.

Leaving in an emergency and returning after it's over because you aren't prepared to be on your own is an understandable pattern. But it doesn't mean you have to follow it the rest of your life. The previous chapters should have given you some ideas about gathering information and deciding how and when to take action. Here are some other practical matters to consider if you're going to leave permanently.

Protect Your Money and Property

Property rights in marriage differ from state to state and are even more uncertain for cohabitants, so you'll need the advice of a lawyer to get an idea of what you'll probably be awarded by the court and what you can legally take with you. (See Chapter 8, Making Legal Decisions.) Then plan how you will get the items you're entitled to.

Take as many (as possible) of your personal belongings out of the house beforehand, especially things of sentimental or financial value or those your partner knows you especially like. If you're going to risk staying with him a few more months you can take important items for safekeeping with a friend. Tell him, if necessary, that it's clothing to be cleaned, family photographs to be framed, jewelry to be reset. However, if the man is very observant and suspicious, it might not be safe. It's important that you know your man and whether he'll notice how long it takes for things to come back after cleaning, etc., before you take this risk.

If he is suspicious, you'll do better to make a list of the important items, gradually move as many as you can to two or three places in the house, and plan what suitcases, boxes, or bags they'll go into so when you do leave you can pack them quickly. Include items important to your children, too. Try not to leave anything behind that will cause you misgivings if he threatens to seize or destroy it.

Find out if community service officers in your police department or another agency will stand by while you remove your personal possessions. Take care of it while your partner is safely away from the house, but have a friend go with you in case he comes back sooner than anticipated. Even if he's never destroyed your property before, once you've left him he's likely to use any tools at hand to threaten or punish you.

Unless you have different legal advice, take half the money in checking and savings accounts and any other assets, such as charge card accounts, that can be quickly redeemed. If you believe you're entitled to more, ask a lawyer about it. Be sure not to leave your share of the money in joint accounts to take out later. After he learns you've left him your partner may withdraw all the money from the accounts, take your name off credit cards, or change all the locks on the doors. Many women have refused to believe their partners would do that, only to find themselves with no resources twenty-four hours after they left. If you have little knowledge of what assets you and your partner jointly own, spend some time looking around for papers that indicate what stocks, property, insurance, pensions, or other assets there are, as well as any loans. Write down all the information or, if you can safely do it, make copies of the papers. If necessary, put all papers and lists in the safe hands of a friend. It isn't mean or cruel to take what is yours, so don't deprive yourself or your children because of unwarranted guilt feelings.

Plan Where to Go

If possible, find a place to live before you leave, whether it's a temporary shelter or Safe Home for battered women, the home of a friend or relative, or a new apartment. Try to decide where you'll settle permanently, whether it's in a different neighborhood or a new city (in which case a shelter may be able to arrange for temporary shelter there). Check the papers for housing ads so you'll know what to expect in your price range. This will make your later search for a permanent place easier.

If you think you may need welfare assistance or public housing, get all the information you can before you leave. Find out what papers you'll need and get them together to take with you.

Many of the practical problems you'll encounter by leaving are discussed in detail in Section IV. That information may help you make effective plans now. By learning to look squarely at what you can and can't do to make a new life for yourself and your children, you can form a realistic picture of your options.

If, at each suggestion, you've been saying something such as, "Yes, but I can't do that . . . " because of no car, no money, no friends, or other problems, look at what these answers mean. You're saying there is no way to protect yourself from abuse and the fear that accompanies it. You're saying, "I accept a life of periodic violence. I'm not going to try and change it." Are you willing to accept that? If not, you'd better make plans to leave.

SECTION II

GETTING PROFESSIONAL HELP

THE PROBLEM OF SEXISM

Professionals can heal your bruised body, increase your safety, guide you through the legal system, advocate for your rights, and assist you in reorganizing your life. The special skills and knowledge of doctors, police, lawyers, and counselors—and the community's recognition of them—can make a great difference in whether your crisis has a permanent and damaging effect or is the motivator to start constructing a new and satisfying life.

Professionals can also make things worse for you. Some of them are not competent in their work, regardless of formal training. Others are competent, but their social attitudes and ways of relating to clients have damaging effects that sometimes outweigh the good they do in the operating room, courthouse, or counselor's office.

You can maximize benefits and minimize harm from professionals by knowing as much as possible about what the law or professional ethics require of them, or prohibit them from doing, by carefully choosing the people you hire, respecting your own responses to them, and knowing your rights. In this section I'll present some guidelines on when to hire a professional, how to choose one, and how to evaluate services.

Sexism, in its extreme form, is the belief that males and females have completely different characteristics, inherent rather than learned, that males are superior to females, and that males have the right to make decisions and laws that govern women's lives. "Men's work" is defined as more important and more difficult than "women's work" and therefore higher paid. This fits into the sexist idea that men are the providers for families, and thus not only deserve higher pay, but need it more. Women are viewed as inherently attuned to emotions, relationships, and intuition. The belief that those inherent qualities make women superior to men is a form of "reverse sexism." Because sexist ideas have been threaded into all our institutions and absorbed by us all, it's impossible to divide people neatly into categories of those who are and who are not sexist. We can only talk about those who are more and less so. As a shorthand I'll use the terms "sexist" and "nonsexist" to mean more sexist and more nearly nonsexist. It's important to understand the sexist biases of many professional people from whom you'll be seeking help.

During the past few decades, therapists, doctors, and lawyers have become much more aware of women's rights and abilities, although here and there you might find pockets of resistance. Some religious counselors believe women and men should adhere to traditional roles while others are open-minded. Few professionals openly admit to blatant sexist ideas. But their old biases, maybe not even conscious, may play out in subtle ways. Some social workers may believe that as a mother you are more responsible than their father for protecting your child. They may want to punish you for being unable to do that. They may think you should be strong enough to just walk away from a violent abuser, yet paradoxically see themselves in a role of rescuing you, a helpless, dependent woman. You might even find that attitude appealing. At the time you see a therapist, lawyer, or doctor—a time of crisis—you may welcome a strong shoulder to lean on. That is all the more reason to be alert to inappropriate, patronizing caretaking on the part of a professional you have hired.

To a large extent, institutional sexism still determines the jobs that men and women work at. The highest-paid and highest-status jobs—often incorrectly assumed to require higher risks and greater stamina than "women's work"—have historically been reserved for males. Although some women have been admitted to all professions, you're likely to find mostly men working as doctors, police officers, and lawyers, especially outside big cities. Among counselors, there is more of a possibility of finding women, though most psychiatrists and psychologists are still men. (More social workers are women.)

Women can be just as sexist as men, but the sexist roles we've all been taught are more likely to be played out by male professionals in relation to female clients. A male attorney who believes he, as a male, is more capable than women will tend to take over much more than is necessary, making decisions that should be yours. If you feel helpless, share his ideas about male and female roles, or are intimidated by his masculine power, you may let him take over. These reactions are not as likely to occur in relationship to a female attorney—or other professional—even if she's quite sexist. A female professional may be condescending, patronizing, or downright insulting to your intelligence, each of which may be an aspect of sexism. But the impact won't be nearly as powerful as when such treatment comes from a male in authority. To the extent you're victimized by your own sexism—as we all are in some degree—you'll interpret the male professional's attitudes as indicating something wrong with you, and you'll begin to doubt your own judgment.

It's not unusual for professionals to use their position and the client's vulnerability to take advantage of clients sexually. This unethical and often illegal practice is nearly always perpetrated by males who exploit their women clients. It's often presented as something good for the client, and her loneliness, mixed with sexual need and the status of the professional man, places the woman client in a vulnerable position. She is nearly always hurt by such a relationship.

For these reasons, it's safer for you to hire a female professional, assuming you can find one who is sensitive, relatively nonsexist, competent to solve your specific problem—and within your budget. Each of these characteristics is important. If your choices are limited by time, money, or the community you live in, it's important at least to recognize the person's inadequacies so you can guard against them. The following chapters will help you through the process of finding, hiring, and evaluating professional workers.

CHAPTER 7

EMERGENCY HELP FROM DOCTORS, POLICE, AND PROSECUTORS

Even if you're not ready to leave your partner, professionals can provide important services that will make your situation more bearable and that may help you prepare to end the relationship. Once you've made the break, they can contribute to your safety and help you start a new and satisfying life.

This chapter will help you decide what you want from doctors and police and give you ideas on what to do if you're not getting the services you want.

MEDICAL HELP

The Emergency Room
If you need immediate medical treatment, it's likely to be in the middle of the night or on a weekend, and you'll go to the nearest hospital emergency room and take whoever is assigned to you. Try to get someone to go with you, as it may be a long wait. Tell the receptionist or nurse you've been assaulted by your husband or lover. Then describe your pain and injuries as accurately as possible. At this point, the staff will know how much pain you're in only if you tell them.

Ask for an estimate of how long you'll have to wait for an examination. It may not be accurate, because in an emergency room those in most severe danger are treated first, regardless of who arrived first. But knowing how long you'll be waiting will allow you to relax without feeling you're being purposely ignored or neglected. Now is the time to ask if there's a special program to help victims of domestic assault. If there is, a social worker may be able to give you a referral to a shelter or other service, as well as some comfort, while you wait for medical treatment. If your condition worsens, tell the person at the desk right away.

The Family Doctor—Pros and Cons

If it's not an emergency, you may decide to see your family physician. A family doctor can be particularly useful if she or he knows you well, cares about your welfare, and respects you. You may have good reason, though, to avoid your usual doctor. Perhaps she or he is so close to your spouse you don't think you'll be believed, or you might feel embarrassed or want to protect the man. (Try to keep in mind it's the violent man who should feel ashamed or embarrassed, but if you'd feel better talking to a doctor who's a stranger, go ahead and do it.) Or perhaps you know from past experience that she or he will pressure you to either report to the police or separate from the man before you're ready, or not to prosecute, even though that's what you want to do. The doctor may have a sexist attitude toward you, implying you deserve to be hurt or asked for it because you've continued to stay with the batterer.

You're likely to feel at the time you get medical treatment that you'll never go back to the man. When a doctor or nurse advises you to stay away from your partner, you may agree with enthusiasm. They'll believe you and when you come back the next month with another injury they'll feel disappointed, discouraged, and afraid for you. A feeling of hopelessness might turn to resentment or thinly disguised hostility as they realize their careful medical treatment may have to be repeated the next time you're beaten. They see only the results of the man's worst treatment and the evidence of his destructive character. It's hard for them to imagine that there are some needs being met in the relationship.

If you do want to try a new doctor, put some effort into finding one who's sensitive, who respects women, and who understands the problems of women victims of violence. Ask at a shelter, women's clinic, or other service for abused women, or try a rape crisis line for a referral. Even if they don't have an official list of doctors sensitive to women's issues and battering, you may get an informal recommendation from a staff person.

What to Tell the Doctor

Many women are ambivalent about telling the doctor what happened. You may want the doctor to know, but be embarrassed to blurt out, "My husband beat me." You wait for the doctor or nurse to coax it out of you and wonder why they don't at least ask when you appear month after month with unexplained bruises. When you explain that you just bruise easily, you may half hope the doctor will call you on it, but some doctors don't want to know what happened. They may find it embarrassing, might be afraid of your feelings spilling over if you start talking about it, or they may be afraid they'll have to appear in court. So if you want the doctor to know, you'll have to tell. Get the physician's attention by saying, "I want you to know how I got these injuries." Once started, you'll probably find it fairly easy to go on and a great relief to have it off your chest.

Not telling the doctor what happened may relieve you of a few awkward moments, but you may be sorry later. There's a good chance the medical record will be admitted as evidence in an assault charge and will impress the judge with the seriousness of your situation. If you have a custody dispute, the record of the father's violence can be an important factor in your favor and in some states it can help you get a better divorce settlement. You may hope to avoid any such court actions but there's a possibility you'll be involved in them whether you like it or not. If you never have to make use of the medical record you can just ignore it and nothing will be lost.

When you've found a cooperative doctor, say at the outset that you'll want a full description of each injury included in the record and that you'll want to see the record when it's completed so you can have important information added if necessary. It will be useful to have a friend or advocate handy when you make these requests. You needn't feel guilty for taking extra time. It's the doctor's job to give you respectful and competent treatment—at public health agencies as well as at private clinics.

If you're very timid in the face of medical authority, take a friend with you and ask her to back you up in exercising your rights. You can tell the doctor you want her to come right into the examining room with you. And stick to that plan, regardless of whether the doctor objects. Keep in mind that you are hiring the doctor and if you don't like her or his treatment or attitude, you can take your business elsewhere. The mere presence of another person sometimes makes a difference in a physician's attitude.

Depending upon your relationship with the doctor, your emotional condition, and whether or not you have other people to ask for advice and help, you might want to listen to a doctor's counseling. If you think the doctor has your best interests at heart and understands the situation, get what you can from the counseling. But keep in mind you're there for medical care. The doctor shouldn't continue to give advice about your relationship if you don't want it. You have a right to say you don't want to explain what happened beyond medical necessity and that you don't want to discuss your plans.

POLICE INTERVENTION

In some communities, police are extremely slow to answer domestic-violence calls, and many calls are not responded to at all. Their reasons vary from fear of being killed (not surprising, since about one-fifth of police homicides occur when they respond to domestic-violence calls), to discouragement when they answer the same call month after month and nothing seems to change, to pure and simple sexism ("If she's getting beaten up by her old man, she must deserve it.").

On the other hand, some police are protective in the best sense of the word and will take victims to a shelter or hospital, refer them to special services for battered women, and give careful, precise advice about how to follow through with the case.

Should You Call the Police?

Decide ahead of time, if you can, whether you'll call the police the next time you're assaulted or the man trespasses on your property. Think about what result you'll be looking for. Will you want an officer to stop the man from immediate attack and calm him down, arrest him, remove him from the scene, or take you to a safe place? When you've answered those questions, call a shelter for battered women, a women's rights group, or the county Bar Association to find out what you can reasonably expect from police and prosecutors in your community.

You may think it's not worth it to call the police if there's little likelihood of arrest or jail time for the batterer. He may reinforce that feeling by making a show of nonchalance, but few people are casual about being confronted by police, even when they're not taken to jail.

You may be reluctant to call the police because you feel sorry for the man who battered you and don't want him punished by being sent to jail. Your fears about his being jailed are probably unfounded unless he's already in trouble with the law. If he has a criminal record and is on probation or parole, fears related to his serving time may be more realistic. But if you blame yourself for that, remember it's his own actions that result in jail time. Or you may fear that a jail term will make him angry at you and that when he gets out, you'll be confronted with more violence than you face now. To protect yourself from his anger, you might have to find a secret place to stay while he's out of jail on bail. It may be months before the case comes to court, so find out from the prosecutor whether you can get a "no contact" order (see the end of this chapter, How Can You Keep the Batterer Away?).

Even when it's extremely hard to do, filing a complaint may be worth it. Taking legal action and following through regardless of the consequences may be the only way you and other women can persuade batterers and justice system personnel that you won't tolerate men's abuse. If the man doesn't have a criminal record he might be sentenced to alcoholics' or batterers' counseling and that might be the best thing for him as well as you.

If you decide to call the police, be as calm as possible. It's extremely hard to do that in an emergency, but if you practice saying a few sentences beforehand, you may be able to say them automatically when the emergency arises. The main things you want to do are to get your address across clearly and accurately and make sure the police know it's an emergency. One or two short sentences should be enough. "I'm being beaten up. I'm at _____." Don't say it's your husband or boyfriend who's attacking you.

HOW TO GET THE MOST EFFECTIVE POLICE RESPONSE[1]

1. Be as calm as you possibly can be.
2. Don't be afraid to ask the police to make a report.
3. Tell them about the assault in detail.
4. Show them any injuries or bruises or damaged property.
5. Let them know if there were witnesses.
6. Tell them about other violent incidents.
7. Show them any court documents you have such as "no contact" or "restraining" orders.
8. Ask them for community resources such as shelters, hot lines, counseling, and advocacy.
9. Ask for the case number of the report and a phone number if you want to follow up on the case.

WHEN WILL POLICE MAKE AN ARREST?

Police may legally make an arrest if they have "probable cause" to believe a crime has been committed that involved injury to a person. "Probable cause" means there is some evidence of the crime, such as a bloody nose or other obvious injury. However, they will probably not make an arrest unless:

1. There is a warrant out for the abuser. Tell the police if you know about any outstanding warrants.
2. The assault was very serious, involving a weapon or major injury.
3. The abuser attacks the police or attacks you in their presence.

COOPERATING WITH THE PROSECUTOR

You don't have to worry yet about whether charges will be pressed because that decision will be made later by the prosecutor. But to be prepared in case the prosecutor does need the information, make sure the officer writes down your description of what your partner did to you and of any injuries you received. But first do whatever is necessary to be safe. Even with an officer right there, that could mean leaving the house right away. If that is necessary, try to get the police to help you get to a safe place.

If charges are pressed and the man is convicted, there can be some advantages for you and for him. The court can order the man to have no contact with you for the duration of the sentence (six months to a year), to get batterers' counseling or alcoholic treatment, and to pay for your medical treatment or replace stolen property. Some batterers are concerned enough about what will happen in court that they stop threatening and attacking the women while the case is pending. If the man does assault you again while the case is pending, police are more likely to arrest him. If he assaults or threatens you, call the police to get additional charges reported and let the prosecutor know right away.

Once you've decided to cooperate with the prosecutor, it's important to follow through. It's a way of making a strong statement that the man must change. It's a way of saying to both of you that you're taking care of yourself.

If you reconcile with the batterer before he is brought to court, he may pressure you to "drop charges." But only the prosecutor can do that. That can be an advantage for you, since you can honestly tell the man it's out of your hands.

What Do You Want to Happen?

When you've gotten some ideas from a shelter or women's organization about how police and prosecutors in your community are likely to interpret the law and how they'll treat you, ask yourself more questions. Consider what you'll want to happen and how you'll probably feel about various results.

• *In addition to the possible results mentioned above, what are your personal reasons for wanting charges to be pressed?* Do you want punishment, revenge, to have the man taken away or ordered to have counseling? Do you want your action to stand as a public statement that men will no longer be permitted to batter women without some legal consequences?

• *Have you said before that you wanted charges pressed? Did you cooperate with the prosecutor?* How did the outcome affect you? Did you feel let down or betrayed by the system? It may be that the courts weren't as responsive to battered women as they are now. Find out from women's groups or Legal Services whether there have been important changes in your district.

Perhaps you decided you still loved the man after all and didn't want him to suffer. Or maybe you felt guilty for "putting him in jail," even though it was only for a few hours. He and family members may have persuaded you it was your fault; perhaps you were afraid of even greater violence; the continual stress wore you down or you believed he had changed.

• *Which of your previous situations are different now?* If nothing much happened as the result of your action before, is there reason to think the judge will make a different decision on a second charge? Is there better evidence? Might the prosecutor take your case more seriously, now that you've gone through it once?

How can you be sure you don't still love him, even though you feel hatred or indifference right now? Or are you willing to go through with it, even though you still love him? Do you have reason to believe you handle guilt and emotional turmoil better now, and that you can't be persuaded to change your mind? Is there a reason you won't be afraid of worse violence or can rise above those fears enough to follow through this time?

• *Where can you get emotional support and practical aid?* Is there a special project at the prosecutor's office or a shelter? Will a friend go through the whole process with you, accompanying you to interviews with the prosecutor and court proceedings? Will you have access to one particular prosecutor who will answer your questions as they come up? Is there a safe place to stay, in case the man does become violent?

Enlist a friend's help in going over these questions. Have her pretend to be a persuasive or threatening person—your partner, a relative, or the prosecutor—who plays on your guilt feelings and ambivalence. Try to respond honestly, as if she really were that person, so you'll get an idea of how vulnerable to persuasion you are. You may decide you don't want to cooperate with the prosecutor after all. Or you might decide to keep practicing your responses so you'll be able to resist whatever pressures you face in the future.

You might believe you don't need such help. Maybe charges were pressed before, but when your husband pleaded with you to go back to him, you didn't cooperate with the prosecutor. If you're persuading yourself there's no point in testing out how you'd respond to his pleading because this time he definitely doesn't want the relationship, consider it again. Even if he's acting hateful or ignoring you and has a new woman, the moment he believes you're serious about taking action, he's likely to come back to threaten or sweet-talk you, or both. Even if you believe there's no chance he'll ask, a little practice in resisting both his threats and promises will make you stronger.

WHAT THE PROSECUTOR CAN AND CAN'T DO

Many women are confused when they discover how little power they have over whether the violent man will be prosecuted. They expect the prosecutor to be mainly concerned about the victim's safety. But the prosecutor's job is to preserve the peace and order of the state, rather than to protect the individual; it's to redress public wrongs, not private ones.

Because prosecutors are authoritative figures, it's easy to imagine they have more power than they do. You may think you're getting the runaround when they tell you court dates are unknown or delayed and that the prosecutor hasn't taken you seriously if the man doesn't get jail time. Whether the case is successfully prosecuted depends upon a great many factors, including how good the evidence is, the man's history of violence, the attitudes of the community and judge, and how hard the prosecutor was willing and able to work on it.

The man who battered you can be prosecuted whether or not you're married to him, but because it's technically the state's case, it's the state's decision what to do about it. Jennifer Baker Fleming, in *Stopping Wife Abuse,* describes the situation this way:

> Prosecutors have a great deal of latitude in deciding which accusations will become the subject of a formal charge and which will not. There is virtually no review of this decision and virtually no guidelines, so prosecutors tend to exercise this power of "prosecutorial discretion" on the basis of their own values, their perception of society's view of the crime charged, and the likelihood of success in getting a conviction. Their calculation of these factors and their decision to prosecute or not is final. . . .

> Usually the decision about whether to prosecute is made on a case-by-case basis, after considering four or five basic issues: the extent of the injuries and their seriousness, the defendant's apparent intent, the victim's desire to prosecute, the defendant's history of similar or other violent conduct, especially whether he has a criminal record— and the prosecutor's own estimate (based, among other things, on the existence of tangible evidence and other witnesses) of the likelihood of success at trial.[2]

The decision is complicated by the fact that prosecutors often don't realize how much their personal values, including sexist attitudes, affect their judgments about matters that are supposedly factual and objective.

DEALING WITH THE PROSECUTOR

Nevertheless, you may be able to influence the decision. Your enthusiasm for going ahead with the case and understanding of just what it involves for you will help. You might have said in the past that you would cooperate with the prosecutor, but then when he or she pressed charges you changed your mind. The prosecutor may be reluctant to press charges because of fear you won't follow through. If that's the message you're getting from the prosecutor, try especially hard to have someone with you to help you state your case. Carefully list the reasons things are different this time, so if you forget to mention some of them, your advocate can help out during the interview with the prosecutor. If you pressed charges before and got no support or information from the prosecutor's office, explain what happened as thoroughly as possible. Use statements such as: "When you insinuated I asked him into my house, and that's why I got beaten up, I thought you didn't believe me and weren't interested in my case," and "If your office can tell me what's happening as we go along and give me some encouragement and emotional support, it will be easy for me to follow through."

If the prosecutor tells you the office is understaffed and can't give you the support you want by keeping you informed and helping you understand the legal process, give yourself time to consider whether it will be worth the struggle. While you're rethinking the situation, talk to women's organizations (National Organization for Women, YWCAs, a city, county, or state office of women's rights) as well as a shelter to enlist help. One of them may be able to pressure the prosecutor to take your case seriously or give you the support and information you'll need to get through the ordeal. They may be able to put you in touch with other women who've been through the court process. It's easy, under these circumstances, to feel isolated and in the wrong. Knowing that women in similar situations successfully used the system will help you gain a healthy perspective.

In any case, if you get vague answers from the prosecutor, or if your telephone calls aren't returned and it looks as if no action is taking place, keep politely, but firmly, asking questions. Sometimes the case is going along as it should, but nothing much can be done until a court date is assigned. In that case the prosecutor is doing an adequate job but is insensitive to your feelings or hasn't time to call back.

When you're angry and hurt it's hard to realize that a prosecutor has numerous other cases that are just as pressing as yours. It may seem you're being ignored, but the prosecutor may know she or he can't get to your case until a few days before the court date because other cases are demanding a similar amount of work. Nevertheless, let the prosecutor know how you feel. You might want to add that the better informed you are, the more confident you feel about following through and being a good witness. The prosecutor wants to win the case and must have a good witness to do it.

If you're convinced you're not being taken seriously or if the prosecutor is blatantly sexist, ask for a different prosecutor or to speak to her or his supervisor. In some communities you might be assigned to someone more compatible, sensitive, and nonsexist. In others, you will get nowhere with your request. It may be that there are no prosecutors in a particular office who are sensitive to the problems of battered women. An additional problem is that there is frequent reassigning of cases in some offices. If you just wait it out, you may get someone better by the time you go to court. You might want to consult with knowledgeable women's groups before you decide how far you'll go in fighting the system.

HOW CAN YOU KEEP THE BATTERER AWAY?

There are many legal methods of ordering a violent person to stay away and stop abusing or threatening you. But you don't need any special methods unless you have a legal relationship with the man, such as marriage or a child in common. If a boyfriend, former lover, or husband from whom you're legally divorced enters your house without permission, forces you to have sex with him, threatens or assaults you, you have all the rights you'd have if he were a stranger. In some states, he can be charged with trespassing, rape, or whatever would be appropriate if you had never had a relationship with him. Call the district court to find out what charge can be legally made.

If you do have a legal relationship with the man, you may need a legal order to keep him away. The type of order and what it's called varies from one jurisdiction to another. It may be a temporary restraining order, a no contact order, or an order of protection. For some of these orders you don't have to consult a private lawyer or a prosecutor. Call your county Bar Association or district court to find out what the proper order is called, whether you need a lawyer to get it, and how to go about getting it.

The order in itself might not keep the man away from you. But the combined action of consistently calling the police whenever it's violated and following through with calls to the prosecutor may frighten the man into staying away.

These ways of using the criminal law system will help you in certain ways, but they don't cover everything. You might have other legal problems that don't have to do with crime. They are the subject of the next chapter.

CHAPTER 8

MAKING LEGAL DECISIONS

For most of us, the law is a mysterious set of rules and regulations, a system of reasoning that's often confusing or intimidating. When we're faced with legal problems and have only a hazy understanding of the system, we may not know when to go to a prosecutor, how to find a trustworthy private lawyer, what to ask them, or how to evaluate them. Some of those lessons will be learned by experience, but I'll try in this chapter to make suggestions that will spare you the most expensive lessons.

WHEN SHOULD YOU HIRE A LAWYER?

A prosecutor takes cases only in which there is an allegation of a crime against the state, such as battering. Property division and custody disputes are civil matters, not the responsibility of the state, so you are on your own with those issues. The law is complex and it is important to have the advice of someone who understands the system, usually a lawyer. It is possible to get a "do-it-yourself" divorce or legal separation. But when you are dealing with someone who has battered and controlled you, that process can be very, very dangerous. If you have children in common the stakes are especially high. If your husband tries to make you appear to be an unfit parent, that question could then become a concern of the state. You probably will want the advice of a lawyer. See the section on Children's Visits with Their Father in Chapter 28, Nurturing Your Children: Safety and Resilience.

Your spouse may find other ways to use the courts to continue intimidating and controlling you, so you might have to counter his legal maneuvers. To do that you will need the legal expertise of someone who also understands domestic violence. That in turn may cost you more money than you can afford, and there is no easy resolution to that dilemma. A local domestic-violence advocate may have suggestions about how to find free or low-fee legal advice.

DIVORCE

You'll save a lot of money if you get a divorce by yourself, without an attorney. If you can agree with your husband on custody, child support, and property division, a do-it-yourself divorce might be for you. However, if you have large amounts of real estate or personal property, if your husband has been able to manipulate you in the past, has hidden his and your assets, or makes vague promises about what he'll do for you in the future, be careful. Not many batterers are willing to talk reasonably about these difficult problems and to be honest and fair in arriving at decisions. If your husband is the exception, by all means consider the possibility. For details on the do-it-yourself process, ask your local county Bar Association or women's organizations about kits that tell how to get a divorce without a lawyer. The availability of self-help legal materials varies in different localities.

If you decide to hire an attorney, ask a number of friends for recommendations or call those organizations mentioned above for suggestions of someone who's particularly experienced in and concerned about wife-beating cases.

When you call for an appointment, say you want to discuss the possibility of hiring the lawyer and ask if there's a charge for the initial interview. Try to find a lawyer who doesn't charge for the exploratory interview.

Before your first appointment, try to make decisions about exactly what you want. You may have mixed feelings about what to do, because you both love and hate your husband. A private lawyer has little time or ability to help you with your emotional seesaw and will charge a great deal of money to listen to you or discuss it. If you can't sort out your feelings by yourself, a counselor can help. But first, try answering these questions:

Do you want a divorce? This is usually an agonizing decision, and to think it through you may want to review Section I. It's essential to examine your fears and obligations as well as the roles of love and loneliness in your life.

If you do get a divorce, is this the right time? Will the degree of stress and anger you feel give you the strength to go through with it or will it create such a feeling of helplessness that you'll back out before it's completed and be left at square on—with a large lawyer's bill?

If it isn't the right time, what do you need to do first? What changes can you begin that will prepare you to make the break? Do you need to make friends, consult a counselor, get a job, or go to school? What can you do to begin those changes right now?

CHILD CUSTODY

Arranging custody of the children is one of the most difficult of legal problems and even more so when the father is violent. This subject will be discussed further in Chapters 15 and 18. Meanwhile, continue asking questions, this time about how you feel about custody.

Do you want custody of the children? Are there some reasons to fear you'll lose custody? If your husband is an influential person in a small community, if you have a history of mental illness, emotional disturbance, drug, alcohol, or child abuse, or a criminal record, you may have good reason to be concerned. But don't assume it's hopeless. The father may be using the threat of winning custody only to keep you in line, and if you resist, he may give in quickly. You have no way of knowing whether you'll have a problem getting the custody arrangement you want until you consult with someone who knows the law, the community and its judges, and the details of your situation. He or she can discuss with you what you might expect under various circumstances as well as what you can do to make a good case for yourself. The lawyer can make a more educated guess about the outcome, but no one can be sure of it until the case has gone to court.

If you believe you haven't been a responsible parent, now is a good time to begin changes. Enroll in parenting classes, join AA, or do community volunteer work—whatever is appropriate to establish yourself as a good parent and citizen. Maybe you don't want custody, but you're feeling guilty about it.

It may seem to you now that you can barely take care of yourself. Your energy and self-confidence may have taken a dive, so that the thought of caring for your children on your own seems overwhelming. You may even consider giving up custody to your husband. Before you make such a decision, read Chapter 28, Nurturing Your Children: Safety and Resilience, and try to get a copy of Lundy Bancroft and Jay Silverman's book, *The Batterer As Parent.* It explains the damage that most abusive husbands and fathers do to their children. Then ask yourself these questions: *Will my child be physically safe? Emotionally cared for? If I give up custody, how often will I be able to be with my child? How will she or he react and how will that affect me? What if I change my mind later?*

Within a few months of separating you may feel much better and want the children to live with you. But once your husband has even temporary custody, you may not be able to persuade a judge that you are a responsible parent. Think about what help you might get from counselors, nursery schools, friends, family, and agencies such as child-protective services. Maintaining custody doesn't necessarily mean you have to do everything all by yourself all the time. If you have to or choose to give up custody later, that will not be anywhere near as difficult as trying to get it back once you've let it go. The safest decision for you and your children for now is to do everything you can to maintain custody.

PROPERTY DIVISION, ALIMONY, AND CHILD SUPPORT

If you shared property with the man who battered you, it would be wonderfully simple to divide it in half and each go your separate ways. That doesn't often happen, especially among people who aren't rich. If you were married and you both worked, your husband may have earned much more than you did. Perhaps you worked part time, or perhaps you stayed home with your children; you own part of a house, car, and some household goods, have a good-sized mortgage and some hefty monthly bills. Perhaps you have some small savings and investments, and, if you're like most Americans, you live pretty much from paycheck to paycheck. Items of significant value, such as a house or car, don't lend themselves to being divided in half. If you sell one to divide the profit, you'll both think you have to buy another, and you probably can't afford it.

In many divorces when property is contested, a lawyer would advise you to insist on your economic rights, which might be an obviously good idea for most women. But when you deal with a batterer, safety may be a more pressing issue. Fear of your husband may tempt you to give in immediately to his demands in order to be free of him. On the other hand, if you think that he has already robbed you of years of your life, you might be willing to fight for what you believe is rightfully yours. If you make the first choice and let him take the property, you may be losing a lot. But if you opt for the second one, you could be letting yourself in for an extended legal tug of war. That could keep you legally and emotionally involved for an extended period. It could jeopardize the freedom from abuse you are seeking. A good argument can be made for either one of those positions.

It is essential for your lawyer to understand that staying involved with the abuser, even if only through third-party negotiations, may threaten your physical safety. Other hazards are more subtle. If extended legal arguments encourage your husband to think he can win you back, that could spell serious trouble. You need someone who understands both law and domestic violence to talk over the ramifications of either decision.

Alimony and Maintenance

Money will very likely continue to be an important tie to—and a problem with—the man. If you've been married a long time and own a home, if you haven't worked much outside the home, or you have custody of young children, you'll probably be awarded the house and perhaps your former partner will have to make payments on it for a certain time. He may also have to pay you temporary maintenance (until your divorce is final and the property divided or until you've had time to complete an educational or job training program) or alimony if you live in one of the states that allows for it.

Alimony can be a great help to women who have few job skills, but even in states that still assign fault to one party or the other, less than 5 percent of divorced men are ordered to pay support to their ex-wives. Of those who are ordered to pay a very small number pay anything.

If you've shared living quarters, property, or expenses with a man you're not married to, your legal situation is uncertain. Even if you decide not to take your case to court, a lawyer who has experience in such cases might be useful in negotiating a property settlement.

Child Support

Although laws and judges' attitudes are changing along with social customs, it's still common for women to be awarded custody of children, especially young ones, and for the custodial parent to be awarded the family home until the children are grown. But situations and communities are so varied one can't be sure what a particular judge will decide.

Both parents are obliged to support their children, so even if you are not married to the father of your child, he is obliged to contribute to his child's support. But as in every other interaction with a batterer, a decision to push him to fulfill his obligations is risky. It depends first of all on whether he is likely to interfere with your degree of safety and the safety of your kids. If your husband is ordered to pay child support, he may use your dependence on that money to harass you. If you decide to hold him accountable for his share of your children's expenses, it will help to have him pay through a third party. Get advice from an advocate on how to do that, but don't be surprised if he finds some way around it. If a court does award you child support, try hard to budget your money so that you can get by without his money. Then if he doesn't pay, you won't be in a desperate situation and won't be tempted to contact him to make him comply.

If he doesn't pay, you may be tempted to withdraw visitation rights. But you have no legal right to do that. Child support is legally unrelated to visitation rights. Unfortunately, all efforts to hold him accountable may lead to contacts with him. Each time that happens you may be in danger. The danger could be of being assaulted or it could be in becoming reinvolved with him emotionally.

COSTS AND BENEFITS OF SUPPORT FROM THE MAN

When you finally break free after months or years of financial and emotional dependence, it would ease the pain if you never had to look back and had no strings or qualifications on your freedom. Continued financial dependence will be hard on you and very likely be used by your former partner to threaten or cajole you into going back to him.

Whether you exercise your right to ask for support from your ex-partner for yourself or your child will depend on how dangerous the man is and whether you think a continued financial relationship will put you in danger. You might also consider whether he's been generally financially responsible. If not, there may be little point in your taking any risks at all unless you're willing to carry out a lengthy fight for your rights as a matter of principle.

Even men who are generous with money and dedicated to their children are likely to be much less dependable after separation than before. You'll be in a better position if you can get your share of the property or a lump sum of money right away. Even if it's less than the total you'd receive if he actually paid monthly support through a period of years, you'll have it in your hands. You won't have to wonder each month if your payment will arrive early, late, or not at all.

If you do ask for support, keep in mind it's your right and the children's right. Their father is not doing you a favor, regardless of whether he thinks he is. If you have custody, it costs you money to support the children. You're putting in many hours of child-care labor worth hundreds of dollars and may be paying for additional care while you're at a paid job. (If he has custody and you have a job, you may want to pay child support whether the court orders it or not.)

Find out if payments can be made through the court or automatically taken out of his paycheck and put into your credit union or bank account. That will ensure that it's there on time, and you won't have to speak to him about it each month. Whether such arrangements can be made depends on your state law, his employer, and in some instances, his willingness to comply.

OTHER LEGAL PROBLEMS

Is there something else you want that doesn't fit neatly into any of these categories? There are other legal procedures and goals that may help you. You may want to sue for damages to you or your property, have your husband ordered out of the house, restrained from destroying property, harassing you, or even coming near your house or workplace. You may also want something to happen that can't be done through legal procedures. The only way to find out whether your goals can be accomplished through the law is to ask a lawyer who specializes in domestic relations and who's experienced in wife-abuse cases.

If you're not going to get a divorce or permanent separation, what you can do is increase your safety. Can you stay away long enough to get your partner well started on counseling, AA, or other constructive action? Is there any way you can protect your children from witnessing at least the worst of his abuse?

Considering each of these legal options and your questions about them with the aid of a friend should help you make some decisions. Write the answer to each question, including partial answers such as "don't know," "probably yes," or "ask lawyer about this one." If you have many vague responses go back to the beginning and review each question. When you can't answer any more of them, list the questions you will have to ask an attorney. When you know the possible legal consequences of certain actions, you'll be able to answer the questions you're uncertain about now.

INTERVIEWING THE LAWYER

If possible, take a friend with you to the lawyer's office to act as your advocate; that is, to help you speak up for your rights. You may find it difficult to understand and remember the attorney's advice and explanations. Your friend can take the notes that you might be too nervous, confused, or distracted to take down. If you're embarrassed to ask questions and admit your ignorance, your friend can help by asking for clarification. She can also give some objective feedback when you leave the office. She must, of course, be someone you trust. If you can't find an advocate, don't hesitate to take notes yourself and, when necessary, to say, "Please go more slowly so I can write down what you're saying."

Questions to Ask the Lawyer

Going into the office with a clear idea of what you want, what you don't want, what you're not sure of, and questions for the lawyer to answer will put you on a more even footing. Don't be embarrassed at having your lists of questions in hand to check off. The attorney will probably be pleased at your businesslike attitude, and the efficient use of the lawyer's time will save you money. Give her or him a duplicate of the questions so you don't get rushed out of the office before they're all answered.

Begin by asking the lawyer these questions:

1. What is your fee?
2. Does the fee include time spent on telephone consultation? What else? Are filing fees included in the initial fee?
3. Will you send an itemized bill at least once a month?
4. Will you estimate for me the time you expect to spend on specific tasks as they come up?
5. Will you answer my questions even when they seem unimportant or difficult?
6. What period of time will be required to complete my case?
7. What role will I have in decision-making? (Then state whether you want to be an active participant or leave it up to the lawyer to decide questions about the case.)
8. Will you let me know what problems you encounter and plans you're making as you go along?

Lawyers are expensive, depending on where you live and the experience and status of the firm. A few lawyers charge on a sliding scale according to income. Most lawyers won't take certain cases until they're paid money in advance (a "retaining fee"). If you have no access to money but your husband has a good income, you may find a lawyer to take your case at no charge to you on the assumption the settlement will include payment of your attorney's fees by your husband.

Most lawyers charge for any time they talk to you on the telephone as well as for time in court and working on your case in the office. Clients usually underestimate charges because they don't remember that three twenty-minute telephone calls may add up to a substantial charge, and they don't realize paperwork takes many unseen hours. The attorney's agreement to keep you informed of charges as you go along will save you from the shock of unexpected large bills at the end of the services.

If the attorney doesn't give specific answers to questions about fees, if you think the fees are too high, or if you're not satisfied with answers to your other questions, don't feel you're obliged to continue with that person. Say you'll let her or him know your decision later or state your objections. You might find there's a misunderstanding. If necessary renew your search for a lawyer you can feel confident in working with.

What to Do if You Don't Understand the Lawyer

Some legal ideas are hard to translate into layperson's language, but it can be done. Some lawyers are thoughtless about speaking the language of law, which is foreign to most of us. Some of them purposely speak more "legalese" than is necessary to increase their authority.

Make it clear from the beginning that you want the lawyer to speak plainly and you want to understand everything. When the lawyer uses vaguely familiar legal phrases, you may tell yourself you should know what they mean or that you'll look them up later rather than appear stupid by asking for clarification. There's no reason why you should know legal terminology, so ask.

If you ask for clear explanations and the lawyer ignores your request or says not to worry about legal details ("Just leave it to me"), this may be a form of sexism and is certainly disrespectful. Say, "Thank you for your time, but it's important to me to understand what's happening, so I'll find another lawyer." Then do it. Shopping for a lawyer can be stressful, but so can hiring someone who doesn't respect you.

EVALUATING THE LAWYER

As with all professionals, keep in mind that you're the one who's hiring the services and that you have a right to ask for what you want. Continually review what you want, weigh it against what the lawyer advises, consult with friends and advocates at shelters or other women's organizations, and then make up your own mind what's best for you and what's best for your children. If you believe your attorney isn't taking your case seriously enough, say what you think and insist on an explanation. If it doesn't seem adequate, let the lawyer know you'll have a hard time following through with action unless something changes, or that you're thinking of hiring someone else.

It's difficult to start over with someone new, but it may be even worse to continue with a person who's doing an inadequate job. Many lawyers are competent in some kinds of cases but not others, so if you're not satisfied, give notice and don't feel guilty about leaving the lawyer. Your business now is to take care of yourself in the best way you know how. You need a lawyer you can count on to help you do that, and there are many of them who will, so keep on looking until you find the right one. Then let the lawyer do a lot of the worrying for you.

The Attorney Doesn't Know Everything

Like doctors, lawyers are often asked by clients under stress to help them make decisions on matters other than their area of expertise. Eventually, some of these professionals begin to believe they're experts in a great many areas, for instance, finance, politics, or human relations. Sometimes their work does afford them an opportunity to develop expertise in these fields, but often their alleged understanding of human relations is little more than the sum of their accumulated biases.

If you've answered carefully the questions on previous pages about your legal options, you'll be clearer about what you want to do and whether your doubts are related to positive feelings for the man, fear of him or of other things, considerations of what's right and wrong, or lack of sufficient knowledge. This self-awareness will enable you to weigh whether your attorney's advice is based on personal feelings or politics or on strictly legal issues.

Let's suppose you're one of the fortunate people who earns enough money to support your child without help from the father. You understand you don't have to contact the father to get child support. But you also know yourself well enough to realize if he owes you money every month, you'll use the situation as an excuse to contact him. Even though the children have a right to support, and he has the obligation to pay, you may decide not to ask for support. That decision might be safest for you and in the long run for your child.

If your lawyer tries to change your mind about it, listen carefully to the reasons. There may be a number of facts you don't know, and if you're in crisis you won't have the broad perspective your attorney has on your own and your children's rights. It's appropriate for your lawyer to tell you what rights you have, and what you might expect to happen if you exercise them. Then it's appropriate for you to decide whether you'll exercise them.

Any time you're in doubt about a lawyer's advice or plan of action, ask why she or he considers it the best one. "Is that strictly a legal decision, or are you considering other things, too?" Or, "What will be the effects if we do something different from what you're suggesting?"

Many male attorneys have sexist attitudes and are paternalistic toward women in distress. You may get an answer such as, "Well, we wouldn't want a pretty girl like you to go without, would we?" Or, "You don't want him to get away with this," or "Later on you'll wish you'd gotten a divorce." Don't let an attorney treat you like a child or define for you what you want or how you feel. What may seem like welcome protectiveness may just be another form of sexism. (He or she might legitimately tell you how most women in similar situations feel, and then you can decide whether you're enough like most women to make that information useful.)

If you find you're being persuaded to change your mind about an action you were pretty sure of when you started out, be a little suspicious. Are you changing your mind because of legal considerations you weren't aware of? Or have you, because of your feelings of helplessness and confusion, developed the idea that the attorney knows best even about your personal choices, such as whether you will divorce? If you've been persuaded to change your mind about one of those major questions, it might feel wonderful to let someone else be in charge. But when you leave the lawyer's office, you might gradually return to your original position. Then you may feel too embarrassed to explain your changed mind to the lawyer. It's your right to change your mind, but to save yourself from that awkward situation, whenever you have any doubts about taking an action, say you'd like a day to think it over.

Legal Advice Doesn't Include Emotional Support

Your attorney may be so emotionally supportive while you're consulting in the office that when you're in stress you'll be tempted to call her or him rather than a friend, counselor, or support-group member. This can result in disappointment, since your attorney will probably be busy with other clients, often in court all day, and unlikely to return your call unless there's something specifically legal that it's necessary to talk to you about.

If the attorney does call and listens to your troubles for twenty minutes, you may later be surprised by a bill for the time. It's important to distinguish the roles of each person who can give you advice or treatment and to rely on attorneys for legal help only.

If you find yourself frequently crying on the shoulders of your lawyer or friends, and thinking continually about your troubles yet not able to make headway in resolving them, you may want to seek professional counseling. The next chapter tells you how to go about doing that.

CHAPTER 9

GETTING HELP FROM A COUNSELOR

You don't have to be "crazy," "sick," or "neurotic" to seek help from a counselor, and the fact that you've been abused doesn't mean there's something wrong with you that a counselor can "fix." But living in a violent situation—or leaving it—creates practical and emotional problems difficult to sort out alone. As you'll see in the next chapters there's a great deal you can do for yourself or with the help of relatives and friends. But if you're depressed or isolated, or there is no one you want to talk to who can be counted on to be sympathetic, consider a professional counselor. She or he can help you decide whether or not to leave your partner and give you courage to carry out your decision. After a separation you might discover long-standing problems you want resolved before you become involved in another relationship, or you might just want short-term counseling to ease your way through the crisis period.

WHAT DO YOU WANT FROM A COUNSELOR?

Finding and choosing a counselor who is right for you may be difficult. Perhaps you're vaguely unhappy, fearful, tense, confused, and unsure of what you want or could reasonably expect from a counselor. Will she tell you what to do, help you make decisions, make you feel better? She may do most of those things and more, though you'll need to be wary of a counselor who tells you what you should do.

The following sets of questions are designed to help you decide what you want. *Check the appropriate spaces, keeping in mind there are no right, wrong, or best answers.*

Activity 13A ✂ What I Want from a Counselor

1. I want to know
   what I'm feeling .... _____
   why I'm feeling it .... _____
   other .... _____

2. I want to stop feeling
  confused . . . . _____
  trapped . . . . _____
  angry . . . . _____
  sad . . . . _____
  lonely . . . . _____
  afraid . . . . _____
  other . . . . _____

3. I want to learn to express
  anger . . . . _____
  fear . . . . _____
  sadness . . . . _____
  joy . . . . _____
  other . . . . _____

4. I want help in making decisions . . . . _____
5. I want help in solving problems . . . . _____
6. I want help in becoming more confident . . . . _____
7. I want to become more employable . . . . _____
8. I want to know what I want . . . . _____
9. I want to be able to ask for what I want . . . . _____
10. I want to be able to say "No" to unfair requests . . . . _____

11. I want to get along better with people, which includes
  knowing why I have trouble getting along with people . . . . . . _____
  ending involvements with destructive men . . . . _____
  having better sexual relationships . . . . _____
  finding men who treat me with respect . . . . _____
  making better friends . . . . _____
  coping better with children . . . . _____
  being a better parent . . . . _____

12. I want to
  gain more control over my life . . . . _____
  be more disciplined . . . . _____
  make better plans . . . . _____
  stick to my plans . . . . _____
  learn to take better care of myself . . . . _____
  other . . . . _____

If you checked a number of items, you have a good start on knowing how to ask for the right counselor for you. But other questions will help too. Check these desired counselor traits as honestly as you can, even if you think you shouldn't care about them.

Activity 13B ✧ What Kind of Counselor Do I Want?

I want to see a counselor who:
1. is objective and unemotional . . . . _____
2. is friendly, warm, and casual . . . . _____
3. is younger than I am . . . . _____
4. is older than I am . . . . _____
5. is about my age . . . . _____
6. is a woman . . . . _____
7. is a man . . . . _____
8. has experience with abused women . . . . _____
9. won't say it's my fault I got hit . . . . _____
10. believes women should have as many choices as men . . . . . _____
11. believes in traditional marriage relationships . . . . _____
12. shares my values . . . . _____
    political . . . . _____
    religious . . . . _____
    sexual orientation . . . . _____
    ethnic, racial, cultural traditions . . . . _____
    other . . . . _____
13. is a parent . . . . _____
14. other . . . . _____

From the answers to the two sets of questions, *circle* the counselor's characteristics that are most important to you, and what you want her to help you do. *Underline* the things that are definitely unacceptable. Perhaps you'll compromise on the desirable age or parenting experience but not on values or counseling experience. As you read the next part of this chapter, you may want to add to those lists, and you can refer to them when you're ready to call or see a prospective counselor.

FINDING A COUNSELOR

Ask friends and coworkers if they know of good counselors. Try to find out what they liked about them, what problems they were useful with, and whether they seem to have the qualities you're looking for. If they're willing to answer your questions, friends can be the best referral source.

If you're living in a big city, you may find therapy referral services or counseling services that are specifically directed to women or to abused women. There may also be agencies that charge according to income. Look in the telephone book yellow-pages section under "Social Services," "Social Work," "Psychology," or "Therapy." Check in the white-pages section under "Abuse," "Battering," "Women," "Feminist," "Rape Counseling," and "Child Abuse." You may find agencies that have expertise in domestic violence or who can refer you to the best person.

Settle down for an hour or two of phone calls. You'll probably get a mix of answering services, receptionists who have little information, receptionists who have a great deal of information, recorders, and people who say so-and-so will call back in thirty minutes or who refer you to four other numbers. It will help if you think of this as an exploration to find the best counselor for you rather than as making one quick call to make an appointment.

If you continually postpone making these calls, consider the possibility that you're scared. Most people are nervous about their first contact with a prospective counselor, so give yourself permission to feel what you feel.

Have pencil and paper with you when you call, so you can note the fee, address, and other pertinent information. When you call, tell the counselor right away that you have a number of questions to ask so she'll know she has to allot more than a couple of minutes for you. If she says she hasn't time to answer your questions, ask when would be a good time to call back.

Interviewing the Counselor by Telephone

Your first questions might be, "What are your fees?" and "Do you have a sliding scale?" If you don't have much money, you won't want to waste your time interviewing someone you can't afford to see anyway.

If transportation or time is a problem for you, get that settled right away by asking where the office is and whether the counselor is available at the times when you're free.

Before you ask more questions, give a general idea of what your goals in counseling will be. Use your answers to the questionnaires as a guide. Then ask, "How would you approach that kind of problem?" The counselor might say she has to know more before answering and then you'll have to decide whether to take a chance on an exploratory interview to answer that question. Some counselors will be willing to give you a very clear answer as to how they would work with you.

If you've never talked to a counselor before, your nervousness about her specialized language may cause you to have trouble understanding her. Don't assume it's your fault. Tell her you don't know much about counseling and ask her to explain what she means.

Sometimes it's hard to understand professional people, so don't expect to get a perfectly clear picture right away, even when you've asked for clarification. But you should expect the counselor to try to help you understand and to use ordinary language rather than the special jargon of therapy. After a couple of questions are answered, you should have an idea of whether you can expect counseling that's mostly talk or that includes a good deal of direction from the therapist, or activities designed to help you relax, express your feelings, or explore your potential. Take notes on what the counselor says.

You might want to ask the following questions also, either on the telephone or at your first interview when you can get a clearer impression face to face.

About how many battered women have you counseled, and have you had any special training in working with battered women? Your counselor should be experienced in counseling battered women and should have attended at least one workshop or class that dealt specifically with the issue.

What do you think is the main reason men batter women? There's room for a variety of opinions on this, but the counselor's opinion should have some reference to the sex-stereotyping and socialization of men and women; that is, she should understand that women are taught men are boss and men are given permission to control women and to express their anger in violent ways. She should put the responsibility for violence squarely on the shoulders of the person who does it.

Deciding on a Counselor

At this point you might have a definite impression and be ready to hang up or to make an appointment. If not, feel free to ask more questions. Some of the people you talk to might be gracious about answering them at length, others will be brusque, and still others willing, but too busy at the moment. You'll have to decide how important it is to you to get the information you want before making an appointment.

After each call, write your impressions, beginning with both pleasant and uncomfortable feelings you had as you talked or just after you hung up. Your first response might be "ugh" or "I feel awful" or something equally vague. Try to remember what was said or what attitudes were subtly expressed that caused the feeling. For instance, you might note "seemed hurried" or "laughed when I was funny." Then write other comments or information about fees, neighborhood, and so on, and rate each counselor as "No," "Possible," or "Yes." Note any questions you'll want to follow up on in your first session, and be sure to take them with you at that time.

If your telephone interviews give you two or three people that seem to be good prospects, make an appointment with the one who sounds the

best: the one who understands what you want, is easy for you to understand, is open to answering questions, and has considerable experience in
counseling abused women. Beyond these criteria, each woman's opinion
will vary. Explain that you want your first visit to be a mutual interview
to see if you want to work together.

THE FIRST COUNSELING SESSION

Each of the previous steps will increase your sense of control over the initial interview, though if you've never talked to a counselor, you may still
have some nervousness. The best way to dissipate it is to simply state that
you're nervous, have never been to a counselor before, and don't quite know
what's expected of you. The counselor will probably say something reassuring and then ask you to say why you're there or what's troubling you.

If you have more questions to ask, say so. If you ask them at the beginning of the hour you'll be sure not to run out of time before you get to
them. Additional questions may arise during the session. Ask when the
interview is scheduled to end so you'll be sure to have time to say what you
want. Have your written questions in front of you and don't feel embarrassed about making notes as they're answered. The more nervous you are,
the more you're likely to forget what was said unless you take notes.

Here are more questions you might want to ask:

How long have you been counseling and what kind of degree do you have?

Psychiatrists and most psychoanalysts have medical degrees as well as
training in psychotherapy. Their fees are generally the highest, unless
they're in public agencies that charge according to income or you're
receiving public assistance. A psychiatrist may be willing to accept medical coupons for payment. Their training tends toward upholding traditional sex roles and they're more likely to be interested in why you're
involved with a violent man than in how you can change your life.

A psychologist usually has a Ph.D. degree from a university and often
is trained in research on the behavior of animals and humans, knows how
to do diagnostic testing of intelligence and other factors, and has some
training in psychotherapy.

Social workers have a master's or Ph.D. degree from a university and
are trained in research, community organization, or counseling. A social
worker may have more concerns than other therapists about public policy and social services.

Counselors have degrees in counseling and often degrees in many
other fields. Their backgrounds may include formal training in institutions of higher learning or therapy institutes, private training with other

therapists, or on-the-job training or training in community sponsored workshops. Each profession has its competent and not-so-competent members, and it's impossible to say that one group is better than another. It's the individual who counts.

Paraprofessionals often counsel battered women, especially at shelters. They don't have degrees in counseling but have on-the-job training and much more experience in handling the problems you're faced with than have most professionals. If you have severe problems aside from those directly related to the battering, you may want to see a professional person. But for the crisis period or for problems related specifically to battering, you may get the best help possible from a paraprofessional. Whomever you choose, experience with and knowledge about the problem of battering is essential.

Will you expect me to talk most of the time and what other methods will you use to help me change?

There isn't one correct answer to this question. The therapist may expect you to spend most of the sessions talking while she makes only occasional remarks, both of you might talk, or she'll ask you to do relaxation exercises or to play roles in specific situations in order to understand or handle them better. Or she might ask you to do certain physical movements to help you express emotions.

You'll have to be the judge of whether the methods make sense to you, or whether you have a good enough feeling about the counselor to take a chance they'll work for you.

Is this session, in general, about the same as I can expect from other sessions?

Some counselors gather extensive information at the first interview. In some agencies, this "Intake" interview is done by a special person and will not be the same person you see for counseling. The "Intake Worker" may even assign you to a counselor and if you want to see a particular person or type of person, you may have to be very assertive to get the person you want.

If the counselor indicates the other sessions will be quite different from the first, ask for an explanation. You may want to wait until the end of the second session to make your decision.

You also have the right to ask about the counselor's marital status, lifestyle, and other questions about her personal life and personal values. She has the right to decline to answer and may or may not have good reasons for it. If she does decline you'll have to decide how important it is to you to have answers to those questions. If it is important, you have a right to find someone who will answer them for you.

What to Expect from the First Session

The first interview may provide you with clarification of your problems, plans to resolve them, or increased awareness of your feelings. Or it may take the whole session to relate your story and get your questions answered. How it goes depends on the counselor's skill and methods, on how upset you are, and whether you're well-organized about presenting your problem and clear about what you want. If you have many interconnected problems, one session may not be enough to give the counselor a clear picture. Aim to finish the session with agreement on whether you'll come back, how often, what you'll pay, and on the goals you want accomplished.

Sometimes in an initial interview a client becomes so immersed in her emotions or her story that she forgets to ask questions, has trouble saying what the problem is, and leaves with only a vague idea of what the counselor is like. If that happens to you, continue to follow the suggestions for the first interview in the second one. If by the end of the second session you don't have agreement about what you'll work on and how the counselor intends to help you, something is probably wrong.

Once you've invested an hour of your time in an interview and discussed troublesome and personal aspects of your life, it's difficult to conclude you don't want to continue seeing the person, even when you have misgivings about her. But if you have any doubts about whether you and she can work together, don't make a permanent commitment. If you're clear about what your reservations are, explain them. The problem may be just a misunderstanding. If not, the counselor's response may reinforce your negative feelings, so you'll be able to make a more definite decision. Remember there are other counselors available who may be much more satisfactory for you.

THE SPECIAL CASE OF A SEXIST COUNSELOR

It's difficult to say exactly what the counselor should do for you because the goals are hard to measure and it's not always easy to separate what you can expect of the counselor from what you must accomplish yourself. At a minimum, insist on respect. Among other things, that means sexist attitudes are not acceptable.

In the Broverman study referred to in Chapter 1, it was discovered that both female and male therapists believed it appropriate for men to be more confident, dominant, worldly, and emotionally reserved than women, and for women to be submissive, passive, and dependent. Counselors who accept traditional sex stereotypes such as these can have a powerful and damaging effect, especially on women. A woman may have just begun to gain a sense of what she wants from life, to make independent judgments, or to exercise her rights when she sees a counselor for the first time. If the counselor defines the woman's role for her in a narrow way, the woman may decide she was "crazy" to think she could be independent or make her own decisions. She may retreat from a newly developed determination to get a professional job or training in a trade or to define her own sexuality.

You'll experience special problems if you contract for the services of a sexist therapist. She or he is likely to reinforce your self-blame. If you're already blaming yourself for the abuse, it may not take much for your guilt feelings to lead you right back to the man. You may persuade yourself, or be persuaded by the counselor, that by becoming a better person yourself you can control the man's violence. Sexist therapists often ask battered women, "What did you do to provoke him?" and imply that it's the women's responsibility to change, so the man won't have a "reason" to beat her up again.

Whether they admit it or not, many men (and some women) believe it's the man's responsibility to control his women, especially his wife. Counselors are among the people who believe that, and it may take you quite a while to discover what your prospective counselor's attitudes are unless you ask pointed questions early on, at the first session or even before over the telephone. Try these:

- How do you feel about how women's and men's roles have been changing?
- Do you think mothers of small children should work outside the home?
- Do you think the one who earns the money should make most of the decisions in the household?

Answers to these questions won't tell the whole story, but they'll give you an idea of how similar or different your values are from those of the counselor's and whether she or he is rigid or flexible about sex roles or leans toward traditional or contemporary definitions of what it means to be male and female.

ADVANTAGES OF A WOMAN COUNSELOR

We've all grown up believing males are the people in authority, are knowledgeable, and can tell us what to do, whether they're doctors, husbands, or TV repairmen. That means you're particularly vulnerable to a male counselor, because of his double authority as a counselor and a male, and you'll probably be cautious about confronting him on his sex bias and speaking up for your own ideas.

A woman counselor is more likely than a man to understand and empathize with your feelings about the violent man and also to want to help you protect yourself. She may be more likely to help you get in touch with supportive women's groups in the community that many male counselors won't know about. In addition, she'll be a good role model for you. But many female therapists identify with male values, so don't assume if a female therapist implies you're in the wrong, she must be right.

Not all counselors realize that it's the batterer who must change, that his victim is not to blame, and that her obligation to keep herself safe is more important than an obligation to continue the relationship. You're more likely to find a female counselor than a male who's developed that awareness, but you'll need to ask questions to be sure. Ask, "Do you think one partner can be the only one at fault when there's battering, or is it always both partners who contribute and are equally responsible?"

If the counselor believes the problem is caused by the way the two parties interact and that they have equal responsibility for the battering, you had better look further. Keep looking until you find someone who recognizes that only the person who does the battering can stop it or start it and only he is responsible. (If you also behave in destructive ways sometimes, you are the one responsible for those actions.)

HOW TO EVALUATE THE COUNSELOR

The goals you and the counselor agreed upon at the first or second session give you criteria for judgment. For instance, after two months of counseling you may still feel unhappy, but if you remember that the goal is to gain insight or express your emotions, you'll realize it might be necessary to experience more pain as a byproduct of growth. On the other hand, if your goal is to receive support and validation of your feelings and ideas, and yet you emerge from each counseling session feeling worse than when you went into it, something is definitely wrong.

When sessions aren't going well, allow for the fact that the fault may lie either with you, the counselor, or the relationship between you. Don't assume you're a failure and beyond anyone's help. And don't expect magic of the counselor or blame her when you're not immediately "cured." Perhaps one or both of you is not working hard enough or well enough, or you're not working together well. Don't give up until you've considered each factor.

Express your dissatisfaction to the counselor in terms of the agreed-upon goals and the length of time you've been meeting together. "We agreed that I should work on becoming more self-confident, and after three months I don't feel any different." "I was supposed to be able to express my anger, but after four months I don't even know how I feel."

An open, ethical counselor will explore the reasons, trying to reach a balance of responsibility between you and her, and, most important, a satisfactory way to proceed. It might be you've said you'd do suggested exercises but haven't followed through; the exercises haven't been appropriate for you; the counselor hasn't been consistent in her expectation—has stated one goal but then drifted toward another; or you've continually redefined your goals without beginning work on any. Maybe there's nothing wrong with either of you, but you just don't like her much. That's important too.

Reevaluating the Process

The counselor, ideally, will admit to some questions about her methods and will accept your criticism as possibly valid. The result of such a discussion should be a new plan with a clearly defined goal and an agreed-upon time and method of evaluation. An alternative is to recognize that it's time to end the relationship, either because the counselor isn't acceptable to you, or because of a personality or values clash or, for reasons only dimly understood, because it's just not working. Together you can discuss alternative counselors. You may find that your counselor knows several others and their methods of working and by now knows you well enough to make a good referral.

And what if she isn't that sort of ideal counselor? Suppose you tell her you don't feel any changes are taking place and she says it isn't so, or that you should let her worry about that, or that the problem is your hostility toward her, or any number of nondirect responses? You should be very careful to state what it is you want ("I'd like you to tell me now what changes you see and why you feel that's significant progress") or what she does that you don't like and find out if she's willing to change ("When I get stuck and don't talk, it makes me uncomfortable for you to just sit in silence. Would you be willing to help me get started?").

She may point out a number of changes that you've lost sight of or don't count as important. It's very hard to discriminate between the validity of a counselor's evaluation and your own, especially if you've been depressed for a long time or if one of your problems is holding on to unrealistically high standards. If the counselor can remind you of how you were when you first came in ("Remember when just a couple of months ago you wouldn't even get out of bed for days?"), if she can give concrete examples of positive steps you've taken ("You've stood up for your rights three times this week, found an apartment, started making a friend"), you may have to put your trust in her.

On the other hand, if she's vague about what progress you've been making and thinks the changes she wants you to make are more important than ones you're interested in, it may very well be time to stop seeing her.

Deciding to Leave or Change Counselors

It's extremely hard for most clients to tell a counselor they want to end the sessions, so they find excuses for not coming to appointments, hoping to gradually slip away unnoticed. This is not the most useful method for either party. Your absence will be noticed.

Try to screw up your courage to tell the counselor exactly why it is you want to stop. If she disagrees with your reasons, try honestly to listen to her and weigh her comments against your ideas. Be as frank as you can about your reasons and don't back down just because of her power and authority. She may try to talk you out of leaving, or she may disagree with your reasons but encourage you to act on your own beliefs, or she might come around to agreeing with you. In any case, acknowledged or not, you will have done her a favor by letting her know why you're choosing to leave. And you will have done yourself a favor by standing up for your rights and taking full responsibility for your decisions.

As you choose, work with, and evaluate a counselor, keep in mind that you're buying services. If you're not getting what you want, you have every right to buy them someplace else or to negotiate until you get what you want. After three visits to one counselor, don't let yourself off the hook by saying, "I tried counseling but it didn't help." Keep on looking until you find a person you can work well with.

If you're lucky, you'll find a counselor who shows you how to help yourself. Regardless of what you get from formal counseling sessions, in the end it's up to you.

SECTION III

HELPING YOURSELF
TO SURVIVAL

CHAPTER 10

YOU CAN BE YOUR OWN COUNSELOR

Professionals of various sorts can be lifesavers at times, but ultimately you have to save your own life and create your own destiny—even if you think you're the last person you can count on right now.

You want to get out. You want to stay. You feel dependent on your partner, yet you know he can't be depended on. You want a job, but you do nothing about getting one. You're sad and depressed. There's an angry monster that pops out when you least expect it. You love him, you hate him. You say you couldn't tolerate the loneliness of leaving him, but you're lonely when you're with him. All those contradictions make you feel as if you're going crazy, and they may paralyze your will to act.

But you can help yourself. The contradictions don't mean you're crazy, though many abused women do wonder about their stability. When the most important adult in your life regularly gives you negative feedback about the kind of person you are, you're in a "crazy-making" situation: a situation that continually causes you to question your judgment on things you previously felt secure about; a relationship that causes confused thinking, a mass of contradictions, and a frequent feeling that nothing makes sense anymore. It's especially so if you've been isolated and get no balancing positive messages from other people.

It's true that some women stay in the situation long enough to go a little crazy. But it needn't be a permanent condition. Changing your situation, either by leaving the man, or by expanding options and activities within the relationship, can begin important changes in the way you think and feel about yourself, enabling you to start believing in your sanity.

You can begin to recapture the will to act, even when you're still feeling confused. You've already started by reading this book. This section will help you learn how to be a good counselor to yourself.

CHANGING HOW YOU TALK TO YOURSELF

Any woman involved with an abusive man hears a great deal of verbal abuse directed against her. Few women can take it for long without beginning to agree. Often, unknown to the man, his woman begins to talk silently to herself the same way he does. After a while, he doesn't have to give the negative messages any more to keep her in line. She does it for him.

If she has friends or relatives who give emotional support and believe she's a good person, she may eventually begin to trust their judgment. But if she thinks her man is far more important or knows her much better than they do, she won't hear the supportive, positive messages that come her way. If she spends little time with people other than her man—a common situation—there won't be other messages to hear.

All of us counsel, or coach, ourselves in ways that are either useful or damaging. It's easy to get into the habit of coaching for failure, but that can be changed. You can begin by modifying your "self-statements," the things you say to yourself, about yourself. If you give yourself messages to the effect that: "You don't deserve to eat well or dress well because you're too fat and ugly," "You're helpless and stupid and can't take care of yourself," or "Nothing is ever going to turn out right for you," your life probably won't get better. You may make dozens of promises, weekly, or even daily. "Tomorrow I'm going to look for a part-time job, learn to type, clean the house from top to bottom, enroll in a class, be a better wife, a more patient mother." You won't be able to fulfill any of these promises if you constantly tell yourself you're hopeless and incapable of change.

The next series of exercises is designed to combat the hostile messages that are probably coming from you as well as from the man who abuses you. You may not be able to change his behavior, but at least you can stop verbally abusing yourself.

The Importance of Writing

Many of the activities below require writing, and some people resist them because they don't like to write. They think the writing is "just a gimmick." No one but you will see what you write, so it doesn't have to be correct. Writing is a gimmick, but it has a purpose. In fact, several purposes.

Writing things makes them concrete. If you're of two minds (you want to leave, you want to stay; you have rights, you deserve nothing), your conflicting ideas can be confusing and discouraging. Writing can help clarify them. It can also make you more aware of your unconscious thoughts. Because you don't always hear the things you tell yourself, saying them out loud helps; writing them down helps even more. If you try to repeat back exactly what someone said two or three minutes ago, you'll realize how easily the spoken word drifts away. (A tape recorder will help too, if you really hate to write, but there are important advantages to writing that I think will become apparent as you do the exercises.)

You may be afraid of the changes necessary to get out of your painful situation, and you may rather stay hurt and bewildered than face a frightening unknown. But if you don't do the written exercises to give yourself an opportunity to see your thoughts more clearly and to understand the changes that can be made, there's a good chance you'll remain confused and unable to take action. If you continue making excuses for several months, you may need professional counseling to get started.

WHAT DID YOU DO RIGHT TODAY?

Make a list of all the things you did right today. You'll have to decide what "right" means to you, according to your own values, but here are some questions you can ask yourself and some ideas about what you can take credit for. Even if they don't seem like a big deal, they're still things you can feel good about.

What did you do to try to make things better for other people? Perhaps you prepared a meal, comforted a child, controlled your temper, shopped for a sick friend, taught a neighbor to crochet, listened to someone's troubles, smiled at the letter carrier.

This question is placed first, not because it's the most important kind of thing to do, but because you're likely to do things for others and value them more readily than what you do for yourself.

What have you done to begin getting more control over your life? Have you made a decision, tried something new, enrolled in a class, started learning to drive, made a phone call to get information, stayed away from a destructive person?

Any action, no matter how small, that moves you a little further in the direction you want to go, is "right."

What have you done to make yourself feel better? Luxuriating in a long bubble bath, walking for the joy of it, taking the time to look at the sunset, going out to listen to music, playing cards with a good friend.

Notice I haven't listed activities that can be done without much conscious choice, or time-passers that seem pleasant at the moment but later leave you feeling you've wasted your time. In this category are alcohol, drugs, watching whatever happens to be on television, looking through magazines you aren't interested in, and passively talking with people you didn't choose to be with.

Women who've been abused often find it extremely hard to think of anything they've done right. When they do remember it, they're afraid to say it out loud. Writing about your activities helps you to be honest and precise, so when you read what you've accomplished, you're confronted with the fact that you're not hopeless, not a total failure.

If you want to gain some control over your life, you have to start giving yourself credit for things well done, which doesn't necessarily mean you succeeded in exactly what you wanted to accomplish. If you've been sitting around in a depressed funk for a few months or years and then decide to take up jogging, you may not get farther than one block. What you did well was to make a change. You made a decision, got up off your chair, got some exercise, and started moving in a different direction. As you increase your awareness that you've done some worthwhile things already, you'll gain courage to try more activities and a greater sense of what's possible.

Note whether you've added any negative qualifiers to your positive statements. When women are asked to make positive statements about themselves, they often qualify the self-compliment with a criticism or by discounting its importance. "I have a good disposition—except I get mean when I'm depressed." "I'm a good mother—but anybody could do that." *Draw a line* through the qualifiers.

Activity 14 ✒ Do Right List

	Day 1	Day 2	Day 3
HELPED OTHERS FEEL GOOD	Listened to elderly, lonely neighbor		

	Day 1	Day 2	Day 3
GAINED CONTROL OVER PART OF MY LIFE	Called for info on class		

	Day 1	Day 2	Day 3
DID WHAT FELT GOOD	Went shopping		

Go back over your list one more time. What have you left out? Did you fix the children a nutritious meal? Get to work on time? Do the laundry? Are you telling yourself those accomplishments don't count, because "It's something any responsible mother/employee would do"? Of course it counts. The way you're feeling, you could have thrown together jelly sandwiches and Cocoa Puffs to keep the children happy and off your back. You could get to work late, take long breaks, and leave early. What else did you do that you didn't list because you thought, "It had to be done, so why give credit for it?"

Sometimes you have to get out of bed but it takes a gigantic effort, and perhaps there have been days when you've just refused to cope and stayed in bed or stared at the television all day. If you felt like that but got up and went on with your day, give yourself credit for it.

Remember that "doing right" means doing the best you can at the moment. Look again to see if you omitted anything you tried to accomplish but that didn't work out well. There might be times when you take hours (or days) to work up your courage to make a phone call, and the person you call is out of town. That can be a letdown. But at least take credit for making the call, which you could control, and don't blame yourself for the result, which you couldn't do anything about. You ought to have at least thirty items on the credit list for the first three days. Keep listing them every day.

WHAT ARE YOU TELLING YOURSELF?

List your self-criticisms exactly as you say them: "Dummy!" "Oh my god, you screwed up again." Some may be single words: "fat," "ugly," "gross," "stupid," "hopeless." Others may be whole sentences or paragraphs that demolish your ego: "You dimwit! You really are a hopeless fool. Everything you touch, you ruin. You never learn. You keep saying you're going to reform, but you never get better. You're ugly and fat, too, because you don't have any willpower."

Activity 15 � Self-Criticism List

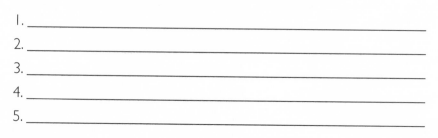

1. _____

2. _____

3. _____

4. _____

5. _____

6. _____

7. _____

8. _____

9. _____

10. _____

This kind of inner monologue may be nearly constant and such a familiar part of your being that you're no longer aware of it. To appreciate how damaging this slanderous self-talk can be, consider how you would feel if someone else continually insulted you that way. Perhaps you heard something like it from a parent or spouse and can remember how small and helpless it made you feel.

However bad that may have been, what you say to yourself can be much worse. No one else can equal the many opportunities you have to hurl insults at yourself all day, every day. Another important difference is that other people's insults are spoken aloud, so that however hurtful they may be, it's possible to fight back. Your own criticisms, in contrast, are often silent; so you may be unconscious of them and unable to contradict them. If you continue to be unaware of what your self-criticisms are, they can make you a very effective one-woman demolition squad, chipping away at your self-esteem a little more each day.

You may find it difficult, at first, to notice what you're saying, but just making the decision to record the statements will improve your awareness. If nothing comes to mind the first day, don't give up. Get a nice drink, settle into a comfortable chair, and recall the last twenty-four hours in detail. Form a picture in your mind of each event, recapture the mood, try to experience again what you felt at the time, and pay special attention to what you said to yourself when you were bored, angry, disappointed; when you forgot something or failed to follow through on a plan. If even one slightly self-critical word comes to mind, write it down.

If you can recapture a negative mood but can't recall any specific statements, ask yourself what you might have said if you had chosen to put the mood into words. Never mind whether the words are rational or accurate. You're not trying to find the absolute truth; you're getting a process started. Putting these imaginary statements on your list will help you form the habit of listening to yourself.

THE DIFFERENCE BETWEEN THE GENERAL
AND THE SPECIFIC

Generalizations have a very different effect from statements that criticize only particular acts or single aspects of your character. ("You were selfish about going out to dinner." "You're not good at gardening.") The general statements speak of who you are, the others describe a specific behavior or failure in a particular area. It's easy to forget that sometimes smart people do dumb things and good people do bad things.

For instance, the generalization "You're so stupid!" leaves no room for change or improvement. In contrast, "That sure was a stupid thing to do" allows for the possibility that you're not generally a stupid person and can correct your action. In the following example, the woman:

1) accuses herself of being a stupid person,
2) writes it down,
3) analyzes the self-accusation and realizes that she was referring to one action that seemed stupid, and
4) states what happened: She burned the toast.

This exercise is a modified version of Sharon Berlin's model of self-criticism reduction.

Activity 16 ∿ Substitution List[1]

Self-Critical Statement	What Happened
1. You're sure stupid!	burned the toast
2. Oh, my god, you're never going to change; you'll always be a fat useless slob.	ate double ice cream cone
3. _____	_____
_____	_____
_____	_____
4. _____	_____
_____	_____
_____	_____
5. _____	_____
_____	_____

A simple statement of what you did takes the comment out of the realm of blame and praise. No intellectual or moral evaluation is made of the act of burning toast. If you do this exercise regularly, you'll avoid the guilt, depression, and anxiety that often follow self-blame, and you'll be free to consider how you can change the behavior. Blaming won't improve your life, but changing what you don't like will.

Self-criticism can be useful, but not if it implies that you're destined to remain lazy, idiotic, and ugly until you die. It can be put to use only if it's specific and not so constant that you become overwhelmed with the number of things to be changed.

Substituting the Specific for the General

Continue to take the steps of (1) Increasing awareness of self-criticisms, especially general or total characterizations, (2) Recording, (3) Analysis, (4) Restating. Do it every day. It may take several weeks to progress to (5) Developing the habit of automatically substituting a statement about a specific action for a generalized insult.

First, work on corrections, noting each day how many times you remembered to correct each general criticism as soon as you made it. Soon you'll be able to substitute the more specific, rational statement for the general criticism. Your inner monologue may go something like this: "Well, fatty you did it again! . . . Whoops! I mean . . . let's see, what did I do? Correction: I had potatoes and gravy." After several weeks of these kinds of corrections, you'll find yourself skipping over the "Well, fatty" remarks entirely and substituting a factual statement about what was eaten.

The ability to skip over the general self-criticism to the substituted specific statement isn't necessarily a continually improving path. There will be setbacks, but gradually there will be more items in the substitution column than in the correction column. Sometimes it takes weeks for that to happen.

EVALUATE YOUR RULES

Take another look at your self-criticism list. How many criticisms imply rules about what you should do, or what you should be like? If you're confused about what the rules are, try writing them. *Write* one criticism at a time, then *write* the rule you seem to be trying to obey. Rules usually demand that you must never do something (lose your temper, be late for work) or must always do something (remember to call mother, stick to your diet, be nice, be sensible, etc.).

Where do your rules come from? Your mother? Your father? Your husband? Your children? School? Friends? Who said you should have a complete hot dinner and dessert on the table at 6:00 every night? Who insists you be clever, competent, and unruffled? Who said you should be smart? A good housekeeper? Able to handle money well? Write the name of the rule-giver beside the rule.

Activity 17 ᧖ Whose Rule?

Self-Criticism	Rule	Whose Rule
I'm just a slob. The house is always a mess.	The house must be uncluttered at all times after 10:00 A.M.	Mother's

_____

_____

_____

_____

_____

_____

_____

_____

You may have trouble deciding where the rule came from. Perhaps you're thinking it doesn't come from anyplace special. "Everyone knows you shouldn't leave dishes in the sink," or "That's just the way people are supposed to be." If so, shut your eyes and try to visualize a house that "looks the way it should." If it's your mother's house, the rule probably came from her, whether or not it was stated in so many words. If you still don't have a clue, ask yourself what person could drop in unexpectedly—however unlikely—and cause you embarrassment at the condition of your house? A neighbor? The minister? That person may never have made any sort of rule, yet you may be trying to live up to a standard you think the person demands.

What Are Your Rules?

You'll do better if you try to live up to your own standards. Suppose no one except you ever saw your house? Would you still try to abide by that rule? If not, what would *your* rule be? Maybe only part of it suits your lifestyle. Perhaps you like the kitchen clean because you don't like the looks of kitchen mess, but you'd rather keep the bedroom doors closed than make the beds. Maybe you'd prefer to clear away the clutter at the end of the day than at nine-thirty in the morning.

Give some thought to what it feels like to try to live up to other people's rules. Does it make you nervous? Bad-tempered? Defensive? Do you feel guilty? Inadequate? If you experience some of those feelings, consider whether the rule itself might be at fault, rather than you.

Write your own rules now, noting it's your own decision this time whether you'll follow each one or change it when it seems unreasonable.

Activity 18 ᘒ Your Own Rules

New Rules	Whose Rule?
Wash dishes after each meal.	Mine
Pick up general clutter between 10:00 A.M. and noon.	Mine

_____

_____

_____

_____

_____

_____

_____

_____

All the activities in this chapter work together: giving yourself credit for what you do right, reducing self-criticism, and establishing rules that are your own. The next chapter tells you how to begin making changes, one at a time, even when you don't want to take action at all.

CHAPTER 11

A COURAGEOUS ACT A DAY

Perhaps your picture of a courageous act is restricted to the drama of saving people from a burning building, leading a platoon into battle, or donating a kidney. If so, you'll need to broaden your definition. Any worthwhile activity you do in spite of the fact that it causes you nervousness, anxiety, pain, or insecurity is a courageous act. Worthwhile simply means an activity worth doing. The range might be from asking a friend to come for dinner to job- or house-hunting or to asking a social worker to help you stop abusing your child.

You can probably see that the last example takes courage, but you may argue that the other two are nothing to be nervous about.

THE USES OF DENIAL

It's natural to deny feelings of insecurity or anxiety, because you think there's something shameful about them or they're painful to live with. You deny their existence, hoping if you ignore them they'll go away.

Denial does work that way sometimes for some people; more often, however, it has an opposite effect that goes something like this: "I shouldn't be nervous about a little thing like apartment-hunting. So I'm *not* nervous about it. It's just that I don't want to do it today, because I think I'm getting a cold. I'll wait till tomorrow." And when tomorrow comes: "I'd better stay home and mend this dress so I'll look nice when I go apartment-hunting tomorrow." And tomorrow and tomorrow.

Flimsy excuses will increase your confusion and sense of helplessness. "I couldn't call emergency housing because the line was busy" won't wash. Nor will "I couldn't look for work because I missed the bus." Those are excuses, not reasons. Excuses may explain why it was hard to do something (going out in the rain when you have a cold, getting up early even though you didn't sleep well). They don't explain why you didn't do the difficult task.

When you reorganize your life, you may have to talk to many people with whom you've had nothing to do before (lawyers, crisis counselors, rental agents, welfare workers, employment interviewers, plumbers).

Most people are anxious, in varying degrees, when faced with unfamiliar contacts and new roles. So don't be surprised if "just" talking to a plumber makes you nervous. If you were once accustomed to handling money and making business contacts, but your partner has "protected" you from all that for several years, it may be especially difficult to accept the fact that you are now uncertain and scared. Admitting it would make you feel as though you'd regressed, and that might be humiliating.

Are You Denying Your Feelings?

If you make a decision to do something that seems right for you, and postpone doing it several times, that may be a clue that you're playing a denial game. Listen carefully to the explanations you give yourself and determine whether they're really excuses.

Suppose you're asking yourself why you put off house-hunting. "Well, without a car it's hard, and Monday it was raining." Note that the lack of a car and the rain make it hard, but they don't say why you didn't put on your raincoat and get on a bus. "Tuesday I thought the baby was sick. It turned out she wasn't, but by then it was too late." Perhaps you really couldn't go if she was sick, but did you take her temperature or take her to the doctor as early as you could? Did you try every way you could think of to find a babysitter? Could you have gone to one or two places after you learned she was all right, even though it was later than you wanted it to be? A second postponement is cause for suspicion, even when the reason seems valid.

"Wednesday my friend came by and I didn't want to hurt her feelings by leaving." Did you think of asking her to come with you? Did you have any special reason to think she'd be hurt? The third postponement in three days almost certainly indicates you're not being honest with yourself.

One way to catch yourself at that game is to ask if you really mean "couldn't." Usually "couldn't" means "I didn't want to" or "I was too scared, but I didn't want to admit it." Reasons are honest. Excuses are partly true (you really did miss the bus), but they don't explain much and may even turn the truth upside down (maybe you missed the bus so you'd have an excuse not to job-hunt).

UNCOVERING YOUR FEARS

When you suspect yourself of denying your feelings, some further questions are in order:

- What are the feelings I most dislike experiencing?
- What kinds of situations usually cause me to feel that way?

- If I *were* feeling that way about this situation, why would I feel that way?
- What's the worst thing that could happen in this situation?
- What's the best thing that could happen?

Suppose your husband has done the shopping for the past ten years, including all the groceries. Now he's gone and it's up to you. You postpone going to the supermarket and get by with what the children pick up at the corner mini-market, but you're concerned because it's so expensive to shop there. The first few times you put off shopping, you give yourself excuses. Finally you admit you just don't want to do it. Then you get to the questions above and answer them like this:

- I most dislike feeling inadequate or confused or stupid when out in public.
- I feel inadequate when I don't know how to do something and when people expect me to know certain things that I don't.
- Maybe I'd feel this way because of not knowing what are reasonable prices, not remembering how to pick out good meat or fruit, some young customer or clerk asking my "expert" opinion.
- The worst thing that could happen is I wouldn't be able to answer, or I'd start crying, or I would wander around, feeling so anxious that I wouldn't be able to find anything, make a fool of myself, be carted off to a mental hospital.
- The best thing that could happen is I'd remember it all and just start doing it again like I used to.

Now you can be pretty sure it's your fear of feeling inadequate, foolish, or crazy that's keeping you from the supermarket. "But that's ridiculous," you may think. "I used to handle everything, I even gave public speeches and terrific dinner parties until he took over everything and we stopped seeing anybody. I can't be putting off shopping because I feel like some dumb little kid when I think about trying to find my way around the supermarket." But apparently that's the reality, and now that you know what it is, you can deal with it.

Suppose you have to look for a new place to live. Maybe you've been staying with friends or at a shelter and now it's time to move out on your own. "Anybody," you say, "should be able to look for an apartment, right?" Maybe you've put it off because it's boring and you'd rather sit in the sun. That's probably true as far as it goes, but it's not far enough. If you ask those same questions, you might realize that you most hate feeling poor, and you feel poor when you live in dingy places or have to admit you can't afford to live where you want. You're afraid you'll only be able to find a place that's cramped and depressing. So boredom is only part of the picture. If you thought your hunt would reward you with a wonderful place, you'd gladly suffer the boredom of looking.

Answering the last question, "What's the best thing that could happen?" may surprise you. If the best thing that could happen is finding a place to live by yourself, and the feeling you hate most is loneliness, it might be you're afraid you'll succeed in finding a place. When you move into that wonderful place by yourself, you'll miss the people you're staying with now. Perhaps you're not quite ready to be on your own but you haven't wanted to admit it.

As long as you continue to deny your fears, you can postpone action indefinitely with a series of excuses that hide the real reason even from yourself. But when you recognize the fears you can force yourself to rise above them and that's what takes courage. As you'll see in the following pages, there are things you can do that make it easier to be courageous.

The days you force yourself to get out of your chair and go to the supermarket, regardless of your feelings of anxiety, confusion, and frustration, the days you pound the pavement for a new place to live, even though you dread moving, those are the days you act with courage. If you didn't have those feelings about the tasks, they wouldn't be remarkable at all. It's the feelings, together with your willingness to rise above them, that make those acts courageous.

REDEFINE THE TASK

If you're promising yourself you'll go out to get a job, rent an apartment, or make a new friend, you may be afraid you'll be even more depressed if it doesn't work out. You need to reword your intention so that it states only what you know you can do: "I'm going to *look* for a job or apartment." "I'm going to *invite* someone out for coffee." Perhaps these seem small distinctions, but they're important. Although you can't control other people's responses, you can take responsibility for your part of the interaction. If you don't get the job or the house, you needn't be depressed over failing. You can give yourself credit for working hard and intelligently, even though you couldn't control the result.

Choose your task carefully. Make it one you're willing and able to carry out, and then hold yourself accountable. That does not mean building up a lot of anxiety about failure to succeed. Nor does it mean putting yourself down if you don't carry out your plan. It means you're clear about your intention, and clear about whether you carried it out. It may mean figuring out why you didn't do it.

Once you establish the reason you haven't acted, you can begin to work on changes. Not by telling yourself you should be brave or should want to do it, but by choosing a task that's the least threatening to begin with and getting help from a friend in carrying it out.

Suppose you've been telling yourself you'll enroll in a community college and learn to be a computer programmer. After you postpone applying for admission several times, your self-questioning tells you you're afraid you can't do the work. Maybe you've been at home with several children for ten years and feel your brain is frozen.

Stop thinking of your task as getting through one or two years of schooling without flunking out or making a fool of yourself in comparison to all those bright young students.

Start thinking about the first step. You'll need to talk to a counselor at the college about requirements, how you can prepare ahead of time, how other people in your circumstances manage, and so forth.

If you postpone doing that two or three times, choose another step for an easier task. It might be just walking through the campus a few times to make it familiar and noticing how many older students there are. Maybe it's talking to a friend who's a student or looking up the number you'll need to call for an appointment. Or each one of these, one each day.

"The longest journey begins with a single step" is a saying with much truth. Your job is to concentrate on that first step.

TAKE CREDIT FOR EACH COURAGEOUS ACT

You probably accept the idea that it's right to be good to other people, especially those you care about most: your children, your husband, parents, friends. Yet you may object to being good to yourself, insisting, "That's just selfish. I don't deserve it."

Women have a way of copping out when credit is due. If husbands, lovers, children, or friends come to us saying, "I'm a failure, I didn't do well at all," we quickly run to their defense, attempting to rescue them from despair with words of comfort and reassurance, reminders of things done well, and efforts made. Why don't we do that for ourselves? It doesn't seem appropriate to toot our own horns or to promote ourselves.

If you care about yourself, you'll treat yourself well. If you have hostile, punitive, disapproving attitudes toward yourself, then you'll see to it that one way or another, you're deprived of things that make you feel good. Make up your mind to behave as if you like yourself and deserve to feel good. If you're willing to change your actions for awhile, you'll find before long you're beginning to believe you're as deserving of respectful and nurturing treatment as anyone else.

Often you're the only one who knows what task you've assigned yourself, and you're certainly the only one who knows just how much courage and energy goes into goading yourself to get started at it and follow through. So you're the best one to assign credit. (Review the Do Right exercise in Chapter 10.) Your own encouragement is the only response you can control, so make the most of it. When you appreciate yourself, you'll appreciate others. When you value yourself, others will value you. Start taking credit now and giving yourself specific rewards.

BE GOOD TO YOURSELF

Being good to yourself may mean rewarding yourself for courageous or other worthwhile acts, or it may mean allowing yourself pleasures for no special reason. Either way, you have to know what things make you feel good. Does listening to your favorite music cheer you up? How about going to a fashionable restaurant for lunch? Or seeing a good movie, walking in the park, lingering over a letter from a friend? See how many pleasures you can find or invent, especially things that aren't expensive, fattening, illegal, or potentially dangerous.

If you've been in a brutal, restrictive relationship for a long time, you may have trouble thinking of something you enjoy. If you married or had a child shortly after you finished school, you may never have had the opportunity to explore what you want. If you haven't known many people, read many books, had many jobs, or tried many sports or arts, you may think you don't want much of anything or that it's impossible to find out what interests you.

Think about the people you like or admire or envy, men or women, old or young, in fiction and history, or real and alive. What is it about their characters, abilities, or lifestyles you find attractive? If the excitement of a TV detective's life or a mountain climber's opportunity for bravery and risk-taking are what appeal to you, don't assume you could never do anything like that. Consider less dramatic, more available activities that provide opportunities to learn skills and experience similar feelings. Imagine yourself learning to ski or mountain climb, with the long-range goal of becoming an instructor or part of a rescue crew. Never mind that it could take years to become proficient, that skiing can be quite costly, and that in real life you think of yourself as "chicken." You don't know exactly how chicken you are until you try some slightly risky activities and give yourself a chance to overcome your fear gradually. Start with a low-risk sport to get in shape and gain more confidence in your body. When you find you're becoming a little braver, you'll be motivated to consider how you can earn or save money for skiing or climbing lessons. The point is, there's no need to give up any dreams or fantasies until you've thoroughly explored how they can be made real and what you'll need to begin the process.

Suppose you want a long vacation by yourself or with another adult. If you are tied to children for a number of years, that may very well be an impossible dream for the near future. But with some imagination, and careful planning, you may be able to get away for a weekend, or a day, or arrange to have a few free hours each week.

Be wary of sentences that begin with, "Yes, but . . . " and finish with all the reasons you can't give yourself pleasure: "I'll never have time, energy, money, or opportunity to do what I want." When you have few opportunities, it's certainly painful to be aware of all the things you'd like to have and do. But suppressing awareness of what you might want dulls the senses and increases depression. It also almost guarantees the depression will last longer, because if you don't know what you want, you can't begin to get it.

Find Out What Would Give You Pleasure

Make three lists:

1) pleasures you enjoy and want more of,
2) pleasures you used to have (at any stage in your life), and
3) things you might like but have never tried (caviar, gardening, black satin sheets, bowling). Be sure to include small pleasures such as reading in bed, watching a plant flourish, putting up a shelf, browsing in a bookstore.

Activity 19A ⋙ Pleasure List

Pleasures I Enjoy	Pleasures I Used to Have	Pleasures I Might Like
Watering plants	Roller-skating	Riding river rapids
Visiting	Crocheting	Writing poetry

Put a check next to each of the pleasures you might have in the next week. Include those that require you to give up something else, plan, or get some information. If you haven't at least ten activities that are possible to do almost immediately, go back and see what you can add to the list.

Make a list of pleasant events you can look forward to early in the morning, sometime in the afternoon, and in the evening.

Activity 19B ✌ Daily Pleasures

Morning	Afternoon	Evening
Lingering over newspaper	Read mail	Telephone (Sue)
Water plants	Crochet	Write poetry

You now have the possibility of waking up each morning with some-

_____

_____

_____

_____

_____

_____

_____

_____

thing to look forward to immediately, again later in the day, and of finishing the day with the knowledge you can have some pleasures in life if you'll take them. Make it a reality by giving yourself some joy at least three times a day.

BE PHYSICALLY SELF-SUPPORTIVE

When you're depressed or worried, frightened or overworked, it takes special effort to remember that your body is as much a part of your self as your mind and your feelings. It's affected by the way you think and feel, and its condition will, in turn, dramatically affect your thoughts and emotions.

Eat Well

Don't let yourself forget meals, and don't eat junk food. If you must have a sweet, take the time to go to a special store or restaurant where you can get something really worth spending extra money on and worth gaining the extra pound. Or fix something delectable at home. Allow yourself to plan and thoroughly enjoy it without guilt. Otherwise, eat what's good for you: fruit, fresh vegetables, protein. Prepare them so they taste wonderful. Set the table and sit down to eat in a leisurely way. Don't grab food on the run.

It's easy when you're feeling down to form the habit of eating food that's neither delicious nor good for you, nor even the right price. Make up your mind that anything you eat should have at least two of those characteristics.

Sleep Well

If at all possible, get somewhere near eight hours of sleep each night. If you have trouble getting sleep, pay attention to what you can do that's relaxing. Anything that calms rather than stirs your emotions and that doesn't fill your head with disturbing ideas is good to do during the hour before bedtime. A warm bath and milk will help, but if you can't shut your mind off from worry, anger, or confusion right away, accept the fact that it may take a while to learn how. Meanwhile, rather than tossing and turning and gnashing your teeth, try to turn that time into an enjoyable period. Turn on the radio and just let yourself listen without purpose. Read something light and entertaining. Without becoming restless and irritable, use the time to stretch and rest without trying to sleep. Learning relaxation techniques or meditation will help.

Recognize that although a regular good night's sleep will help you to feel your best, you won't collapse from lack of sleep. Don't dramatize the situation. Avoid talking to yourself (or others) with phrases such as, "I hardly slept last night," or "I was awake all night." You and your friends will both become bored by it and continually thinking about it will make you more aware of the negative aspect of your life.

If you become desperate and threaten yourself with messages such as "I've got to sleep tonight or I'll fall apart," you'll find it even harder to relax and sleep. If you begin to feel pretty ragged because you're really sleeping just a few hours a night for a long period, get medical advice. If your doctor prescribes tranquilizers or sleeping pills, you may want to use them during the crisis period, but stop taking them after a few weeks. You may be surprised to find you don't need them after all. You can't necessarily count on the doctor to tell you whether the pills are addictive or have side effects that are dangerous if taken for a long time. This is a time when you may be tempted to overuse pills or alcohol, so pay close attention to any new habits you're forming now.

Even if you feel as if you "just got to sleep" at 8:00 A.M., don't sleep past ten in the morning and don't take sick leave unless you're really sick or are planning a pleasure-filled day. Get up and get some tasks accomplished and then, if you must, take a short nap later in the afternoon. Plan it for a time when you're certain to be awakened within thirty minutes. If you sleep until noon, or nap for several hours, you'll easily fall into a demoralizing cycle of feeling half awake at night and half asleep all day and "never getting anything done." Forcing yourself to be up during the day will help you get back on a schedule that helps you feel good.

Exercise

Many forms of exercise help you feel optimistic and invigorated. Running and swimming have the advantage of being available whether you do them by yourself or with others. If you like to compete, you can join a team or enter a marathon, but if you'd rather keep it noncompetitive, that's easy too.

Running is available to almost anyone, almost anywhere. The exercise is good for you, but that doesn't mean that the more you suffer, the better off you'll be. If you're out of shape, begin by walking a mile or two, then running a short distance. Concentrate on the pleasure of being in motion and continue running only as long as it feels good, even if it's only a few yards. If you stop while you're still enjoying it, you'll probably do it again.

Follow the same principle whether you swim, do calisthenics, or join a soccer team. It's no longer strange for a woman to jog alone or to play team sports. Take advantage of the times and do something for yourself.

Look Well

The way you look affects the way you feel. Start the day by getting fully dressed, arranging your hair, and putting on whatever makeup you're accustomed to wearing, whether or not you're going to leave the house or see anyone. This is one way to banish the demoralizing habit of glowering at the mirror and saying, "Ugh! See? On top of everything else, I'm ugly too."

Looking well doesn't have to take a lot of time, so don't use that as an excuse. Clean, combed hair, clean jeans, and no-iron shirts are minimal. Add a bit of bright color somewhere and splash cold water on your face. You'll feel better. People will react positively to you too. But do it first of all for yourself.

If you find it difficult to ask for what you want, if you believe you must always be nurturing, sensitive, and giving, and are quick to label yourself "selfish," it will take courage to follow the advice in this chapter. Giving yourself rewards for tasks and pleasures for no reason at all and treating yourself well physically may make you nervous at first. So those turn out to be courageous acts, too.

In addition to treating yourself well, find people who will distract you from your troubles, entertain you, and who have the potential to become good friends. The next chapter is about how to start that process.

CHAPTER 12

AN END TO ISOLATION

If you've been involved with an abusive man for a long time, it's likely you have few, if any, friends. A man who abuses a woman often senses, correctly, that the fewer relationships she has, the more easily he can control her. Through a period of months or years he'll demand that she be more and more available to him and less available to friends and relatives.

When you've been beaten and humiliated by the one special person who says he loves you, before long you'll probably feel pretty worthless and unlovable. Even if you know you've let your friendships go because of his demands, you may reinterpret events so it now seems it's your own fault you lack friends.

Some women are certain that friends can never provide the security and degree of caring nor the stimulation that a lover relationship brings with it. It's true that there's a great difference between the kinds of relationships, but some of the differences exist only because we place arbitrary limitations on our friendships, because we believe we can find intimacy only in sexual relationships. We can change those attitudes if we choose.

To begin that process of change, you can become more discriminating about a potential new lover and less critical of potential friends.

HOW CRITICAL OF OTHERS ARE YOU?

People who are overly self-critical often have similar attitudes toward other people. This is especially likely if they have few friends. The self-loathing is turned defensively onto others, sometimes toward those acquaintances and colleagues who are potential friends. It's as if the lonely, friendless person says, "I'm so uninteresting that no one would want me for a friend, but that's too painful to accept completely, so I'll keep reminding myself that there's something wrong with everybody I know. I'll reject them before they have a chance to reject me." And so begins a habit of criticizing and blaming other people.

To find out if this is something you habitually do, *make a list* of at least ten people you know or see frequently, no matter how casual or fleeting the contact is. Ask yourself these questions about each one:

- Is this a good friend?
- Is she sometimes a friend but sometimes not?
- Is this someone I've wished were my friend?
- Is it a relative who might become a friend?
- Is this an acquaintance—someone I work with, see in the neighborhood, at church, school, or where I do business—but who I've never considered as a potential friend?
- Is this an acquaintance or relative who I'm sure could never become a friend?

Activity 20 ॐ Why Aren't Acquaintances Friends?

1. Mary   sister-in-law; lives in San Diego

2. Betty   neighbor; gossips too much

3. _____

4. _____

5. _____

6. _____

7. _____

8. _____

9. _____

10. _____

If there are quite a few acquaintances who are potential friends you'll have a good pool to draw from. If you dismissed many as impossible to develop friendships with, you have a problem.

Think about those people who you indicated are not potential friends and *complete this sentence* for each one: "She or he hasn't become my friend because. . . ."

Your sentence completions might include anything from descriptions of the person's faults ("mean," "flighty," "stupid"), to reflections of your own sense of inadequacy ("not interested in me," "she's too popular"), to an assumption that certain differences make friendship impossible (age, income, educational level, marriage, parenthood).

Perhaps you haven't pursued relationships among many of these people because of what you perceive as their faults and inadequacies. You're either so critical of others that no one seems quite good enough to be your friend and you haven't made enough effort to find people who share your interests and values, or you're so anxious to spare yourself rejection that you've persuaded yourself they're impossible.

If you've made critical judgements of quite a few people, notice whether they're generalized criticisms such as "she's crazy" or "she's stupid." If so, you're discarding the possibility of any kind of relationship, even a limited one. You can use the same techniques you learned for reducing self-criticism in Chapter 10 to develop a more balanced attitude toward other people.

Give careful attention to what you say about other people. Change generalized criticisms to specific descriptions of behavior. "She's a fool" will become "She giggles when she's nervous" or "She's too loud." After a little practice, you'll be able to substitute the description before the generalized putdown even comes to mind.

While you're practicing, you can also begin to look for positive aspects of the people you know. Begin with potential friends who've sometimes seemed friendly to you. *List* all the positive qualities of five of these people. If you have trouble thinking of anything desirable about them, try looking at the way they relate to people other than yourself. How do they treat their children, neighbors, parents, husbands, bosses? *List* anything they've done that you approved or liked. *List* the skills and abilities they have, whether they're pertinent to your relationship with them or not.

Activity 21 ◌ What Can You Appreciate about the People You Know?

1. _____

_____

2. _____

_____

3. _____

_____

4. _____

_____

5. _____

_____

This doesn't mean you have to like everybody. If someone is a fine parent or hard worker, she still may not be someone you want to be with much. The point of looking for positive traits is to counteract the tendency to see everything and everyone in negative terms. When you break that habit you'll be able to make better judgments about potential friends.

START WITH THE PEOPLE YOU KNOW

Consider again whether each person on your list of acquaintances has enough positive qualities for you to spend even a little time with them. A woman who's tiring for an entire evening may provide an entertaining half hour over tea every week or so.

If an acquaintance is interesting but is a nonstop talker, enjoy brief conversations before or after a movie with her. Maybe there's a pleasant person who's so shy she makes you nervous. Go to a sports event or the zoo, so the structure of your activity will reduce some of the nervousness and give you both something to talk about. If there's a tennis partner in the neighborhood whom you don't like well enough for a long conversation, play with her and limit your after-game visits to a half hour.

Many people are pleasant to be with on the job or in the neighborhood. If you never thought of associating with those people outside of the situation where you regularly see them, think about it now.

Perhaps there's someone you once liked but later became bored with. Why not revive the relationship now, but plan to keep it on a once-a-month basis? What about someone you poured out your troubles to and then avoided because you regretted imposing on her? When you're feeling very positive, call and make a point of listening to her and saying some cheerful things about your life.

Look for people who can momentarily give you some pleasure, help you feel less lonely, and expand your interests, rather than waiting until you meet someone who looks as if she'll be the perfect intimate, long-term friend. Casual relationships may begin in surprising places and may take years to develop, flourish, and become solid friendships.

If you don't want to risk placing all your emotional needs in the hands of one person on whom you'll become increasingly dependent, you have to take the risks that go with creating friendships. When several acquaintances have become good friends, you'll enter relationships with a man from a position of strength rather than vulnerability, knowing that romance is something you want rather than something you'll die without. You'll then be able to make clearer judgments about the men you become involved with and the decisions you make in regard to them.

MEETING NEW PEOPLE

Learn to look at all the people you meet as potential friends. Rather than assuming none of those relationships will grow into friendships, consider that they might. Take a fresh look at the drugstore clerk you've passed the time of day with for years. You know her pretty well and enjoy your periodic short conversations. Is it possible you'd enjoy more of her company? Ask her to have coffee with you during her break.

How about the secretary in the next office, the one you had a delightful conversation with when you accidentally shared a lunch table in the cafeteria? Why not invite her to join you for lunch? See how many old acquaintanceships you can revive or develop into friendships. Virtually none of us are so isolated that we know no one. Even if you moved to town yesterday and you have two small children who make it difficult to get around, you have to go to the grocery store or laundromat at least. Eventually, one of the children will get you to a doctor's waiting room and the drugstore. You may have to wait in a welfare or food-stamp or public-housing office. With a little energy, you can turn these situations into opportunities to socialize and to learn more about the city or neighborhood.

Perhaps it sounds unrealistic to think you'd connect with someone you'd like while standing in a Safeway line or riding the city bus. Have you ever known anyone who met an exciting man in that sort of situation? Why not an interesting woman, then? It's especially likely to happen if you have small children, since strangers often talk to and about them and if you meet another woman with a baby or child the age of yours, you already have something to talk about.

In addition to considering all the people you meet as potential friends, go to the places where the kinds of people you'd like to know are likely to be. Picture the people you like to be with, or if you've never been around many people that you liked, what they *might* be like. How would such people spend their time, and where would they be?

CHOOSING JOBS, CLASSES, ORGANIZATIONS

Although you can make friends almost anywhere you go, some places are easier than others. Classes and volunteer organizations are two of the best. Social clubs you find through your church or in your neighborhood are also good possibilities. Paid employment is another.

Paid Employment

Not many people evaluate job opportunities in terms of social contacts. The rate of pay, chance for advancement, opportunity to learn, and the satisfaction or stimulation of the work are most important.

But there are other considerations as well. You may be looking for a challenging, absorbing, and well-paid career, or a stopgap job to pay this month's rent. Of course, whether the salary will pay your expenses is the first requirement, but in pursuing any of those goals, you can also consider the social possibilities of employment.

Whether you work as a fast-food cook, administrative assistant, store manager, nurse, or receptionist, think about the neighborhood you'll work in. It might determine the type of clientele you'll serve, the size of the company, the lifestyles of your coworkers, and even, perhaps, the type of management. In a downtown financial district, dress will be high style, speed and efficiency greatly valued. A university district, tourist area, or neighborhood shopping mall may offer informality and flexibility in a slower-paced atmosphere. When you apply for work, notice the social atmosphere as much as possible. If it isn't visible, ask for a tour of the workplace. If your job would be joining workers at rows and rows of desks with telephones constantly ringing, it may be an unpleasantly noisy atmosphere, yet there ought to be someone among so many workers who you'll find compatible. On the other hand, if you would be the only nonprofessional person in a five-person office, or if you're forty years old and everyone looks twenty-one, you're likely to feel socially isolated.

If you're able to find a job that's interesting, challenging, pays well, or allows you the opportunity for advancement, you may very well decide to take it even if there are few opportunities for developing friendships. In that case, keep in mind that you'll need to make more than the usual effort to make friends outside of work, since you won't have that potential during the bulk of every day. For example, you can reduce the loneliness by finding friends who work or live nearby to have coffee or lunch with every day. That's especially important if you work alone, if you have a nontraditional job that until recently has been available to men only, or if the male workers are hostile to you because of your sex.

Classes

Long-range goals are most important in determining what classes will be most useful in developing skills and planning or changing a career. But consider other opportunities besides the value of learning the skill. One major consideration should be whether you're likely to make friends in the class.

Although it's certainly possible to develop male friends in a class, friendships with other women are easier to make and maintain because they're less subject to the unpredictable whims of romance and sexuality. Look for women's classes first. Neither you nor the others in the class will be distracted by the pressure of trying to impress male classmates, and you can assume some of the women are there partly to make friends. In a mixed class, you can be sure some of the women are there partly to meet men. That doesn't preclude their responding to a friendly gesture from you, but if you're feeling shy and insecure, you'll want to be among people more interested in you than a man.

It's stimulating to break out of old habits and meet new kinds of people, but it's also frightening. You may want, at first, to try to find a class where the members share some of your values and lifestyle. You can't be sure you have a true image of the women who attend particular classes at a church, YWCA, or community college until you've attended for awhile. But you can get an idea of how you'll fit into the group by asking direct questions of the agency or the teacher. You might want to explain your particular concerns, whether they're about being shy, being with people of a different age or economic class, or who are too feminist or not feminist enough.

Ask the instructor whether the class is formal or informal, large or small, includes activities and discussions or mostly lectures. You'll have more opportunity to get to know people if the group is small, informal, and active than if it's large, formal, and academic. You may, for instance, decide to begin with a rap group at the YWCA or the local chapter of the National Organization for Women or a small church-related group. Later, you can enroll in assertion-training or social-skills classes, where you can develop friendship skills while you practice them.

You should get the information you want, as well as a feeling about the teacher's willingness to explain her technique and outlook and about her warmth and attitudes toward the women she teaches. If you don't have a good feeling while talking to her, try to figure out why so you can get more information on the spot. If it isn't clear what bothers you and you have alternatives, follow your hunches. But if you live in a small community where the choices are few, take a chance. It's better to go *somewhere* than nowhere, better to know *someone* than no one. Above all, don't sit twiddling your thumbs waiting for the perfect situation to come your way.

If you decide that your most immediate need is for the kind of formal education that can be found only at a community college or university, you can still plan your first-quarter program along these same lines. Check out the Women's Center, now a fixture at many colleges. There you'll be able to meet other women in an informal atmosphere and get information about which teachers are good and which classes are likely to be useful for you. The centers usually provide a lounge for informal interchanges as well as structured activities.

If you plan to take classes for a couple of years, you'll have plenty of time later for the difficult ones, the large lecture courses, and those that seem intimidating. What you need to begin with are courses that are fairly easy and have plenty of opportunity for interaction. Once you've started a support system and have proved to yourself you can manage in an academic setting, you'll have a base from which to take more challenging classes.

Volunteer Work

If you're able to work without pay, a great number of challenging and educational jobs are available. To find out what's right for you, use roughly the same criteria that you used in finding the best classes. Of course, it's important that you do something worthwhile and meaningful to you, and you should also weigh the experience in terms of your career goals.

But these shouldn't be your only considerations. Think, too, about what organizations and what kind of work will bring you into contact with potential friends. For instance, working as a volunteer coordinator or assistant program developer at a women's center or YWCA will provide dozens of contacts with many women in a context where you can get to know them fairly well rather quickly.

If you're a low-key person who likes to take things slowly and form relationships in a structured environment, you might join a library group or club and learn to maintain and care for books with other people who have similar interests. If you like dramatic personalities, try helping out with the scenery or fundraising events at a local theater. If you crave intellectual conversation with friends, see if there is some unpaid work you can do for a department of a graduate school or a museum. In any case, choose a place and a particular kind of volunteer work in which you are likely to meet compatible people. Watch the newspaper for notices of where volunteers are needed, or call the local United Way for lists of such organizations.

To recapitulate: Consider everyone you're in contact with as a potential friend. Analyze what you like and don't like about each. If you're overly critical, use Activities 15 and 16 in Chapter 10 to make your criticisms more rational and precise. Spend limited time with people who make you feel bad. But if they're somewhat interesting or pleasant, find out what you can do together that will maximize their assets. Choose classes or volunteer and paid work partly on the basis of whether you can find potential friends there.

CHAPTER 13

REACHING OUT

So there you are, on the job, at the laundromat, or in a ceramics class. How do you make a new friend?

First, you must think well enough of yourself to realize that people will want you as a friend. If you're still full of self-blame and convinced you're too dull to interest anyone, it will be hard to reach out to other people or even to recognize and accept their friendly gestures. To paraphrase Woody Allen, "Why would I want a friend who would talk to a person like me?"

RISKING THE FIRST STEPS

There are risks involved in initiating friendly gestures, and there's no point in pretending they don't or shouldn't exist. The biggest risk is the ego blow if you're rejected. Many of us act as if the sky will fall down if anyone turns us down for anything, and the devastation will be especially great if it's clear someone doesn't want to be our friend. It may not even matter that it's someone we aren't much interested in, or even a person we actively dislike. If we learn she doesn't like us, we're wounded.

Women are particularly vulnerable in this respect because they usually have fewer experiences in sticking their necks out than men have. Because males have learned it's important to win and be successful, they start early—usually in sports—learning to risk failure and rejection and to handle it smoothly when it happens.

As a woman, you probably have little experience in risking the implied rejection of your offer of friendship being turned down. I say "implied" because even though it may be only your specific invitation that's rejected, you're likely to experience it as rejection of *you*. To determine which is true, you'll probably have to take further risks.

When you think about extending yourself to someone, remind yourself of these facts: It's okay to fear rejection; there are specific things you can do to reduce the fear; even if your worst fantasy comes true, you'll learn from the experience; your wounds will heal. But keep in mind the satisfactions that will come your way if your friendly gesture is welcomed.

Something else that may inhibit you from reaching out, especially if you're very critical, is the fear of unwelcome success. Suppose your invitation is accepted and the other person turns out to be a bore or worse? Then you're in the position of having first extended yourself and then of wanting to reject the other person.

This is really borrowing trouble. The person you invite for coffee, lunch, or a movie may not turn out to be completely entertaining nor compatible enough to be your closest friend, but that's not what the invitation is about. When you ask someone to have coffee with you, it means just that, not that you'll have coffee every day or that you're obligated in any way after that.

You may fear the other person will accept your invitation but find you boring or awkward or stupid. If, under pressure, your anxiety level tends to get so high that you become tongue-tied and really do appear stupid or awkward, now is the time to stop complaining about it and get help with that problem. Find an individual therapist or class where you can learn relaxation techniques or social skills. A class is best because it will probably be less expensive, and you'll also have a built-in opportunity to make friends who not only have a similar problem, but who understand some important things about you right away.

If you've lived in the same town all your life, if you have a close supportive family, if you have stimulating work and the time and money to indulge in hobbies, sports, and entertainments, you might be able to enjoy the luxury of letting friendships develop slowly during a long period. In these circumstances there is almost no risk involved; by the time two potential friends go to lunch or the theater together they've been around each other enough to be sure of each person's responses. Often no one even has to invite the other, mutual plans just happen. But that slow, safe process of making friends isn't always available. Reaching out to new people may seem difficult or frightening, but it can be done and it's well worth the risk.

GETTING TO KNOW PEOPLE ON THE JOB

Coffee and lunch invitations are obvious places to begin making friends on the job, but they presume you've had some conversation and friendly exchanges already.

If you're new on the job and have had few exchanges of even the most casual sort, it may be tempting to decide it's everyone's fault but yours. "No one ever smiles or talks to me." "They've already formed into cliques and they consider me an outsider." Some of that may of course be true.

But if you're the new person, you'll need to smile, say "hello," and generally initiate contact to let the others know you're interested in them.

If you've been waiting for others to speak first, they may have interpreted your shyness as unfriendliness, and you'll need to take some risks in the process of changing their impressions. For instance, if your coworker, Mary, is not used to being greeted by you in the morning, she may be too surprised to respond the first time you smile and say "Good morning." That may tempt you to adopt an I-told-you-so attitude, which you can use as an excuse to give up. But if you persist, you may get a response the second time and friendly conversation the third or fourth.

Shy people usually imagine that they're the only people who fear rejection, so when other people don't respond to their first offer of friendship they assume it's coldness or hostility, whereas it may be protection against rejection. This will be especially likely if you've established yourself as a "loner" or a strictly-business person. Give the other workers at least three chances to respond to clear offers of sociability before you give up. With some people it will take even more.

If your friendship is rejected by one person, resist the temptation to generalize. When you hear yourself saying, "Oh, they're a bunch of snobs," "No one in the office has time for me," or "They all have lots of friends already," *list* what evidence you have that your general comment applies to each one. You may be surprised that your judgment applies only to a few people, or maybe even to one. Our minds are endlessly imaginative when we want to avoid risks. *Make a list,* too, of each friendly gesture you've made to each person. Return to these two checklists whenever you make negative generalizations about coworkers or other groups of people.

Activity 22 ᧖ Social Checklist

Why I think they don't like me	Friendly gestures I've made
1.	
2.	
3.	
4.	
5.	
6.	
7.	

Now that you have a record of your own efforts to initiate social gestures and you've modified your judgments about their attitudes toward you, you can begin a program of taking social risks.

Choose specific actions in particular situations that will be somewhat risky but that you're sure you can do. For instance, you might decide to say "Good morning" to two coworkers, or ask one question of your supervisor, or give one compliment to the person at the next desk. These are better self-assignments than "talk to group for thirty minutes at lunch" because you're more likely to do the lower-risk actions. You can build on your success until you're ready for that thirty-minute group conversation. And remember that "success" is accomplishing what you promise yourself to do each day. It has nothing to do with the response of other people, which you have no control over.

Eventually you'll get some built-in rewards from the people you befriend as they respond to you in friendly ways. But for now, appreciate the fact that you're being brave enough to make those first gestures. You can also give yourself rewards for your efforts, as suggested in other parts of this book.

GETTING TO KNOW PEOPLE
IN CLASSES AND ORGANIZATIONS

These same principles apply to making friends through classes, church volunteer work, or other occasional meetings. It may be difficult to cultivate friends in these situations because you don't have a new opportunity each day. You may have to make a specific request ("Can you have lunch with me Tuesday?") rather than seeming accidentally to sit with a fellow worker at lunch. This means you don't have the luxury of waiting for exactly the right moment or the ideal mood to approach them. If you postpone action six times, weekly class sessions might be over before you even get started. In a volunteer organization you may not work with the same person each time you volunteer. You may encounter an attractive person at a mailing party and then not run into her again for a month or more. So get in the habit of making some kind of friendly gesture at the very first opportunity.

How to Begin

When you're anxious about joining any new group, arrange to arrive ten or fifteen minutes early. The few minutes before a class or meeting provide a perfect opportunity for informal friendly exchanges. As new people arrive, you can introduce yourself and others so that everyone feels included. Early arrival will let you be among the first to meet people and to get to know them a little better than is possible in large group exchanges. You'll feel more secure by the time the group begins. This will help you take the risk of being outgoing right from the start.

If there's an opportunity for each person to introduce herself to the group, use it to say you're open to new relationships. "I'm Jane; I'm new in town and would like to know more people." "My name is Sarah; I'm looking forward to getting to know other people who are interested in ecology." If there's no such opportunity, you might assert yourself by asking the instructor or leader to start off with introductions. Many instructors will be pleased with the suggestion and grateful to you for opening up a more friendly atmosphere.

Look around the room, listen, and decide who you're interested in getting to know. At the first opportunity, whether it's when you're asked to pair up for an exercise or at the coffee break, cross the room and say something friendly to her. I specifically state "cross the room" because that's hard for a shy person to do. To avoid being conspicuous, you may let yourself interact with the uninteresting person next to you rather than walk over to someone you'd like to know. It may be only twelve feet, but it can feel like a stage ramp with 20,000 pairs of eyes glued accusingly on you. When you've exchanged a remark, relax and look at your "audience." You may be astonished that no one is glaring or pointing at you after all.

The content of your first remark is not too important. You might ask, "Have you taken classes here before?" or "How long have you been volunteering here?" Or be braver and say, "I wanted to talk to you because you said you had lived in San Francisco and I hope to go there for a vacation" or "I liked what you said about being nervous in groups; I am, too." A friendly tone will give the message, "I'm inclined to like you and that's all I'm trying to convey at the moment."

Following Up

If all goes well, you'll get into a pleasant conversation. You may have an opportunity to continue it at length (at a coffee break, for instance), but possibly you won't. In that case, be sure to say something when you leave, even if it means crossing the room again. "I enjoyed talking to you. I hope to see you next week." If you want to be very brave, you can offer her a ride next week, ask her for a ride, or suggest you come on the bus together (assuming you live somewhere near her). Or say "I'd like to talk to you some more about . . . Would it be all right to call you?"

This is moving fast, perhaps faster than you want to. But you're not sticking your neck out very far. Your invitation doesn't require a high degree of intimacy, nor much time, and it's closely tied to the activity you're both involved in. It's true that you won't have much time to feel out the situation, so you'll have some uncertainty about how interested the other woman is in getting to know you. If she says, "Thanks, but I'll be coming from another direction," you'll probably wonder whether she's telling the truth or doesn't want to become involved with you.

If you're easily hurt or given to feeling rejected, you might have trouble with this situation. You'll have to make a special effort to be open to the woman the next time you see her so she knows you're still interested. It may be that she took you literally, thinking you wanted transportation rather than recognizing your gesture as one of offered friendship. At the next opportunity, you can make another overture that's more obviously friendly. If you get a second cool response (or if you're convinced the first was a negative message) you can look for someone else to befriend.

It might be that a person you approach is not interested in exploring friendship with you. Don't take that as a commentary on your personal worth. It may say more about her: She's extremely shy and can't quite believe you really want to know her; she's too involved in her career to have time for friends; she's wrapped up in her family or already has enough friends. Perhaps she's suspicious or critical of people and rarely sees good in anyone. If you want to play it safe, approach women who are new in town, newly separated from mates, or who have indicated they're looking for new relationships.

Plan to use each opportunity that comes your way to do a "Courageous Act a Day," such as smiling and saying "Hi!", or asking about yesterday's lecture, or inviting someone for coffee. If you make a friendly overture five times a day for five days to the same or different people you'll soon begin to get rewards.

MOVING FROM ACQUAINTANCES TO FRIENDS

Each time you increase the depth of a relationship, you'll be in a new risk situation, but you'll also have some successes to build on so remind yourself of them often. By "depth" I mean a combination of these factors: length of each contact, frequency of contact, amount of unstructured time spent together, and degree of trust for sharing intimate conversation.

If you're very lonely and have some initial success, it may be tempting to move quickly from a brief, casual acquaintanceship to daily or hourly intimate exchanges, especially if the other person is in a situation similar to yours. If you allow yourself to do that, it might be awkward to withdraw later, especially if you work closely together. It's better to build the relationship gradually. Don't leap from a casual conversation in the company cafeteria with an acquaintance to inviting her for dinner and a long evening of intimate talk. First try shorter, more structured, and less personal contacts. Ask yourself whether you enjoy them and whether you feel you have more to say.

It takes time and some work to develop an intimate but nonsexual relationship—more work, perhaps, than one that quickly develops into sexual intimacy. Close friendships may also feel too risky in the short run, though ultimately a sexual relationship is much more likely to involve higher risk.

Working to develop a close nonsexual relationship requires continual alertness to the other person's boundaries, taking risks to judge the relationship at each new step in the direction of openness, and calming one's fears after each new opening of a previously private personal space. ("Did I reveal so much that she'll think I'm a terrible or ridiculous person or feel burdened by my problems?" "Did she reveal so much that she'll retreat to cover her embarrassment or fear of vulnerability?")

These risks present problems in a sexual relationship also, but they're made easier by the more readily available reassurance of a touch, a kiss, or a few words. Most of us need to work at developing comparable verbal skills to express caring and reassurance to friends. For instance, we can reassure ourselves when we're nervous about the growing openness in a friendship by saying, "I'm really glad we decided to get to know each other better," or "I feel good about finally talking to someone who feels the same as I do." We can learn to be more direct in checking out concerns: "We really talked about some intimate stuff today. Do you feel okay about it?" "I've got a personal problem I'd like some feedback on, but if this isn't a good time, let me know and we can talk about it another time."

It may seem alarming to say such things out loud. Perhaps your fear stems from the idea that speaking directly about feelings will be looked upon as an unwanted escalation of intimacy. Occasionally that happens, but most of the time the other person will be pleased and flattered. If she does feel it's too much, it can hurt, but in the long run it's valuable information. If you want to form a close friendship, the person who readily feels intruded upon is probably not a candidate and it's helpful to know that early. (She can still be a welcomed casual friend.)

Even though it's new to you, you can learn to be open and direct about feelings and what you want and enjoy in a friendship, and you can incorporate this into your self-concept, just as you do any other skill you learn. The emotional risks of intimate friendships may seem difficult or frightening, but they are usually much less damaging than disappointments in sexual relationships. And very often the rewards of friendship are more lasting and rewarding.

HOW MUCH DO YOU CONFIDE IN A NEW FRIEND?

For many years, women usually remained silent about the abuse they suffered. But with battering out of the closet, attitudes have changed in some circles. But it's difficult to predict how people will react to hearing about your experience, whether they're new acquaintances or close friends or family.

When speaking to acquaintances, proceed with caution, protecting yourself from criticism. Many people still don't understand the reasons that women remain with abusive men, and you may be subjected to hints that you "must have asked for it," or that you were a fool not to have left much sooner.

You can protect yourself from these comments by starting a conversation about abuse in general to find out how the other person feels before you put yourself in a vulnerable position. If you don't think she'll understand your feelings or be sympathetic, wait until you know her better before exchanging intimacies.

This may be difficult if one reason you want the friendship is to tell your troubles to a caring person. But if you give it a little time you'll gain more. It may turn out several people you enjoy spending time with give no indication they'll understand. That's not necessarily a reason to drop the relationships, since they can still give you pleasure and help you keep loneliness at bay. Later, when they've gotten to know you and realize you're neither a fool nor a person who "deserves to be abused," they'll probably be able to listen with more understanding.

If you do find someone who's willing to hear about your past suffering and current problems, it will be tempting to spill your troubles out once the emotional dam breaks. It may be such a relief to finally tell it all to someone who believes you and cares about you that you'll want to tell every horrifying detail. First check out whether your friend is up to hearing it all and be sensitive to signs of boredom or impatience.

Having laid it all out once, don't go over it again and again. Even if you have the good fortune to meet someone who has had similar troubles so that you can trade stories, you may easily perpetuate each other's "poor me" attitudes by continually repeating the painful experiences of the past. Those "horror stories" will be a welcome relief at first, but if they continue, ask yourself, "Do I feel better or worse after telling them?" When you become aware of feeling worse, you'll need to explain the situation to your friend: "You know, I really get myself on a downer when I talk about being battered. I'm going to try not to talk about it anymore, and if I start, please stop me." That kind of declaration will usually be met with agreement and a similar request from the other person.

GETTING HELP FROM THE FAMILY

At a time when you most need their help, family members may not be supportive. If you've kept secret your man's abusive behavior, the family may have a great deal of trouble believing that he threw you against the wall or went after you with a knife. Their disbelief may indicate their confusion rather than their opinion of you. It may reflect their confidence that a woman as strong and wonderful as you would never put up with such abuse. They'll need to be educated about the problem of abuse, and they'll need time to absorb and understand what is happening.

You'll have to strike a fine balance between understanding *their* problem and protecting yourself from unsupportive attitudes and blame. Explain what happened if you want to, but give them some time to understand your revised marital history. ("Remember that time I said I was too sick to go to Thanksgiving dinner? I really had two black eyes." "That night we were at Mom's and everyone was congratulating each other on having such good marriages—How could I break in and say that Joe had raped me the night before?") If they react by saying, "Somebody's crazy, and I'm not sure if it's him, you, or me," don't be surprised. If they want to hear his side, try to be patient, but make your situation clear.

If you're still trying to protect the man's reputation by telling only about one or two of his lesser abuses, expect people to be skeptical of the necessity of your leaving. This doesn't mean you have an obligation to tell all or even to tell anything, but that information and the time to absorb it will make it easier for many people to support you. The best choice may be not to talk about it at all, depending upon your family relationships. In that case, you have a right to ask that family members trust you've made the best decision you could after long, careful, and responsible thought. They don't have to agree with your decision, only to accept that you're doing your best.

Perhaps you've confided in the family all along and they've not only urged you to get out of the relationship but have insisted that as long as you stay, you deserve to be beaten. Now that you're leaving, they may be impatient if you express concern for the man's welfare or complain of loneliness. They might even seem contemptuous of you and your feelings. Even though you're feeling punished by them, try to place yourself in their shoes. They care about you, have worried about you, tried to help you, and felt helpless when you decided to stay with or go back to the dangerous man. When you say something positive about him, or speak of your loneliness, they may be prone to instant panic, fearing it means you're going back.

Trying to understand their pain and frustration and confusion doesn't mean you should listen to their negative reactions. If you find you're subjected to negative reactions after two or more attempts to explain what has happened and what you're trying to do, protect yourself by not discussing the subject.

Sometimes the family's reaction will be subtle. You can't put your finger on any specific thing, but you find that after a visit to your sister or your father you feel vaguely depressed. When this happens, remove yourself from the people who cause you to feel sad, to question your good sense, or otherwise start you on a downward emotional spiral. You don't need evidence or reasons; your feelings are your feelings. Simply tell your family you find you feel better if you spend more time alone. Suggest they do some reading about wife battering and check every now and then to see if they've changed their outlook. Don't write them off forever. You may find you need them when you've all recovered from the crisis.

Dealing with Kindness

Families who do their best to be supportive can also be difficult. They may be so overprotective they reinforce helpless feelings you're trying to overcome. If you ran crying to them for help in the middle of the night and were rescued, you may now feel you have no right to reject further help. If you've taken refuge at your parents' house, they might encourage you to stay indefinitely. If you're afraid of the man, insecure about your ability to make wise choices, or you're without other supports, it will be soothing to indulge your dependency feelings. Soon, though, you may find that while you don't feel ready to move out on your own, your family's protectiveness is stifling you. Your ambivalence may be masked by concern for your parents, who "need" you to be there.

If you find yourself in a situation something like this, accept the fact that sometimes you like being dependent and that you're in the situation because you chose it. Become aware of what events increase your helpless feelings. Does your dad encourage you to talk about your fears and to enjoy his promise of protection? Notice whether that momentary increase in security is followed by a wish to curl up in bed rather than to start organizing your life. When you talk of getting a job, do your parents or other relatives persuade you to "wait another week till you're feeling better"?

If you're faced with these seeming kindnesses that ultimately prolong your status as a dependent person, you'll have to tell your rescuers you appreciate their concern but must stand on your own two feet. You'll have to ask them to encourage your steps toward independence. Let them know that part of you wants to be helpless and that's why it's hard to resist their indulgences. If they won't change, explain that you'll have to leave.

If you have a warm, supportive family who can extend support without overprotecting you, count yourself lucky and by all means accept what they have to offer. When you're in the process of leaving an abusive man it will help to be almost constantly in the company of friends, acquaintances, or family.

The knowledge that there are people who care for you nearby will be important during the months after separating from an abusive partner as you adapt to a new style of life. In the next section I'll discuss some of the problems you'll encounter during the year or years after you separate and various ways of coping with them.

SECTION IV

AFTER YOU LEAVE

CHAPTER 14

THE FIRST WEEK

The first week you're on your own will be stressful and possibly filled with fear and anxiety, but you can use those feelings to get your life reorganized. The scope and details of your immediate problems will vary depending on how badly you were hurt, whether your relationship was short or long, and whether you have children. It will make a big difference whether you're unemployed or have marketable skills. Where you stay right after you leave the man will have an impact on how you feel, how you interpret your situation, and how you start planning your future.

STAYING IN A SHELTER FOR BATTERED WOMEN

A stay in a shelter for battered women may be your best protection from the dangerous man as well as from your own temptation to go back to him. You'll be surrounded by people who immediately understand why you had to leave. You'll get support for not contacting the man, and he may not be allowed to call or visit at all if the location of the shelter is kept secret from the public.

There will be someone in the shelter nearly all the time to help you sort out practical problems related to money, school or work, childcare, and finding reliable professional help. Many shelters also have counselors available to talk to, and public assistance workers often make regular calls so you won't have to spend a day standing in the public assistance line alone. Talking with other women in similar situations will help reduce your loneliness and fears. Women who would ordinarily never meet because of differences, interests, and lifestyles can be marvelously helpful to each other when they have the problem of a battering man in common. If you have children, it can be a great relief to get help in caring for them while you arrange to reorganize your life. Some shelters have full-time childcare, others have occasional volunteers. If it's not available on a regular basis, you can always trade childcare with other women in the shelter.

A shelter may have the disadvantages of lack of privacy, crowded conditions, too many children, and too much stress in small quarters. But you may not have time to ask, or care, about those conditions if you're escaping from an immediately dangerous situation. Even if you think you won't choose to stay in a shelter, it would be a good idea to get information now about the services they offer and how to arrange for housing in case you need it in an emergency.

There are also other kinds of shelters available, usually run by churches, the Salvation Army, or YWCAs. These provide temporary housing to men, women, and children who have no place else to go, and while they offer some of the same advantages of shelters specifically designed for battered women, they lack the special community feeling that often develops among people whose situations are similar. If you have to wait a few days to get into a shelter for battered women, this other kind of shelter is a good option.

Safe Homes

A Safe Home offers many of the advantages of a shelter but provides a calmer environment and the support of one or two people who may or may not have been in a situation similar to yours. This is someone's private house, which she offers to share for a limited period, often two or three days. Usually, you'll find yourself a cared-for guest, and you may be provided advocacy, information, referrals, and sometimes even counseling on an informal basis. Safe Homes are often available in small communities where there are no shelters.

How to Find a Shelter or Safe Home

Find out all you can about shelters in your community long before you will need to make use of one. Gather information now, even if you think it will never be necessary to use it. You have several ways to find a shelter in or near your community. Call the National Domestic Violence Hotline at 800/799-SAFE (800/799-7233) or 800/787-3224 (TTY). The staff there can answer questions about domestic violence but their main service is to tell you how to contact shelters in your community. You can also go to its website at www.ndvh.org, where you can find the telephone number of your state domestic-violence coalition; that office will probably have information about shelters in your area, but it will probably be open only during business hours. A lot of effort goes into making shelter information easily available while also maintaining confidential locations in most cases. Even so, when you call the hot line, you may have to wait on hold a few minutes before you reach a hot-line advocate, so that is another reason not to wait until you are in an crisis. If you are in a crisis, call 911, not the hot line.

When you reach someone at a shelter, you can ask her for information about whatever aspect of battering you need to know about. The shelter may have a legal advocate, for instance, or a child-care specialist. If you want to leave the area or think that is the only way you can be safe, she can probably help you arrange to go to a shelter in another city. If there is no shelter right in your city or town, the hot line can find one that is nearby. The shelter may be a large house with several bedrooms for one or more women and their children in each. It could be a downtown YWCA or a Safe Home system, where you can spend a few days or longer in a safe private home. Some shelters are able to give out vouchers for a few nights in a motel. A few others have transitional houses where a few women, most of whom have children, can stay for a year or longer.

The hot-line advocate can tell you about the services the shelter provides, what the place is like, whether there are activities for children, and what the shelter expects of residents. She can also tell you about other choices in your area. She can help you sort out what you want to do and explain how to arrange for a safe place to stay if you decide to leave your partner either permanently or for a short while. Once you have all that information, you can act right away if an emergency arises.

STAYING WITH FRIENDS OR RELATIVES

Most of us are wary of being with strangers, so given a choice, we would avoid a shelter in favor of friends or relatives, even if we don't have very good relationships with them. It's an advantage to be with someone you feel close to; however, that very closeness can seem to give the person permission to tell you how to run your life: "You should have left him long ago." "If you were more assertive (or less assertive) these things wouldn't happen." "If you go to work, you'll be in good shape." "Above all, you shouldn't try to go to work now." The bond between you and your friend or relative may mean there is no time limit on how long you can stay, but it may also set up feelings of dependence or guilt in you, and resentment in them, especially if you're staying with a parent or someone who has helped you in the past.

Once you've made your choice, accept all the help you can get as graciously as you can, without apologies. Let your mother babysit while you go to the doctor, lawyer, or counselor. Borrow your friend's car to look for permanent housing or even to get away to a distracting movie. Just be sure you're both clear about the conditions for giving, lending, or providing services, and when in doubt, ask. Don't keep talking about how grateful you are, but let your host know you appreciate the help and you plan to return it when you're settled. You might mention some specific payback such as offering childcare.

Your host probably won't mind some complaining and crying the first day or two, but soon it will become tedious. Avoid playing a "poor me" record, repeating your troubles, your fears, and the awful things the man did to you. Friends and relatives are often glad to listen if they think they're helping you improve your life, but if nothing changes they soon feel helpless and frustrated, and that's often followed by resentment. The resentment may yield to guilt and then more resentment over the guilt.

You can make it easier for them if you say what you want and encourage them to do the same. If you want advice, ask for it; if you want to be left alone, or just listened to, say so. Ask whether your host is willing to do what you want, and set a time limit, even if it's completely arbitrary: "I need to be alone tonight, is that okay?" "I might be ready to hear some advice in a couple of days, but until then could you just listen and support the way I feel? Or tell me you've had it if it gets to be a bore?" This will be particularly hard to do with parents or friends who may be eager to point out that you'd be all right now if you'd listened when they "told you so," but at least give it a try.

For your own sake, do as much as possible to help around the house, no matter how hard it is to get moving. This may be doubly difficult if your host insists you "just take it easy because you have enough to do to reorganize your life." "Reorganizing your life" may then take the form of lying on the couch brooding. You'll be much better off baking a cake, sweeping the floor, or painting the front porch. You can explain that to your host.

STAYING ALONE

You may decide to live alone, either in the home you shared with the man or in a new place. Even if you had to leave your home temporarily, for safety, don't assume you'll have to give it up permanently. If your children are in contact with your ex-partner, you may not be able to keep a new address secret and you might feel strongly that you refuse to be forced out of your home. If so, stay in the home and assess the risks carefully.

Even if you're pretty sure the man won't pursue you, it's a good idea to change locks, secure windows, and perhaps to change your telephone number. If there's a chance the man will try to break in, add double-bolt locks on all outside doors, including the basement and garage. You'll be safer if a friend or relative can stay with you until your situation is stabilized. Even having friends over frequently for part of an evening will let the batterer know—if he regularly drives by your house—that you're not often home alone. Stay away from the places he frequents and from his friends.

Even though it's embarrassing, let your neighbors know what has happened. If the battering has gone on for some time, they probably realize it anyway and will feel relieved to know you're doing whatever you can to ensure your safety.

If you've moved to a new place you might be reluctant to confide in neighbors you barely know, but a little embarrassment may mean the difference between life and death. Spend a few minutes talking to several neighbors, sounding them out on the subject of battering. Then tell them your situation and ask them to call you or the police if they hear anything that sounds like violence. Even though you may feel awkward in the telling, it can give you more sense of control, since you won't be worried about the man disturbing neighbors with his demands to be let into your house at 2:00 A.M. Instead, you'll be hoping they'll hear the commotion and call the police. Be more cautious in speaking to your apartment owner and manager. If they're determined to avoid trouble in the building at all costs, noise in the middle of the night may cause them to evict you. Get to know them a bit before you explain your situation.

As soon as possible, remove all of the man's personal property and store it out of view until you can get it to him. Where the signs of his absence are most noticeable, rearrange things so you don't have to look at empty spaces where his raincoat used to hang, his pipe, toothbrush, or book used to be placed. Put something of your own in those places, and arrange things the way you want them, making it *really* your home.

Start projects that will take your mind off him and give you a sense of satisfaction. Paint a room or sand some furniture. Choose television programs that you really want to watch, but be very careful not to get hooked on one uninteresting program after another. TV can be just as much of an addiction as alcohol and drugs or love if you're susceptible, and right now you are. If there's always one more program to watch, you may never get out of your chair to make new friends and create a new life for yourself. The sooner you contact friends, relatives, a counselor, or support group, the better. You need to know there is someone out there to call on if you're in need. If it isn't possible to arrange those connections quickly, post the number of one or more crisis lines by your telephone, and don't wait until you're desperate to use them. Review Chapter 12, An End to Isolation, and Chapter 13, Reaching Out.

GROUPS FOR ABUSED WOMEN

Unless you're in a shelter that provides regular group meetings, try to find a weekly battered women's group in the community. You may be a bit nervous at the thought of being with a group of strangers, but once you're there, you'll find they're not so strange after all. They'll be like you in many ways and are likely to understand your feelings better than most friends or family members because they've been in similar situations and felt some of the same feelings you have. Some will have started new lives away from their abusive partners and will be an inspiration to you. Most of these groups charge no fee, and you can attend as often or as irregularly as you like.

CONTACT WITH THE MAN WHO BATTERED YOU

Should you or shouldn't you call, write, or meet this man? You can give yourself lots of reasons to make contact with him, each of which seems absolutely essential: You owe him an explanation or at least some information about your plans; you need to talk with him about seeing the children; you have to get some things out of the house. Your imagination may work overtime rationalizing your reasons for speaking to him. Don't do it. Wait. Ordinary considerations don't apply when it's a matter of your physical or psychological survival.

It's probable your man will get along all right without you, but if you have doubts review Chapter 3. Later, when you're sure you'll be safe, you can arrange for visits with the children. As difficult as it is to risk having your property taken or destroyed, if you can't get it without encountering the man, you'll have to remind yourself that most of it is replaceable, but you're not.

Give yourself the same advice you'd have for an alcoholic who decided it's okay to have just one drink. It's not worth the risk. Whether or not you've decided that you have a classic case of addictive love, at this point you'll almost certainly behave like an addict. So make new rules for yourself appropriate to *this* situation, *this* week.

The first rule is not to see the abusive man under any circumstances. The second rule should be not to talk to him on the telephone under any circumstances. Give yourself at least seven days to think about your situation without his self-interested comments.

If you have a good friend who's looking out for your best interests and who's strong enough not to give in to your "reasons" for needing to contact the man, make an agreement with her that you won't call him unless she agrees it is both necessary and wise. If that kind of friend isn't available, you'll just have to promise yourself not to get in touch with the man for at least one week. If there's something that he *must* know, put it in a letter without a return address. The letter should be strictly business. No "I love you" or "I'm sorry" or "I hope you're all right." Just "the cat must have medicine three times a day. The prescription is on the kitchen table. Sue." Before you mail it, try to get a trusted friend to read it and to take out any hints that you want him back. In ordinary circumstances you can trust your own judgment, but this is an emergency situation and you're under a lot of pressure. You need to be protected from yourself, as difficult as that is to swallow.

If, in spite of this advice, you're determined to get some things from your house, be sure to go when the man is away from the house and take someone with you. A friend will help you take as few chances as possible and her or his presence may discourage the man's violence if you unexpectedly encounter him. In some communities, public service officers of the police department will stand by while you remove your things. If you decide to meet the man to discuss business, take a friend with you and meet in a public place such as a restaurant where there are lots of people. Under no circumstances go anywhere in his car with him. If you aren't willing to take these precautions, you're likely either to be coerced or seduced into going back; if you recognize that danger, rather than pretending you're beyond temptation, you can at least guard against it.

These may seem like easy precautions to follow the first few days after you've left. You may be able to both see and feel your injuries, and probably you'll swear this time you won't forgive or forget. But sometime during the first or second week, the memories of the good times will begin to surface and the evidence of damage he's done will begin to fade. This is a very crucial time, so be ready for it. Here are some simple but effective ways to keep your perspective on the relationship and on why you decided to end it.

Most Dangerous List

Make a list of the most humiliating and dangerous things your partner has done to you. Then put it in the form of a letter not to mail but for you to keep. Writing in the first person ("I hate you for . . . " "I resent the times you . . . ") can help you recapture your anger. Most important, don't leave things out because they're too awful to remember. Describe the pain and humiliation he caused you. Include the things he said to you afterward, whether they were cruel or loving. It won't be long before you hear these "loving" promises again, and you'll need to refer to this sheet as a reminder of how empty the promises are and how little the loving words mean in the long run. This exercise will be painful, but it is extremely important. If you don't want to do it, or get too busy, or forget, be suspicious of your motives. You probably don't want to remember the pain of the past. That's understandable, but if you let yourself forget, you'll be extremely vulnerable when the man tries to sweet-talk his way back into your life. You won't remember these are the same words you heard the other times he abused you. You won't remember they weren't followed by loving *action,* or that the honeymoon period lasted only a few days or a couple of hours.

At this point you may think it's not a question of choosing to remember or not. You may believe you can never forget what the man did to you. But didn't you forget before, the last time you wanted to take him back? Write it all down whether you believe you can forget or not.

Activity 23 ⁓ Most Dangerous List

_____

_____

_____

_____

_____

_____

_____

_____

_____

Best Memories List

But, what about the good times, you wonder. *Make a list* of them, too. All the happy moments, the good conversation, the hopes, the dreams, and the qualities that you like or admire about your former partner.

Activity 24 ⁓ Best Memories List

_____

_____

_____

_____

_____

_____

_____

_____

_____

_____

    Look at both lists and decide whether it's worth it to put up with one to gain the other. If the positive list is very short, it may be a little too soon to try to remember the good. If, after being separated for a week, you still can't remember many good times or things you like about your partner, you're probably hooked on a fantasy about the relationship rather than on the real thing. You may be mourning the lost dream, what you hoped the relationship would be. To check that out, compare your hopes and dreams at the beginning of the relationship with the way it really has been. How often and how recently did any of your dreams materialize? Let yourself mourn the loss of that dream, and then get on with your real life.

Change List

You may find yourself saying, "If only he would . . . we could be so happy." Put those "if only's" on paper and *underline* the ones that are essential to change. Turn that list into a letter to him that spells out what he would have to change for you to risk going back. Never mind, for the moment, whether it would be easy or hard for him, how long it might take, or what things you ought to or want to change in yourself. This, too, is a letter you won't necessarily mail, so don't worry about whether it's "nice" or fair. It's a list of things that would have to happen for you to be respected as a person who can make choices and who has a life she can call her own in addition to the relationship with the man.

Activity 25 ༀ Change List

_____

_____

_____

_____

_____

_____

_____

_____

_____

_____

When you turn your Change List into a letter it may look something like this:

Dear Tom:

If I were ever to consider going back to you (which I wouldn't), this is what would have to happen. You would have to:

Never hit me, no matter what I do.

Not insult me or make fun of me, especially in front of other people.

Not put me down when we're alone.

See a counselor or go to a batterers' group for at least six months.

Go to AA for at least six months.

Not drink at all for at least six months.

Not interfere if I want to see my friends or go to school or get a job.

Give me a certain amount of money every month that I can spend with no questions asked (amount negotiable).

Joanne

The items that have a minimum time are the most useful. It's easy for him to say (and even to mean it, at least for the moment) that he'll quit drinking or start counseling, but the real test is whether he follows through. If you return to him as soon as the promise is made or the first appointment for counseling is kept, he'll have no incentive to continue. If he quits, you may entreat or threaten, but you probably won't leave until he's beaten you again.

This list, like the ones that preceded it, is for your own use right now. When you're tempted to call the man, look at the list of changes you said he must make and note any he said he'd do but didn't, as well as those he flatly refuses to consider. Face the reality that he's unlikely to comply with any of them unless he's already made an impressive start. Realize that even if he did agree, it would be months before you could be sure he was following through. The point is that you won't return until he's proven his good intentions by action.

How to Use the Lists

Make a commitment to yourself that you won't even talk to him without reading the other lists first. Read the Most Dangerous List out loud and force yourself to live through the experience emotionally one more time. Remembering won't be as painful as living through it physically again. Keep the list near you so you can read it as often as you need to. Read the Best Memories List too, so that you can keep the two in balance and avoid an unexpected sentimental memory that eclipses everything on the Most Dangerous List. You'll then be in a position to keep a balanced perspective: "Sure, that vacation with Bill was the most romantic time of my life, and yes, he's often been very nurturing. But those times don't come close to making up for the miscarriage he caused, the day he knocked me down the stairs, and the daily hammering away at my self-esteem."

If you're tempted to go back to him even after you've reviewed your lists, if you're trying to persuade yourself he's changed, take a look at your Change List and mark the items he's actually changed and for how long a period. Compare what's actually happened with what you said he'd have to do for you to feel right about going back. The answer to what you should do will be right there.

COPING WITH FEAR

To feel afraid is a natural response, but it doesn't mean the things you're afraid of will happen. Statistically, there's small chance your husband or ex-boyfriend will hunt you down and kill you. But the possibility doesn't have to be very great to make you extremely frightened, and you might become a prisoner of that fear.

Even if your worst fear is improbable, you can't be sure, so you should take precautions to protect yourself. Spend as much time as possible with other people. If sometimes you have to go out alone, try to be on streets where there are lots of people. But once you've decided what reasonable safety measures you can take, start working on reducing your fears.

Pay close attention to what you say to yourself when you feel very afraid. The more you tell yourself terrible things will happen, the more frightened you'll feel. Statements such as "He'll find me and kill me" and "He'll beat me even worse than before" are certain to increase your fear.

Start changing those fear-inducing statements to reassuring comments that reflect and reinforce your ability to cope. "He didn't come after me yesterday, and he probably won't today." "I protect myself by staying near populated areas when I'm in public and keeping my address a secret." "I can handle what happens, just as I handled frightening situations in the past." Remind yourself over and over that if you'd stayed with him you'd still be living in fear and it might continue for the rest of your life. But if you stay away, you'll endure heightened fear for a relatively short period and a time will come when you'll be free of it.

Check out your level of anxiety each day. Without your realizing it, it's probably diminishing as you make it through each day without your fears materializing. Many women who've left an abusive man find their fear steadily diminishes during the first few weeks after they leave. Then one day they realize with a start that it's gone. They can barely remember what it was like to be so afraid.

If the man does find you and attack you, double your efforts to find a safe place to stay and consider some big changes such as shared living quarters, leaving town temporarily, or changing jobs. Don't hesitate to call the police. If you've been giving mixed messages for months or years, it will take time and require some firm and consistent action on your part to persuade the man you're serious about wanting him to leave you alone. This is a good time to start.

The odd thing is that when you're living with an abusive man you get used to a certain level of fear, and much of the time you believe it is only temporary. "It will all be different tomorrow or next time—or next week." After you leave, you might feel as if the new kind of fear you experience will never end. You think you will be afraid for the rest of your life. Like any kind of pain, fear is endurable if you know it will last only a short time. Remind yourself that this fear really will pass, and probably soon.

LONELINESS

If you're at a shelter or with friends or relatives, you may not have too much trouble with loneliness at first. Keeping busy will help and that shouldn't be too difficult. You may have to see a doctor, lawyer, or counselor and look for a place to live in addition to working every day or applying for work or public assistance.

I'd like to tell you that loneliness will pass quickly, but probably it will get worse before it gets better. If you expect separation to be painless, you'll set yourself up to go running back to a dangerous situation. It's better to know that you can expect to suffer for quite awhile and that you can endure it because in the long run you'll suffer less.

Coping with loneliness is still another area in which you can affect your feelings by what you say to yourself. Instead of "I'm so lonely, I can't stand it," try "I'm lonely and I can handle it" or "I was lonely with him, but now I have a chance to learn how to change my life so I won't be lonely." There's more about coping with loneliness in Chapter 20, The Long Haul.

For some women, the first week is the easiest and they assume they've licked the problem of loneliness. It's important not to deny your feelings, so you'll know when you should make a point of being with people and when not to risk contact with the man.

CHAPTER 15

PROTECTING YOURSELF AND THE CHILDREN

It won't be so hard to end the relationship cold turkey if you don't have children in common. Children make separation more complicated, but you can overcome the difficulties by careful planning. Not all the problems will revolve around the children's relationships with the father. A long abusive relationship and the children's separation from their father or father figure can also create problems between you and the children. Children's methods of coping with a violent environment may be quite ineffective now that the violent man is no longer present. This chapter gives you some ideas about how to minimize contact when the father visits (or when you visit, if he has custody), how to deal with typical post-battering family problems, and when to get help from professional counselors.

VISITATION

Arranging for your children to visit their father will be difficult in the best of circumstances, and guilt about the separation can make it even harder. The father will know how to manipulate those guilt feelings and the children might also.

If you've been involved with several men who became important to your children and then lost contact with them when your relationship ended, you may be particularly vulnerable to guilt feelings. It's true that children suffer when they're separated from a father figure, but they suffer even more when they live with a role model who is violent to their mother.

Your involvement with an abusive man or with multiple "fathers" of your children has been a mistake and may have had destructive results for them. But that's not a reason to continue subjecting them to contact with a violent father figure. That would be a perpetuation of the same mistake and more likely permanent damage to the children.

If you're going to find it hard to stay away from the man, his visits with the children will create special risks for you unless you set them up very carefully. You can be pretty sure he'll use his visitation rights to try to lure you back by threats, by his charm, or by playing on your guilt feelings.

During the first few months of your separation, arrange for him to pick the children up at someone else's house. Even if it's awkward or expensive or inconvenient, take them to a friend or relative's home, hire a babysitter, or make arrangements through a child-protection agency to leave and pick up the child there. Do whatever is necessary so you won't be forced into contact with him.

He may object to that procedure, or he may agree but then fail to come at the appointed time and try to persuade you to let him pick the children up at your house "just this time." At that point you're likely to feel angry at him, disappointed for the children, and frustrated about your own ruined plans. It may be impossible to redo your arrangements on the spot, or you may feel so defeated you don't want to take the time or trouble. It can then be very tempting to give in and concede that this time he can pick them up at home. That's an understandable reaction, but if you do that even one time you not only place yourself in a vulnerable position by meeting him in person, you also give him a message that he can manipulate you to get what he wants. He may interpret your conciliation to mean he can eventually persuade you to go back to him.

If you've left without the children or made the hard decision to give up custody, your problems may be greater, but they are essentially of the same kind. If the father fails to show up with the children at the appointed time and place, you may be so eager to see them you'll give in to almost any plan of their father's. In the long run you'll be better off if you follow the same inflexible guidelines advised above. The father probably has looked forward to being free of the children and if you're absolutely consistent even when it's very hard, he'll eventually believe you mean it when you say you'll pick up the children only at a certain time or place. Giving in to his demands even one time will give him hope and then you'll have to start all over again to make him understand you're serious.

You don't have to give him reasons for your tight regulations on visitation and you don't have to listen to his complaints. If you've followed the advice in Chapter 8 to have the specifics or visitation arrangements written into the separation or divorce decree, the situation will be much easier to handle. You can find more on visitation in Chapter 28.

CONTACT WITH THE BATTERER

A few weeks or months after separating, you may feel calm and friendly toward your ex-partner. Maybe you've relaxed your restrictions on visitation arrangements and have begun to talk to him for brief periods, either when he visits the children or to discuss other affairs you still share an interest in. If he's being reasonable and considerate and you're not afraid anymore, you might even have coffee or a drink with him now and then. You may begin to believe you can trust yourself, maybe even him.

You probably can't. To the extent that you've lost your fear and anger, you're vulnerable to his seductive promises and to your own wish to believe him. Perhaps you're feeling down, that you're not much good for anything, that no one loves or could love you. Your ex-partner will tell you you're wonderful and lovable and that he cares for you even if no one else seems to. Because you're emotionally isolated and dependent on him, you cling to him like a drowning person to a lifesaver. What you forget is that you wouldn't be in such desperate emotional need if he hadn't beaten you into believing you're worthless and hadn't insisted on isolating you from caring friends in the first place. His ability to nurture you takes on such importance because he's put you on an emotional yo-yo.

You'll find it difficult or impossible to stay away from him if you talk to him on the telephone or if you're around him and the children together. Once he sits down to chat about Susie's reaction to the animals at the zoo, or Johnnie's reading problem, it may begin to feel like the good old days (with the bad parts of those days forgotten). Before you know it, you may ask him to dinner and then encourage him—or be persuaded by him—to spend the night. It will be easy then to imagine he's a changed man, especially if he's considerate and romantic, or if he reads the children a bedtime story. It will be easy to persuade yourself they need each other and that you haven't the right to deprive him of his children.

If you don't have children in common to provide a reason to visit with the man, you may invent others. Keep in mind that it's a short step from the dinner table to a few drinks together and an even shorter step from these to the bedroom. The longest road on a destructive journey, as well as on a worthwhile one, begins with a single step.

You probably won't go back to your ex-partner if you don't go to bed with him. You won't go to bed with him if you don't cook dinner or go out drinking with him. You won't be tempted to cook for him or drink with him if you don't listen to his troubles or promises. And you can't listen to him if you're not in touch with him at all.

Don't Give In to Your Impulses

Refer to your Change List again (Activity 25 in Chapter 14). If you haven't kept it, question your motives. Losing it may be one way to avoid facing reality. *Make a new list,* being honest about your earlier demands. If you decided he needed six months of therapy or AA or one year of not drinking or three months of treating you with respect, don't reduce those times now. He may have taken a small step in a constructive direction, but you'll have to wait at least several months to be sure of what it means. You'll also need verification of his changed patterns. You can insist on permission to talk to his counselor or other people who can tell you whether he's been living up to his promises. You may want to see his counselor once (which he should pay for), either together with him or alone, to be sure the counselor understands the degree of battering you were subjected to. More than one man has seen a counselor for months and months without mentioning battering, or related problems such as drinking, as behavior he wants to change.

Activity 26 ⌇ What Changes Has He Made?

Your former partner may try to make you feel guilty by accusing you

_____

_____

_____

_____

_____

_____

_____

_____

of not trusting him. Your response should be, "Of course I don't trust you, after the abuse you put me through and the empty promises you made." He may play on your guilt feelings by insisting, now that he's taken steps in the right direction, that he needs your support to continue. Tell him he'll have to change because *he* wants to, and he'll have to do it by himself. If he won't do it by himself, he's even less likely to do it when he has what he wants—you. For your own safety and to be sure of how serious he is about changing, it's important to stay away from him. If you feel sorry for him or guilty, remind yourself that the best thing you can do for him is to stay away so he'll have the motivation to change. Providing him with an opportunity to be violent and destructive does neither of you any good.

You Can Control the Relationship

If you've gradually slipped into a friendly relationship, you may have to retrench; if you feel yourself getting more involved you'll have to retreat from once-a-week dinners to occasional coffees or from coffees to nothing but telephone arrangements about the children. This might be hard to do and perhaps he's been treating you reasonably well, but it's much too soon to tell whether it will last and you have a right to stay away. *You don't owe him an explanation.* Say something such as, "I prefer not to go out with you anymore. I don't want to explain or answer questions about it. It's just the way I want it now." He'll probably act as if you're punishing him and try to make you feel guilty if you say you don't want to talk to him for awhile. If so, he hasn't changed because that pattern of inducing guilt and demanding explanations so he can talk you into going along with his plans, or batter you into it, is typical of abusive men.

If you do continue seeing him for any reason at all, you're in for another period of turmoil. He'll most likely want more and more from you until he gets you "back home where you belong again." And you'll have to battle not only against his arguments, but also against your own vulnerability and guilt feelings. "He's trying," you'll tell yourself. "At least I could give him a chance." "He needs some motivation if he's going to change." "After all, I owe him something."

These are the ideas you have to get rid of, and you'll find it much easier to do if you don't hear them from him. You have to find out what life is like without him, and you won't be able to if you're sleeping with him once a week, or even involved in telephone conversations that keep you wondering when he'll call again. You have to get him not only out of your life, but out of your mind. Look away from him toward a new way of life. Start by convincing yourself you owe him nothing. This is a rigid attitude and may seem harsh, but it's necessary. You don't owe him another chance. You've probably given him too many already.

WHAT YOU CAN DO FOR THE CHILDREN

It's hard to tell the children you're afraid of their father, but they need to know the truth. With the possible exception of very young infants, all children will have been affected by the violence and fear in the household. If they haven't seen it, they've sensed that something threatening was happening. Vague apprehensions can be more frightening than the fact of violence itself. If they've seen it often, they've probably begun to accept it as a normal way for married people and parents to act toward those they love most. They may have begun to incorporate it into their own ideas of themselves as future spouses or lovers.

Children sometimes repeat the pattern of violence they learn at their parents' knees. You can reduce that likelihood by taking a strong position right now that violence is not acceptable, their father is not safe to be around, and that you're going to protect both yourself and them. You don't have to go into detail, nor need you talk about what a monster he is. You can explain that you do love him, which is why it's been too hard to leave before, but that now you're determined to stay away.

That determination is important for the children as well as for yourself. They can adapt to living separately from their father, but being separated and reunited and separated again is confusing to them. They may get a message that either it's not important to protect yourself or them or that you can't do it.

Tell the children that when you believe it's safe they can see their father if they want to. Whether or not he was violent to them as well as to you, they may be too afraid or angry to want to see him, at least for awhile. Make it clear they don't have to see him until they feel safe. (If the court has ordered visitation you may have to seek a modification of it.) Sometimes children have a hard time saying that they don't want to see the father. If that's how your children feel, help them to know that their feelings are natural, that they may change, and they have no reason to feel guilty about them.

Coping with children's problems can heighten your stress, but the responsibility can also distract you from your grief. Taking care to entertain and nurture your children will help them and you by keeping all of you busy. Let them know they can count on you to be there when they need you, and try to have meals, bedtime, and school routine as "normal" as possible.

If the children complain about the move you've made or their father's absence, try to be both sympathetic and firm. You might want to say you're not going to see him even though you miss him, or that because he hurt you, you're glad he's not there. Encourage your children to discuss their feelings and let them know they don't have to feel the same way you do.

One of the most difficult aspects of your situation may be that your children are frightened, depressed, or angry and need more attention than usual at a time when you want to be mothered yourself. Try hard to get your emotional needs met by friends, family, or shelter staff. Do it for yourself so you'll have something to give to your children. You may also want to arrange time for them to share with relatives or caring friends. Just be sure they know they have a place and a person in their lives that are stable. You may have to give the same reassurance over and over again, so try to be patient.

Old Coping Skills Need Revision

You may have developed a pattern of overprotectiveness toward your children in an effort to protect the children from the father's violence as well as to compensate for his harsh discipline or indifference. Perhaps the children received so much irrational and undeserved punishment from their father that you've been reluctant to discipline them. Another common pattern is to be overly punitive or even abusive to the children. You might have done that as a way of expressing the rage you didn't dare let out at the man, or in hopes of shaping the children's behavior to avoid the man's anger. You may have directed anger at your children because you were jealous of the father's devotion to them while you were ignored or abused. Still another way of coping is to become so depressed you don't notice or care about much of anything, including the children.

You may have to pay a price now for your previous ways of dealing with the children as you tried to survive an impossible situation. In addition, the children have developed their own ways of coping with a frightening, dangerous, unpredictable environment, which may have worked reasonably well for them in a chaotic household but is counterproductive in the family now and in other relationships.

When you make a great effort, and rise above your lethargy or anger to provide good parenting for a week or so, you may hope to reap some rewards. If they're not forthcoming, you may slide back to your old patterns. It might be hard to realize that even the best of parenting won't necessarily get good results right away. Try to remember that your children have lived a significant part of their lives in a state of tension (whether or not they actually saw the battering) and that they'll take a long time to recognize and respond to consistent treatment. Some professionals who work with children of batterers say it take two years for their mothers to establish credibility as parental authority. You'll need lots of emotional support and the ability to reward yourself during this transition period.

CHILDREN'S REACTIONS TO VIOLENCE AND SEPARATION

Each situation in regard to children presents different problems and different advantages. If you or the batterer moved to a distant city and cut off contact, or if he isn't the children's father and doesn't choose to see them, you'll avoid the emotional turmoil that the absent parent's visits often cause. However difficult life may be for you and the children, it has the potential of at least being stable. Everyone can become used to being part of a one-parent family without the emotional upsets of the father's visits and eventually can learn to appreciate its advantages.

On the negative side, the children may long to be with their father. This will be especially hard for everyone if other children in the family have different absent fathers who come to see them and take them on excursions. If that's the situation, try to arrange your own special activities to coincide with those outings.

The children may also blame you for their father's absence. Even when they've seen him beat you, they may start rewriting family history, which will make it even harder for you to remember the past accurately. Try to help them keep a balanced picture and you'll help yourself. "Yes, it was sometimes more fun around here before Daddy left, but it was too dangerous." "Yes, I did tell him to leave, even though I still love him. He can't come back unless he can prove you and I will be safe, and he hasn't been willing to do that."

The children may blame themselves for the breakup of the relationship or even for the violence, particularly if they once called the police or tried to intervene. If they've frequently been disciplined by the father they may simply explain his absence as one more thing that's their fault. But often children don't need any reason at all to blame themselves. If you suspect that's how they feel, try to get them to talk about it. Ask, "What do you think you did that might have caused the violence or made him leave?" Listen carefully to the answer. Don't tell the child immediately that she or he is wrong, because that will probably shut off further talk. Encourage the child to express feelings about the father, whether they conform to your picture of reality or not. Then encourage careful reasoning by asking questions such as, "Does hitting somebody—or leaving home—seem like something a person would do for an extremely important reason, or because another person didn't do the dishes?" You may have to say several times, "Daddy left because I told him he couldn't stay." After you've talked about feelings, you might want to say, "I used to blame myself when he beat me, but then I finally realized that he's responsible for what he does. I'm only responsible for what I do." Tell your child you don't think she or he is to blame, but that you understand the reasons for their feelings.

It won't hurt to limit the amount of violence your children watch on television, but when they do see it, you can use the opportunity to find out what they feel and think about rights and responsibilities in regard to violence and to tell them what you think about it. If a child is having a hard time adjusting to the new situation or persists in taking responsibility for the father's absence or his violence, consider professional counseling with a person experienced in working with children of batterers.

When a Child Becomes Violent

Your child may have learned by watching the batterer that the way to get what one wants is to bully: to take, to intimidate by loud shouts or threats, to hit, to break things. It may be especially hard to tolerate a bullying child when you've just broken away from the person the child mimics.

Consistent intervention is the key to changing this pattern. Ideally, each time the child bullies a person, you will step in and calmly state that she or he isn't allowed to do that and either physically remove the child or send him or her to another room until the child's self-control is clearly established. It's important to react the same way each time and not to hit the child to "teach him a lesson." The lesson the child needs demonstrated is that violence and coercion are no longer tolerable. If you want the child to take you seriously about this, don't strike her or him regardless of behavior. If you've had the habit of controlling the child's behavior by spanking, you'll need to learn other ways to discipline. This may be hard at first, so if you do slip up, be sure to explain that you're all learning new ways to treat each other, that you're working hard on it and when you fall back on old ways, it doesn't mean it's right. It just means you have to try harder. If this problem doesn't get much better soon, you'll need to get professional help, perhaps both to show you how to manage your feelings better and to teach you skills in coping with difficult children.

When you're upset about the way your child is acting and feeling sad or angry about your own life, it's hard to notice the positive. It's important that you try hard to appreciate a child's gentle and cooperative behavior, even when it seems nonexistent. Force yourself to acknowledge that the child is behaving well even if you're still angry about a recent outburst.

If your young child is persistently violent or subtly manipulative and controlling toward you or others, you may want to get a professional evaluation from a children's therapist. Consider having the child go to a special school or therapy program. If the violent child is a teenager, you may have difficult decisions ahead of you. You'll want to give her or him time to adjust to the new family life and learn new habits. But there may come a time when you'll have to consider your own or other children's safety and well-being and take drastic action such as foster-home placement. That will probably be a last resort, but keep it in mind as an option. It may be the best thing you can do for the child as well as yourself—the strongest way of putting across the message: "No more. You must not treat the people you love violently."

When a Child Withdraws or Is "Too Good"

It's easy to overlook the good child who makes it her or his business to stay out of everyone's way and to be very obedient. This is the child who may be most helpful to you now, caring for younger children, comforting you when you're sad, easily forgiving your irritation. If you're nearly paralyzed with depression or fear, or drowning your sorrows in drink or tranquilizers, this child may start playing parent to you. Although it might be tempting to be comforted, keep in mind that the child needs to be a child and should know there's an adult in charge. You're probably the only anchor the child has now.

A child may also withdraw from everyone, escaping into books, television, or drugs. You may vaguely wonder where the child is or how she or he feels, but as long as there are few demands on you, it will be easy to ignore the child. Though it takes a lot of energy, make a point of spending time with a withdrawn or "good" child. Talk about violence, fear, and the new ways of living you're all learning. Encourage the child to express feelings and be alert to hints about self-blame.

A withdrawn or overly good child may suddenly begin to act quite differently, expressing a lot of anger or destructiveness toward you or others or being generally disobedient. You may also find that one or more of your children uses the same psychological methods of control as the batterer, and you may react in the same way as you did to the batterer. Or the child who reminds you of him in other ways may trigger reactions that are not appropriate.

When to Get Professional Help

Many children outgrow problems and most probably don't need therapy, but children who have been exposed to violent and emotional abuse among the people who they must trust may develop lifelong scars. One way to avoid them is to get a third party to intervene. Don't worry about the child suffering from being labeled "sick." Rather than "sickness," it's a matter of learning or relearning skills in problem-solving and relating in constructive ways. If you're not sure what to do, find a children's therapist who has worked with children of batterers and get an evaluation.

The child may find it much easier to express feelings to a skilled professional than to you. Even if there are only a few sessions with the therapist, you'll be giving a clear message that it's okay to ask for help and that there are people outside the family who can provide it.

CHAPTER 16

THE PRACTICAL QUESTIONS OF WELFARE AND HOUSING

Soon after the first week you're on your own, you'll probably begin to plan where you're going to live and how you'll manage financially. If you've had a paid job, some of your immediate problems will be solved, but it's likely you'll still suffer a big drop in income and have to make decisions about whether the house or apartment you've been living in is affordable as well as safe.

If you have neither a good job nor other sources of income, you may have to make some shifts in lifestyle and some compromises with your values. You might, for instance, have to rely temporarily on welfare or move from a comfortable house to an apartment or shared housing in someone else's home.

WELFARE

If you've never received welfare funds—and perhaps if you have—it may bring to mind pictures of unkempt children, harried or depressed mothers, and snooping social workers. It's hard to dispel that image because like all stereotypes, there's some truth in it. The welfare grant is usually so small it's hard to dress children in clothes that haven't been patched over patches, and it's easy for parents to become depressed trying to make ends meet. Although social workers are no longer permitted to investigate the intimate lives of recipients, they do have to get some information from applicants that you might think is personal. Nevertheless, welfare can be a lifesaver in an emergency.

Categories of Aid

Old Age Assistance is available for anyone sixty-five years and older who lives outside a public institution. Aid to The Blind is for partially or totally blind people. Aid to Permanently and Totally Disabled is for people who cannot work because of permanent physical or mental disabilities. These payments are all made through Social Security and recipients are automatically entitled to Medicare. Temporary Assistance to Needy

Families (TANF) supports families that include at least one child or pregnant woman. Each state has its own eligibility standards, programs, and options but under the federal Family Violence Option, TANF might wave certain requirements for you as a victim of domestic violence.

Applying for Welfare

What is commonly called the "Welfare Department" may be listed in various ways in your telephone book, and you can find out how by looking under "Welfare." The more you can learn ahead of time about what to expect, what your rights are, and what information you need, the easier the process of applying for welfare will be. You may be required to bring birth certificates for yourself and your children, receipts for rent, utilities, medical bills and other expenses, and check stubs or other papers that prove your income or proof of residency. When you call for general information, ask what papers you need and be sure to take them with you. Arriving without the necessary papers will mean more delay and perhaps another frustrating morning standing in line.

Take a friend or welfare advocate with you and try to arrive fifteen minutes before the office opens. If you get there at ten or eleven in the morning, you'll wait a long time and soon be hungry for lunch but afraid to lose your place. If you get there in the afternoon, your name may not come up at all. In any case you're likely to have a wait so try to minimize it by arriving early. Having a friend to talk to will help to pass the time. If you're alone, take along a magazine, stationery, or a crossword puzzle. If you can't leave your children with a friend, be sure to take along several small surprises for them to pull out at intervals when they've become bored.

As you wait in the welfare office, you may find yourself looking around skeptically, thinking that all these people must be losers, somehow different from you, or worse yet, you must be a loser too. There will be a lot of people like you in that they have low incomes, they're women with children, people who have troubles. If you talk to some of them, it will help pass the time, and you can learn about the system from old hands.

Some welfare workers will act as if they're doing you a favor so it's important for you to keep in mind that you have a right to public assistance. Others will go out of their way to help you. Try not to let your frustration get the best of you, because you'll get better service if you stay calm.

Computation of "Need"

Welfare funds are a combination of federal and state funds and subject to regulations of both levels of government. State welfare guidelines indicate how much the department is willing to budget for various expenses such as rent, food, clothing, and utilities. Don't be surprised if the amount they allow you is well under the "poverty line." What the welfare department calls your "regular recognized need" may be much less than what you recognize as your need, especially if you've left home with little but the clothes on your back.

Even after the state figures your "regular recognized need," it may not be willing to pay the full amount. Some states figure the need and then deduct a percentage from the actual grants given; others have a maximum payment per family or per person. Some have extremely complex systems that are difficult for most people to understand.

Once they've established an amount they think you can live on, the welfare department will subtract your regular income from child support, unemployment compensation, employment, or other income sources to determine the amount of the grant you'll receive. You'll be obliged to report any income while you're a recipient of a welfare grant, though in some instances you may be able to keep a small part of earned income.

If you have a full-time job but are barely scraping by, it will be worth your while to call the welfare department to see if you qualify for welfare assistance for medical care or childcare while you work. Those extra costs might make the difference between a tolerable income level and financial disaster.

If you think you're being treated unfairly, it's unlikely you'll have the energy to fight the whole system, but you can work at getting what you're entitled to within the system. If you have questions or doubts about your grant, ask to see the rules that apply to your situation. Ask also whether there are special allotments for someone in your circumstances. There might be special allowances for transportation to doctors or for people who are old, blind, disabled, or pregnant.

Know Your Rights

Don't be afraid to ask how each decision is made, what you're entitled to, whether there are exceptions, why you're being turned down, what you need to do to qualify for general or special aid, and what the department regulations are that apply to your case. They must let you know in writing within forty-five days if your application has been approved. Your first check will arrive within that period.

If you are applying for Temporary Assistance to Needy Families (TANF), the welfare worker will ask for the name and address of the children's father so the department can see that he pays child support. But be sure to ask the caseworker how you can get an exemption from this requirement under the federal Family Violence Option. Explain to the social worker that you're in danger, if that's the case, and ask if there are special rules that apply to your situation. The caseworker may ask you for evidence of battering, such as court records. A letter from a counselor or shelter may be enough. At a later time the department may want to go after the man for child support, and you'll have to persuade the staff that he's still a danger to you, if that's the case.

If you're refused aid, you must be given a reason in writing. If you think you've been unjustly refused, or given too little money, call your local or state Welfare Rights Organization or the Urban League in the nearest large city. They can help you decide whether to appeal the decision.

If you have nothing to live on until the first check comes, explain to your interviewer that the grant will help next month, but you have nothing to live on for the next few weeks. You may get an emergency grant for rent or food stamps, or if you have a notice that utilities will be turned off, you may receive enough to pay them. If there are no emergency funds available, ask for referrals to agencies who will help with money, food, clothing, or other necessary items.

It's Not Forever

It's demoralizing for anyone to be financially dependent on others. It's hard not to feel incompetent, helpless, and that you have no rights. Sometimes a bureacracy seems like the most difficult of all dependency situations, because it's a giant machine that neither sees nor cares about individuals, whether they're workers or clients.

When you feel discouraged by it, remember the different kinds of hardships that accompanied your life with the man who battered you. The welfare department at least has regulations that you can see in writing, and it will give you notice of them when they do change. Checks may sometimes be late, and welfare may take away some of your grant when the government decides it needs the money for something else. But there won't be changes and new unkept promises every day or week, and you won't be emotionally abused or beaten up.

Most important, it's not forever, unless you want it to be or you're elderly or permanently disabled. Even then there may be some hope of finding better solutions once your life has calmed down. As hard as it is to have so little money, you can at least clear your head and begin to look at alternatives, which is almost impossible to do when you're involved with a violent man.

OTHER BENEFITS

If you received welfare payments you automatically receive Medicaid, which will pay for many medical expenses. You may qualify for Medicaid if your income is quite low, even if you're not getting welfare money. To find out if you're eligible, call the welfare department of your state, a Welfare Rights Organization, or your local Urban League.

If you're over sixty-five or disabled or blind you may qualify for Supplemental Security Income (SSI), a government program to aid poor people. To qualify, you must have a very low income and few resources other than a home. Apply at your local Social Security Administration.

Social Security is designed to assist retired workers in their old age. A small monthly payment is available even for those who have never paid into the social security system through paid employment. You must be sixty-two years old to receive it and if you wait until you're sixty-five you'll receive more. If you were married for at least ten years, you're entitled to half of the amount your husband gets after he's sixty-five, or sixty-two if he retires then. Even if you worked for pay most of your adult life, you may be entitled to more from his account than your own because you may have earned a great deal less than he did. Get information about your individual situation from the local office of the Social Security Administration. Take your husband's social security number and your marriage license, as well as your own social security number.

Food Stamps

Food stamps are available to people with low incomes, which nearly always includes welfare recipients. To find out how much you're entitled to, call your welfare department. Be sure to ask whether your age, the type of assistance you receive, or particular expenses you have affect the amount of food stamps you're allotted.

Employment and Training

Special employment and training opportunities may be available through the welfare department, or even required by it. If you're willing and able to go to work, but have no marketable skills, ask about subsidies for training and assistance in finding on-the-job training. When you get the information about special welfare programs, compare them with those available through other community agencies.

After what you have been through, you might need a lot of help getting started in a paid job. A caseworker can make the task easier by showing you how to find a state program that includes such an opportunity. They vary by state, and may pay only a very low wage. Their main advantage may be to get you out of the house and among people on a daily basis. In the long run you'll need to get training for a skilled job unless you already have it. There is more about searching for rewarding jobs, career planning, and long-term goals in the next chapter.

THE HOUSING SEARCH

Looking for housing takes a lot of energy. You have to get up early (when perhaps you'd rather not get up at all) and read the paper first thing. It's likely to be a discouraging process at best, but it will be even worse if you start answering ads at one in the afternoon. By then, the best apartments will be taken. If you don't have a telephone, ask a friend if you can use hers regularly at the same time every morning. Then you won't have to worry about feeling guilty for asking another favor every day. If you must use a telephone booth, be sure to get more than enough change the day before you call.

If there's an afternoon paper in your community, don't wait for it to be delivered. Find out where you can get it at the earliest possible time, and go there, even if it's the newspaper office itself. You'll be ahead of everyone who's waiting for the delivery at home or work.

Telephoning can be difficult. If you're feeling nervous or insecure, know that it's a normal reaction. When you need something very badly, it's easy to feel you're being personally rejected when you don't get it. Continually remind yourself it's okay to feel like putting off those calls, it's okay to feel rejected when an apartment owner says, "We don't take children," or "We need the first and last month's rent and a damage deposit." It's okay to feel that way, but you still have to make the calls. After being turned down several times, or rejecting the places yourself, you'll feel like giving up. But sooner or later, something will turn up if you keep working at it.

Review Chapter 11, A Courageous Act a Day, and define this task not as finding an apartment but as "Now I'm going to make four phone calls." After each series of calls, reward yourself.

Don't neglect the possibility of walking or driving around desirable neighborhoods. In a tight rental market, many apartments and houses never get advertised but are rented as soon as a sign goes up. You might be lucky enough to see the sign go up yourself.

Look into public housing. There are plenty of reasons it might not be your first choice, but it won't hurt to put your name on a list so if worse comes to worst you'll have some place to go. Public housing will give you some breathing space until you find something you really want. If there's a long waiting list, call every day, and politely but firmly explain that you're in physical danger and your situation is critical. You may be moved to the top of the list. I have known this to happen a number of times when abused women explained their situations.

SHARED HOUSING

Sometimes two women in a shelter hit it off right away and decide to find a place together. It seems wonderful to know someone who's in a similar situation and understands the problems. But the relief of gaining understanding about abuse and shared feelings of loneliness and fear may temporarily blind each woman to differences in values, lifestyles, attitudes toward children, and other important matters. One woman may be afraid to tell the other about her doubts, and the other may have her own misgivings. If neither speaks up, it's impossible to find out whether their doubts are important enough to drop the plan or if they can be worked out through talk or compromise. Sometimes they go ahead with the plan because each is afraid to hurt the other's feelings, and eventually this leads to mutual hostility and the loss of a housemate as well as a potential friend. If you speak up about what you want and how you feel, you should at least be able to save the friendship.

Another thing to consider in sharing housing with an abused woman who's just left her man is whether she's likely to go back to him in a week or a month, which will leave you with half an empty house and may demoralize you and weaken your own determination to stay away. There's no reliable way to make that prediction, but you can at least think about your probable reactions if it does happen. You might prefer to share housing with someone who's in a more stable situation.

You might decide to move in with an old friend, or answer an ad for group living, or invite someone into your home in exchange for rent or childcare. Whatever the situation, talk frankly about your similarities, values, and habits. Be sure you do this even if you think you know all about the other person. Many old friends have been surprised at what they learned about each other when they began to live together.

Major differences, such as the type of work you do, people you associate with, and how you entertain can be problems, but sometimes they're much easier to cope with than with who left the frying pan dirty. Insofar as such things don't impinge directly on you, how tolerant are you? Will you express disapproval if your housemate spends all her spare money on records, or if she dates men you believe aren't good for her? How will you react if she gives you a bad time about your habits or associates?

QUESTIONS FOR A POTENTIAL HOUSEMATE

1. How much company do you like at meals, in the evenings, on weekends?

2. Will you be unhappy if I'm rarely home for dinner and the evening, or if I'm not always sociable when I'm home—or if I'm almost always home and almost always sociable?

3. How will you feel if I have guests several times a week, or if you do and I almost never do?

4. How will you react if I have a male or female friend spend the night, or if I object to your having a frequent overnight or dinner guests?

5. What can we agree to do if the man who battered one of us comes to the house or calls?

6. What will happen if one of us invites an ex-partner to come to the house?

7. What are the things that bother you about other people's housekeeping habits and what bothers them about your habits?

8. What are your attitudes about money, e.g., payment of bills, sharing expenses, impulse buying, etc?

9. How much common involvement do you want in the household, sharing expenses, childcare, cooking, etc?

10. If you have children, how do you want to divide space and expenses?

11. How similar are our lifestyles and values and how tolerant are you of differences?

12. What time do you like to go to bed and get up, and how do you feel about noise (conversation, music, etc.) at night and in the morning?

13. Will you or your friends smoke, drink, or take drugs at our house?

Working Out Differences

As you and your potential housemate answer and discuss these questions, try to remember how potential problems were worked out with other people you lived with. Don't dismiss problems with the thought that it wouldn't come up with anyone other than your mother or your former partner. Instead, remember the things that bothered you and that bothered others about you. Be as honest as you can about whether you've changed in respect to those previously troublesome areas.

You won't see eye to eye on everything, nor can you predict how you'll feel about some of these things a month or a year from now, since life with a batterer tends to distort one's reactions to many situations. You'll go through many changes in the first year when you're physically and emotionally separating from the man and will make decisions about what's so important to you that it can't be compromised. If it's completely unacceptable to spank your child, you won't want to live with a woman who spanks. If it depresses you to be greeted by a sink full of dishes in the morning, you probably won't want to take a chance on someone who tends to put off washing dishes, even if she says she'll try to do better. You don't have to defend your likes and dislikes or feel guilty for being too demanding. It's better to live alone than to start each day irritated by the habits of your housemate.

Once you each decide what items are not subject to compromise, you'll know whether you should continue talking. What are some of the compromises you can make? If you're a night owl, you might agree not to play music after 10:00 P.M. during the week if you can play it as late as you like on weekends.

Most important is a plan for discussing disagreements and problems. If you've been with an abusive man for some time, you may have formed the habit of walking on eggs, trying to predict moods and behavior, and never asking for what you want. That can result in depression or smoldering resentment that periodically bursts out in angry shouting. You may have to do some hard work to learn to know how you feel, and then to tell your housemate about it and ask for what you want. If you at least agree about wanting to learn those skills and if you give each other permission to comment when one of you is sulking, irritable, or otherwise indirectly expressing resentment, you can learn to clear the air before it gets too thick.

Sharing Your Home

If you decide to share your own house or apartment in which you've previously lived with the man, you'll have some special adjustments to make.

Even if you think you hate everything about him right now, there are certain habits of living together that you developed with him that may still seem the obvious or only way to do things. When your new housemate has different ideas, it may automatically seem wrong or ridiculous just because it's different. If you're alert to this possibility, you can prevent yourself from reacting until you've thought it over.

When setting a price for renting part of your home, include the cost of wear and tear on your things and put your agreement in writing. If all the furniture and household goods are yours, you'll start your relationship with more power in setting rules about how things are used and treated. You'll need to discuss this difference and sometimes you'll need to bite your tongue when you see mud on your light-colored rug. If you remember that the rental charge allows for that, it will be easier to take.

Shared housing presents the possibility of both expanded horizons and increased stress. If you haven't experienced group living outside the nuclear or extended family, you may be reluctant to try it. But shared housing may be your best choice for a while because of the opportunity for low-cost rent and other household expenses and the availability of people to diminish your loneliness. Once you've determined where your immediate income will come from and where you'll live, you'll be able to look at some long-range financial planning.

CHAPTER 17

THE ECONOMICS OF SINGLE LIFE

When you're separating or divorcing after a long relationship, you might feel overwhelmed by the thought of starting over emotionally, socially, or financially. If you're in a new city or neighborhood without your customary friends and relatives, or even familiar landmarks, you may feel especially bewildered. If, in addition to all that, you've lost a home and furniture, personal possessions or a job, you'll have some struggles ahead of you in establishing a new style of life.

On the other hand, starting over can have an exhilarating effect. Financial responsibilities that are frightening can also become a new adventure. Learning new things is stimulating and can give you a sense of accomplishment and build your self-esteem.

Even if you were once confident about handling household finances, don't be surprised if they seem overwhelming now. Men who batter usually insist on controlling the money and persuade women they're not capable of making sound decisions or adding a column of figures. The longer you've been involved in such a situation, the more helpless you're likely to feel. This might be true even if you're the one who handled the money or if you were the principle breadwinner.

PAID EMPLOYMENT

Costs and Benefits of Working

If you have the luxury of choosing whether to be unemployed or to work outside the home, it may be difficult to decide what to do, especially if you have children. Once you're separated from the abusive man, rest may be the most appealing alternative. You'll certainly need to recover from your emotional turmoil and physical abuse, but a vacation from work may not necessarily be the best way to get it. A lack of structured activity may add to loneliness, depression, or fear. Paid work often creates a healthy tiredness at the end of a day that can distract you from a repetitive cycle of emotions.

If it's been quite a while since you did paid work, don't assume that you're too old, not qualified, or that you can't work because of commitments to children. One or the other might be true, but you can't be sure until you've taken a fresh look at your situation and the current job market. You might not be sure until you've actually worked six months or more. Don't underestimate the emotional impact of paid work and its contribution to your self-confidence. Maybe you don't like the idea that our values are closely associated with paychecks. But that's the fact for most of us, and it's important to recognize it.

How Valid Are Your Fears?

Some jobs are better for self-esteem than others. Perhaps one of your fears is that you'll be stuck in a dead-end, tedious job forever—with some emotional abuse from your boss thrown in. Perhaps that's the only kind of job you've had, and you didn't think about working toward something better because you thought you could depend on a man to save you from all that. Now that you're beginning to realize you can't count on a man's economic protection, what are the reasons you still believe a boring, low-paid, low-status job is your only choice? *Write* them down. They might look something like this:

Activity 27 ⁀ What Are Your Fears about Job-Hunting?

1. I have no education or skills.

2. I don't know what I want to do.

3. Employers discriminate against women, minorities, single mothers . . .

4. I'm too young, old . . .

5. _____

6. _____

7. _____

8. _____

9. _____

10. _____

Look carefully at each reason you've listed. How many of your statements are specific and objective?

It's not objectively true that you have no skills, training, or educaion, though you may feel that way if your skills are not easily marketable or if they won't get you a high-paying job. To say you're the wrong sex, age, or race is not precise enough to be useful, even though being nonwhite, under nineteen or over thirty-five, and female may be a disadvantage on the job market.

You may be too old to be accepted as an apprentice in certain fields, and you may not have the right kinds of skills or education to be a secretary or an engineer. These are different statements from the first very general ones. To make your statements precise, you need to ask: "Too old for what?" "Not enough education for what?"

Formulating Goals

To evaluate your strengths and weaknesses regarding employment, you need to have a specific goal in mind. What do you want to work at? What are your minimum financial requirements? Suppose you want to be an administrative assistant at a minimum salary of $18,000 a year. Assess the situation:

Goal: Administrative Assistant

Requirements	I have	I need
Data entry; Excel	Some skill	Brush up course; practice
Typing: 80 wpm	40 wpm	Speed practice
Shorthand	None	Introductory shorthand course
High school graduate	High school graduate	—
Some college preferred	—	Community college
Usually under 32	8 extra years of life experience	Courage and assertiveness
Neat, attractive, etc.	Not bad	One job-hunting outfit
Ability to organize time and work	20 years' experience in family	—

Activity 28 ॐ Evaluating Your Job Goals

Goal: _____

Requirements	I have	I need

Instead of getting depressed over what you don't have to offer, concentrate for a moment on what you do have. Rather than think you'll never be trained for the job, or that by the time you are you'll have one foot in the grave, consider how you can start getting what you need.

Traditional and Non-Traditional Jobs

I've chosen the traditional woman's job of administrative assistant in the example to illustrate how to evaluate a career goal because many women feel it's possible to do the job, the training period can be fairly short, and jobs are plentiful. Moving into the responsible position of executive secretary offers special challenges with appropriate rewards in some businesses.

Nevertheless, the financial rewards in a secretarial job will rarely be as great as those in the traditionally male-defined jobs in the skilled trades such as electrician, machinist, plumber. Just because you don't know anything about these trades doesn't mean you can't learn. Although women once were barred from almost all apprenticeship programs, it's possible to get into them. So along with checking out the secretarial and technical courses at the community college, why not see an adviser at the counseling or career center or women's programs office about training in the trades? Find out what each job pays, how long the training is and other pertinent information, as well as making arrangements to visit the classrooms. Don't overlook the possibilities in sales jobs either.

If you have several children to support or if you don't want to depend on a man to provide a house, car, or good life for you, it may be necessary to challenge the traditional employment system. To live well, you'll either have to be assertive and imaginative about creating a responsible job for yourself, or move up through the ranks, enter a traditional male trade, or spend several years getting professional training at a college or university.

For the earlier example, you could find out what computer skills are most in demand in your community, and what courses are offered at a community college, and gather information about costs and financial aid. Call the college to get information on courses and find out whether there's a women's center or a women's program office or career center. These often have special scholarships or information about financial aid and childcare. They may even act as your advocate with the financial aid office, and if you go there in person you'll probably meet other women who are in situations similar to yours. If you qualify as a "Displaced Homemaker" you may get help from one of the special programs designed for women who have been out of the job market while raising children. Perhaps the most important aspect of such centers is the warmth and understanding of both women staff and participants, many of whom have been where you are now.

GETTING AHEAD ON THE JOB

If you're already working at a job that seems dead-end, there are two major ways to change it without completely redirecting your career. First talk to your supervisor or personnel manager or the boss of the whole business about what you'd like to be doing and how you can work toward it. Suppose you're working in a fast-food restaurant at minimum wage. Tell the general manager you want to make more money and have more responsibility. If he or she replies to the effect that you would need managerial or technical skills, ask for specifics. Would you need classes, more experience, or to change the way you relate to coworkers now? Try to get specific answers and a commitment that if you did X, Y, and Z, you'd be given an opportunity to step up to management.

Whatever your job, make it clear you want to advance, find out how to do it, and arrange to have periodic evaluations on specific criteria. Even if you've mentioned to your boss that you'd like a promotion, you might not be taken seriously unless you follow through with a specific plan. Perhaps, like many people, the boss automatically assumes women aren't ambitious. He or she won't deliberately discriminate, but your ambition will have to be called to management's attention. Every time you read a book about your field or take a class, a workshop, or hear a lecture related to your job or the one you want, tell your boss about it. Put all those things in writing and have them available when you're evaluated.

Perhaps your company doesn't often promote from within its ranks or your boss doesn't happen to like you or appreciate your abilities. In that case, apply at other similar businesses or agencies. When you're interviewed, ask specific questions about what promotions you could expect within a specific time if you do the job well. Make it clear that you want to go as far as you can and don't be afraid to say how much you'd like to be earning a few years from now. Even if you're sure you don't want to leave your company now, it's a good idea to know what opportunities are out there. If you get a good offer it can do a lot for you even if you don't take it. You might want to tell your current boss about it, emphasizing that you want to stay where you are but that it's costing you money. (Whether this is good strategy depends on your individual circumstances.) Even if you don't want to use it as a bargaining tool, the fact that you know you can do better can give you much more confidence.

Another strategy for upgrading your job skills is to look for a company that has its own training program, pays for the education of certain employees, or gives you time off from work to go to school. Sometimes those opportunities go to men partly because women don't make it clear enough they're interested.

If you have evidence that management in your company discriminates against women, you can take your case to one of several government antidiscrimination offices or look elsewhere for a more promising job. The U.S. Equal Employment Opportunities Commission or your state or city office of Women's Rights, Human Rights, or Human Relations Commission will tell you your rights, how to establish acceptable evidence, and how to file a formal complaint. This takes a long time to gain satisfaction and can cause a good deal of emotional stress, so you'll need support from friends during that period.

Many books are available about how to succeed in business, how to decide on a career, and how to present yourself in the best possible way to a prospective employer.

HOW TO BUDGET YOUR INCOME AND EXPENSES

If you're not used to working from a household budget, it may seem too restrictive. But remember, it will tell you what you can do with your money as well as what you can't.

Activity 29 ᔧ Making a Budget

First, *list* all income you can count on for the next twelve months. Include wages after taxes and other deductions, child and spousal support, gifts, welfare, interest and investment income, and income tax returns from last year. If you're uncertain about the amounts, estimate low. If your husband has paid child support in the past, but only about one third of the amount that was court-ordered, that's the figure you should project. Divide the total by twelve so you'll know your average monthly income.

_____

_____

_____

_____

_____

_____

_____

_____

Next, list your fixed expenses for the next year, converted to monthly averages:

Housing: rent or mortgage, payments, upkeep . . . . _____
Utilities: heat, light, water, garbage, telephone . . . . _____
Medical and dental . . . . _____
Insurance: house, car, medical, life . . . . _____
Taxes: house, income . . . . _____

Now subtract the amount of your fixed expenses from your projected income, and decide how you'll distribute it for these day-to-day expenses:

Food: at home, school, and in restaurants . . . . _____
Clothing: yours and children's; cleaning and repairs . . . . _____
Transportation: bus, gas, car upkeep, car payment . . . . _____
Entertainment: evenings out, liquor, cigarettes, childcare . . . . _____
Household supplies: replacements, cleaning, supplies . . . . _____
Education: self, children. . . . . _____

Organizational dues and contributions. . . . . _____
Newspapers, magazines, books, records. _____
Vacations . . . . _____
Gifts. . . . . _____

If your monthly day-to-day expenses total more than the amount you got from subtracting fixed expenses from income, you have a problem. Unless you were supporting the man you recently left, you'll probably have a smaller budget after separation than before. But don't lose sight of the fact that you'll have total access to whatever money is available and total control of how it's spent, which can feel very good.

Go over the day-to-day expenses again, cutting here, adding there. Consider a job if you don't have one or a second job for a short while during the transition. Borrowing may be an option if you're sure you can pay back the loan on time. The main thing is not to pretend to yourself you're going to spend less or earn more unless you have a very concrete plan. Don't, for instance, cut out cigarettes if you've never been able to quit in the past. Don't cut out all entertainment, because you probably won't stick to the plan, and if you do, you'll pay a price in depression.

If your adjustments of day-to-day expenses still leave you short, review your fixed expenses for possible changes. Consider moving to a smaller apartment or sharing your house with someone. You might want to sell your car and buy a less expensive one that uses less gas or take a bus until you're in a better position. If you're tempted to let insurance policies lapse, consider very carefully. In addition to the risks that go with being uninsured for a period, you'll find it hard to get insurance after being uninsured and you may pay a premium three times what you're paying now. However, you might want to get different kinds of coverage than you've had.

WORKING FROM A BUDGET

During the first couple of months after separation, you might have to make adjustments in your budget as you discover previously hidden costs and adjust to changes in some expenses. You won't always have to account to yourself for every penny, but during this period of transition it's important to keep a careful record of expenditures. In a month or two you'll know what you can handle on your current income, and you can plan what to change so you'll have more options.

If you are an impulsive buyer, or careless or impatient about keeping records, you may want to put a certain amount of money in an envelope labeled with each category of day-to-day expenses. If you're dipping into the wrong envelope to pay for something not budgeted, at least you'll be forced to acknowledge it on the spot. If you leave an IOU, saying what the money was used for, you'll be able to adjust your budget at the end of the month to reflect reality.

An alternative is to pay almost everything with a check or put it on a credit card. When your monthly statement arrives, go over each item to find out how much you've actually spent in each category and compare it with your budget. If you do this, take careful note of how much you're paying for bank charges or interest, and consider what you might buy with it at the end of the year if you shopped with cash.

The Importance of Saving

You may think you can't possibly save on your limited income, but the more difficult it is to do, the more necessary it is. Even five dollars a month will give you a cushion for unexpected expenses. You'll feel more secure if you have a small amount set aside for a car repair or doctor's bill. As you earn more money, raise your regular savings deposit and put part of the extra income from bonuses, income tax refunds, and so on in the account. Try to build it up to an amount twice your monthly salary, and keep it in an interest-bearing account you have immediate access to. Money Market Mutual Funds are available free. They pay much higher interest than banks or savings and loans and don't tie up your money for any length of time. If you're like most people, you'll never put money in savings if you wait until you have enough extra. Take it right off the top, as soon as you're paid. In other words, "Pay yourself first."

Loans

If you're caught between the maxim "Neither a borrower nor a lender be" and the temptation to accept every offer to buy now, pay later, look for a middle ground. It makes sense to borrow, either for a special purpose or by regular use of a credit card, if you're sure you want or need the item and if you can be sure you can make the payments when they're due and without increasing whatever stress you already have. Add the total interest you'll be paying to the price of the item and then decide whether the combined figures are what you're willing to pay.

At the time you separate you might have a number of unusual bills for medical care, moving costs, or lawyer fees. Several bills may come in at once or be past due. If you're billed for insurance, medical care, and house taxes, try first to negotiate terms. Write to your creditors, suggesting a schedule of payments you're sure you can manage. If they agree, find out how much they will charge you for a longer payment period. If they don't accept your plan, consider borrowing. Gradually, you can get onto an evenly spread payment plan for all creditors and major expenses, either putting cash aside each month for such annual expenses as insurance, or paying a fraction each month. It may take a year to get your new system working smoothly.

When you borrow, you're paying to use someone else's money, and in general the longer you use it the more you'll pay. But interest figures vary from place to place and sometimes change within a very short time. If you decide to borrow, either through a loan or by buying a major item on credit, shop around. Find out what fees will be charged in addition to interest, and get precise information on interest rates. If you don't understand the complexities, ask how many dollars you will be paying out by the end of the payment period. You may be shocked to learn how much it is. In some cases you might be still willing to pay it to have the use of the item much sooner or because it's a necessity. Insist on a written statement of terms, read the installment contract carefully, including the small print, and when you've signed it keep your copy in a safe place. If you tend to get anxious about small print, take a copy to a friend you trust and go over it together. Don't be pressured into purchases (of money or things) by threats that this is the last time such a great offer will be made. You won't be able to tell if it's a great offer until you've compared it to some others.

If you borrow from a friend, relative, or man you're involved with, you may pay in ways other than money: You may postpone payment beyond the time necessary and set up feelings of guilt and resentment in both parties. Consider the possible consequences carefully, and put your agreement in writing, so you'll each know when the repayment will be made. You might want to pay a small amount of interest to emphasize the businesslike aspect of the relationship and so that the lender gets something in return.

HOME MAINTENANCE

If you own property or investments you'll need to learn or relearn how to handle them. Before anything goes wrong with your property, ask friends, neighbors, and coworkers to recommend carpenters, plumbers, electricians, and other repair people. Call all of them, ask their hourly rate, terms of their guarantees for materials and labor, and whether they charge for estimates. Find out if they'll come to your neighborhood on emergency calls and how long they usually take to respond to such calls. Unless you've been keeping close track of the cost and quality of work done on your house and have reason to trust the people who serve you, compare this new information with the costs and type of service you've had before. There's an advantage to continuous service, but you may also have paid top rates when it wasn't necessary.

If you have a major home maintenance problem, be sure to get several estimates before you contract for the job. By the time you've talked to the third person, you'll begin to understand the problem and you may want to talk to the first company to ask more questions. The lowest estimate isn't necessarily the best, but you won't even know what's low and what's high until you've talked to several companies. Ask them to put the estimate in writing and to itemize it. You may then be able to use the language of the estimate to get several more rough estimates by telephone, though you shouldn't accept a final one until the job site has been inspected.

If you can, watch the repair person at work so you can understand the problem and, if it's a minor job, do it yourself next time. Your interest will also be an extra incentive for the person you hire to do good work.

You'll be surprised at how much you can do on your own. Buy a few books on simple household repairs, invest in the tools the books suggest, and take a risk or take a class in household maintenance. You'll find that once you stop being anxious and have the right tool in your hand, you can do many repairs yourself.

If you need major expensive repairs on your house, don't panic. The loan picture changes so rapidly it's hard to know what to do other than to keep inquiring. A bank that gives no loans when you call at the beginning of the month may give you a different answer at the end. One bank may say "No," and another or even a branch of the same institution— say "Yes." If a credit union turns you down, a bank may accept you. Save yourself time and stress by calling a number of places and getting as much information as possible before you apply in person. Say whether you want a mortgage on your house, a home improvement loan (often available when others aren't), or a personal loan, and ask what, in general, is necessary to get such a loan or how they decide who will get it. They may give you a formula such as maximum mortgages are two and a half times your annual income or that your total debts, including the new loan, can't go over thirty percent of your income. To get that information, let them know you realize they have to look at your total financial picture before they can give you a loan, and be a little pushy about asking for their formulas. Ask what papers you should bring with you when you go for a personal interview.

When you consider where to invest money, or whether to refinance your house, or to buy for cash or credit, you'll need to understand the economy as it changes on a week-to-week basis. You may not know much about it now, but you can learn. Ask friends and colleagues to recommend a financial adviser. You may want to interview two or three before making a choice. Even if you're not sure which of them is giving the best advice—and like all professionals, they're likely to disagree—you'll have different feelings about how they do or don't explain things, or how closely they listen to what you want, and whether they understand your values. Your financial future is your future—get expert guidance from someone you feel is really concerned with your best interests.

OVERCOMING FINANCIAL IGNORANCE

If you find yourself resisting the opportunity to learn more about money, give some thought to why that is. It may be that, like many women, you've bought the message from the time you were very young that girls don't understand math, that women are frivolous and extravagant about money and really can't be expected to understand it. You may believe high finance is men's business. You may be scared and quite uncomfortable with feelings of inadequacy The way to overcome those feelings is to take one piece of the financial picture at a time and learn about it. There are many classes designed specifically for women to help them overcome their fears and ignorance. And it is ignorance, not stupidity, which means it can be overcome.

Another reason you may resist learning is that you still have the fantasy someone will take care of you all your life and that you'll be spared taking responsibility. Many men also feel that way and aren't good at handling practical matters. Men are forced to pretend they're knowledgeable so they won't appear less than masculine, but women are let off the hook. It's also easier for men to cover their mistakes because of higher salaries. Some women really have been taken care of by their men, but many find out too late that they weren't cared for at all. Just because your man made all the practical decisions doesn't mean he made the right ones. If you're willing to admit your ignorance and seek advice from various people, you may make much better decisions now that you have the chance.

At first you may see only the pitfalls of making decisions on your own and the burdensome aspect of responsibility for the consequences. You'll forget that you can find experts, as well as friends and family to consult with, and that your friends will help you pick up the pieces when things go badly. Later, you'll find yourself looking at some risks as the potential for success and an exciting challenge. You'll wonder why you ever let that man take away the good feeling that comes with standing solidly on your own feet.

CHAPTER 18

SEXUALITY

For many women, the decision to end an abusive relationship with a man means an end to sexuality as well. This is especially true if sexuality has been narrowly defined as orgasm through intercourse, and not as a combination of needs and desires that include affection, sensuality, and romance. Yet according to research, even orgasm hasn't been the reason most women engaged in intercourse, and it is not always what women miss most about the lack of sex.

Shere Hite, in a survey of more than three thousand women, found that only about 30 percent of the respondents experienced orgasm as a result of intercourse (though some had orgasms during intercourse but as a result of manual stimulation). Yet most women (87 percent) said they did like intercourse and that sex was important to them.[1]

Hite says, "The most frequent reason for liking intercourse by far was that it was time of great affection and closeness."[2] Many of the women she quotes speak of *being one with a man, of warmth, love, closeness, wholeness, security, feeling loved, wanted, important, and powerful.*

This chapter will give you some ideas on how to get your needs for intimacy and sensual stimulation met without intercourse. A first in that direction is to look closely at your own sexual desires and how they were satisfied—or not satisfied—in the relationship with the man you've left. As an aid in doing that, write the answers to these questions:

Activity 30 ✑ What Have You Enjoyed about Sex?

1. Do you enjoy affectionate touching?_____
What people do you especially enjoy touching, and which of them would you like to touch or be touched by more? (Think about friends, relatives, children, men, women, and even pets.)_____

_____

2. Do you ever touch someone or want to be touched for sexual arousal,

without wanting it to result in orgasm? How does it work out?_____

---

3. Did you ever have sex with the man you just left or another one mainly for the intimacy, closeness, warmth, security, or romance, rather than for orgasm? How often were you successful?_____

---

4. How important is sex in your life?_____

---

5. How often did you have orgasms with your ex-partner? Did they usu-ally come about as a result of intercourse, clitoral stimulation by him or you, or other sexual activity?_____

---

6. Were you unable at times to have orgasm with your ex-partner dur-ing intercourse? _____ What would have helped?_____

Did you ask for what you wanted? _____ If not, why not?_____

---

7. How often were you left disappointed or frustrated after intercourse?

Did you ever fake orgasm? _____ How often? _____ Why?_____

---

8. Were you ever sexually abused or humiliated by your ex-part-ner?_____ How often?_____

9. Are you ever left feeling frustrated or disappointed after masturbat-ing? _____ How often? _____ Why?_____

10. What other sexual activity do you enjoy? How important to you are kissing, breast stimulation, caressing of hips and thighs, general body touching, caressing of vagina, oral vaginal contact, your caressing of your partner? _____

Which are important in reaching orgasm?_____

11. In the best of all possible worlds, what would sexuality be like?_____

LEARNING TO TRUST YOUR EXPERIENCE

If the questionnaire has been difficult for you to complete because of lack of knowledge about your own body and the nature of orgasm or nonorgasm, don't give up yet. Orgasm is a controversial topic when it comes to women. Through much of recorded history it hasn't been acknowledged that women could even derive pleasure from their sexual activities. Intercourse was seen (and still is by some) as a procreative function, entered into unwillingly by the female, forced by the male.

Whenever the subject of female sexuality and particularly orgasm has come up, the so-called experts have disagreed. Sigmund Freud promoted the idea that only immature women had clitoral orgasms whereas mature women had vaginal orgasms. Not until the 1966 Masters and Johnson study was there scientific evidence that women orgasmed through clitoral stimulation. Millions of women who had doubted the reality of their own experience were validated, yet more recent findings indicate that women are capable of vaginal orgasms as well.[3]

Experts can both dispel myths and create new ones, which makes it hard for us to know how much to take on scientific "faith," when to doubt authorities, and when to trust our own experiences. And that's complicated by the fact that some of our beliefs directly affect what experiences we have.

Many of us have been persuaded by experts that women aren't nearly as sexual as men and that men, because of their greater sexuality and vast experience, know and understand more about female as well as male sexuality. So we treat our male partners as experts and listen to them rather than to our own feelings. We do the things that seem sexiest to them, without saying what we want, for fear of seeming strange, wrong, sexually immature, too loose, or too prudish—or for fear of hurting or embarrassing them by casting doubt on their expertise.

There is clearly one area you're an expert about and that's what feels good to you and what doesn't. Regardless of whether it "should" feel good, or whether you've been told it's normal or the way women are supposed to feel, you're the authority. If you've been hesitant to tell a sexual partner what makes you uncomfortable or what you'd like him to do, this is a good time to get clear about what you do and don't like and to resolve to ask for it the next time you're in a sexual relationship. On the other hand, you may be without a sexual partner for a while either by choice or through lack of an attractive enough opportunity. Such a condition can be tolerated, and even enjoyed, if you give yourself options to gain pleasure in a variety of ways.

SEXUALITY ISN'T JUST SEX

Sexuality is made up of affection, sensuality, eroticism, intimacy, and romance and probably almost everyone would like to have a relationship that includes all of that. But if that's what you're longing for, there are some important questions to be asked: Was your partner affectionate? Sensual? Erotic? Intimate? Romantic?

Although it's true that there is a magical quality to life when these five components of sexuality come together in one relationship, it doesn't happen very often, so it will be useful to look at each separately to determine how to meet each need independently.

Affection

Affection can be expressed verbally, but more often it is a physical expression of caring for a person by hugging, patting, or stroking. Some people are quite free with their affectionate touching, others reserve such expression for intimate family members or long-term friends. If such an expression of friendship or concern is important to you, look at your patterns of getting those needs met and consider changing them if necessary.

For instance, if you've reserved affectionate contact for the family or friends you're close to, let yourself open up to touching new acquaintances and potential friends. Women in many groups—for instance, at some YWCAs or NOW chapters—interact in an affectionate style. You may want to explore several groups before becoming involved with the one that best suits your needs.

If you do have friends you'd like to touch more, don't assume that they don't want it too. Let yourself stroke a friend's arm, or put your arm around her shoulders, or give her a hug when you're feeling good—or sad, or lonely, or especially close to her. Pay attention to whether she feels uncomfortable. Ask her how she feels about expressing friendship by touching, or say, "I'd really like to hug you now, okay?" And unless you get a negative response, do it. You might want to review Chapter 13, Reaching Out.

If, like many women who've been in abusive relationships, you have no friends or family available, there are still some things you can do to meet some of your affectional needs. Get a cat or dog or another pet that has almost unlimited pleasure in being stroked and makes virtually no demands. Of course, it's not the same as what you can get from a person, but it will help. And after what you've been through you can stand some affection from a creature who expects very little from you and doesn't criticize you at all.

Sensuality

Sensuality is an important part of sexuality for many people and on a continuum of stimulation or excitement it falls somewhere between affection and eroticism, having some of the characteristics of both.

Sensuality refers to the gratification of the senses or appetites. The more intensely you become emotionally involved with the pleasures of your five senses, the more sensual you are. For instance, hearing music, smelling or tasting food or drink, looking at paintings, sculpture, or snow-covered mountains, or touching or being touched may give you great sensual pleasure. Though the context is different, the feelings may be similar to those you have in a sexual relationship.

What are the greatest sensual pleasures of sex for you? The touching of an entire body by another whole body, exploring crevices, curves, and angles that otherwise you hardly know exist? The sounds of juices flowing, of your partner's panting, satisfied moans, or your own gasps or cries? The smell of your partner's body? The salty taste?

Think about other activities in which you gain similar satisfactions. If there are few, consider which ones you might develop. You might indulge in a weekly full body massage. If a professional is too expensive, trade massages with a friend. Or massage yourself slowly and lovingly with an aromatic body cream. Contact sports, running, and swimming can also provide satisfying physical stimulation.

Develop your appreciation of visual and auditory experiences by really looking and really listening. Put aside some time for visiting art galleries, looking at lakes, or mountains or sand or trees—just looking without any purpose other than the visual experience, without analysis or judgment. Do the same with music, experimenting with symphony, jazz, rock. Let yourself feel sad or lighthearted or excited. Dance to it if the spirit moves you. When everyone else has gone to bed, read poetry aloud.

It may take some time to develop your sensual nature fully, especially if you've previously relied on sex with a partner to satisfy you completely. Part of this development is remembering to notice. *Notice* when you enjoy running your hand over a velvet pillow. *Notice* when a singer's high note or a trumpet's call sends "chills up and down your spine."

The next thing to do is *enjoy*. Often, when you unexpectedly experience a sensual reaction, you'll immediately sense that a surge of longing threatens to follow it, a longing for that particular man and sexual intimacy with him. When you feel that threat, you're tempted to stamp out the sensual urges to deny the longing. Maybe for a while that's what you'll choose to do, but you don't have to. You can learn to enjoy sensual experiences for their own value, not just as a prelude to, or reminder of, sexual intimacy. And if you want to, you can let them build in an explicitly sexual way until you're ready to treat yourself to an orgasm.

Eroticism

By eroticism I mean orgasm and the explicitly sexual arousal and tension that is most often associated with it. For some women this may be the aspect of sexuality that is longed for most, yet it's the easiest need to meet without a partner.

If you've been telling yourself that the "right" or "normal" or "mature" way to have orgasm is during intercourse with a man, start telling yourself now that the "right" way is the way that satisfies you without hurting anyone else. And if you haven't learned the pleasures of masturbation you might want to begin now. If masturbation is something you "give in to" and try to get over with quickly, consider looking at it a different way. If you think of it as something shameful, either because of moral or religious training or because it's something only sexual "losers" do, you might want to reevaluate. Almost everyone has masturbated at some time, religious and nonreligious people, those who are in good relationships and unsatisfying ones, and those who have no sexually intimate relationships.

If you're going to masturbate, you might as well get the maximum pleasure from it. You probably don't appreciate a "Wham bam! Thank you, ma'am!" approach from a man, so why treat yourself that way? Use your sexual urges as an opportunity to appreciate your physical and sexual being. Take it slowly and be loving and affectionate to yourself. Once you become used to your own caring and satisfying touch, you'll be less likely to settle for less.

Intimacy

Intimacy implies first of all closeness; it also means warmth, depth of relationship, familiarity, and affection. Shere Hite's research indicates that women enjoy sexual intercourse because of the intimacy they experience. Here are some of the things women wrote about the reasons they like intercourse:

"The touching and tenderness then makes me feel warm and secure, safe and close."

"I love intercourse. It feels really close, like he is really mine and cares for me."

"It is a time when I get his individual attention, and feel very loved and secure. "[4]

These and the other answers quoted from *The Hite Report* indicate that reassurance of a special man's love, and being close, are important aspects of sex for many women. We can assume that for many of Hite's respondents, intercourse caps a relationship that is warm, close, and reassuring in other respects. But it's also clear that a certain number of women feel close to their lovers only during intercourse.

Take a second look at your responses to the questions at the beginning of this chapter and consider them in relation to the satisfactions, care, communication, security, and intimacy you experienced in other aspects of your relationship. If it was rare for you to experience those feelings except during sex, perhaps that indicates a serious flaw in the relationship. If you didn't get those satisfactions even during sexual intimacy, then you're not missing so much after all. When you're tempted to believe you're missing an intimacy you actually had, read the list of pleasures you did and didn't get and consider whether you're longing for a lost dream rather than a reality, or even a potential reality, with that particular man.

All of this doesn't mean there isn't a special wonderful quality to sexual intimacy, but there are other close relationships that, if not quite as exciting, are sometimes more reliable and ultimately satisfying. Review the section on Moving from Acquaintances to Friends in Chapter 13.

Romance

Regardless of how well you organize your life, neither your successful career, your delightful children, good friends, sports or art activities, nor the joys of masturbation provide quite the same excitement as does romance. It's this special quality of romance and the search for it that gets many of us into trouble.

In defining romance the dictionary uses these words: "heroic," "colorful," "chivalrous devotion," "supernatural appeal to the imagination." Another definition is: "A baseless story usually full of exaggeration or fanciful invention." Synonyms for romance are "story," "fiction," "falsehood," "fable."

Our longing for romance is often a longing for the unreal. Real life is hard for many of us. It can be tragic, boring, lonely, frightening, or oppressive. Sometimes there's nothing we can name that's wrong with life, so we tell ourselves we shouldn't feel depressed or restless, yet there's something missing. What we crave, often, is that unreal something called romance.

As discussed more thoroughly in Chapter 5, romantic love is often a kind of addiction that lifts us out of our everyday doldrums. Falling in love is a very special experience, one that ought to be treasured but not expected to continue indefinitely. A continuous fall will eventually end in a crash. At this time of your life, if you think you're too vulnerable to risk falling in love, you need to look for other ways to rise above the tedium of everyday life.

There's an overlap between sensual and romantic pleasures, and you can experience both through drama, music, and art, which lift you out of the daily rounds of chores and nuts-and-bolts reality. They put beauty into your life and help you make imaginative leaps. If you have a little money that you normally spend on beer or the hairdresser or lessons for the children, set aside enough instead to go to a movie, concert, play, art exhibit, or dance program. Choose whatever is likely to grip you, whether it's country music, ballet, a sculpture exhibit, or science fiction film. Let yourself be transported without indulging in a fruitless longing for the other kind of romance. Enjoy the experience for itself.

If you really have no money to spare, plan your television-watching carefully so that you're not using it to kill time but watching something that truly captures your interest. Avoid the "soaps," which focus on the tragic aspects of love and problems like your own.

An important part of romance is the suspense. Will he call tonight? Does he love me? What if he finds out I'm not as wonderful as he thinks? The very things that often make a new romance tortuous are the same tensions that make it deliciously enticing. And to the degree we allow ourselves to be transported, we risk serious damage to our egos, careers, life goals, and the ability to be in control of our lives if the object of the romantic feelings doesn't feel the same way. Yet this is one of the few risks in life that most women don't hesitate to take.

There are ways to compensate for the lack of that romantic excitement in our lives. Any activity that carries with it the risk of loss, rejection, or failure and of winning, acceptance, or success can provide a similar titillation.

Sports provide the best arena, since they allow for the sensual pleasures of the body as well as the opportunity to win or lose either publicly or privately, alone or with teammates.

Art also provides suspense. Art doesn't necessarily mean the creation of a great painting. Writing a poem or experimenting with watercolors or modeling clay will stimulate you to develop skills you may think you're "not good at" but may never have tried. Art includes many media: crocheting, cabinet-making, playing the recorder, creating macrame, ceramics, photography, woodwork, upholstery, and many, many other activities you can do at home alone or with friends.

Business or other career involvements also may include excitement and risk. Any career, including parenting, can involve you in learning, creating, risk-taking, and the stimulation of peak experiences. Short-range, one-time adventures can give you a thrill that's similar to romance. Anything you've been afraid of trying, whether it's climbing a ladder or a mountain, can provide a feeling of suspense and anxiety, success or failure. The "small" pleasures you can find daily or even hourly are at least as important as those occasional dramatic happenings. A sunny fall day can be experienced as a sensual marvel rather than as wasted because you can't share it with a lover. Remember that romance is sometimes low-key and don't compare each small pleasure with the fireworks at the height of romantic excitement.

An important part of romance that often makes the risk worthwhile is the ego-enhancement of knowing someone really believes we're the most wonderful person on earth. Even though our minds tell us the absurdity of such a view, it feels mighty good. To be adored, to be thought brilliant and clever and good and beautiful is intoxicating, so what can substitute for that?

Nothing, really, except some drug, perhaps, that allows for an equal amount of fantasy. But part of the joy of competing in sports or of developing other talents is in basking in the praise and appreciation of others. You don't have to be the best to get it, either. If you knit a sweater or create a beautiful garden that gives you pleasure, your friends will tell you it's terrific and you're clever to have done it. Not that you're perfect, no. Still, it feels good. That, and developing the ability to admire yourself, will help you to get along better without a lover's romantic illusion that you're perfect.

If each week you hug your good friends several times, masturbate, focus on the sensuality of music, nature, food, or art once or twice for several hours, play on a team or run or swim once or twice, and create something of your own, whether decorating a cake, running a small business from your home, or designing a stained-glass window, you're certain to get some excitement from taking risks and to enjoy being appreciated by other people. You won't have much time to pine for that man and the sexuality you associate with him.

LESBIANISM

Much of the discussion in this chapter on sexuality and in the next on romance focuses on women with or without male partners. Yet a significant percentage of women are additionally or attracted only to other women. For some, lesbianism is an early choice, while others come to the realization only after years of relating to men sexually and often after having been wives or mothers. While there still exists disapproval of lesbianism, the last decades have brought greater public acceptance of the reality of women loving women.

Lesbians teach school, win custody battles, are congresspeople, tennis stars, actors. Lesbians are in every field, just as there are gay men. Being openly lesbian is not a decision to be taken lightly, yet many women find they're comfortable for the first time in their lives when they accept their same-sex orientation and adopt a lesbian lifestyle.

A number of women find it easier to form egalitarian relationships and to meet their needs for affection and sexuality with other women. Certainly all the problems of intimacy aren't solved. Battering even occurs among some lesbian couples. But many women find that a common style of emotionality, nurturance, talk, and sexuality make it easier to solve problems and bring out the best in each other.

If you think you might be at least as attracted to women as to men, don't deny it. Think back to your sexual impulses as an adolescent and young woman. If you were attracted to other women at that time, it might have been "just a phase" or it might have been the truest expression of your sexuality. You're the only one who can know that, and it may take you awhile to think it through.

Wanting to touch or hug another woman doesn't mean you're a lesbian. If you're afraid of being misunderstood you can avoid it by being sensitive to the other's feelings. If your affectionate gestures are met with a cool or ambivalent response, you have only to back off to reassure the other person. You don't have to act on your affectionate or sexual impulses toward a woman any more than you do if you're attracted to your friend's husband or a strange man on the street. You might feel sexually aroused and want to follow those feelings or you might want to pass right on by them in favor of building a good, solid nonsexual friendship.

What if you do want to follow through on those feelings, not only toward a particular woman but women in general? These days there are many books published, by and for lesbians, that explain what lesbians do and how they feel. Most cities have at least one gay or lesbian organization, and colleges and universities with women's resource centers have referral and drop-in services. There are networks for lesbians living in rural areas and many newspapers and periodicals to connect you to others.

It is important not to be threatened by your feelings and to realize that even if you do decide to act on them you may not be a lesbian.

Throughout history, societies have recognized that people can be bisexual. That is, they're capable of being attracted to both sexes, even though most people deny or repress attractions to people of the same sex.

This book is about, among other things, making real choices. You can't make choices until you investigate your feelings and learn to accept them. Fortunately we live in a time when choosing a woman lover can be seen as a healthy and positive option. Whether you choose to exercise that option is up to you.

CHAPTER 19

THE NEW ROMANCE

They say there's nothing like a new romance to heal the wounds of the old one. If you're lucky and careful enough to find a man who treats you well, your lonely hours may be reduced to a tolerable level. You'll have concrete evidence that men can be loving and affectionate without threatening or abusing you. If you don't let it become addictive, such a relationship can be helpful in getting you through the rough times after your separation from the batterer. Whether or not it turns out to be forever, you'll want to be careful who you choose this time.

WHAT ARE YOU LOOKING FOR IN A PARTNER?

The first step in developing a healthy, nurturing relationship is knowing what kind of man you want. And the best time to think seriously about the question is when you have no special man, so you won't pretend to yourself that your new man perfectly fits the description of what you want.

List the characteristics you'd want in a man, including those you think you have no right to. For instance, if you don't consider yourself smart or good-looking, you probably won't think you deserve a smart or good-looking man.

Activity 31 ∽ What I Want in a Man

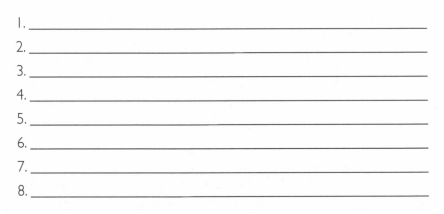

1. _____
2. _____
3. _____
4. _____
5. _____
6. _____
7. _____
8. _____

9. _____

10. _____

11. _____

12. _____

Now *add* to the list whichever of these characteristics you find attractive in men: dominant, worldly, confident, aggressive, unemotional, independent, funny, affectionate, smart, sexy, dependable, personable, expressive, dependent, submissive, insecure, modest, artistic, interesting, family-oriented.

Put parentheses around each characteristic you'd be willing to do without if there were other important ones. *Underline* the ones that are absolutely essential.

List the characteristics of the men you've been involved with, including the man who abused you. How many of them had the traits you now say are essential? If few of them did, what are the other characteristics they had in common, if any? In other words, what was it about those men that "hooked" you even though they didn't have the qualities you say are most important?

Activity 32 ♋ Characteristics of Men I've Been Involved With

1. _____

2. _____

3. _____

4. _____

5. _____

6. _____

7. _____

8. _____

9. _____

10. _____

If there's a pattern, you can use it to be wary of certain kinds of men and suspicious of your reactions to them. For instance, if essential characteristics are "kind," "considerate," and "good-natured," yet you were involved with three men who lacked those qualities but who were either "sexy," "good-looking," or "good dancers," recognize the contradiction between what you want and who you actually choose. Then you can be especially careful when you're attracted to that kind of man. The man you choose to go dancing with may be very different from the one you want to live with. If you're attracted to a good dancer who's bad-tempered, then dance with him, but don't invest yourself emotionally and if he begins to mistreat you, walk quickly to the nearest exit. If you're romantically or sexually attracted to a man, it doesn't follow that you should love or marry him.

Consider the possibility also that you're not attracted to kind, considerate, good-natured men. Maybe you just think you ought to be, but usually you find such men dull. Perhaps you've bought society's message that a "real man" must be adventurous, tough, and keep you guessing. If you added to your list quite a few of the first six characteristics listed after Activity 31, you're looking for the stereotype of what a male is supposed to be. The trouble is that a man who's developed most of those characteristics is likely to be a controlling kind of supermale, and he is likely to expect you to be a superfemale—that is, to have the opposite of his characteristics. He might be the kind of man who abuses a woman who doesn't conform to his expectations.

WHAT IF YOU KEEP FINDING THE SAME KIND OF MAN?

If you've frequently become involved with abusive men, it's either because you tend to find them in more or less the same places, something about them attracts you, or something about you attracts them.

Abusive men are found in all classes, races, ages, at all educational levels, and in all employment categories. However, there are families, neighborhoods, taverns, and social groups in which it's looked upon as okay for men to beat their women and battering may be more common there than in groups where at least lip service is given to the idea that battering is unacceptable. Men who drink or use drugs excessively probably batter more than those who don't, even though their drug use doesn't necessarily cause the battering. Women who abuse drugs or alcohol are more likely to be beaten, simply because they may lose control of their environment. If you're in a high-risk environment, you'll have to look hard and be extremely careful to find a gentle, considerate man. It will be safer to move to a different neighborhood, stay away from certain crowds, and make an entirely new set of friends. If that doesn't change things, then you should look into yourself.

Family Patterns

Although a few women who've attached themselves to several abusive men may believe they deserve punishment, it's not a typical pattern. There are other reasons for a woman's involvement in more than one battering relationship. Many people find mates with whom they repeat the kind of relationships they formed with a parent. This sometimes happens even when they didn't like that earlier relationship and consciously looked for something different.

If you were emotionally or physically abused by a parent, you may unintentionally continue to find abusive partners because that's the intimate pattern most familiar to you. You meet a new man and feel some sense of excitement or comfort or both. It's warm and familiar to you, a little bit like coming home. Only later is it clear that the comforting familiarity is similar to what you experienced as a child. Whatever else it may be, the feeling is known to you and therefore seems safe. It may even be that a nonpunitive intimate relationship is so alien you feel insecure and uneasy with it and don't know how to react.

List the characteristics that best describe you, your mother, and father (or parent figure) and compare them with those of your intimate partners (Activity 32). Pick out the ones that most of the men in your life have in common and see whether they are much like those of a parent. That will tell you whether you have a tendency to find partners like your father or your mother—or whether you seek the opposite traits of one of them.

Activity 33 ᗡ Your Family Characteristics

1. _____

2. _____

3. _____

4. _____

5. _____

6. _____

7. _____

8. _____

9. _____

10. _____

If you regularly become involved with a person who's similar to an admired parent and yet who abuses you, consider whether there's a previously unrecognized streak of abusiveness in the parent. Perhaps you've called it independence, humor, protectiveness, or strength and when you've found it in your romantic relationships, it's more like selfishness, sarcasm, control, or stubbornness. In that case, think about the precise meaning of each of those traits and when you meet a new man, consider whether there's evidence of that trait. You may not be able to tell for sure until you've seen the man in a number of situations, including stressful or embarrassing ones.

In your search for the opposite of a parent who was abusive and who was also alcoholic and lazy, you might make the mistake of assuming an energetic nondrinker can't possibly be abusive. That might cause you to overlook some early signs of a potentially destructive relationship.

Repetition of Patterns

If you were in love with a man who seemed quite different from your abusive parent and discovered the similarity too late, think back to an early point in the relationship when you felt uncomfortable about how he treated you but let it go without complaint. Ask yourself what it was you wanted that caused you to overlook the discomfort. Keep pushing your memory back to the earliest point. Do the same thing with each relationship in which you didn't realize what kind of man you had until you were already deeply involved.

Define as precisely as you can what you wanted or were trying to avoid. Perhaps you were afraid to risk hurting the man's feelings, so you didn't say you disliked his plan for your evening. If you're often compliant because you're afraid of hurting someone's feelings, start being considerate of your own feelings and heighten your awareness of what you want and enjoy. Review the Rights List (Activity 6) and the Be Good to Yourself section in Chapter 11. Maybe you didn't want to pay your way, so you felt you had no right to object to the restaurant he wanted to take you to. Maybe you were afraid that if you told him you were hurt or insulted he'd become angry and leave, or if you asked a question he'd think you weren't very bright. Is it a pattern you learned trying to prevent abuse from a parent? The man might have interpreted your passivity to mean you cared so little for yourself that he could easily abuse you.

If there's a clear pattern, you'll find it easier to know where to begin making changes. If you habitually let people's unacceptable statements go unchallenged because you're afraid of appearing stupid, you can begin changing now. Enroll in an assertion-training class or force yourself to begin speaking up in a variety of situations and with different people.

When you have some practice, you'll be willing to tell a new man your opinion whether you expect him to like it or not. You'll find out at the beginning of the relationship whether he's going to use the opportunity to insult your intelligence. If he is, you can leave before he becomes seriously abusive and before you're so involved it's hard to do.

Avoid the Appearance of a "Soft Touch"

Many women are drawn to men who call forth their nurturance and protectiveness, which makes them vulnerable to the very men who may be especially likely to mistreat them. Men who had difficult childhoods, were mistreated emotionally or physically by parents, served time in jail, or have drinking problems often seduce certain women into feeling sorry for them. The women believe they can compensate for the men's troubles by loving them. Many abused women have said, "I thought if I just loved him enough for long enough, finally he'd believe in me and trust me and learn to love himself—and he wouldn't want to hit me any more." If you have the urge to rescue, steer clear of men who call forth that response in you. If you're prone to guilt feelings, you're doubly vulnerable, because when you want to separate he'll trigger the guilt by saying he can't get along without you and you're cruel to abandon him.

If you're the woman on the block to whom children bring stray cats or wounded birds, if your heart—and money and time—goes out to anyone who has suffered, abusive men will spot you very quickly. When you're with someone new, there's nothing wrong with being warm, but try not to let him know your weakness for troubled and inadequate people. Part of the problem here is that you let men choose you, rather than deciding who you want to be with.

None of this means there is something wrong with you or that you want to be punished. It does mean you have to take special precautions to avoid abusive relationships. It means you should go slowly in becoming involved with new men and continually question yourself about their behavior and motivation, your feelings and responses, and the character of your interactions. When you find yourself "falling" for a new man or being sought by one, use the list of traits for your ideal man from Activity 31 to evaluate whether he's really the one for you. If he isn't, don't stay with him while waiting for someone better to come along. Stay uninvolved and begin an active search in the places you're likely to find a man who will be good for you.

You can't always predict whether a man will be a batterer, because some are gentle and considerate during the dating phase but change radically soon after marriage or when the woman becomes pregnant. But if you let the relationship develop slowly, in most cases you can save yourself heartache and injury. Here are some other things to look for.

Activity 34 ❧ Questions to Ask Yourself about a New Man

1. Can you state particular characteristics of his that you love?. . _____
2. Can you give examples of them?. . . . . _____
3. How many essential characteristics of your "ideal man" does he have?. . . . . _____
4. Does he accept your right to decide if you'll use birth control?
5. Does he think it's a wife and mother's right to decide whether to work at a paid job?. . . . . _____
6. Is he willing to have you spend time alone, even if he'd like to be with you? . . . . _____
7. Is he glad you have other friends? . . . . _____
8. Is he pleased at your accomplishments and ambitions? . . . . . . _____
9. Does he think women can and should be as wise, worldly, confident, strong, decisive, and independent as men? . . . . _____
10. Does he sometimes ask your opinion? . . . . _____
11. Does he both talk and listen?. . . . . _____
12. Does he tell you when his feelings are hurt?. . . . . _____
13. Does he think it's okay for men to show they're weak or vulnerable and to cry sometimes—aside from right after he's abused you?
14. Is he able to express affection aside from the times he's sorry for abusing you and when he wants, or you're having, sex?. . . . . . . _____
15. Are there some special traits about women (ability to express emotions, willingness to be vulnerable) that he admires? . . . . _____
16. Does he like and admire his mother or sister?. . . . . _____
17. Does he have good friends?. . . . . _____
18. Does he have interests besides you?. . . . . _____
19. When angry does he break or throw things?. . . . . _____
20. Does he lose his temper suddenly over small things, especially when he doesn't perform as well as he'd like?. _____
21. Does he ask you about other men in your past life?. . . . . _____
22. Does he want to know where you've been when you've been out?. . . . . _____
23. If you stay out late, does he insist on an explanation? . . . . _____
24. Does he believe husbands should make the important decisions?. . . . . _____

25. Does he think there are any circumstances in which it's okay for a man to hit a woman (for instance, if he finds "his woman" with another man)? . . . . _____
26. Is he jealous of your friends or relatives? . . . . _____
27. Does he think you're with another man if you're not home when he calls?. . . . . _____
28. Does he think you're going to "cheat" on him when you talk to a man or dance with an old friend?. . . . . _____
29. Does he think men should earn more than women? . . . . _____
30. Does he especially want boy babies and associate fathering boys with masculinity? . . . . _____
31. Does he think you have enough education, even though you want to go to school?. . . . . _____
32. Does he get angry if meals are late, or the food isn't just right? . . . . _____
33. Does he have the traits that often "hook" you into involvements with abusive men?. . . . . _____
34. Does he take over when you're having trouble doing something, whether you want him to or not? . . . . _____
35. When he's hurt, does he act angry instead?. . . . . _____
36. Does he silently sulk when angry? . . . . _____
37. Does he drink or take drugs almost every day or go on periodic binges?. . . . . _____
38. Does he ridicule you for being stupid or for characteristics that are "typical of women"? . . . . _____
39. Do you like yourself less than usual when you've been with him?. . . . . _____
40. Has he spent time in jail?. . . . . _____
42. Was he abused as a child?. . . . . _____
42. Does he sometimes put you on a pedestal, saying he doesn't deserve you? . . . . _____
43. Are there some qualities you especially like about yourself that he disapproves of or ridicules? . . . . _____
44. When you've acted independently, has he sometimes called you a "women's libber" or "dyke?" . . . . _____
45. Has he been in fistfights or hit other women he's been involved with? . . . . _____

If you have many "no" answers for the first eighteen questions, if you haven't many answers to question three, or you have many "yes" answers to questions nineteen through forty-five, the man in question is likely to be abusive. Look especially at the answers indicating anger that comes easily and is expressed destructively, that is, he breaks things or sulks rather than stating directly what has made him angry and asking that something be done about it. Be wary of a man who's jealous or doesn't want you to be well educated or to have many friends. Look out for a man who shows contempt for women or thinks it's unmanly to express affection or admit vulnerability or hurt feelings. If you can't name the characteristics you love in him and you don't feel good about yourself when you're with him, be suspicious of yourself. Be especially suspicious if he has some of the traits that attracted you to other abusive men.

GIVING UP CONTROL

In the beginning of a relationship it may be difficult to spot the ways you give up control. It feels good to be with a new man and you think nothing could possibly go wrong. But listen carefully to the things you're careful not to say, comments that might break through illusions he has about you, point up a difference in opinion, or risk having him think you're wrong or stupid. Count the times you're silent about your legitimate grievances because you're afraid of hurting his male ego. Notice the times you shrug and say, "Oh, well," to yourself. For instance, "I disagree, but . . . oh, well, I guess it doesn't matter, so why say anything?" In the long run all those little things will become big things that do matter.

The first thing to go might be your opinions about politics or other subjects you think he knows more about than you. Next you become silent when he criticizes friends or family members. You don't tell him much about how you spend your time or money because you're afraid of his criticisms. Then you begin to "walk on eggshells," waiting for him to be in a good mood before bringing up certain topics. He makes more and more of the decisions about the things that concern you both (whether to go out to dinner or stay "home" at your house) and becomes more decisive about the things that should concern only you ("You don't need to go to school; I like you just the way you are.").

Perhaps each time he makes a decision about an aspect of your life, you interpret his action as wisdom, leadership, superior intellect, or an ability to rise above mere emotions. Like many women you've looked for a man who's smarter and more experienced than you to fulfill your romantic ideal. You then have an investment in maintaining that image of the man, and it becomes important for him. You confuse superiori-ty—real or imagined—with control and being controlled with being taken care of.

From Control to Abuse

Control and abuse are closely intertwined, though physical violence is not always a part of the picture. Control, in itself, seems to be almost addictive for some men. The more they get, the more they need. Their self-concept is severely threatened when their women seem to be slipping out of their control. These men begin by making decisions about how to spend the couple's money; soon they decide what the woman should wear or how she should act. Since the scope of approved activities becomes very narrow, the occasions for doing the "wrong" thing and being punished by psychological or physical abuse become frequent. And that increases a feeling of helplessness and dependence, which in turn causes resignation to even more control.

PROTECTING YOURSELF

To avoid becoming involved with a man whose "protection" becomes control, develop your own ability to protect yourself and to control your own life. That means a whole range of activities—from moving furniture or understanding something about how your car works to carrying out plans for a better-paying job and managing on however little money you have.

We all want to be taken care of to some extent, in some ways, at some times. If you're occasionally depressed, a good man will fix you some tea, rub your back, and do the laundry (and you'll do the same for him). He'll take care of you *when you want it,* without taking advantage of those low times to increase your dependence on him. He won't try to make your decisions or take over your jobs when you've made it clear you want to stand on your own feet even when it's hard. If you have mixed feelings about maintaining your independence because you feel weak but want to practice being strong, your new man may be confused about how to act. Talk to him about your feelings (and about his probable ambivalence toward rescuing you). Either he'll have to be very sensitive to your attempts to be independent or you'll have to negotiate an agreement that he'll resist the impulse to take care of you unless you directly ask. You'll have to agree not to give him mixed messages by frequent hints for help or helpless sighs when you don't know what to do next.

When you do need help, it needn't always be from a man. You can find women who teach mechanics, repair plumbing, and who are willing to share their knowledge and skills. Each time you successfully struggle with something alone, or accomplish a "masculine" job together with other women, it strengthens your belief that you don't *have* to have a man but can choose one when you want to. That's part of your self-protection.

Establish Limits

Remembering that you can choose when you want to be with a man will help you to involve yourself slowly. Even if you want to spend every night with him, don't do it. Several evenings a week tell him you have other things to do. Practice enjoying a good book, doing some work around your home, or sharing the company of women friends. If he insists on knowing what you do when you're not with him, or if he tells you he can't be parted from you even for a day or two, he's probably becoming addicted. If you give in early in the relationship you'll find it hard to exercise independence later. When you try, he'll probably feel threatened and in turn threaten you. You'll be right back where you started, but with a new man.

The beginning of the relationship is the best time to establish limits, although it's hard because you may want to please the man and be with him constantly. It's important to separate what you want from what he wants, even if at this point nothing seems to matter much but being with him. If one evening you feel like going to a movie and he wants to stay at your house to watch TV, you may be tempted not to mention the movie or immediately list the reasons why you'd rather stay home after all. *Don't do it.* Establish right now that you're a separate person with desires of your own, apart from his. That doesn't mean you shouldn't compromise. Just be sure you state your preference and that you get what you want some of the time. This is even more important if he's paying for the date. If you think that gives him the right to make all the important decisions, you're setting the scene for a relationship in which you'll never have equal power.

If you feel you're losing control of decision-making, it's far better to go out less but pay your own way more. However, if he earns three times your salary, there's no reason you can't agree that he'll pay three quarters and you'll pay one, and each of you will have an equal part in the decision-making.

Don't take on wifely or motherly duties right away, either. It's fine to invite the man to dinner occasionally, but don't let him assume he can join you for a meal any time he drops in. When he does come for dinner, ask him to do the dishes or part of the cooking. The important thing is to keep some time and space and decision-making to yourself. Once you let him make certain assumptions about your availability and compliance, it will be difficult to establish your independence.

One of the ways women are sometimes seduced into destructive relationships is through the comforts a man with money can provide. When you're tired, discouraged, and struggling to make ends meet on a welfare budget, late child-support payment, or meager paycheck, a generous man can be hard to resist. And when he pays, it's tempting to let him have his way, take you to the places he chooses, buy you clothes he likes to see you wear, and pay for vacations that would never be your first choice. Or it's easy to go along with other things he wants of you because he buys you gifts, helps with the rent, or takes you to places you could never afford on your salary.

If you tolerate activities or statements you would normally challenge because you're afraid of losing the man and all those nice gifts and the outings you can't afford, you'll be putting yourself in a position for potential abuse. To change that situation, renew efforts to earn more money by taking classes or making other long-range plans. Work double shifts for a while, ask for a raise, or find pleasures that aren't expensive. Women are often underpaid and this advice isn't easy to follow, but in the long run it pays off in better feelings and more control.

If you tend to let men do as they please as long as they pay your way, ask yourself what the money means to you. Is it important only for what it can buy, or is it tempting because you enjoy the feeling of being taken care of, of not being responsible? If the value is mainly in being taken care of, remind yourself that sooner or later the bill comes in and with an abusive man it's very high. You'll need to protect yourself by making friends who are interested in mutual caring and who don't exact a price.

What Do You Tell a New Man?

Another way to protect yourself from a controlling or abusive man is to keep your previous relationship with the abusive man to yourself. When you're with a new man, you may have the urge to pour out your life story, especially the terrible experience you had with the man who battered you. Resist the temptation. No matter what he says about it, no matter how hard he tries to convince himself otherwise, you take the chance that such an admission will reduce his respect for you, especially if you continued a relationship with a batterer for a long time. Even though you both agree it shouldn't have that effect, in the back of his mind the idea may lurk that you were abused once and you could be controlled and abused again. It may rise to the surface at a later time when he wants you to do something you don't want to do.

Even if you're in love, even if you're going to marry eventually, there's no rule that says you have to tell a man everything about other relationships. If he asks, you needn't make up a story but can simply say, "It's past, and I'd rather not talk about it." If he persists in questioning you about past relationships, it may be a warning that he's unreasonably jealous and possessive. Later, when it's clear you've become an independent strong person who cares for herself, telling him will have a different effect.

Proceed Slowly

Perhaps you're beginning to see why I advise not being closely involved with a man during the first year of separation. It's much easier to struggle with the hundred-pound sandbag if there's no one ready to toss it easily into the sandbox. It's easier not to cry too often if there's no handy shoulder to lean on. It's easier to make mistakes and learn from them when there's no one to relieve you of that responsibility. And it's much easier to learn to get along on a very slim paycheck if there's no one near to slip you a five-dollar bill, buy you a television, take you out to dinner, pay the babysitter, buy your cigarettes. You can pay your own way if you have to, but if you don't have to, it's tempting to say, "Well, why *not* be dependent? Why *not* let him take care of me?"

Pay special attention to the difference between wanting a rest and wanting to retire. Even if it's satisfying to take care of yourself most of the time, there will be times when you're sick, feel tired, burdened, overwhelmed with responsibilities. These are the times when you should be especially careful. Along comes Mr. Right, he helps you make some important decisions, pays off one of your debts, and oh, it feels so good to lean on someone. You like being taken care of.

Don't confuse this momentary restful lull in your exhausting routine with a lifetime of being financially and emotionally dependent. If the man says he'll marry you and you can quit work and devote yourself to the children, does that mean he will want more children? Do you agree about that? Does it mean that when you're ready, you can go back to work without the least objection from him? Does it mean that when you want more independence he'll feel as good about your taking care of yourself as he does now about taking care of you? Don't just think about those questions, and don't just ask him. See how he reacts when you spend time with other people, when you do things for yourself, when you refuse financial help.

Give the relationship at least a year before you make a decision to move in together, or marry, or have a child together. Not only does love blind people to the loved one's faults, those faults often temporarily disappear. When they're newly in love, stingy people suddenly feel generous; gloomy people become cheerful; rigid people flexible. A big part of the intoxication of love is the changes in one's self. One tends to believe the changes are permanent. The best way to tell whether they are is simply to wait a year.

If you live alone for a year, without complete involvement with another man, you'll begin to know yourself. If you don't like all that you come to know, you'll begin to change some things and as you become better company for yourself, you'll become better company for other women and men. You'll get pleasures out of being by yourself sometimes as well as from being with friends and coworkers.

When you meet an attractive man, you'll say, "I'd like to be with him," rather than, "If he doesn't want me, I'll die." If the attractive man begins to take advantage of you, control or threaten you, you'll tell him immediately that you don't like it and won't put up with it. If he persists, you'll say good-bye and mean it. You'll be going ahead with your life, even if you'd like to be involved with a man, but if you can't find a man who's good for you, you'll make it just fine on your own.

CHAPTER 20

THE LONG HAUL

You're finally free. You've gotten safely through the crisis stage of leaving and reorganizing your life. You keep telling yourself you should feel great . . . and you wonder why you're depressed instead and if the emptiness you feel will ever go away.

Believe it or not, there are some benefits to being in a continual state of crisis. There's always something that must be done immediately, and feelings of fear or rage can sometimes mobilize you into action. If you've had to make several moves, job-hunt, cope with the children, deal with your ex-partner, and learn quickly how to survive on your own, you may not have had much time to feel depressed or lonely. But sometime after you've finally settled into a more stable routine—a week, a month, or three months after you leave the man—you may begin to experience the hardest period of all.

LEARNING TO COPE WITH LONELINESS

Perhaps when you're lonely you become irritable, or keep to yourself, or are especially self-critical, or find it difficult to sleep. Maybe you get a perverse pleasure from looking sloppy or having a cluttered house. Each person has a different way of coping with loneliness. If your individual ways are destructive and increase the problem, try behaving as if you're not lonely. Make a point of talking to one person a day in person or on the phone and make at least two plans for the weekend with other people.

If your lonely moods aren't immediately obvious to you, learn to recognize their early signs in order to control them before they get out of hand. Notice changes in your sleep, TV-watching, eating, and drinking patterns. Increased consumption of food or alcohol or lack of appetite are likely signs of depression, which in turn may be a sign of loneliness. When you notice one of these patterns developing, substitute an opposite activity or something that will give you the same satisfaction without the guilt. When you feel like an afternoon nap, go for a walk. When you want an extra piece of chocolate cake, treat yourself to a bubble bath.

Make a coping plan during a time when you're feeling on top of things. Write the plan out, so that when you first notice you're slipping into a lonely state you can put it into action.

Activity 35 ∽ Coping Plan for Loneliness

What I Do When I'm Lonely
Snack all evening alone

What I Can Do
Brew some special tea, start that long historical novel I've always wanted to read

_____

_____

_____

_____

_____

_____

_____

_____

Loneliness may never completely leave you. It haunts nearly everyone occasionally, whether we're actually alone or not. So don't assume a love affair will necessarily banish the empty feeling. Remember, too, that even an excellent relationship can end with sickness, death, or unexpected divorce, so your ability to create your own satisfactions and excitement is the best insurance against loneliness in the future. That same capacity for enriching your life as a single person can add to the quality of a new love relationship when the opportunity arises.

The satisfaction of having responsibility for your own life is also the anxiety of having to take care of yourself. It's a new experience, almost a new job, and it will feel frightening for a while, so allow yourself time to become used to it. The fears and loneliness won't go on forever, and in the meantime, you're learning how to cope with them. Here are some more ideas for getting through the hard times:

Find out what makes you feel up and down. Anything that makes you feel useless, lazy, helpless, or out of control will contribute to your feeling low. Be especially alert to self-critical statements that accompany your low periods (see Activity 15 in Chapter 10).

Pay attention to how you feel after you talk on the phone or in person to your friends or family. If you feel sad when you hang up or leave them, ask yourself if that's the way you usually feel after talking to that person. If so, stop calling or seeing them. If it's someone you really must speak to regularly, keep the conversation short and refuse to discuss things that make you feel sad, angry, guilty, or lonely. Do something that lifts your spirits as soon as you hang up or are alone.

Notice if there are special times of the day or the week when you miss your man more than usual. Do something different at that time from what you did when you were with him. If he sat across the breakfast table from you every day for twenty-five years, have breakfast in a different room or go out for coffee. Try to change the habits that are associated with being with him, so it isn't as noticeable that there's someone missing.

Be equally aware of what makes you feel good. If it's been a long time, you may have to experiment with new activities. Go to places where you feel comfortable or pleasantly excited. Get a radio or CD player. Play music that cheers you and makes you feel energetic, not music that reflects your low mood. Never play love songs.

YOU MAKE YOUR OWN LIFE

You may go through a period in which you're not acutely miserable, but life has lost its savor. You ask what happened to the ecstacy that comes from intimacy, the trust and security that come from long-standing friendships and the stimulation of new experiences.

The short answer is, "It's where you make it happen." You have to make those friends, then risk letting the relationship deepen to a more intimate level; you have to work at overcoming difficulties, developing trust and allowing yourself to be vulnerable, until new friends become old friends. You have to look for new experiences, take the risks, and find new rewards. You also have to know what you want from a lover and see that you go where you're likely to find the right kind of person.

It's up to you, but you don't have to do it all by yourself. The right person, or better yet, the right group, can give you both support and courage.

Group for what? Courage for what? Possibly you don't know yet. The longer you've been involved with an abusive man or married or a mother, and the longer you've been out of the job market, the less certain you probably are about who you are and what you might enjoy. So this is a good time to find out. You're free to do what you want without the constraints of a man who easily feels threatened or who says everything you want to do is too independent, expensive, or silly. (I'm not forgetting the constraints of children and poverty for a single woman. They're important but can be worked around.)

Reactivate Your Dreams

Now is the time to rise above the sameness of your days and explore the risk of testing your abilities, the expansive feeling that comes from intellectual, physical, social, career, or psychological growth. Perhaps you've been taught that while everyone, of course, wants all that, it's just adolescent nonsense to expect it. Maybe you believe mature people settle down to a dull life and make do with what they have.

It may, indeed, be impractical to recapture and act upon your girlhood dreams. This may not be the time to go (with or without the children) off to Hollywood to become a star. But don't count it, or anything, out until you've come up with some good reasons why you can't or don't want to do it. If you really "always wanted to act," don't go to your grave saying that regretfully. Get out and join a little theater group or take acting lessons at a community college.

Acting is just one example. It could be mountain climbing, skiing, learning archaeology, dress designing, studying medicine, sailing, painting, coin collecting, car racing, horse grooming, landscape gardening, hairdressing, hiking, nursing, joining an encounter group, camping, "swinging," singing, teaching, being a mathematician, taking up ballet, upholstering furniture, skydiving, gourmet cooking, car repairing, interior decorating, skating, biking, white-water canoeing, visiting different churches, getting into politics, joining a rap group, or joining the neighborhood campaign for good government.

The list can be endless when you let your imagination play. But you may have trouble getting started, so think back to the things you wanted to be, do, or have when you were young. Turn back to Chapter 2 and look at your answers to Activity 1. *Make a new list,* using ideas from your previous answers and your own memory. *Underline* all the items you might like to try if there were no obstacles in the way. *Put a $ sign* after each one that requires money, a T after each that takes more time than you seem to have, a C for each that's difficult because of child-care responsibilities. *Put an A* after each that requires more ability than you think you have (brains, beauty, personality, strength, etc.), O for any you think you're too old to begin, and P for those you might do if you lived in a different place.

Activity 36 ᎭᎭ Recapturing Your Dreams

1. _____
2. _____
3. _____
4. _____
5. _____
6. _____
7. _____
8. _____
9. _____
10. _____

If age or ability or place are major factors holding you back, chances are you can overcome those barriers with enough determination. Lack of time and money are likely to be more difficult to contend with. But before you give up, estimate how much time, money, or other items you lack. How much of it do you need? Be as specific as possible. Decide what you're willing to sacrifice in the short run for long-run satisfactions. How much money would you need to go to school, how many years would it take to develop a particular ability? If you don't know the answers, call an employment or educational counselor, community college Women's Center, travel agent, or whoever might give you specific information. You may want to review Chapter 17 for ideas about how to solve money problems.

Abilities Can Be Acquired

If a specific ability is the big thing you think you lack, it's probably a skill that you can acquire with practice and some instruction. Some people do have what seems like a natural gift for certain achievements, but often we don't know what our "natural" talents are until we try them out for awhile. Have you ever admired a craft done by an amateur or read a story that was not great literature but that pleased you? Have you watched the thrill of a child when a blob of clay resembles— even slightly—an animal? If you'll let yourself, you can recapture that childlike pleasure. It's not the great product or prize at the end of the rainbow that's the thrill—it's the process of getting there. You can feel yourself growing as you learn new skills, whether your small steps are visible to anyone else or not.

If you're going to escape boredom, loneliness, and depression, you have to take some chances—though the risks won't be nearly as great as those you took each day of your involvement with a violent man. More important, you can be in control of just how much risk you're ready to take at any particular time, and you can arrange to have supportive people and other rewards available to comfort you when you feel scared or don't measure up to your own standards.

Take each item on your list that you wish you'd done when you were younger and note which ones still appeal to you. That is, if you could have it happen magically—if, with a snap of your fingers, you could have the brains, talent, beauty, youth, or time to make those dreams come true, which of them would you still want?

Modify Your Dreams

Modify each of those dreams to something related that you can easily do now. If you always wanted to be an opera star, you can still take singing lessons or sing alone with a recording. If you wanted to build houses or cabinets, you can scrounge some scrap lumber and make a dollhouse for the kids or put together a bookcase for yourself. If you wish you'd studied architecture, you might enroll in a community college drafting course or start reading books about architecture from the public library. If you'd like to be a world traveler, but lack time and money, find out where you can see travel films, send for maps of places you'd like to go, and start planning and saving. Meanwhile, explore the parks, museums, and neighborhoods in your own city. If you "would have been an artist except that you lack talent," take some drawing courses, or try pottery, jewelry-making, or macrame. Don't assume you lack talent until you've worked hard to develop a skill.

WHAT CAN YOU DO NOW?

List all the things you'd like to do that take only a little energy, time, money or skill. *Add* activities that will develop skills related to the "talents" you wish you had. *Mark* two of them to begin this week. If there are others that appeal to you, but that would take elaborate planning or a good deal of money, don't discard the ideas. Later you can make a long-range plan to encompass them.

Activity 37 ᴄ᷍ Start Now List

1. _____

2. _____

3. _____

4. _____

5. _____

6. _____

7. _____

8. _____

9. _____

10. _____

Never mind, for now, which you're most interested in. Choose the one you can start tomorrow. The sooner, the better. If you find you're stalling, saying you don't want it enough, do it anyway. Act as if you're eager to devote the time or money to it. Get started. Make the telephone call, gather the materials, check out a book from the library—but get going. Right now it's not so important what you do, as that you do something.

Whatever you've chosen will probably be hard work at first, but as you see yourself developing you'll discover new activities and interests can be very exciting and rewarding. You'll then be on your way to creating your own life's excitement.

From time to time it may be difficult to find energy for new activities. Read Chapter 11, A Courageous Act a Day, as often as necessary. As soon as possible get involved with other people—through classes, clubs, or special-interest groups—who have similar interests. There's an excitement that comes from talking with others about shared work, paid or unpaid, that can be as stimulating and intimate as a love affair.

I speak of "work" where others speak of recreation or hobbies, because to gain the most satisfaction you should treat the activities you do like a job. Devote yourself to them regularly, take them seriously, and try to improve your skill. This doesn't mean you can't do many things lightly as well. But if you haven't been able to find paid employment that valuable and absorbing, you need to develop another activity that's important to you.

Most of us live narrow lives without taking advantage of opportunities to learn or to be stimulated. Check your newspapers for coming events. Note how many you're not interested in and ask yourself how many of them you've never actually tried and know almost nothing about. List those you might experiment with and try one new thing at least once a month.

When you do take up a new sport, hobby, or "work," don't stop until you've given yourself a chance to practice it quite a bit. Then if you're satisfied you're not going to like it, try something new. Even if you take up something different every couple of months, it will be valuable to find out what you don't like. It's one way of getting to know yourself better and learning to appreciate your individual tastes. When you meet lots of people and have new experiences, you'll be too busy growing, learning, and changing to be bored or depressed.

Remind yourself that it will take time to build a new life and that whether you're feeling good or not, you can tough it out. Even with ups and downs, in the long run you'll have a much better life than the one you left. In the next chapter you'll get some ideas about how other women adapted to their new lives.

SECTION V

THE ONES WHO GOT AWAY

CHAPTER 21

THE ONES WHO GOT AWAY

Why do they leave and why do they stay away?

Very little is known about what enables women to develop the strength to leave an abusive man and to create a life that is satisfying. Theoretically, women who leave and stay away should have the opposite characteristics of those who continue the relationship. We ought to be able to say about a woman who left a man after years of battering, "She reduced her economic dependence by getting a job," or, "She stopped feeling emotionally dependent on him ," "She stopped loving him . . . felt better about herself . . . changed her ideas about traditional values and the role of the father as head of the household. . . ." But it isn't necessarily so. Many women leave *in spite of* continuing feelings of emotional dependence and love, and in spite of poverty, isolation, and traditional values.

To get firsthand descriptions of what it's like to break away from a violent man, to stay away, and to discover a new way of life as a single person, I asked nine women to tell me their stories. They answered my questions about their feelings and relationships before, during, and after their involvements with the men.

Most of this chapter is about their lives as single women, but so that you may know something of what they endured in the abusive relationships, I'm including very abbreviated versions of their life stories. In some cases I have used initials, in some fictional names and slightly altered facts, and in some real names, according to each woman's preference.

LIFE WITH THE BATTERER

Jan

Jan was married at seventeen, right after high school graduation, and has worked and attended school for most of her married life. Her husband, Ron, was often unemployed and floundering in his career as a salesperson. Jan, at twenty-four, is an exceptionally assertive person and has been as long as she can remember. No one would have called her dependent at the time of her marriage, yet now she has questions about that. "I would say I was not dependent. Yet I felt the only way I could get out of that situation (living with her mother and a violent stepfather) was to marry someone. I didn't think I could get out by myself. I was feeling real scared, even though everyone said, 'Oh, Jan, she's such a strong person.' "

Jan, in fact, was the dominant person in the relationship with her husband. She was the worker, the planner, the organizer. Unlike many abused women, she was neither socially isolated nor economically dependent. She was convinced that she could overcome the marital difficulties by "persistently loving Ron and talking to Ron." "He didn't hit me all that often, at most, six times a year. Sometimes, he might go five or six months, so that gave me hope. I was very much afraid of his outbursts, his uncontrollable anger."

Jan left him several times, once for nine months, after which he didn't hit her for two years. But when it happened again, she left him for good. She has made a very satisfying single life for herself.

Sandi

Sandi says of herself, "I was so introverted in junior and senior high school that no one ever talked to me, only Ernie." He fathered her twin sons, who appeared on the scene shortly after her eighteenth birthday. But that relationship didn't last long. Bringing up mixed-race children alone was not easy and when Merle came into her life, she was glad to have some help, to be "rescued," in fact. She had been dating him only a short time the first time he hit her. "I opened the door and his arm came at me, he just smashed my whole body to the floor and broke my nose." After a couple of other hits, Sandi retreated to her parents, who sent her to Tucson to stay with an aunt. She was so lonely there that she called Merle, who brought her back to Seattle. Periodically, she called on him to rescue her, but she always paid a price in physical or emotional abuse.

Merle never hit her during the times she lived with him, but he found other ways of abusing her. Sandi, who was on welfare, was expected to pay all the household bills, even though Merle had well-paying jobs with the city. He refused to admit that the twins needed food or clothing so that she had to sneak these basic necessities to her children.

The second time Sandi went to a shelter was final. She has now been away from Merle for more than two years and is discovering exciting things about herself in community college classes.

Patricia

Patricia met Tim when she was in a foster home at the age of fourteen. "Tim came in saying, 'I'll be your mama, I'll be your daddy, I'll be your world.' " And I never had one, and I took it. I felt like I knew him and we were of the same cut or something. In the beginning we had fun together and we were two wild ones, let me tell you, he could keep my pace. He's still the same. I grew up.

"I was with him for six years, from the time I was fifteen and he was seventeen." During these years Patricia attended high school and worked as a prostitute. "The worst I was beaten was when I was first out on the street. He broke my nose, broke out a couple of teeth, broke my tailbone. After a while people at school knew what was going on, but they didn't say anything."

After several miscarriages, Patricia gave birth to a baby girl. "As the kid got a little older it got to be mind abuse as well as physical abuse, but Tim's physical abuse would be only every three or four days instead of every day, the way it had been."

Finally, Patricia left for the last time three years ago, putting several hundred miles between them. She now lives with a man who is "the opposite of Tim," and she's planning to learn drafting at a community college.

E. S.

E. S. was a twenty-three-year-old radio technician student in her native Philippine Islands when she began a correspondence with the man she was to marry. Pete was an acquaintance of her cousin and had been living in the United States for some years.

After a year of exchanging letters and pictures, Pete went to the Philippines to ask E. S. to marry him. She was almost twenty-five, and having turned down four marriage offers, was becoming concerned about whether she would ever marry. In addition, she had fallen in love with Pete's picture. Almost before she knew it, she was married to this fifty-three-year-old farmer and was embarked on a new life in the United States.

Their life in the States was one of constant hard work in the fields, and E. S. supplemented their farm income by working as a hotel maid. She also cared for their daughter, who was born two years later, and a son, born three years after that.

From the beginning, Pete lied to her, denying, for instance, the existence of his ex-wife and five children, pretending his oldest daughter was his sister, even after E. S. had met them. Insisting that E. S. sit in the cold in the car, waiting for hours while he visited that other family, was one of the first of many humiliations she suffered. The humiliation was worse than the physical abuse.

Four months ago, after thirteen years of marriage, she left Pete. She was no longer able to persuade herself it was God's will. E. S. has already passed her GED test and is starting electronics school through a government program.

Virginia

Virginia had an adventurous life before she became involved with Bob. In the sixties she left Seattle to work in the civil rights struggle in the South. Later, her company transferred her from Seattle to Anchorage. In those days, before the pipeline boom, there were few black people there, which perhaps exacerbated the loneliness she had felt. Nevertheless, she did have some friends, and it was through them that she met Bob, who was gentle, kind, and romantic.

After they were married he continued to display those traits at times, while at others he was morose and uncommunicative. His was a "Jekyll-and-Hyde" pattern common to many abusive men.

Virginia was twenty-five when she married this thirty-five-year-old father of four boys. Immediately after the marriage, she became an instant mother to three of his children and maid to the household of males. Although she felt used and demeaned by Bob from the start, the physical violence didn't begin until they had been married several years and the boys had returned to their mother.

It took Virginia three years to regain the confidence she had lost during the first five years of her relationship with Bob and to gather the courage once again to strike out on her own. She has now been divorced for three years and is a student, with plans to be a counselor or teacher.

Marilyn

Marilyn, now in her early thirties, loves a good time. Married at nineteen, she was "true blue" for the duration of that six-year marriage. But once out of it, she devoted a good deal of her nonwork and nonparenting time to partying. Monty, whom she met during the first year after the divorce, became a part of that life. He was "sneaky" from the start, and the relationship was volatile, but not violent.

Only when Marilyn said she wanted to break off the relationship did Monty become physically abusive. He had said, "Once you tell me that you're going to be mine, I'm never lettin' you go," and to her sorrow, she later realized that he had been serious. He followed her, harassed her, and threatened both her and each new man she began an involvement with. The reign of terror culminated in his forcing her car off the street with his car and threatening her with a gun. Neighbors intervened.

Marilyn took him to court and now feels relatively safe as a result of the "no contact" order she obtained. She has begun a new relationship with a man she enjoys being with, but she worries that he too is destructive to her. For the first time in her life she is beginning to think about making real choices about her life.

Corrine

Corrine says she cried at her wedding. "I felt I'd betrayed myself and realized I didn't like Marty enough. I was wretched, but my mother and sister encouraged me to go through with it anyway."

During the first year of marriage she became pregnant, she and Marty "fought and fought," and there was "emotional upheaval all the time." Although Marty hit her "in fun" during the first few months of their involvement, it wasn't until the fourth year of their marriage that he struck out in anger. Her injuries during the next seven years included small cuts from broken glass, a black eye, bruises, and a broken nose. Perhaps even harder to take, he was involved with four women in a period of four years.

Although Corrine acquired a bachelor's degree and a teaching credential, she "couldn't imagine taking care of the kids"—two girls, now nine and ten—"without a partner, having to do everything myself."

Corrine, at thirty-five, is divorced, has lost custody of one of her children, and has not spoken to Marty for well over a year except on essential business. She has an unsatisfying relationship with another man, has not been able to find a teaching job, and is still undecided about whether she wants to be an artist or a social service worker. Nevertheless, she has no questions about her decision to break up the marriage.

Shirley

Shirley grew up in the South and is still very much a traditional Southern woman in some ways. At forty-five, she has been a suburban housewife and mother of two for twenty-five years.

Shirley speaks of emotional abuse and sexual humiliation as the intolerable aspects of life with Clarence, her engineer husband. Only when questioned specifically about it does she say offhandedly that yes, he was physically abusive, too. One of the things he did to her was to push her down the stairs when she was pregnant.

He criticized her cooking, her housekeeping, and everything about her. He was so rude to everyone that they had no friends. Through the years, Shirley became convinced that she was incompetent to do anything, so that now, six months after leaving him, she worries about whether she'll even be able to rake the leaves adequately.

Shirley had several strokes, which she attributed to the stress of living with Clarence's abuse, yet even long hospitalizations didn't worry her enough to propel her out of the marriage. But when Clarence put their thirteen-year-old daughter out of the house, Shirley finally gained the strength to separate from him. After six months she is slowly learning to regain her ability to handle everyday tasks, her health has vastly improved, and she's considering taking up the nursing-school classes that she dropped twenty-five years ago.

Valerie

Valerie, at sixty-four, has also had a struggle learning to take care of herself after forty-two years of being alternately protected and slapped around by an alcoholic man with whom she fell in love at twenty.

Valerie still admires Jim's mind, his ability to understand international politics and remember the information he absorbs from his reading. For forty-two years he was her window to world affairs. But almost every weekend he was drunk, and periodically she would become the victim of his violence.

Two years ago she left him for good, and she now enjoys handling her own money, meeting new people, and learning new things. Although she is partially disabled from a youthful bout with polio and a later stroke and heart attack, she is managing a fairly independent life in a senior citizens' apartment building. She would take Jim back in a split second if he would stop drinking, but she doesn't believe he will.

THE UNEXPECTED

In earlier chapters I noted what you might expect to experience right after leaving your man and at various periods during the first year or so. Those experiences are common to many women.

You'll find, though, that you can't predict quite how you'll feel or what you'll do. Each woman's experience is both the same and different from others'. Below are some of the surprises that these particular women have experienced after leaving violent men.

Although Shirley often feels sad and lonely since leaving her twenty-five-year marriage six months ago, that's not the whole story. She says, "My health is surprisingly good since Clarence left. And I sleep so well. I thought at first something must be wrong with me, because I can go to sleep at night. And my daughter said to me that I ought to be sorry. My whole family has broken up, so why am I so happy?"

Now, after eight months of total distance from Monty, Marilyn says, "I never thought I'd feel so good about being on my own and sometimes I really feel great about it. It surprises me that there are times when I can't even imagine being involved in a relationship with a man."

Patricia was surprised to find that leaving Tim didn't solve all of her problems. "There were things I blamed totally on him 'cause he was messin' with me so much. I think a lot of women will do that. They think the grand person who they are, inside, will just bloom once they get out. Everything will be just fine. But no, I still have a lot to change. Like, I drag ass. I have to be inspired to do something. I always thought it was him holding me back from doing the things I wanted to. It's just me. I don't push myself when I should. For a while I was in a stage where I thought, 'He did it to me!' Now I realize it's up to me to change it."

Virginia had a similar rude awakening when she finally got away after six years. "I thought I would be happy and I wasn't. I thought I would be independent and self-confident and have high self-esteem and really enjoy life. But I didn't. I thought it was the marriage that made me depressed. I thought the anxiety was around the boys and Bob, but I'm still (three years later) quite anxious. I thought marriage would just solve everything and it didn't. And then I thought divorce would solve everything and it didn't. It was sort of a low blow to my ego that I had a couple of problems, too. I'm working on them, but I still have them."

Corrine also found a number of unexpected difficulties. The most profound disappointment was that one of her daughters chose to remain with Corrine's ex-husband. "I never considered that either girl would leave me. It was a great shock." In addition, Corrine at first felt "anger and shame about public assistance, social workers' investigations, the legal system, and the divorce trial," and there were continuing problems in finding or choosing stimulating relevant work and being always poor or broke and worried about money and the kids.

Nevertheless, when Corrine was asked what things have been easier than expected about being a single woman her emphatic answer was, "I've had no regrets about leaving." She was also surprised that some very immediate fears of retaliation from her ex-husband didn't happen after all. "He hasn't hunted me down yet. Apparently, he's respected the authority of the restraining order, and after coming to my house three times, has taken seriously my threat to call the police."

Jan thought she'd never be able to manage rugged backpacking trips again, since she and Ron had always done them together. "A few weeks later I met Mary (who also was used to taking such trips with a battering man whom she'd just left) and I realized I could do it without him. I realized I did have the skills and those I didn't have I could learn. And I could make up for muscles with the right kind of equipment."

Jan had other pleasant surprises during the first few weeks after leaving Ron. "At first I thought I'd be lonely. That lasted just a couple of weeks, though. I started taking all those classes. I took six different classes, a different one every night: "What to do when your husband or wife walks out," "Intimacy," "Wilderness camping" . . . then after I was away for about a month I started liking living by myself. I didn't expect that to happen. I think I thought I'd just keep myself busy until I went back to Ron."

Jan had been pessimistic about her future. "I was damned sure last fall (one year ago) that I was never going to be happy again—not until I got back to Ron. I did not expect to do all this growing this year."

THE GOOD OUTWEIGHS THE BAD

As you can see, it's not at all unreasonable for you to fear being lonely, poor, depressed, or otherwise unhappy after you leave that violent man. Almost no one says it's a bed of roses, and nearly all admit to having bad times at first, with some continuing for quite a long time. But, on balance, all say the bad times are worth it, because the rewards of the new life are more lasting or more important than the painful times.

Shirley: "I'm about as lonely (after six months) as I was when Clarence was here. But I think it's worse when there's somebody in the house with you and you're still lonely, and you know it shouldn't be this way, but it is."

Virginia: "I like myself better, with all my flaws. I used to hate myself. I hated myself for being there. For believing all that crap. At least now I'm not worrying about, 'Oh, why am I doing this.' "

Patricia: "I had a lot of fear (before I went into court over custody). I guess what you'd say is my soul is washed of him. I don't carry around that fear anymore."

GETTING THROUGH THE STRESSFUL DAYS

One of the things that all these women have learned is that even though some bad times must simply be endured, there are ways to cope with the

stressful and dreary days so they're less painful or don't last so long. The
methods of coping exhibit some striking similarities, as well as a high
degree of individual imagination.

Loneliness, especially on weekends, nights, and holidays, is a pervasive problem for many women during the first year that they're not part
of a couple.

Patricia: "Weekend nights would be the hardest. I'd see couples going
out and stuff. I'd just grab up my kid and go to a girlfriend's house who
had kids and me and my girlfriend would let the kids play and sleep while
we had a good time. If I was at home I'd try to find little things to distract me. I'd try to be real good with the kid, so I wouldn't feel guilty
when I put her to bed. And then I'd write big plans about what I wanted to do."

Shirley: "I cannot go into Fred Meyer's on weekends when it is such a
husband-and-wife store. We used to go there on weekends and buy tulip
bulbs and grass seed or whatever. I don't want to go there on weekends
'cause it will make me feel bad. All those couples . . . and they probably
go home and fight like cats and dogs!"

Virginia: "Holidays and weekends were hard. I didn't stay home but
spent them with friends. I lived with a friend who was divorced and we
helped each other. She was really supportive to me."

Sandi: "I can con myself into being in a good mood. I can recite what
things are good about me and what I really want to be and I like that. I
don't depend on somebody else."

Valerie: "I was a little bit depressed but I found Barry, a good friend.
He took me under his wing and we became fast friends. I think he's filled
in the gap of being lonely. I've got to have somebody and I'm still fighting that, but I'm getting better. Now I can stay home two nights a
week—maybe three—by myself, instead of running to Barry. I'm also
going to the library and reading books, which I never did before."

Marilyn: "At first just being alone was real hard to accept. I can't really remember when it stopped being hard."

Jan: "I had a real hard time last Christmas. I didn't send out any
Christmas cards last year. I didn't know how to sign my name—Jan?
Ron? Thanksgiving I volunteered to work and in the evening I went to
Donna's house for a nonfamily Thanksgiving. It was fun but it just was-
n't Thanksgiving. I had always spent it with Ron's folks."

Corrine: "I've done volunteer work, made new friends, I write letters
to old friends, write in my journal, swim, walk, read, paint, take courses,
job-hunt."

HELP COMES FROM UNEXPECTED SOURCES

In the relative isolation of an abusive relationship, it's hard to imagine that you won't be alone if you separate from the man. Yet, help comes through agencies, shelters, and friends and relatives, sometimes unexpectedly.

Patricia: "My girlfriend from Utah moved here. Hot mama, one and two! That's just somebody who knows everything about me! We're like teenagers sometimes. Somebody said we're like primates picking out fleas, and we are. We give each other that kind of attention. She's the only one I'll do without for. She sat in court with me every day for eight hours."

The group leader at the shelter was helpful to Patricia, too. "I asked myself how flowery was she going to be. I was suspicious of social workers in general. And then here she was, cussing and confronting people and I thought *this* woman's for *real.* She's not going to feed me a line. So when she told me something I trusted it.

"The shelter was real helpful. They would come up with things I never dreamed of, and when somebody is that willing to help, you get real enthused about helping yourself. For a long time I only socialized with people at the shelter. I didn't want to go 'out there' yet."

Shirley (separated for six months) doesn't yet socialize much and found it hard to tell the few neighbors she talks to that she was getting a divorce, but it finally came out. And after twenty-five years of being told she couldn't even rake the leaves right, she gains solace and encouragement from seeing how these other women manage. "Marion is very nice . . . . She comes over and helps prune away a dead bush. She's very capable because her husband doesn't do a darned thing so she's had to learn all these things. Sandra raised four kids by herself and I guess she had to learn absolutely from scratch. Her husband was one who had done everything before. It can be done, I guess."

Particular women at a shelter had a positive impact on Sandi. "Every time I left, I intended to stay away forever. I think the only reason I did the last time was because of the people at the shelter. I was saying to these people, 'How could you go back? And they were saying, 'How could *you* go back?' I was saying to Vera, 'God, someone did that to you and you still care about him?' She got mad; she said, 'Look at *you.* Who do you think you are to tell me that when you do exactly the same thing?' And she was right. But not just anybody who hadn't been hit could say that to me and get away with it.

"Joan never talked much, but she had a real impact, being around someone who's been in that situation for twelve years and got battered for twelve years. It's easy to do it little by little but when you see somebody who's done it for that long it's easier to say, 'I'm not going to do it for twelve years. One more is going to make three.'"

Valerie finds solace in the friendship and help of a man. "Barry's eighty-six years old; he's a big-hearted fellow willing to do anything. We all need a man to fix this or fix that and he does it for every woman in this building. We have a nice friendship going and that fills the void of talking to a man. I've got to have . . . no, 'got to' is the wrong word, but it's *nice* to have a man to talk to."

E. S.: "I got lots of friends. If I need help they can help me. They're giving me more support. All the old friends we had, they didn't change.

"I call the telephone counselors at the Abused Women's Network and I just talk and talk; it makes me feel good, not hurt anymore."

The Second Phase group (for women who have determined to stay away from abusive men) at the Abused Women's Network was helpful to Marilyn. "It's all a learning process about myself and if I screw up at all, I can't go in there and lie, can't cover up. I feel that when I do, I'm not fooling anyone."

ADVICE TO WOMEN IN ABUSIVE RELATIONSHIPS

For the most part, these women admit to bouts of depression and loneliness varying from moderate to great. Some are beset with illnesses that have limited their activities, have chronically incapacitated them, or are life-threatening. Nearly all are continually beleaguered by money problems. Yet none regret the decision to leave, and when asked for their advice to women who are involved with abusive men, their responses are almost identical.

Shirley: "Can this marriage be saved? I have one word: 'no.' It's not going to get better. It will only get worse and you'll get older."

Virginia: "Get out quickly. The longer you stay in it's just more defense for the opposition to say, 'You can't make it.' And you begin to believe that, and it is tough. But you only get out by doing something for yourself. That's the hard part, getting out by yourself. Going to a shelter is a big step—that phone call."

Sandi: "Go to the shelter. Be around people who are in the same situation. It helps to be around people who are also debating or in the process of leaving and saying 'Yep, we did have good times. When things were good they were *great*, but when they were bad they were *awful*.'"

Valerie: "I say to a young girl or even one twenty years married, 'Get out of it while you're still young enough to start again, even to finding another man and starting another marriage. Get out before you're too old and sick.' I'm not that old, but I'm too old to start again in a marriage."

E. S.: "Think it over. Think of your future. If he's doing that all the time you can do something, say something, get a divorce."

Marilyn: "Get out. I feel very strongly after what I've been through, that the situation is not going to change. It might be all right for a while. It's the exception that battering stops."

Corrine: "You might as well leave now as later. My situation did not improve. But then I left when I was psychologically ready and I have had no regrets and no temptation to return."

HINDSIGHT

Corrine's philosophical aceptance of her need to leave when the time was right typifies many women. It may even help some women to leave if they can accept their past decisions as inevitable and to accept or forgive themselves for staying with the man. Those who can't forgive themselves may think they must stay and stay until they can turn the frog into a prince.

I asked, "What would you change if you could live your life over again?"

Patricia: "I would have stayed with the foster family and gone to school. I wouldn't have gotten involved with Tim if I'd stayed there. And even if I had, I would have left the first time he ever laid a hand on me."

Shirley: "I think I would have left [years ago] instead of now. I would not have left nursing school, but I suppose better late than never is the only thing I can say now."

Virginia: "I would have had counseling before we got married. I would have had him bring his boys up *before* we got married, instead of becoming instant wife, mother, and maid. I think I should have left in the first week."

Sandi: "It all formed me, who I am now and I really like myself more than I did. So whatever it took, it was good. I don't think if I hadn't of went through that relationship, I would have had the strength to be who I am now. I wouldn't have had the drive."

Valerie: "If I had my life to live over again, I'd be a more educated person. I used to read any kind of cheap novels. Now my mind is changing to the point that what I'm trying to do is increase my knowledge, which I never felt like before."

Marilyn: "I guess if I had never even fraternized or gone back at all, it would have been easier. But I think every time I did, I learned something. And because I did, I have no regrets. I mean I know how terrible it can be. I don't have any question marks in my mind as to maybe if I'd stayed, it might have been wonderful and maybe he'd of really straightened out. All those questions are answered for me. I *know* what it would be like."

Patricia: "I wish there was some way I could have known how to get from point A to point B without going through all the shit I've gone through. But there's no way I could have known, and I had to go through all that. I would have filed for divorce the day after I left Tim for the last time if I had known what I know now. But there was no way I could have known that and if someone had told me that, I would have told them they were downright wrong."

ADVICE TO YOU IF YOU'RE THINKING OF GOING BACK

In spite of the seeming complacency of some of those answers, these women want you, a woman who is separated from an abusive man, to consider carefully the temptation to go back.

Virginia: "Think about the worst thing that has happened to you. It will probably happen again. Think about how you didn't like yourself when you were there. Think that it's a hell of an environment for kids to stay in, watching their mom being kicked around."

Shirley: "Think about how you're going to pay for what you've done while you were gone: the money you've spent, the embarrassment you caused your husband. And no magic is going to occur, unfortunately."

Patricia: "Do whatever you can to keep yourself busy, and hang in until you can build yourself a new life. Socialize a lot with women who are trying to get out of it, too. If you haven't got that, the best thing to do is to pack up and move many miles away, so it takes a couple of days to get back, 'cause he may call. And your heart will go flutter, flutter and you might want to dash right over there, but wait a couple of days before you go back. After the emotion passes, your head will take over."

Some other things that might help you endure staying away and the feelings that sometimes overwhelm you:

Patricia: "When I first got away from him I enjoyed it every day 'cause I'd get up in the morning and I'd say, 'Today I can change my life and there's nothing he can do about it.'"

"I make a list every week, still, and some of the things hang over from week to week, so then I ask myself, 'Why is it so hard to do?' And then when I think about it, I see what was hard and it's not so hard after all. And I just go do it. And if it *still* looks hard, I make sure I get up in the morning and go do it, just get it over with."

Shirley: "I'm not sure I'm ready for church yet. I think I would cry when I heard the songs. But if I keep hiding behind this, 'I'm not ready for it,' I will never get out from behind the kitchen table. That is something I'm going to have to do. Take a chance and do it."

Sandi: "Every time I felt like I needed him I would think about a certain situation and getting hit and how I felt, and then I got into those feelings and then I didn't want to go back.

"I knew that even if he went into counseling and changed I would still feel the same. I would always be afraid.

"It was really hard for me to start being less introverted. School helped a lot. The immediate reinforcement of school helped. That 'A', that '85' on a paper that kept telling me I was okay, the accomplishment of being in a man's field, finding out it's nothing."

Valerie: "I've made a lot of my own friends, I'm going to church every Sunday which I didn't do before, and going to potlucks and meeting people. I go swimming and to Bible study and when I wake up and get out of bed I look forward to my exercise class, and I am glad to get up."

E. S.: "Before, I don't know what to do. I don't know whether I can make it or not, if I and my children have a future or not. Now as long as I can get my training and get a job that makes me secure."

Jan: "At first I thought I was deserting Ron when he needed my help, really not believing that leaving him was the best thing I could do for him. It took probably about six months for me to believe that. I realized I had to work things out for myself and then I realized, 'Oh, yeah! It's the same thing for Ron.'

"Now I have other people who are closer to me than my family, and because of that, this holiday season is not going to be as difficult. I've redefined family, I guess.

"During the first four months after I left Ron I used the drop-in group at the Abused Women's Network. I also used my mother as an example. I told myself, 'I'm not going to live with a jerk for twenty years like my mother's been doing.'"

Corrine: "I wish I'd told all his relatives exactly what had happened instead of being discreet. I think they believed his stories that I was emotionally feeble and unstable, a lousy mother, and having an affair. I think you should tell *everyone* about him. Visit with friends, go to groups, get counseling for yourself and your kids, do enjoyable things with your kids. Get the best lawyer you can find, don't listen to the man, don't visit him, don't call him, and don't let your kids talk to him."

LIFE IS BETTER NOW

In spite of loneliness, poverty, and depression, these women who have stayed away from violent former partners—whether for several years or a few months—are unanimous in their assessments that life is far better now.

Corrine: "I *love* my independence. I'm relieved and *glad* to be away from him. I consider it an accomplishment that *finally* after so many years I *did* leave. No more arguing, scapegoating, and blaming in front of the kids. I don't have to listen any more and I don't. Life, even including the routines (which I don't have too many of), is more of an adventure, a challenge, and more rewarding."

Jan: I miss the intimacy of just being held—and yet . . . I just realized . . . I can get those needs met right now with my friends Betty, Nan, and Doris.

"Another thing I like is getting off work and getting a yen to go to the park to feed the ducks, not having to make a phone call to say, 'I'm going to be a couple of hours later tonight,' not to get permission, but just to let him know. And being able to do with my money what I want.

"Now I know what's important to me, and I do what's important to me. A trip is more important than a house, reading a book is a higher priority than washing dishes, going canoeing is more important than vacuuming."

Marilyn: "The best part of being away is being free, not having anybody criticizing me or telling me what to do. When I'm out and it's late I don't have to call anybody to make up an excuse about where I am.

"At work I can concentrate, because I'm not in crisis all the time.

"I think I'm in the process of probably making major decisions which I've never done. I never made decisions about what I'm going to do with my life. I'm wondering about that now and I'm very slowly looking into possibilities. I'm asking for what I want. I never felt like I could do that before."

E. S.: "When you come home you're not scared. I have lots of things I can accomplish. Before if I'm talking on the phone, I'm laughing and if he's here he says, 'What?! Are you laughing like a kid?!' Before I could not even say what I want, express what I want. I'm always in fear before.

"Now I like to go to school. I'm free. Even if I'm poor, I'm happy. I can feel happiness inside now."

Valerie: "I'm getting away from that loneliness. I can talk to anyone. When he took care of the money, I didn't have that responsibility; I didn't think I wanted it. But now that I've got it, I know a little bit about how good it can feel to have your own and do as you please. I use my money for a little entertainment and trips. I'm going to get along on what money I have and not depend on a man to take care of me."

Sandi: "I wake up in the morning and maybe I'm depressed for about a half an hour and then I say, 'Wow, you know you got to get up and do things or of *course* you're going to be depressed and it's going to be a boring day.' So, I get up and have a good day, usually.

"I'm twenty-four but I never had a chance to be a kid. Now I go to school and I think a lot. This creative writing class is making me get into my head and making me express things I never could express before. I really want to be able to do that, tell people how I feel. I've never taken a class before that I was really wanting to put everything into. I want people to understand me. Before it's always been, 'I'll understand you, I'll listen to you,' and now I want to take turns and I really want to know what to say when it's my turn.

"Being mostly without a man for almost two years is really lonely sometimes and it's real depressing sometimes, but I don't think I could have developed who I am with somebody around, or it might have taken real long and I'm in a space where I really appreciate me. I can believe that I can make decisions on my own, I can raise my kids on my own. And you know? Everything I have is more than anybody else I know has, and they all have men!

"And they all look to me for advice. They think I know it all. I don't know *anything,* to me. That's really good for people to respect me, and I like that a lot. It's independence in a way. I can deal with my kids without saying, 'Wait till your father comes home.'"

Virginia: "The best thing is my privacy. Before, the boys were always there, or he was always there, I couldn't say, 'Hey! I want to have Sunday to myself.' I would say it but I never got it. And I really treasured my privacy. I like not worrying about so many people—four boys and a man and their games and their schedules—and I don't know, somehow there wasn't time for my schedule, my problems. I had so many mother-type shoulds, ball-game shoulds, PTA shoulds, and wives' club shoulds, the things you're supposed to do if you're married or a wife or a mother.

"I'm planning to get a four-year degree and to be a counselor or teach teenagers to work with victimized women. On the good days I like myself."

Shirley: "I watch TV, I go to see my counselor twice a week, I go to Safeway a lot, you know, maybe to just buy one thing, and I go to the post office box twice a day. I'm going to be in the phone book in my own name next year, isn't that nice?

"I don't think much past Christmas right now. That's better than it was before, when I didn't think past next week. Things are better for me now because at least there's hope. Before I left Clarence, it was a hopeless situation. It could only get worse."

Patricia: "I'm living with a man who is totally the opposite of what I had before. It's give and take now. I've learned that. I live a normal life now. I have a normal relationship. I guess that's what I was always looking for, that was the void. I never had those normal things through childhood. I kept on feeling that loneliness. I put all that dependency on him, instead of learning how to give and take with another person. That's one of the best things.

"I feel like I fit in the world. I'm not being kept in the basement."

None of these women found it easy to get away, or to stay away, or to make a new life. Many of them still don't find it easy. But none of them regrets leaving. Several refrains stand out:

I'm learning . . .

I like myself . . .

I feel free . . .

Their message is that you can learn new ways, you can like yourself, and you can get free.

SPECIAL CHALLENGES

CHAPTER 22

EMOTIONAL ABUSE

If you've been physically assaulted by an intimate partner, you're almost certain to have been subjected to emotional abuse as well. Perhaps the worst of it has been the continual or chronic terror of being beaten or killed. Maybe it's been the more subtle erosion of your self-esteem and capacity to act independently, or the daily shame and humiliation you endure. Perhaps, like nearly all women who are subjected to both, you experience emotional abuse as even harder to take than the physical abuse.

It might be that you've rarely or never been physically assaulted, but threats have kept you in fear and caused you gradually to lose your sense of identity as you've given in to the ideas and demands of your partner. If the abuser has neither hit nor threatened you, but has used more subtle methods to manipulate, control, and debilitate you, you might feel more submissive, confused, and given to self-blame than many women who've been severely beaten. A woman who has a black eye or broken bone knows something has been done to her, but emotional abuse is sometimes so complex and bewildering it is difficult to name. If it can't be identified clearly, the person it's directed toward may believe she's imagining it.

Much of *Getting Free* implicitly provides ways to defend against or recover from emotional abuse. A continuum of emotional abuse is described in the introductory Who This Book Is For and How to Use It. But you won't find an analysis, a refined definition, or a special section on the subject. When *Getting Free* was written I was still struggling, as were many of the women subjected to emotional abuse, to identify it in specific terms. We were searching for ways to delineate it from the ordinary irritability and occasional name-calling that most couples engage in from time to time. In fact, much of that behavior is abusive, but it may not be permanently damaging until it reaches the level of a campaign to reduce the partner's sense of self-worth and to maintain control. Because the abusive person may establish control over the other, it is most damaging when it is a pattern of behavior on the part of just one partner, though it may also be harmful when it's mutual psychological combat.

UNDERSTANDING THE CHART OF COERCION

Because it's so hard for many of us to get a clear view of emotional abuse, in this chapter I'm going to use a framework that creates some distance from it. In her book, *Rape in Marriage,* Diana Russell reprinted a Chart of Coercion from an Amnesty International publication, *Report on Torture,* depicting the brainwashing of prisoners of war; she suggested that it also describes the "torture of wives." Most people who brainwash their intimate partners use methods similar to those of prison guards, who recognize that physical control is never easily accomplished without the cooperation of the prisoner. The most effective way to gain that cooperation is through subversive manipulation of the mind and feelings of the victim, who then becomes a psychological, as well as a physical, prisoner. These methods form the core of emotional abuse. In the following discussion of brainwashing and the exercise to help you identify it, I have modified the language of the Chart of Coercion categories for readability, but I have maintained their essential meaning.

Biderman's Chart of Coercion

General Method	Effects and Purposes
Isolation	*Deprives victim of all social support [for the] ability to resist.* *Develops an intense concern with self.* *Makes victim dependent upon interrogator.*
Monopolization of Perception	*Fixes attention upon immediate predicament; fosters introspection.* *Eliminates stimuli competing with those controlled by captor.* *Frustrates all actions not consistent with compliance.*
Induced Debility and Exhaution	*Weakens mental and physical ability to resist.*
Threats	*Cultivates anxiety and despair.*
Occasional Indulgences	*Provides positive motivation for compliance.*

General Method	Effects and Purposes
Demonstrating "Omnipotence"	*Suggests futility of resistance.*
Degradation	*Makes cost of resistance appear more damaging to self-esteem than capitulation. Reduces prisoner to "animal level" concerns.*
Enforcing Trivial Demands	*Develops habit of compliance.*

Isolation

Isolation is the most effective way to set the stage for brainwashing, since once the victim is away from emotional supports and reality checks, the rest of the process is relatively easy. A prisoner may be placed alone in a cell to increase dependence on the guards and a subsequent willingness to obey. Religious fanatics sometimes surround a potential recruit and repetitively hammer into his or her consciousness a rigid ideology, while the victim is cut off from previous relationships and competing ideas. Women who are battered are often kept from contact with almost everyone except the person who batters, so that the self-interested, demeaning, or threatening messages can saturate her senses.

A man who batters often carries on a process of gradually weaning a wife or girlfriend away from everyone else she is close to through a combination of demands, threats, and manipulation. He may complain about her maintaining a friendship with a former boyfriend, then make critical remarks about her divorced women friends being a bad influence, and later insist that she not talk on the telephone when he is home. He may insult her friends, acquaintances, and relatives, so that they voluntarily stay away or the woman feels too embarrassed to invite them into her home. He may stay at the woman's side except when he is at work, and if he does decide to leave her alone he either telephones periodically to be sure she is at home or convinces her that he has spies who watch her and report to him. Sometimes he does have spies. The woman may unwittingly collude in his campaign to isolate her because she is either too depressed to want to be with other people or too ashamed to let others see her if she is bruised. The violent partner may also threaten that if she talks to anyone he will beat or even kill her.

Lesbians may abuse their partners in similar ways. There are often additional excuses for abuse. For instance, a lesbian who is afraid to claim her identity may demand that her "out-of-the-closet" lover drop her lesbian friends and, in effect, join her in the closet. The abused partner may be coerced into hiding many of her true ideas and feelings because they seem threatening to the abusive woman's job or relationships.

The abused woman, whether lesbian or heterosexual, may be allowed to see people, especially if the abuser wants her to work, but the isolation may still occur on a more subtle, emotional level. For instance, she is not allowed to speak of what is done to her behind the closed doors, and she may be terrified of the abuser's violence if she inadvertently lets someone know what she is subjected to. To be on the safe side, she becomes unnaturally silent or superficial. She may also be convinced that if her friends or colleagues knew about the violence they would believe it was her own fault. Under those circumstances she is emotionally and socially isolated from everyone, because she hides her feelings, her thoughts, and the pattern of her life from them and they don't really know her.

Humiliation or Degradation

Once the woman stops interacting openly with other people, the abuser's influence becomes paramount. She is bombarded with misinformation and distorted values, and there is no one to reinforce her own ideas of the truth. This process of isolation and the self-doubt it creates are effective in gaining power over another person. But there is more. The abuser may criticize the woman for minor flaws, sometimes in public, or remind her of humiliating experiences. He may continually tell her she is bad, stupid, and crazy, as well as a slut, cunt, or worse. He may also subject her to sexual innuendos about her behavior with other men, flaunt his relationships with other women, insult her, or simply ignore her.

Lesbians may, in addition to those abuses, call their partners names that demean their sexual orientation and the very relationship that in happier moments is treasured. The abused lesbian is called a goddamned dyke or "femme" or "butch." Or she's accused of really loving men.

Some abusers find extreme and bizarre ways to degrade a partner, such as raping her in front of the children or forcing her to eat from a pet dish. The sense of extreme humiliation makes the woman feel she deserves to be treated as less than human and may also cause her to think no one but the abusive partner would ever want anything to do with her. When the abuser occasionally treats her well, she is so hungry for any crumb of care that she accepts it gratefully. Eventually, the awareness of her dependence and her gratitude for the smallest attention contribute even more to the woman's sense of degradation, and she abuses herself with litanies of self-blame.

Trivial Demands and Focus on the Whims of the Abuser

The abusers insist on compliance with trivial demands related to all facets of life: food, clothing, money, household arrangements, children, and conversation. They monitor their partner's appearance, criticize her values, her language, and her child-care practices. They insist on precise mealtimes with prescribed menus, which may change and be contradictory from day to day or moment to moment.

The abused woman may at first think that her partner is unreasonable and argue back. Later, either because she wants to live in peace or because she is afraid, she tries to comply. After all, what difference does it make if the dinner has to be served at precisely 5:00 P.M., after 6:00 P.M., or if she is forced to wear yellow even though it looks ghastly on her? In the long run maybe it's good for the children to always have their toys put away when their father is home. A woman with an abusive male partner tries to read his mind, anticipate his wishes, and deflect his wrath. Soon it becomes apparent that there is no end to his demands, and her time and energy are focused on him and his imminent rage over anything she does that may turn out to be "wrong." Everything becomes important in terms of how it will affect him, and her desires, feelings, and ideas become insignificant. Eventually she doesn't even know what she wants, feels, and thinks. He monopolizes all of her perceptions with his trivial demands so that she loses her perspective on the enormity of her total situation.

An abusive lesbian might insist she knows what is "correct" about the lesbian lifestyle, as if there is only one. She will criticize her partner's clothes as being too "femme," too "butch," or too "dykey" and her sexual practices as being "sick" or too much like heterosexuals'. A woman who is just coming out as a lesbian may be particularly vulnerable to these verbal assaults. Her focus changes from her own preferences in style and habits to what she projects will keep her partner from being displeased with her.

Demonstration of Power and Threats

The abusers persuade the woman that they are the ones who know the correct way that everything should be done. When their behavior results in disastrous consequences, as it often does, the partner is blamed. Abusers may even claim to have supernatural powers. Usually they claim to be superior intellectually and to know the ways of the world. Because the abused woman has been brought so low herself, she may come to believe this. As early as the initial honeymoon period she may have developed the idea that her partner is brilliant, worldly, accomplished, and knowledgable, and he or she will have done everything possible to encourage it. Abusers may also have moments, especially after a beating, when they "confess" that they think they're inadequate or worthless; the contrast of these moments of vulnerablity with their usual pose of being all-powerful endears them to the woman and gives her hope for some open communication. Their supposed superiority and her inferiority reinforce their power over her and inhibit her ability to create change.

Threats are an almost natural concomitant to all of these processes. The person who batters threatens to leave the partner, threatens to harm her children or other family members, tells her "I'll fix you so no one will ever want you," and threatens to kill. Since some of these actions are carried out, the woman can never be sure when the abuser will follow through on the others. She is coerced into obedience to unreasonable demands and increases her attention on the abuser and away from herself. Her focus is on what she can do to preserve her short-term safety, and it distracts her from considerations of how to work toward a plan for real security in the long range.

The person who is not physically abusive may first force the woman into actions that embarrass or humiliate her, then threaten to tell her family or friends about it. A lesbian may threaten her closeted partner with making their relationship known to her boss or family. An abusive man may tell his partner that he will take her children away, destroy objects of sentimental value, or harass and humiliate her in the presence of her work colleagues or boss or use other methods to cause her to lose her job. He often controls all the money even if she earns it and may periodically take her car keys or checkbook away if she doesn't obey him. If she doesn't give in to his demands, he may begin to put into practice one of these threats. Emotionally abusive people are sometimes remarkably imaginative. They can be just as frightening to their partners as are physically violent partners.

Helplessness and Exhaustion

The chronic physical injury from beatings creates an ongoing state of exhaustion. The woman who is subjected to these techniques of brainwashing becomes worn out by her tension, fear, and her continual rushing about in the effort to arrange her partner's world effectively enough to avoid abuse. She must also strain to keep her fear, sorrow, and rage from showing, since any display of emotion is likely to be ridiculed or punished. Physical weakness, self-doubt, and self-loathing, reinforced by her partner's insistence that she is stupid, crazy, and does not know how to do anything, finally convince the emotionally abused woman that she is incapable of taking care of herself or of making a move to sever her relationship.

Occasional Indulgences

If there is a moment in which the woman sees hope of escaping or becomes desperate enough to take any risk to get away, the abuser often senses it and comes through with some form of indulgence, whether a new car, a night out, or a seemingly loving, affectionate offering of time together. Hope that the abuser will change replaces the woman's fear or despair, and she decides to continue working on the relationship.

Some of the brainwashing techniques in each of the categories mentioned above are extreme, but not uncommon. Some abusers use them in a disciplined and regular manner, some sporadically. But even mild and occasional use of the techniques is often effective in gaining power. When they are combined with physical abuse they are reliable methods of keeping a woman in a relationship and guaranteeing obedience. These methods are not the only means of emotional abuse. There are no doubt countless ways a person can manipulate the emotions of an intimate partner in negative ways, but I will mention only two more.

Emotional Distance

Psychological unavailability or emotional distance is known to have an extremely devastating effect on children, but little is known of its impact on adults. It is such a common complaint of women about their male partners that it has been a standing cartoon subject for many years. The man sitting behind the newspaper at the breakfast table while his wife sets fire to it to get his attention is just one of the many variations on the theme. A woman often thinks there is something wrong with her for wanting the man she's involved with to be present. She wants him to talk, to listen, to express feelings, to understand the nuances of her conversation. If he is focused on the paper or the television or only pretending to listen, then the woman begins to feel like a nonperson. If she doesn't have other people in her life to let her know she is heard and understood and cared about in a way that reflects who she really is, she may eventually begin to doubt her judgment and her worth.

"Crazy-Making"

Another method of emotional abuse is "crazy-making." It is difficult to describe because it has many manifestations. In the movie *Gaslight* the husband regularly turns down the gaslights and when his wife complains about it, he says she's imagining that they've changed. In its extreme form, such a man may remove his wife's possessions from their usual place, and when she says they are missing, complain of her inability to keep track of things. Then he replaces them and accuses her of imagining they were missing. That's expert "crazy-making."

Many people who abuse their partners deny and minimize their faults, and they often tell lies about such trivial matters that the woman wonders if she is mistaken about what she thinks is true. "Who would lie about something so unimportant? I must have misunderstood." When she has "misunderstood" numerous times, and that notion is reinforced by her partner—"I never said that. You must be imagining things"—she begins to doubt her judgment. Small contradictions—"I never eat well-done steak"/"I always want my steak well-done"—can have a similar effect.

Because there are no socially prescribed roles for lesbians, an abusive woman may use her partner's ambivalence or confusion about who does what tasks to confuse her with continually shifting ideas or demands about what, if any, roles they each should play. Being dependent or doing domestic tasks, for instance, may be rewarded on Friday and demeaned on Saturday. A transfer of guilt from the abuser to the victim sometimes causes the victim to feel crazy. "You brought it on yourself. You love to be beaten," the abusive man says, and eventually the woman asks herself, "Could I love it, subconsciously? Is it my fault?" Abusers may often be troubled by fears, anger, and depression and may try to get rid of those feelings by blustering, threatening, and dominating a woman or an entire household. Then they feel some release, and the others feel frightened, angry, or depressed. They may then be criticized for those feelings while the abuser brags that he or she doesn't let feelings get out of control that way. When the others wonder what's wrong with themselves, they're beginning to get a little "crazy."

Some abusive people are adept at picking out a trait that a woman is most pleased about and using it against her. This can happen two ways. Treasuring her independence of spirit or her analytic ability, for instance, can be made to seem like a flaw. Independence becomes rejection or selfishness, and analytic ability is called "logic-chopping," "coldness" or "showing off." When the woman begins to believe that her virtues are her flaws, her ability to make other judgments becomes impaired as well. Another tactic is to convince the abused partner that she really isn't humorous or smart or artistically talented. A lesbian who is pleased by her growing comfort with her lesbian identity may be told by her abusive partner that she has no right to call herself a lesbian unless she comes out to her boss, her grandmother, and her neighbors. When an abused woman begins to doubt that she has that one special trait she has always felt secure about, the rest of her self-concept is quickly called into question.

PROBLEMS OF IDENTIFYING ABUSE

Why have workers in the battered women's movement emphasized physical rather than emotional abuse? Perhaps because we recognize that everyone emotionally abuses to some extent, and if we are all guilty then we don't want to blame anyone else for fear we will in turn be held responsible. Or we thought emotional abuse wasn't "so bad," because after all it was so common. We didn't realize "how bad" it can be. A lie? An unreasonable demand? A name called? An occasional manipulation? Not really listening? Oh, come on! Everybody does those things. That's no big deal. There's some truth to that, except when one person is using it as a way of controlling another or frightening her or destroying her self-concept; except when it's a pattern that characterizes the relationship and gives one person almost all the power; except when one person becomes so uncertain of herself she can't trust her judgment and thinks she doesn't have the right to make judgments.

We also didn't know how to name emotional abuse. It's not clear-cut like a black eye. It is often subtle and it's also confusing if the one who's abused is also emotionally abusive. "It isn't fair to call that abusive, because I do that too." It should be remembered that even if both partners do it, it is still abuse. Sometimes it's hard to tell whether a person is being abused by a partner or abuses herself. What about a woman who is neurotic, who has a very low self-concept, who continually defers to her partner, who hands over her power to others? Isn't it possible the emotional abuse isn't really being done to her at all and that she's imagining it? Sure, it's possible, but probably it's being at least reinforced by the partner.

IDENTIFYING EMOTIONAL ABUSE AND USING
GETTING FREE TO DIMINISH IT

If you wonder about whether you're being emotionally abused, *fill out* the following checklist to determine if that's what's happening to you. If you're being subjected to brainwashing, "crazy-making," or psychological neglect, start diminishing its impact by doing the indicated exercises in *Getting Free.*

Activity 38 ॐ Emotional Abuse Checklist

Are You Isolated?

A.

	often	sometimes	never
1. Does your partner ridicule or insult people you like?	_____	_____	_____
2. Is your partner jealous of your friends, family, and even pets?	_____	_____	_____
3. Does your partner intercept your mail or telephone calls?	_____	_____	_____
4. Does your partner become angry or upset, dampening your enthusiasm, just before or during a social event you've looked forward to?	_____	_____	_____

B.

	often	sometimes	never
1. Do you discourage people from telephoning you at home because your partner resents sharing your time?	_____	_____	_____
2. Do you have fewer contacts and activities with friends and family than before you began the relationship?	_____	_____	_____
3. Do you feel uneasy about being with your partner and your friends at the same time?	_____	_____	_____
4. Do you feel nervous or frightened of what your partner will say or do if you are even a few minutes late from work, shopping, or visiting others?	_____	_____	_____

If you have many affirmative answers to the questions above, you're in danger of becoming so isolated from the support and perspective of other people that you eventually won't be able to evaluate what's being done to you, or to recognize a dangerous situation or person. If you had many "Yes" answers to "B," it might be that you've adapted so well to the isolation your partner has imposed that you've started isolating yourself. You can begin to break the pattern by reading Chapter 12, An End to Isolation, and Chapter 13, Reaching Out.

Is Your Attention Monopolized by the Abusive Person?

	often	sometimes	never
1. Do you feel your clothing, opinions, and decisions must have your partner's approval?			
2. Do you feel overpowered by your partner's presence whether or not he or she is with you?			
3. Do you speak carefully, or avoid speaking, so you won't risk upsetting your partner?			
4. Do you time your activities to avoid their being noticed by your partner?			
5. Do you often feel you're "walking on eggshells"?			

If you checked many answers in this group, you're focusing so much of your attention on your partner's opinions and reactions that you'll soon lose sight of your own rights and feelings and desires. This monopolization of your attention by your partner, in combination with isolation from other people, may lead you in the direction of excessive dependence on your partner. If you had several "always" or "sometimes" responses, read Chapter 4 and do Activities 5 and 6 so that you can begin to focus on what you need and want for yourself.

Does Your Partner Claim to Be All-Powerful?

	often	sometimes	never
1. Does your partner claim to be exceptionally bright or knowledgable, or to have extraordinary powers?			
2. Does your partner claim to be more aware of the ways of the world than you are?			
3. Does your partner claim to have friends and contacts who will report your activities when you are away from home?			
4. Does your partner claim to know the "right" way to do things and that you don't know what's "right"?			

If you checked two or more of the items above, you may eventually be persuaded by your partner that he or she is omnipotent or at least greatly superior to you, and that you aren't competent to make your own decisions. Read Chapter 10, You Can Be Your Own Counselor, and do Activities 14 through 17 to gain a more positive perspective on what you do that's "right" or smart or competent or loving.

Does Your Partner Enforce Trivial Demands?

	often	sometimes	never
1. Does your partner insist that activities take place in precise ways or at precisely designated times?	____	____	____
2. Does your partner interrupt your work or other things that are important to you to get her or his needs met?	____	____	____
3. Does your partner demand that you wear only approved clothing, jewelry, etc.?	____	____	____
4. Does your partner insist you perform menial services, or inspect your work and make hypercritical comments?	____	____	____
5. Does your partner demand detailed reports of hourly activities?	____	____	____

If your partner enforces trivial demands, you may feel either like a servant or an incompetent child. You'll focus on the narrow mechanical tasks expected of you and give up making your own judgments about their value. To counter those demands, do the activities in A Courageous Act a Day and consider taking an assertion-training course. (This category is not meant to imply that people who emotionally abuse don't also make outrageous demands. They often start with minor issues, which build up to greater ones, or the abuser may start with something so unacceptable that when he or she moves to something less dramatic, it may seem, by comparison, more manageable. These demands may involve "loans" of money, never repaid, or use of a car that's mistreated or not returned in time for you to keep an important engagement, or a host of other items.)

Are You Exhausted, Debilitated, or Dependent?

	often	sometimes	never
1. Do you feel inadequate doing tasks you used to do easily and well?	_____	_____	_____
2. Do you suffer from minor or major illnesses?	_____	_____	_____
3. Do you have feelings of dread?	_____	_____	_____
4. Do you feel you couldn't manage your life without your partner?	_____	_____	_____

Checks after these questions indicate that the trivial demands of your partner are wearing you down. You may feel debilitated or dependent for reasons that aren't clear. Ask youself how you feel when you're not with your partner. If that hasn't happened in a long time, try to get away even for a few days to see how you feel when the pressure is off. You might have a great deal more energy. If these feelings persist for a long time, see a counselor. Meanwhile, do Activities 15, 16, and 19A and B.

Do You Feel Humiliated or Degraded?

	often	sometimes	never
1. Does your partner force you to do things that are against your religious or moral values?	_____	_____	_____
2. Does your partner ridicule the traits you admire or value most in yourself?	_____	_____	_____
3. Does your partner tell you no one else would want you?	_____	_____	_____
4. Has your partner talked you into doing something and then made you feel guilty or ashamed about it?	_____	_____	_____
5. Does your partner keep you up late, asking about real or imagined sexual or romantic incidents?	_____	_____	_____
6. Does your partner force you to apologize for things you didn't do?	_____	_____	_____
7. Does your partner insist you ask permission to spend money for household or personal items, whether the money is a community fund or your own income?	_____	_____	_____

	often	sometimes	never
8. Does your partner call you names with sexual connotations such as "slut" or "whore"?	_____	_____	_____
9. Does your partner flaunt relationships or flirt with others while in your presence?	_____	_____	_____

The above questions ask about activities and demands that cause you to feel humiliated and degraded. It seems as if such experiences would motivate a person to end a relationship, but often that's not so. People who have experienced such things often stay involved because they're ashamed to face anyone else, and because they hope that they can "fix" the relationship, which will make the humiliation seem to have been for a good cause. A course in assertiveness may help you say "no" to some of your partner's degrading demands. But if your partner is violent, make a plan for your safety before you try something new. Chapter 12, An End to Isolation, and Chapter 13, Reaching Out, will help you find ways to meet people and make friends who will encourage you to feel good about yourself.

Does Your Partner Threaten You?

	often	sometimes	never
1. Does your partner threaten to make public the things you've done or that you've told in private moments?	_____	_____	_____
2. Does your partner threaten to leave you or divorce you whenever you have arguments?	_____	_____	_____
3. Does your partner tell you that suicide or mental illness will result if you leave or withdraw your love or affection?	_____	_____	_____
4. Does your alcoholic partner hint at the probability of drinking again unless you do what is required and be certain not to upset him or her?	_____	_____	_____
5. Does your partner threaten to "punish you or teach you a lesson" if you "misbehave"?	_____	_____	_____
6. Does your partner threaten to take your car keys, money, or checkbook if you			

	often	sometimes	never
don't comply with demands?	_____	_____	_____

7. Does your partner use bodily or facial expressions or noises to show extreme anger and loss of control to frighten you? _____ _____ _____

8. Has being hit or beaten in the past made you fear its happening again if you don't comply? _____ _____ _____

9. Does your partner keep guns, knives, or other weapons close at hand? _____ _____ _____

Whether you're threatened with the loss of your partner, the responsibility of your partner's mental illness or suicide, or injury to yourself, the use of power makes it certain you can't have a relationship of mutual respect and love. If you checked questions 5 through 8, you may be in serious danger. One way to diminish those threats is to ignore them, but you do that at risk of being seriously injured. This may be the point at which you'll consider leaving your partner. If you want help in making that decision, read Section 1, Making the Decision to Leave or Stay, and do the activities.

Does Your Partner Occasionally Indulge Your Wishes?

	often	sometimes	never

1. Just as you are thinking of separating, or when you've been abused, or for no reason at all, does your partner pamper you with gifts? _____ _____ _____

2. Does your partner suddenly do something you have been requesting for a long time? _____ _____ _____

3. Does your partner become unexpectedly understanding about something that would ordinarily cause him or her to exhibit anger? _____ _____ _____

4. Does your partner impress you with exceptional sensitivity to your feelings and desires? _____ _____ _____

5. After your partner has "put you down," are you then indulged with affection or special care? _____ _____ _____

This category of Occasional Indulgences is the one that "hooks you." These things may not happen very often, but there's always the hope that they are expressions of the real character of your partner and that they'll surface on a regular basis. Do Activities 23 through 25 to get a perspective on how the positive things your partner has done compare with the abuse. Be sure to include all the most humiliating, demeaning, and other emotional abuses in the Most Dangerous list. They are dangerous to your mental health.

Does Your Partner Do Things That Make You Feel Crazy?

A.

	often	sometimes	never
1. Does your partner suggest you're "stupid" or "crazy" if you disagree with him or her?	_____	_____	_____
2. Does your partner apologize and say the abuse is a sign of deep love and fear of losing your love?	_____	_____	_____
3. Does your partner insist that the two of you are in a battle against a world full of enemies?	_____	_____	_____
4. After abusing you, does your partner express so much sorrow, guilt, or self-hate that you become the one who comforts your partner?	_____	_____	_____
5. Has your partner burdened you with shameful, embarrassing, or criminal secrets that only you know about?	_____	_____	_____
6. Does your partner lie about insignificant things?	_____	_____	_____
7. Does your partner make contradictory demands?	_____	_____	_____
8. Does your partner contradict the positive things others say about you?	_____	_____	_____
9. Does your partner say negative things about a trait you like about yourself, such as "wishy-washy," "intellectual," "stuffy," etc.?	_____	_____	_____
10. Does your partner do unrequested favors, then get angry or hurt when you don't do something in return?	_____	_____	_____

B.

	often	sometimes	never
1. Do you distrust your feelings about yourself, your partner, or others?	___	___	___
2. Do you feel ashamed of past deeds that once made you proud?	___	___	___
3. Are you afraid no one would like you if they knew the "the real you"?	___	___	___
4. Do you believe you're the only one who can save your partner from ruin, depression, alcoholism, insanity, or suicide—and yet, that you're the dependent one?	___	___	___
5. Does it just "happen" that when you are preparing for an upcoming test, job interview, evaluation, or an important event, you're distracted and worried by a crisis in your partner's life or work that seems more important?	___	___	___
6. Does your partner cause you to question your longtime friendships?	___	___	___
7. Are you confused about what is love and what is hate? Or right and wrong?	___	___	___
8. Does your partner bombard you with words, sometimes of many syllables, until you think he or she must know what he or she is talking about and you give in to his or her position?	___	___	___

Most of these questions indicate that the abuser is doing something to make the partner weak, but checks after "A" questions indicate your partner is engaging in "crazy-making" or "gaslighting" behavior, and after "B" show to what extent you're beginning to take responsibility for it. The latter is especially likely if you're kept away from other people and if the "crazy-maker" demonstrates other kinds of power. Becoming involved with other people will help to validate your sanity. Read Chapter 12, An End to Isolation, and Chapter 13, Reaching Out.

Is Your Partner Emotionally Distant or Neglectful?

A.   often   sometimes   never

1. Does your partner ignore you or grunt
   absentmindedly when you begin a
   conversation?   _____   _____   _____
2. Does your partner groan, complain, or
   ridicule you, when you cry, worry, or ask
   for emotional support?   _____   _____   _____
3. Does your partner refuse to confide in you
   when he or she is worried, hurt, or scared?   _____   _____   _____
4. Does your partner ignore your wish for sex
   or refuse to do what excites or satisfies you? _____   _____   _____
5. Does your partner make light of your
   triumphs, discourage your plans, disparage
   your success?   _____   _____   _____
6. Does your partner refuse to share her or
   his plans or hopes for success?   _____   _____   _____
7. Does your partner ignore your need for
   assistance when you're sick, tired, or
   over-scheduled?   _____   _____   _____

B.   often   sometimes   never

1. Have you given up asking your partner
   for companionship?   _____   _____   _____
2. Have you stopped asking for empathy or
   emotional support?   _____   _____   _____
3. Have you given up asking for assistance
   when you're sick, tired, or need your
   partner's help?   _____   _____   _____
4. Have you stopped asking your partner
   about his or her plans, worries, or
   triumphs?   _____   _____   _____
5. Have you developed a habit of avoiding
   sex whenever possible but enduring it as
   a tolerable routine when it's unavoidable?   _____   _____   _____

If many of these situations are prevalent in your relationship, your partner is psychologically unavailable to you and neglecting you, which is a form of abuse. If most of your checks were in part "B," you may have been minimizing the neglect, since you've learned that it's all you can expect of your partner. You may not be able to get what you want from your partner, but you can diminish the pain of neglect by spending time with friends who pay attention to you and finding work that gives you satisfaction. Read Chapters 11, 12, 13, and 17.

MAKING CHANGES

After you've finished Activity 38 and you're still not sure whether you or your partner is the abusive person, reverse the questions that begin "Does your partner . . . " and do the exercise again to check out what you are doing. If both of you are emotionally abusive, and if you're not being battered, you may benefit from the help of a counselor or another person who has some objectivity. The third person can help you monitor your abuse of each other and provide a relatively safe atmosphere in which you can each admit your vulnerability and ask for consideration.

You may have begun to emotionally abuse your partner in moments of helpless fury, to retaliate against physical or sexual abuse, and it may momentarily have given you a sense of power. But the ability to lower someone else's self-esteem is not real power. It doesn't enable you to live the kind of life you want. In addition, it may cause you to feel guilty or even to believe you deserve your partner's retaliation. The theme of *Getting Free* is that you can make changes in yourself, and this is another example. Decide whether you want to be abusive and whether you want to be free of another's abuse. Then act to make the changes you want.

If you don't have a pattern of abusing your partner, but your partner emotionally abuses you, a counselor might still be useful, if only to back up your position that your partner is abusive and can change. The comments after the checklist urge you to begin expanding your social contacts, and now is a good time to begin. If your partner resists your move to seek professional help or to be active and socialize with other people, that's further evidence that he or she has an investment in keeping you the way you are.

Maybe friends tell you you're brainwashed, but you claim, for instance, that your partner doesn't prevent you from seeing other people, but that you stay home because you like to be alone or because it's your choice to stay with your partner. If friends persist in their opinions, you may want to insist they mind their own business, or you might want to allow for the possibility that if you are brainwashed you don't know it. You could decide to prove to yourself and to them that you're making your own choices. If you want to take a risk and are willing to act with an open mind, you can decide to go out on your own to see friends or enroll in a class. If you're not being brainwashed, your partner will probably be glad you're doing something for yourself and will encourage you. If he or she puts obstacles in your way, complains a lot, or "explains" all the reasons you don't need to be out on your own, it should be clear that you're not free to develop yourself without being made to pay a price.

The worst part of emotional abuse is that the person victimized by it eventually takes on the role of her abuser and begins to demean, degrade, and humiliate herself. That is why it works so well, when it does. Brainwashing causes many women to be so debilitated, so dependent, and so overwhelmed by dread that they look as if they could never become autonomous, active, optimistic people. Yet they do it. They are able to break away from abusive partners and to recover their self-esteem and autonomy.

Since you've read this far, you've probably named the problem and know what changes you want to make. You may feel overwhelmed by the tasks ahead of you, but you've already taken several important steps. Even if you can't affect your partner as much as you'd like, you can begin to react differently and to view yourself in a new light. You can take satisfaction in whatever work you do at home or on a paid job. You can begin to do pleasurable things and to allow yourself to consciously enjoy them. Your particular, individual, inner resources have been untapped for a time, but you're using them now and the more you use them the more they will expand. You're on your way to a new way of life in which you'll struggle, learn to appreciate yourself, and interact with others who appreciate you. You'll find rewards in being with people and being alone, and you'll use new skills to meet conflict and criticism assertively and peaceably. That is the miracle of the human spirit.

CHAPTER 23

TEEN ABUSE

If you're a teenage woman or her parent, this chapter is written for you, though women beyond the teen years who are abused in dating relationships may find it of use as well. It focuses primarily on sexual, physical, and emotional abuse of single, childless teenagers by their boyfriends. It doesn't assume that if you're a teenager you aren't married or don't have a child, but if that's your situation, you'll probably find most of the other chapters of *Getting Free* just as pertinent to your life as they are to those of older women's. This chapter gives information about battering in teenage dating relationships and points out the other parts of *Getting Free* that may be most helpful to read. If you're the parent of a teenage woman who's abused, you can use this book to understand your daughter's situation. (You may also want to give her a copy.) The last part of this chapter is addressed specifically to you.

If you're a teenager, you may experience all of the fears and hardships of older women in abusive relationships, but there are additional problems as well. In your struggle to free yourself from your parents' control, you may find yourself confused by feelings related to your relationship with a controlling man. It's difficult for most women to talk about being abused, and as a teenager you may have even more reasons to hesitate. For instance, you might worry that if you confide in your doctor, minister, or teacher, they will tell your parents, and then you'll have to face their hurt, anger, or punishment. Your parents may refuse to let you continue seeing the man you're involved with before you come to that decision on your own.

If you're the parent of a teenager, you may experience all the fear you would have for an older friend or relative in a dangerous relationship, as well as special concerns because of the relative lack of experience and vulnerablity of your daughter. This may be combined with rage that you can't control her as you "should" be able to and jealousy of the man who does control her. In addition, you may be asking yourself what is wrong with the way you raised your daughter and why she pays no attention to your entreaties to leave the dangerous man. If you're the mother of an abused teenager and have been abused yourself, you may feel special responsibility, even if you left the abusive man in your life some time ago. This chapter offers suggestions on how to help a teenager identify abuse, how to support her, and how to cope with your own feelings.

HOW COMMON IS TEENAGE BATTERING?

The information that battering is widespread among all kinds of married and cohabiting couples began to come out in the mid-1970s, but almost nothing was known about teenage or date battering until the early 1980s. Even now, about all we know for sure is that many teenagers, like adults, are subjected to physical abuse in their intimate relationships. Maria Roy found, in interviews with 4,000 adult women who had been battered, that many began the relationships as adolescents.[1] Surveys of violence among high school student couples are few and the responses give us a wide range of figures. One study of fifteen- to nineteen-year-olds found that 17 percent of the women and 8 percent of the men admitted to experiencing some type of physical violence with a dating partner. In more than three quarters of the cases the violence began after the couple became seriously involved, but most of the couples were only fifteen the first time it happened. For about a quarter of the students violence began in casual dating relationships, and almost 60 percent of them had the courage to end the relationships.[2] Another study found that 35 percent of high school students reported various levels of violence in their relationships. Although some students admitted to extremely dangerous acts, most of them spoke of pushing, shoving, slapping, and threatening. There were no reported differences among races or social classes.[3]

It should not surprise us that violence between high school students is common. Violence between brothers and sisters, more than other kinds of family violence, has often been viewed as inevitable, normal, and acceptable. One study found that 16 percent of children aged three to seventeen beat up their sisters and brothers.[4] If you've been fighting for years with your brother, it might not seem too different to fight with your boyfriend. If an older brother has beaten you up periodically, it might not be shocking to be beaten by a boyfriend. If you're in that situation, think carefully about whether you want to go on living with fear and violence or whether you'd rather start a new pattern.

Among college students surveyed, some of whom were teenagers, about half had been victims of sex aggression during a single academic year. That is, the man attempted to make the woman become sexual in a way that was unacceptable to her, and she resisted. Of those attempts, 40 percent succeeded.[5] Legally, many of these acts would be defined as rape, although the women might not realize it. Only 2 percent of them reported these offenses to police or parents or other authorities.[6]

Other surveys indicate that between 21 percent and 68 percent of college students have been violent to intimate partners or dates.[7] Some women who were hit before marriage say the main cause was their boyfriends' unfounded jealousy and refusal to allow the women to be independent.[8] Many of them hoped that once they were married or living together, the man would feel secure and stop the violence. Unfortunately, marriage is often viewed as a license to increase the violence.

HOW TO TELL IF YOU'RE ABUSED

Sometimes it's harder for a teenager than an adult to tell whether she's being abused. Teens are more likely, for instance, to engage in horseplay and teasing that sometimes can turn into physical or emotional abuse. You might be playfully wrestling with your boyfriend when he gets the upper hand, twists your arm behind your back, and refuses to let you go until you are hurt or feel humiliated or until you grant him a favor. Later he says it was "just play" and that you shouldn't make an issue of it. He might tease you by throwing you into a swimming pool or taking your purse and showing people the private things in it. You feel scared or furious at being forced into an embarrassing or powerless position, but you laugh to show you're a good sport. Your boyfriend insists it's just fun, and you try to persuade yourself you agree.

Cars offer some young men important ways to display power. Some of them speed or drive recklessly to scare and intimidate their girlfriends or to impress them with their courage or driving skills. If you feel frightened or intimidated or helpless when your boyfriend is showing off, you have a right to insist he stop the car and to get out whenever you want to. The range of abuse is wide, from "joking" remarks about women, to tickling, to forced sex, to threatening with weapons and using them to maim or kill. (For examples, see Who This Book Is For and How to Use It; also see the Teen Power and Control Wheel in the back of the book.)

Emotional abuse can be particularly confusing (see Chapter 22), especially when it is in the guise of friendly playing around. Teasing is one example. You may be expected to be a good sport when your boyfriend makes "jokes" about things you've done or said that you're embarrassed about, or when he makes demeaning remarks about your body, your feelings, your friends, or women in general. He might brag about other women he's interested in or who are chasing him. If you feel embarrassed, hurt, humiliated, or inadequate as a result of his comments, you're being emotionally abused.

If you think he can't help being that way because he doesn't understand how it affects you, it's your job to explain it to him. Find a time when you can be alone with him, and explain what bothers you without laughing, apologizing, or flirting, so that he knows you're serious. If he still doesn't understand or tries to tell you you're wrong, too sensitive, or have no sense of humor, you have a right to tell him you don't want him to do that regardless of whether he understands or agrees with you. If he persists, it's a message that he doesn't care enough about how you feel or that he deliberately teases you to make you feel bad about yourself. In either case he is exercising power and control over you, and your self-esteem is in grave danger of being gradually chipped away so that it will get harder and harder to state how you feel or what you want.

WHO'S RESPONSIBLE FOR THE VIOLENCE?

Hitting is always potentially dangerous, because it tends to bring on more violence, and then more, until finally someone may do serious injury to the person he or she cares most about. Even if it's not immediately dangerous, violence is an indication that one person is either out of control or is using a display of anger to control the other person. Either of those situations will turn a potentially good relationship into a battle zone filled with fear and hostility.

Having said that, let's look at what kind of hitting we're talking about. Setting aside the probability of escalation, some hits are worse than others. When men hit women it usually has much more force and is a greater threat than when a woman hits her boyfriend. For instance, if you hit your boyfriend, it may be a punch on the arm or pummeling him on the chest. If he is three to ten inches taller, 30 to 100 pounds heavier and in good physical shape, it may feel to him like playfulness and not at all threatening. He might not even bother protecting himself. Yet, eventually, if he gets angry, he may hit you with his fist, which is likely to hurt and scare you and begin a process of his controlling you. Then he might blame you, because after all you started it.

It's true that you started it, and you should take responsibility for what you did, but that doesn't mean you're responsible for what he did. Only he can start or stop his violence, just as only you can start or stop yours. It might be that you've hurt him with a weapon or your fist, in which case you should take your problem seriously and get professional help to work on it. If it happens when you're taking drugs or drinking alcohol, you should consider that a problem, too, and get help to stop.

There is some indication that teenage women tend to think violence has a bad effect on their relationships, whether they are hit or the ones who do the hitting. Teenage men, whether they're the abusers or the abused, tend to believe violent acts have a positive effect on the relationship or no impact at all.[9]

If you agree with other young women that violence has a bad effect, you'll probably be able to control your anger as you mature. But your boyfriend may not even try, since he may feel it's not important or even a good thing to do. This might be a reason women become less violent and men more violent to their partners as they grow older.

The pattern may also change because of marriage or childbirth. There is a tendency for more violence to take place in marriages that occur when the couple is very young. Women who are pregnant are also at high risk of being beaten by their husbands or boyfriends. Few teenage men or women are skilled enough to acquire well-paying jobs, and the lack of money, sudden responsibility, and insecurity about living up to adult roles can all add stress to a teenage couple's lives. The stress is not the cause of the violence, but it can provide an excuse for the man who is willing to control by violence, and it can mislead the woman who's being abused into believing her partner can't help what he does.

WHAT TO DO IF YOU'RE HIT

If your boyfriend has slapped, pushed, or threatened you, it's important to take it seriously, whether you've been injured or not. It means he's willing to use physical force to control you, and there's a good chance it will get worse unless you make it absolutely clear you won't allow it. You have to do more than just complain. If you're not ready to break up, which would be the safest thing, you can still say you won't see him until he comes up with a plan to stop the violence and stop controlling you. Good intentions are not enough and he will need professional help.

Let him know that you won't continue seeing him unless he enrolls in a group for men who batter. For a teenager, that may be a challenge, and if there are really no groups for teen batterers, you can insist he find an individual counselor *who specializes in battering and abuse.* If he has hit you only when he's drinking, you might tell him you'll agree to continue seeing him only if he stops drinking entirely and attends a program such as Alcoholics Anonymous. You may think you don't have the right to decide he has a drinking (or drug) problem, but if he hits when he drinks, the drinking and the hitting are both causing you to suffer and you have a right to protect yourself. He will probably be angry at you for "telling him what to do." You can agree with him that it's up to him what he does, and add that it's up to you to decide whether you're going to continue seeing him. That is, you will or won't see him depending on whether you'll be safe with the decision he makes. If he says he drinks or is violent only when he's terribly unhappy or when his father beats him or because he lost his job, you can let him know that not everyone reacts to those troubles by hitting the person he loves. Let him know that regardless of his reasons, which are really excuses, you're going to take responsibility for staying safe.

Right after your boyfriend has mistreated you, you might be tempted to tell him he has to do certain things or you'll never see him again. That's a good idea if you're absolutely sure you mean it. But if there's any possibility you'll change your mind when he brings you flowers, turns his irresistible "little boy" look on you, or when you get lonely, don't do it. You could tell him you're getting to the end of your rope and that if he does it again, there's a chance you'll walk out on him. An advantage to saying what you *might* do is that when the time comes to act you won't feel guilty about not warning him. Every time you make a threat and then don't carry it out, he gets the message that you don't mean what you say and he doesn't have to take anything you say seriously. Wait until you are sure you can carry out what you say. Then it isn't a threat, but the announcement of a plan.

ENDING THE RELATIONSHIP

Sometimes it's hard to leave a boyfriend who takes you to exciting or expensive places and buys you gifts, especially if you have very little money yourself. If that's one of your problems, try to keep two things in mind. First, there are lots of other men out there who would probably do the same for you and would treat you in a loving way. You may not notice them, however, until you stop focusing on the man who's abusing you. Second, if it's important to you to own good things and to go exciting places, this is a good time to plan the job training or education that will enable you to buy yourself luxuries. Then you'll be secure knowing that if you're involved with a man it's because of who he is, not what he can buy you.

Some teenage women (and older ones too) are reluctant to end a sexual relationship because they're afraid they can never have another without being considered "loose" or a "slut." If you do separate, perhaps you'll want to take some time before you get involved with a second man, so you're sure you know your feelings and that they're directed to someone who deserves them. You might decide not to become sexually involved again unless you're married. On the other hand, you might decide you have the right to express your sexual feelings in whatever way seems right to you and your partner. The main thing is that you can take this opportunity to think through your own values and decide whether you're going to make yourself stay in this relationship as a life sentence for a mistake, or whether you're willing to give yourself a second chance at finding a loving sexual partner.

There are many other aspects of teenage life that make it especially hard to cope with an abusive boyfriend, and it may take some time to find a counselor or to persuade your parents to understand your situation. But keep trying. Most important, try to find some trusted friends, whether teenage or adult, to whom you can talk about your situation. If you keep talking and keep analyzing the relationship, you'll soon be able to decide what's the best decision for you.

HOW TO USE *GETTING FREE*

A relationship with a violent boyfriend is physically dangerous, yet when you're intimately involved with a steady boyfriend, the thought of breaking up with him can seem like an even bigger risk emotionally. *Getting Free* is designed to help you weigh the pros and cons of the relationship, to decide what's best for you, and to make the most of the consequences. If you leafed through the rest of the book you might have seen references to parenting and long-term marriages and thought they didn't apply to you. But *Getting Free* is designed to fit the needs of all abused women, regardless of age or circumstances. For instance, most of Chapter 1 and Chapters 4 through 7 are just as pertinent to you as to an older women who's more established in family life. They will help you understand the social aspects of battering, your rights, and your feelings of love, and they will give you suggestions on how to decide whether to leave the man or continue the relationship.

You may think that because an example in an activity doesn't precisely apply to you, the exercise itself won't help you. For instance, in Activity 8, the Worst Fears List, I suggest that the worst fear a woman has about leaving her man might be losing the house and garden she's tended for twenty-two years. If you're seventeen years old you may think that has nothing to do with you. But instead of skipping the activity, think of what your biggest fear is. Maybe it's being without a date for the senior prom, or being treated like a "loser" by your friends, or having to admit that your parents were right, or just being lonely all the time. All of those, and any other fears you have, are important. You can overcome them by using the activities in the book to help you recognize them, analyze whether they're likely to happen, and think through the ways you can make things go well. At the same time, if the worst can't be avoided, you can plan how to cope with it.

Some of the activities emphasize long-term relationships and decisions about children, because those are often the most complex situations and therefore the hardest to change. But it's also true that some young people's situations are especially hard to handle. If you're still in school and financially dependent on your parents, you have fewer choices than many adults. In addition, you have fewer recognized rights. The social pressure may be more intense than in adult communities and there's a tremendous emphasis on love and romance. Perhaps like many teenagers you're socially isolated or have lots of acquaintances but few people you can tell about your fears and dreams. So don't underestimate the difficulties you face in making changes.

Many women take on family feelings and values as soon as they become seriously involved with a man. You might feel loyalty and concern for your boyfriend, place his needs before your own, and sometimes even feel about him that he needs to be nurtured like a child. If those feelings seem like signs of being grown up and having adult responsibilities, you might be paralyzed by feelings of guilt and failure when you think of leaving him. It might feel as if you're abandoning a family member; many men who batter, even very young men, know how to play on those feelings. So even if you're unmarried and have no children, Chapters 2 and 3, which focus on family issues, can help you get a balanced perspective.

Section 2, Getting Professional Help, applies to you as a single teenager or young woman, with the possible exception of the chapter Making Legal Decisions. Each state has different laws for adults and juveniles, so you'll have to get local information about how the law applies to you. You might also need information on how your local courts are likely to deal with your boyfriend, especially if he's a teenager. A justice system that is harsh on adult men who batter may not take the violence of a teenager seriously.

All professionals are obliged by federal law to report abuse of children under eighteen to police or child-protection agencies, though this is sometimes interpreted broadly in various communities. Medical personnel, counselors, shelters, and safe homes may refuse to help you without your parents' permission. It doesn't mean they don't care, but that they would be breaking the law if they did. To avoid these situations, some teenagers who can't get help from their families feel forced to make up a name or lie about their age. Try to get information about what to expect in your community before you are in a crisis by calling a battered women's shelter, a teen runaway center, or a crisis line. It's easy to be anonymous over the phone; when you feel that you can trust the people, you can arrange to see them in person.

Parts of Chapters 14 through 17 are more relevant to adult couples who have established households together or who share children than to single, childless teenagers. In addition to the restrictions on shelters and safe homes already mentioned, in most states you won't be eligible for public assistance unless you have a child, so the sections about shelters and welfare grants may not be of immediate use to you. But other parts of those chapters can be important for you to read and act upon. Activities 23 through 26, which include lists of dangerous things your boyfriend has done to you and a Best Memories list, can be extremely helpful in keeping you safe, no matter what your age or situation. Check the table of contents to see which sections you want to read.

The rest of the book, which includes the chapters on Helping Yourself to Survival, After You Leave, and The Ones Who Got Away, will apply as much to you as to adults. You may also want to read the parts of the book that are about long-term marriages and child-custody problems, so that you can see what might be in store for you if you decide to break up this relationship in ten or twenty years after you've had several children. I hope the book will enable you to get free now, while you have many options for the future.

WHAT CAN A PARENT DO?

Few things are more painful than to watch one's children make dangerous choices. If your daughter is involved with a violent man you certainly will be right to consider it a serious situation. There is usually no way to predict whether a man will confine himself to moderate or infrequent violence or whether he is going to do permanent damage or even kill. In addition to physical injury, the emotional damage is often severe. So what can a parent do that will at least not make matters worse?

As with all teenage-parent conflicts, it makes a crucial difference what kind of relationship exists. The age of the teenager is also important. Some advocates of "tough-love" might advise telling your daughter not to come home until she has severed her relationship with the man. Although in certain cases this might work, there isn't any guarantee; by the time you know the results it may be too late to change your mind.

Abandoning or rejecting your child is the most dangerous thing you can do. The man she is involved with is likely to perceive you as a threat already and to try to cut off contact between you and your daughter. If you send her away, you will play right into his hands and take away the very support your daughter needs to eventually break away.

You may be under a great deal more stress than you can easily handle if you patiently stand by or intermittently rescue your daughter when she has been beaten up, and there comes a time when you must take care of yourself. You may need, from time to time, to limit your involvement with your daughter. If you find yourself too angry or too depressed or too critical to be of support to her, try to enlist another family member or friend to stand by and explain to your child in the most loving way you can that you need a temporary separation. Make it clear that you care about her and want her to be safe because you love her, but that your feeling of helplessness, fear, or anger make it impossible for you to be with her and help. Let her know you will be back with her as soon as possible, and be sure she has the names of others she can call on.

If you can, listen to your daughter, let her talk about the man, and swallow your outrage when she tells you how handsome or loving or needy he is. Think of all the ridiculous things you did as an adolescent and an adult, even if many of them weren't life-threatening. Try to understand that she can love her boyfriend at the same time as she hates him, and that you may see her only when she is in pain or feeling enraged because of what her man has done to her. If you won't listen to the positive aspects of the relationship, she will be even more embarrassed than she already is to talk honestly to you. Nor will there be any likelihood she will listen to your advice. The more she is silent, the more it plays into the isolation that will help the man abuse her.

When you do have an opportunity to spend time with her, try to arrange some of it alone together and some of it joining valued friends or relatives. The more time she spends with people who have been important to her, the better the opportunity to remember she can be liked and loved without being abused. Give her an opportunity to do things that help her feel adequate, whether it's making cookies or playing tennis. The man is, no doubt, regularly assaulting her self-esteem, so it's important for you to take the opportunity not to criticize, but to compliment.

You will be fortunate if you can do those things. Some of you may have lost contact with your daughter because her man has taken her away and demanded she not be in touch with you. If she's a juvenile, calling the police is an option, and it's a better one if her boyfriend is an adult who can be charged with kidnapping or statutory rape. The law in each state varies, so get reliable information about what the likely results will be before you act. Your decision will require weighing legal possibilities as well as how your daughter is likely to react. If the police find her, don't be surprised if she refuses to go with them. There may be nothing you can do if she continually runs away to the man. If that seems likely, you may want to quietly find out where she is and then carefully arrange brief contacts. As long as you are in touch with her you can remind her someone besides her boyfriend cares about her and will nurture her if she decides to leave. As ludicrous as it may seem, she probably feels that he is the only one who loves her, so that message must be countered at every opportunity.

There will be a time when it's appropriate to put all your energy into rescuing your child, and you may think you have to go on doing that, even if it's to no avail or counterproductive. Resist the temptation to continue when it seems to be harmful to her or you. Go about your usual activities and also be sure to be in touch with people you can rely on for support. If you and your partner disagree about what should be done, don't let it put a wedge in your relationship; it's a time when you most need each other and when your daughter needs you to be in the best possible condition. Talk to a third party and try to come to a compromise or at least understanding and respect for each other's positions.

If your son is the violent person, do everything possible to get him into a class for men who batter or at least to a counselor, and be sure to let the young woman know you understand he is in the wrong and that she should not stay with a dangerous man, even if he is your son.

Above all, don't let anger overwhelm you. You may feel like doing violence to the man or even to your daughter, but that is the path that I hope we are all trying to change. To paraphrase the prayer, work at developing the courage to change what you can, the patience to accept what you can't, and the wisdom to know the difference.

CHAPTER 24

LESBIAN ABUSE

In the years since *Getting Free* was first published it has become all too clear that violence is a serious and widespread problem among lesbians. If you are a lesbian who's been battered, you may have been one of the many who were reluctant to have that disturbing news come out of the closet. You might now be among those who feel strongly that open discussion is essential, so that you and other lesbians who are battered can gain the support and practical aid you need. It is a sad irony that so many lesbians worked alongside heterosexuals to establish shelters and safe homes and a national movement against battering but that virtually no services are available for lesbians who are battered and only a handful of articles have been published about the subject. The National Coalition Against Domestic Violence has recognized that disparity and doubled its commitment to work against homophobia within the battered women's movement and to promote services for lesbians.[1]

On local levels both the movement against battering and lesbian communities need to take the problem seriously, working together where they can for mutual education and cooperative services, so that lesbian victims can be assured of safe havens and supportive assistance. The women who need help will be reached as a result of lesbian communities' conducting widespread educational campaigns to the effect that the community is concerned, the community wants to help, and that the victim is not to blame. Services also need to be made available for lesbians who batter and who are determined to change the way they relate to partners.

THE QUESTION OF WHO IS BATTERING

You might find yourself confused about whether you or your partner is "the batterer." Perhaps you have struck back at your partner in self-defense a few times, or maybe you're being battered now, but in your last relationship you were the violent one. Possibly you're still carrying that guilt and the identity of "the batterer," which is not accurate in this relationship. It may even be that you and your partner hit each other with about the same amount of force and frequency. In addition, if you are both emotionally abusive, the picture can become bewildering, especially if your lives and feelings have become so merged that you're sometimes not sure where your personal boundaries are.

There is controversy in the movement about whether "mutual battering" exists. Some workers insist that only one person is the "batterer" and that she is always in control of her partner, even though sometimes it may look like "mutual battering" at first. I am among those who believe that pattern is just one among several—that some women who are fairly evenly matched fight each other with about equal force and regularity, and that couples go through a period in which one abuses and batters the other, and then the second one gets the upper hand and abuses and batters the first one. Or a woman may batter and control a partner who never even strikes back and may rarely resist, yet in her next relationship she is the one who is abused and who doesn't retaliate. I make these judgments on the basis of what women have told me, whereas others have said they distrust the reports of women who are in the midst of these relationships, especially those who have battered.

How to Identify Abuse

Until we have more knowledge about these issues, there are several things that can be kept in mind to help you clarify what's happening to you. Ask yourself if you've been physically threatened or hit by your partner. If the answer is yes, you're physically abused. Are you free to be with friends, dress, cook, and speak as you please, or take courses or do work that you like, without fearing punishment from your partner? If not, then you're being controlled by her, which is the core of abuse. Using the brainwashing and "crazy-making" criteria in Chapter 22 as a checklist, ask yourself if you've been emotionally abused by your partner. If you're being physically, sexually, or emotionally abused, you need some time away from your partner, primarily to be safe. Secondarily, you need time alone and with good friends to regain a clear perspective on what has happened to you.

Here is another set of questions for you: Have I hit, emotionally abused, or tried to control and punish my partner? Have I, for instance, insisted she dress, cook, speak, keep house, make love, drive, and otherwise behave in just the way I think is right? If the answers are yes, you are the only one who can stop it, and you will need to get away from her in order not to hurt her while you learn to stop threatening or abusing her and how to relate intimately without controlling her life.

If either one of you hit the other in self-defense, but it was severe enough to injure one of you or cause either of you to be afraid, that behavior is harmful enough to warrant methods of preventing it in the future. If it was with more force than necessary or even if it was just the amount necessary for defense, there is a serious problem to be dealt with.

THE NATURE OF LESBIAN BATTERING

Some people believe battering between lesbians tends to be "mild." It's possible this attitude exemplifies a need to deny or minimize the existence of violence among lesbians. Perhaps it reflects the fact that many counselors and group leaders have heard about lesbians throwing things or pushing and shoving with no evidence of serious injuries. Or that politically sophisticated lesbians, feminists, and workers in the movement against battering tend to be appalled and frightened at even a small amount of violence in their lives. They realize it is likely to escalate and, like other women, tend to seek help from counselors at an early point in their relationship problems. Even if these speculations are correct, it is also true that there are many dangerously violent lesbians. We know that at least some lesbians who batter defend their actions as necessary and are unwilling to change. Possibly the most dangerous women won't admit to their battering practices until they're confronted by the justice system. We will know more about them when large numbers of lesbians take the risk of calling the police, when police and prosecutors take lesbian battering seriously, and when lesbians who batter are court-ordered to groups.

Research on lesbian battering is more extensive than it was when *Getting Free* was first published or even when the chapter on lesbian battering was added. But it is a long way from catching up with research on battering of women by men. Almost no research has been published about domestic violence in relationships of bisexual or transgender couples. Sexual abuse in lesbian couples has scarcely been recognized.[2]

In spite of great changes in both law and social attitudes, lesbians are at a disadvantage in a number of ways. Depending on the community they live in, they face varying degrees of housing and job discrimination. Police tend not to take seriously a partner's battering of a lesbian, transgendered, or bisexual person. Some states do not allow lesbians and gays access to court orders to protect themselves. Lesbian couples have no guarantee of many of the rights of married heterosexuals, which can become a significant problem for a lesbian who is battered and has a child. Custody issues are complex and vary enormously depending upon where the couple lives. Advice from an expert in domestic violence and law is important. In addition, you should look for expert understanding of issues pertinent to same sex couples.

As with heterosexual couples, money, ethnicity, muscle, or social position can be used to underscore the power an abuser chooses to exercise. But additional kinds of power can be wielded against a partner who is closeted, has a child, or is uncomfortable about her sexual orientation. (See the Heterosexism Power and Control Wheel in the back of the book. Then make a list of abusive control tactics your partner has used against you that are related to your sexual orientation or identity.)

One study did attempt to find out if lesbians who battered had resources that were superior to their partners', but there was no significant correlation. There may be an imbalance of resources that wasn't considered. Perhaps one important resource that gives power is simply the willingness to use physical force. Since most women are not trained to react physically, if a woman chooses that method of combat, her partner may become quickly intimidated and start a pattern of giving in, not to superior power, but to the violent woman's willingness to use it.

When lesbian battering began to be publicly acknowledged, there was speculation that it was the "butches" who battered the "femmes," but it now seems quite evident that this is not a widespread or typical pattern. In many couples where there is battering, "butch-femme" roles aren't played at all. When they are present, it's sometimes the "femme" who does the battering.

Responsibility for Battering

Research aside, some things we do know. Whether the battering is alternately done by you and your partner, whether you fight with equal strength at the same time or whether you or your partner is in physical and psychological control, the person who abuses another is the person responsible for it. Only she can stop it. The abused woman is not to blame for what happens to her. If you are abused, you probably will have to leave your partner to break the pattern, and she will have to do some very hard work for a long period to change her pattern of violence and control. Meanwhile, you will have to get some help in rebuilding your sense of self-worth and your social network. You probably will not be able to continue the relationship in a way that is safe and in which each of you has equal power. Where there is a chance of that, you will need some help from a third party after you've done your individual work to negotiate and keep a new style of relationship.

HOW TO USE *GETTING FREE*

When *Getting Free* was first published I discussed with the editors whether we should include information about lesbian battering. After careful thought we agreed that anything I could have said about it would have been based on little knowledge and a great deal of guess-work, so we made the choice not to try to speak specifically to the needs of lesbians. I did hope, as I mentioned in the original introduc-tion, that much of the book would be useful to lesbians and gay men who were beaten by lovers. Many readers have told us it was true. They used their well-practiced skills in "translating" heterosexual reading matter into language appropriate to their sexual orientation, discard-ing what didn't fit.

Except for the first chapter of *Getting Free,* which is about tradi-tional male and female roles and marriages, most of the material applies with language modifications to lesbians as well as heterosexu-als, though there are certain sections that will have special ramifica-tions for you as a lesbian. To know what you can expect of police and prosecutors, for instance, you will have to make inquiries about the current practices and attitudes toward lesbians in your own communi-ty, and they may be changing rapidly. The same is true for child-custody problems, though in general we know that a nonbirth-giving lesbian partner is likely to have few, if any, custodial rights to children. However, the law differs from state to state and is subject to wide vari-ations in interpretation from one location to another, dependent upon the prevailing or most vocal community values and the biases of indi-vidual judges.

Because issues of confidentiality affect all aspects of lesbian life, you will have to use your imagination in applying some sections of the book, especially if you're in the closet. This may be especially true of the chap-ters on Ending Isolation and Reaching Out. In addition, the sections about self-esteem, such as the chapter on How to Be Your Own Counselor, should be read in the context of how your life and self-esteem have been affected by homophobic societal abuse of you as a lesbian by representatives of many institutions. Careful attention should be paid, as well, to self-criticisms that stem from internalized homophobia reflected from that hostile "real world." Because much of the world is homopho-bic and ready to verbally abuse you just because your sexual orientation is not the same as theirs, it is doubly important that you not collude with them by abusing yourself.

EMERGENCY SERVICES

If you need emergency housing your choices in almost all cities will be limited. In rural communities individual families may provide "safe homes" for a few days, but there is no guarantee they will have any understanding of lesbian issues. If you are fleeing for your life, you may not care about their attitudes for the first twenty-four hours, but when you're in crisis it will not improve your state of mind to be the guest of homophobic individuals. So try to develop an emergency plan, before you need it, that enables you to be with accepting, nurturing people.

If you decide to go to a shelter, you'll need to find out whether the staff are conservative about things such as sexual orientation or are open to housing a lesbian. You might find an empathetic lesbian working there, or other staff and administrators who are committed to serving all women and who provide an atmosphere of acceptance. In some shelters there may be open-minded staff members but they may be prohibited by an administrator or board of directors from even discussing lesbian issues, nor will staff attitudes tell you much about how you'll be accepted by the other women. Some lesbians who are battered have pretended they were involved with a man and found welcome sanctuary in shelters, but the deception has certainly taken a toll.

You're probably hoping you won't ever need emergency housing, but if you have ever had reason even momentarily to consider it, that's an indication you might need it in the future. So if you're not in crisis now, this is the time to gather information. You'll have more time to collect it and you'll be in a better emotional state to absorb and evaluate it.

ENDING ISOLATION

In many communities it is difficult for lesbians who are battered to break through the isolation that once was typical of all battered women. But it can be done. If you're out of the closet and a part of the lesbian community, you will know what agencies are available to assist lesbians with various issues, and you might know which are going to be appropriately concerned about your safety. If you're not sure, and you want to preserve your privacy, make a few discreet inquiries, of the "I have this friend . . . " variety or by telephone. The response will give you an idea of the agency stance regarding battered lesbians. If it seems positive, ask whether there's a group, housing, or individual counseling available, and whether the women providing it are experienced in issues of violence as well as lesbian concerns. You might ask about the broad goals of their program. What role do they think they or the lesbian community in general should play in stopping battering? Who do they think is responsible for battering? Where do they stand on involvement of the justice system in lesbian battering? If the agency doesn't have a clear stand that the person who batters is responsible for it, and if it isn't open to discussing the pros and cons involving police and courts, or if its attitudes toward battering are significantly different from yours, look for help elsewhere.

Confidentiality

Confidentiality is likely to be a special issue for you, and certainly you have a right to keep your situation private, though there may also be some reasons not to. But if it is your choice not to have anyone in the community know who is battering you, or even that it is happening, ask agency representatives about their record-keeping and who has access to the files. Don't accept blanket reassurances, but ask to speak to the director or the person who understands how the system works to get detailed information. Where are the files kept? How detailed are they? Who has access to them? How will you gain access to them if you want to read them? If you plan to go to a group or counseling session, find out if there is a community-center atmosphere in which many people may see you come and go. If so, you may encounter acquaintances who will ask innocent, but disturbing, questions. If you're not clever at deflecting questions such as "What are you here for?" you might be better off seeking help somewhere else.

Counseling Services

Once you're satisfied that your confidentiality will be maintained or have decided it isn't an issue, then you need to find out which available service suits your needs. If there is no special program for women who have been battered, you might still get some help. You may want to join a general support or therapy group in which you can discuss your relationship. Talk to the leader about what you want and find out whether she is sympathic to your situation and whether her support will continue no matter what decisions you make. Ask her to think about whether the members of the group will be understanding rather than impatient with you for not living up to their images of what a woman, a feminist, or a lesbian should be. You might ask her to explain your situation and needs to the group or to give you time to do it yourself, postponing commitment until you know what their responses are.

If your need for privacy is great or you don't want to be associated with lesbian-serving agencies, you can make similar inquiries of shelter or safe-home personnel or crisis lines for battered women. Many of them will be able to offer supportive crisis counseling and information about housing, welfare, and the police, but you will have to ask them in each instance whether they have special reason to know that what they are saying applies to lesbians as well as heterosexuals. In some instances, they may not have the information but will be willing to find out for you. If so, let them do it. It will take some pressure off you and give them an opportunity to inform themselves, which will benefit the next lesbian who calls.

Finding Support

It may be that the best decision for you is to be completely open about the battering. To say out loud what is happening can be a strong message to yourself that you are not the one to blame and that you are not ashamed. It can also be a message to the lesbian community that yes, this really is happening right in our backyard, and we need to start taking care of it. Of course, you won't want to take the risk of speaking out unless you have an idea you will get at least some support. You will need most of your energy to deal with your fear, your anger, and your sorrow. There may not be much strength left to fight a difficult political battle within your own community (though for some people that can enhance courage rather than diminish it). Try speaking to one friend or community activist at a time and see what kind of response you get. If it's negative, don't give up, but feel out the next person carefully until you've found a couple of people who will stand by you.

If you decide there is no support for you in the community or you are so much in the closet that you dare not even ask for it, you may be better off to find an individual counselor who is familiar with battering and knowledgeable about lesbian issues or at least willing to learn. No matter what your lifestyle or what decision you make, the support of caring, understanding people is essential to get through your ordeal with the least amount of emotional scarring.

CHAPTER 25

IMMIGRANT WOMEN: CHALLENGES AND SOLUTIONS

"I can't tell anyone outside my community; they'll think we are terrible people."

"I tried to tell my mother but she said I have shamed the family."

"I can't call the police, because they will arrest my husband and deport him."

"If I divorce him, I'll be sent back home, and my family won't accept me."

"I can't speak English, can't drive, and don't have a paid job, so how could I make it on my own?"

If you have had thoughts like those quoted above, you are not alone. Immigrant women involved with men who mistreat them face complicated, frightening situations. It sometimes feels as if there is nowhere to turn without running into even more problems. But in the United States physical and sexual abuse are against the law, which means you can find people to help you keep yourself and your children safe.

Abusive men can use your fears to intimidate and threaten you. Maybe you don't yet know much about United States cultures, don't speak English, or you are dependent on your husband for your immigration status. An abusive man will use all of those factors to gain control over your life. Think about how many of the tactics have been used against you. What other forms of control and abuse has your partner used? You will find information about solving problems and creating a safe environment in other parts of *Getting Free*. But this chapter describes problems that are especially challenging for abused immigrant women and suggests ways to get help in resolving them.

ADVOCATES FOR ABUSED IMMIGRANT WOMEN

Definitions

Under immigration law emotional abuse is considered "extreme cruelty" and not "battering." In law "battering" refers to physical acts of violence. But in this book we use "battering" and "marital or domestic violence" to include emotional and sexual abuse as well as violence perpetrated against a wife or intimate partner. "Mistreatment" and "abuse" are used here to mean power tactics that are meant to control and emotionally abuse an intimate partner. Those terms could include violence. Women sometimes abuse their partners but not nearly as often as men do, and they rarely cause serious injury. That is why most of *Getting Free* focuses on how a woman can cope with a male partner who batters her. Lesbian battering is discussed in Chapter 24. I use "husband," "spouse," and "intimate partner" interchangeably.

"Advocate" refers to a worker in a domestic-abuse shelter or at a hot line who has special training in domestic violence. She might have other kinds of training. In most instances she is not a lawyer. Advocates are trained to offer information and support to abused women. Their job is to show you what options are open to you. They can also help find other experts to advise you about laws related to immigration. If you have questions about your immigration status, it is *not* a good idea to go to the U.S. Immigration office until you have talked to an attorney about your rights and what you might expect. That means consulting an attorney who is a specialist in immigration and well informed about domestic violence.

You may have already talked to officials at the former INS or Immigration and Naturalization Service. That office is now called the U.S. Citizen and Immigration Service or USCIS or just CIS. The change can be confusing so I will refer to all branches as "immigration services" or just "Immigration." If you don't know what your immigration status is or if there is any possibility that there might be a problem with it, you are safer not to contact the office directly anyway. If you live in a small town or rural area where there is no nongovernmental immigration "clinic" that specializes in issues related to domestic violence, an advocate might arrange for you to speak to a specialist in another community. That person can tell you by telephone what you need to know.

If you live in a large city or a town where there are many people from your country, try to find an agency where advocates understand your language and culture. Look for one that specializes in helping immigrants who have experienced domestic violence. Advocates in such agencies will usually know how your local police and courts work. They can give you expert advice on how to make a safety plan. They will not tell you to leave your partner. They can tell you what to expect if you need to call police while you are staying with your partner. If you want to separate, the complications of being on your own might seem overwhelming. But advocates can also help you find people who speak your language

KNOW YOUR RIGHTS

If any governmental official (police officer, FBI agent, INS official) wishes to engage you in conversation, all persons, citizens and non-citizens, have the constitutional right to remain silent and request a lawyer. You should know that anything you say to a police officer can be used against you. Thus, if a police officer or other governmental official wishes to ask you questions about a suspected crime, you have the right to tell the officer: "I wish to remain silent; I want to speak to a lawyer." You do not have to say anything else, and do not sign anything.

Some officers may be insistent, even after you tell them you wish to remain silent. Do not say anything until you have spoken to a lawyer.

If the police, FBI, or INS come to your home, you have the right to refuse them entry, unless they produce a warrant from a judge. If they do not have a warrant, you do not have to not let the police, FBI, or INS into your home. You have the right to close the door. You have the right to say, "I do not want to talk to you until I have spoken to a lawyer." If you give them permission, they may enter legally. If you throw the door open and wave them in you are probably giving permission. You should say politely that you do not want to speak to them, that they do not have permission to enter your home, and that if they leave a phone number, your lawyer will call them. There are lawyers with the Public Defender Association who are on call 24 hours a day at 206-447-3900. You may have to leave a message.

Your skin color, accent, or the language you speak are not lawful reasons for an INS agent or any other officer to question, detain, threaten, or arrest you. Your color or language do not legally justify a presumption that you are not a U.S. citizen. You do not have to speak to an INS agent, and if you do, they will usually claim later that you did so voluntarily. However, if you answer their questions, including questions about where you were born, that may give them a "reasonable suspicion" that you are not a citizen.

You have the right to speak to an attorney before answering any questions or signing any documents (you should *never* sign documents without first speaking to an immigration attorney). If an INS agent or any other officer approaches you, the safest thing to do is to say that you don't want to talk, ask to speak with your lawyer, and remain silent. It is a crime to lie to a federal official or other law enforcement officer, about anything. It is much safer to say that you don't want to talk, and then remain silent until you contact a lawyer.

If you are accused of something that makes you deportable, you will have the right to a hearing with an Immigration judge and the right to have an attorney represent you at that hearing and in any interview with INS (there are no government-paid lawyers, as there are in criminal proceedings, however). Do not give up this right. Insist on a hearing especially if you are detained.

Unless you have already gone through a whole proceeding and already have a final, unappealed, deportation order, the INS cannot just grab you and take you to the plane and deport you. You do get a day in court. Don't sign anything that gives it up.

If you are being questioned by the INS or police about your immigration status or about a suspected crime, tell the officer you wish to contact a lawyer at these phone numbers:

For immigration issues:
National Immigration Law Center
(213) 639-3900
info@nilc.org;
United States Immigration Lawyers Association
(212) 566-5297
info@usila.net

For criminal issues:
your local Public Defender

To report harassment, discrimination or incidents of violence:
your local American Civil Liberties Union;
Arab American Anti-Discrimination Committee
(202) 244-2990

Adapted with the permission from the Northwest Immigration Rights Project and understand your culture. They can help you escape and reorganize your life safely.

Asha's Story

A Somali woman I'll call Asha had no marketable skills and could not speak English. She had little hope of escaping her husband's abuse. But she found an agency specializing in services for abused immigrant women. An advocate showed her how to get a court order to keep her husband away. She enrolled in an English class, and later she took a professional child-care course. Asha now has a job at a daycare center and she and her children are safe.

ASSESSING DANGER

You may have lived with risks for long enough that each time you survive you think the danger is over. You talk yourself into believing that it was just stress, or just job troubles, or just alcohol that caused the violence. At least, you tell yourself, the abuse is not getting worse. Maybe it will never happen again. But in most instances, it *will* happen again. Probably it will happen more often and you will suffer more severe injuries.

At the beginning of this book is a Danger Assessment list. It can help you evaluate the seriousness of the risks you live with. In Who This Book Is For and How to Use It, I suggest ways to use the list. Turn to the list now and then follow the accompanying suggestions.

Studies have found that the more situations or kinds of abuse on the Danger Assessment list that a woman experienced, the more likely it was that her partner would try to kill her. But statistics don't tell us what is true of any individual woman. A few of the women in the studies had not been physically abused at all before the batterer murdered or attempted to murder them. So even if most of the listed danger signs do not match your partner's behavior, *that does not necessarily mean you are safe.* Even if your partner's abuse has not been physical, you still have no guarantee that his power and control tactics won't suddenly escalate. If he becomes violent, there is no way to know whether you will be killed or not.

SAFETY PLAN FOR STAYING OR LEAVING

It is important to take seriously the risks on the Danger Assessment list, even if you have left your partner. But there are many actions you can take to increase your own and your children's safety. The Safety Plan for You and Your Family, appears near the Danger Assessment list because it is important to keep in mind *both* the dangers *and* all the ways you can protect yourself. If you decide to stay with your abusive partner, look carefully at how you can increase your safety. Then, if he threatens your life and you have to leave home suddenly, you will know what to do and what to take with you. You will know where to go and how to get there even it is a safe haven for only a few hours or overnight.

Documents to Keep in a Safe Place

Here are some tips to add to the basic safety plan. If you have to leave in a hurry, you might have to stay away longer than you would like. While you are gone your husband may destroy papers you need for court proceedings. He might take records you will need to enroll your children in a new school or for medical treatment. He might hide documents you need to prove your right to stay in the country. If you know your important papers or copies of them are safe, you will not have to worry. Along with medicines, prescriptions, and eyeglasses, keep these documents, or copies of them, in a safe place:

- Your immigration papers
- Your husband's immigration papers
- Your and his driver's licenses
- Proof of marriage or similar relationship: wedding certificate or photos, love letters, or envelopes, bills, or rent receipts addressed jointly to you and your husband
- Medical records
- Records of police reports
- Children's school records, birth certificates, medical records

Begin to collect the items you can as soon as safely possible

Don't forget to see the longer basic safety plan, Safety Plan for You and Your Family, in Who This Book Is For and How to Use It in the beginning of this book.

Don't wait until the last minute to find and copy and secure the papers. Your husband may suspect you are thinking of temporarily or permanently separating. If he hides immigration papers it will be a challenge to establish your right to stay in the country. But even if he does that, you can find ways to prove your right to file for a green card or work visa. It might take longer and you may need extra help. Call a domestic-violence crisis line or shelter or an immigration lawyer who understands domestic violence. To avoid direct contact with Immigration, ask for a referral to someone who is *not* in the government. You might have to go from one referral to another a few times. But it will be worth it.

Even if you feel sure you will never divorce your husband, secure your documents just in case. Your spouse can threaten you by saying he is the one who controls your status. He might claim he is the only one who has the right to keep papers that prove you signed agreements together, including your marriage contract. If he becomes more violent, you might decide you have to separate after all. Even if you leave for a very short time you may need those papers. But if your husband knows what you are doing, he could become dangerous. So after you copy them, be careful to return the originals to their place.

Leave copies of everything with someone you trust. You might never need them. But if you ever have to leave home, knowing you have access to copies of those papers can give you a feeling of confidence. You are taking away one of your partner's control tactics. Keep reminding yourself that each step of the plan brings you closer to safety. It will feel good to know you have done your best to be prepared. Then you can focus on other tasks, such as gathering more information about your choices. Whether you want to leave your husband soon, later, or never, it is important to know what kind of help you can rely on in an emergency.

TO CALL THE POLICE OR NOT

As an immigrant you might be afraid to call the police, even if your life is threatened. Fear of being deported can keep you from taking action to protect yourself. The events of 9/11 might have made you afraid, especially if you are from the Middle East, India, or Africa, if you have dark skin, or you wear a headdress that suggests your religion or culture. You might have good reasons to be on guard, not only around your abusive husband, but also in contacts with authorities.

Local police are not supposed to discuss your immigration status with immigration officers, and usually they don't. But it won't hurt to be cautious. Immigration policies are opening up for abused women. But at the same time, other laws and regulations are changing in ways that can hurt you. If an officer asks, "Where are you from?" the question might be intended to be friendly. But depending on your situation, it could be safer not to answer. You might, for instance, have come into the country illegally and be living near a national border. Maybe you have learned that police are hostile toward immigrants. Those are the kinds of situations that make it important to plan what you will do.

If you don't speak English you can prepare for such situations. Right now, before you need it, ask an English speaker to prepare a card for you.

Ask her to write, "I do not speak English. I speak _____." Some people advise adding, "I do not want to talk to you without an attorney," and that is your right. But if you need the police, you take a risk in not talking to them, even without an attorney present. Keep the card with you all the time. It might not be necessary to use it when you are the one who called police. But you may find it useful if you are stopped by an officer in another situation. It is important not to answer questions. You have a legal right to remain silent. It is your right not to speak until a lawyer is with you. See the Know Your Rights list at the beginning of this chapter.

You may find dramatic differences between the ways police respond in the United States and in your home country. Some women's former lives in dictatorial countries affect beliefs about police officers here. They say police are there only to "preserve money and power for men." They think the only purpose of police is to "protect the government and maintain the status quo." Other women come from a country where members of the public have to pay off a police officer for every service provided. Those situations are rarely the case here. However, it may seem that way in a city where police are not well trained. An officer who batters his own wife may not take your situation seriously. If the police chief doesn't give officers a strong message that battering is a crime, they may not know what to do in your case. Every community is different. But even in the worst of police systems, an officer should see that you are safe at least for the night. You need up-to-date information from local advocates on how the local police behave toward immigrants and toward battered women. That is especially necessary if you live in a town near a national border.

Calling Police in an Emergency

If you don't have a phone, try to find a neighbor or friend who will let you use hers in an emergency. If you are attacked or threatened with assault, dial 911. Explain what has been done to you. Police officers will be sent to your home. Even if you don't speak English, the 911 operator will be able to tell where the call came from unless you are on a cell phone. If you don't speak English at all and you are likely to call from a cell phone, take time soon to learn a few words so you can say, "My name is _____. I live at _____. I am being attacked." If the 911 dispatcher thinks you are in serious danger, she or he will probably send an officer and a medical team right away. If you need to go to a hospital, they will take you there.

When the police arrive at your home, show them any bruises, cuts, red marks, or other signs of injury, even if that seems embarrassing. Not every police department is able or willing to send a female officer. But if it is important to you, it won't hurt to ask for one. If it is difficult for you to speak English, ask for a translator. Or hand the officer the card mentioned above that says in English what language you speak. It is *not* a good idea to rely on your children for translations. They may feel torn between loyalty to you and to their father. They might be afraid to translate the truth about what happened. They may not have the vocabulary to explain what happened or what you want. Finally, they might be too frightened—of the batterer or the police—to think clearly.

Friends may want to help, but if they translate for you, they may not do it accurately. In some instances, border-town police have asked immigration officers to translate for them. But do not under any circumstances agree to that. It is important to tell police officers exactly what you want them to know. For that you need a professional translator who is not part of immigration services. American law states that you have a right to a translator.

If you want the police to take action, do not tell them everything is fine. Don't say you are safe now, even if your husband is acting the part of a loving, caring person. Officers may believe you. They might leave you alone with your husband, who in reality could be furious and in turn even more violent because you called the police. If the police arrest your husband, they might suggest that you will be safe staying in your home. But that is not good advice. There is no way to tell how long he will stay in jail. You need time and a safe place to heal, rest, and to decide what to do next. It is hard to do that when you are looking over your shoulder in fear every minute. Ask the police to take you to a shelter or to help you find other transportation to a safe place for the night.

If Your Husband Is Arrested: The Police Report and Immigration Issues

The police may arrest your husband and if they do, they should make a report. Some cities require that officers write reports of all domestic violence whether there is an arrest or not. Go to the police station soon, ask for a copy of the report, and keep it in a safe place with other important papers. If at a later time your husband becomes more dangerous, the report can be useful to show a judge that this is not the first time you have been assaulted. If later you decide to separate, it can prove that you need a court order to keep your husband away from you. It could contribute to your gaining custody of your children or to establishing your independent legal immigration status.

But maybe you are not sure of your immigration status or of your husband's. You might be worried about one of you losing the right to stay in the country. If he is not a citizen and is convicted of a crime, he could be placed in deportation proceedings. His leaving the United States could save your life, as well as the lives of your children. But you might not want him deported. Maybe you are afraid of his threatening your family in your home country. You might worry that he will kidnap your children and take them there. If he leaves the United States you could lose access to child support. You have to weigh all those possibilities. What might you gain and lose from his being out of the country? That is why it's a good idea to think ahead of time about what you will do if your life is in danger. You can find more about calling the police, prosecution, and court orders in Chapter 7, Emergency Help from Doctors, Police, and Prosecutors.

WHEN THE POLICE DON'T COME: PLANNING AN EMERGENCY ESCAPE

Even though you are not in danger now, that could change. This is the best time to make a plan to leave quickly in case of emergency. If you are in danger, you might not be able to call the police. The abuser may have cut the telephone cord or smashed the phone. Or the police haven't come and your husband is threatening you with a knife or gun. If you have a car and a driver's license you can try making a run for it. Or you might be able to escape to a neighbor's home. Even if you believe you will never need to call the police or leave home suddenly, it is good to be prepared. See the section Leaving to Protect Yourself in Chapter 6, Making the Decision. Follow the suggestions in Safety Plan for You and Your Family in Who This Book Is For and How to Use It (it is repeated in the Resources section of the back of the book for ease of reference). Gather as much information as you can about what kinds of help are available. Advocates at a local domestic-violence crisis line or shelter can give you valuable information. You can also telephone 800/799-SAFE (800/799-7233), 800/787-3224 TTY. Even though those are national numbers, advocates there can find you information about help in your own community.

Emergency Shelters for Immigrant Women and Children

In your home country there may be few shelters or none at all to help women who are battered. But in almost every U.S. city there is at least one shelter. It might consist of a large building, where several women or a few families can stay for several days, a month, or even longer. An agency could arrange for women to stay with private families in safe homes. Or they might give you a voucher to stay for a few days in a motel. Shelter advocates know what you can expect from the police in that particular community, as well as from prosecutors and programs for men who batter. They know how to find financial aid and housing. They can help you find people who speak your language or who belong to your religious group. They can find experts to advise you about your immigration status. They will provide a safe place to stay for a few days or even for much longer.

You might expect to feel uncomfortable in a shelter that takes in all kinds of women and children. I recently visited a shelter where there was a resident from Lithuania, one from Mexico, and another from Ethiopia. That reminded me of an advocate who said, "In a shelter no one needs to feel 'different,' because *everyone* is different." Maybe you worry about whether you will be able to follow your religious or cultural rules about diet. But avoiding certain foods or ways of preparing them should not be a problem. Almost any shelter can arrange for vegetarian meals or for your food to be served on paper plates. Those two things should take care of most of your requirements. Ask an advocate to explain in detail what you can expect.

DIVORCE OR SEPARATION FROM YOUR PARTNER: IMMIGRATION STATUS

You might want to know whether you can leave your husband permanently and stay in the United States. That depends partly on what kind of resident status you have. It could also depend on his status. But changes in immigration law have opened new doors to applying for legal residency independent of your spouse.

If you are a refugee: You might have found it hard to adapt to the United States. Maybe you came from a village in a completely different culture to a large city in the United States. You might have survived a civil war. Perhaps you ran from guerrilla attacks. Now you are subjected to a new kind of danger from your partner in a place where you don't know the territory. But on the plus side, as a refugee you have certain privileges. Most important, you may have been issued your own green card. If you decide to leave your husband, you will not lose your refugee status. You won't have to worry about being deported. You can also work and apply for citizenship.

If your husband has a green card or is a U.S. citizen: If this is the case, your residential status depends on his willingness to apply for a card for you. Not so long ago you could not divorce him without putting yourself in danger of being deported. Many immigrant women were trapped in marriages to violent partners who refused to apply for green cards for them. In 1990 a study found that 34 percent of undocumented women had experienced domestic violence and almost half stated that the violence increased after they came to the United States.[1] By 1994, some members of Congress discovered that 83 percent of battered immigrants surveyed did not contact law enforcement about their problems. Many of them were afraid the police would have them deported. Congress reacted to that information by modifying the Violence Against Women Act (VAWA). The changes opened a door for some immigrant women to "self-petition." That means they can apply for a green card without a husband's cooperation.

Self-petition—if you divorce a resident or citizen and lack immigration documents: Your husband or partner may have lied to you about filing for a green card for you. If your immigration status depends on his cooperation for your own green card, he might make the application but then revoke it. He might even lie to immigration officials about you, claiming you married him only to get legal status. Whether you plan to stay with your spouse or leave him, you can self-petition for your own residency status. You do not need your husband's cooperation or his signature.

Your husband may not know about your option to self-petition. If he learns about the changes in VAWA, he will probably try to keep you from finding out about them. As long as he thinks you don't know he won't be suspicious of your gathering documents. You don't have to tell him you have found a way to get away from him. It is better to wait until you are ready, which may take quite a while.

The new regulations are designed specifically for immigrants who have been abused by spouses. They could apply to you even if you do not have documents. They can enable women abused by husbands to divorce them without fear of losing a possibility for a green card. But you have to file the petition within two years of the divorce and show that the divorce was related to the domestic violence. The new law is meant to offer you some of the protections available to other battered women.

The "U Visa" for abused women who cooperate with the justice system: If you have been battered by a spouse who is neither a U.S. citizen nor a legal permanent resident, another modification of VAWA might allow you to apply for your own U Visa; the provision could give you access to legal status *if* you have been the victim of a crime. If your children have experienced abuse, they may also be entitled to some benefits under this provision. Battering is a crime and you must be willing to cooperate with the government in its prosecution of the perpetrator. But that does not necessarily mean you would have to testify against him. You would need a letter from a prosecutor certifying that you were subjected to abuse. So if you ever call the police when your spouse has assaulted you, say that you need to get legal help to apply for U Visa status. Do that even if you don't plan to separate or file for divorce. The certification is one more source of security in case your situation changes. It should be kept with other important papers.

If your intimate partner has a work visa: Suppose you and your husband are from a country where highly skilled workers such as your husband are encouraged to apply for work visas. Suppose you are a legally dependent wife. Your visa may not allow you to work. If you divorce your husband, you won't be eligible to apply for a green card that puts you in line for permanent residency or citizenship. Even in that situation, you might have some advantages. Formal education or fluency in English will make it easier to understand how the legal system works. That may provide you with room to maneuver.

The government has not issued clear guidelines on what is needed to apply for the U Visa, and that can make it risky. But it has been invaluable to some women who had no other option. It could be worth trying if other avenues fail. The U Visa has helped a number of women with H4 status to get "interim relief." That temporary status has not allowed them to apply for a green card but at least it allows them to stay in the country and to work. If they divorced a husband who had a work permit, a more permanent status might be approved later.

The laws and their interpretations are complicated. The application process may take a very long time. If you want to become a citizen, it could take many years. You might hear stories from friends about what worked for them or did not. But keep in mind that every situation is different. You need to check your eligibility for a particular immigrant status with a private immigration expert. That person must be familiar with these laws and also with domestic violence. Even then, you cannot be certain of what will happen. You will submit your papers and maybe will be asked for more. Then immigration services must officially inform you of their decision.

Don't give up. The laws are regularly reviewed and frequently change. Women's legal organizations are working to get the provisions broadened. Keep checking to see if modifications make you eligible.

Anju's Story

A woman from South Asia I'll call Anju was desperate to escape from her husband. He had held a knife to her throat and sexually abused her. He was a U.S. citizen. Her four children from a previous marriage were in her home country, and she hadn't seen them for seven years. Her husband kept saying that he would file papers for her green card. But he did not do it. He threatened that if she called police she would be deported. That frightened her because she had entered the United States without documents. Anju's strong desire to separate from her husband was complicated because he was disabled, and she felt guilty about leaving him. He kept her from leaving the house except to go to her job. Her situation seemed hopeless.

But Anju found a way to make occasional phone contact with advocates. They were trained to help battered immigrant women. Through them she was able to get information and advice from an immigration attorney knowledgeable about domestic violence. Whenever she could safely get to a phone she called for more information. It took a long time to gather her documents and prepare to apply for a green card. Then it took about two more years for the process to move from application through VAWA to approval. But Anju now has a green card. Finally she can visit her children without worrying about her right to reenter the United States.

Anju's story illustrates a nearly hopeless situation that turned out—with the help of smart, well-informed professionals—not to be hopeless after all. It also is an example of how much patience you need for this process. Immigration bureaucracies can be very, very slow in making decisions. But immigration and domestic-violence advocates and lawyers were with Anju every step of the way. In many cities such services are free. A legal advocate at a shelter or legal clinic or hot line can talk to authorities for you. She might even sit in on your interviews with them and take notes for you. If necessary she can help find an expert in another town whom you can consult by phone.

PEOPLE'S IDEAS AND ACTIONS CHANGE

Tukata's Story

A Laotian woman I'll call Tukata and her abusive partner lived together for 23 years. Outside their home, they appeared to be a perfect couple. But for a long time they had lived mostly separate lives. Their living quarters were divided by a wall of blankets and each stayed on one side of it.

They cooked independently and rarely spoke to each other. They had not shared a bed for many years. Sometimes Tukata could not avoid walking past her husband. Then he would suddenly stick his foot out to trip her. She once called the police when he threatened her. But people in her community urged her not to press charges. "That's just the way it is," they said. "Husbands and wives fight. Just make it up." So she did not cooperate with the police, and they did not follow through.

Perhaps in the past your appeals for help to your community or police had an effect opposite of what you hoped for. That happened to Tukata the first time she tried. Perhaps you also have been told to "live with it." Or police officers haven't understood the seriousness of your situation. That doesn't mean they will always react that way. Circumstances change. People change.

Five years after the time Tukata tried to get help, her husband threatened to shoot her. He had a gun in his hand, so she believed him and she reached for the phone. But he reached it first and smashed it. She was able to run to a neighbor's house, and the neighbor called the police. This time police cooperation enabled her to get a court order. That kept her husband away.

Tukata thought that because she could not get help the first time she asked, it would never be available to her. But the second time police reacted differently. Her neighbors responded too, even though earlier her own community had not helped. Getting help from others probably saved Tukata's life. Calling on someone in an emergency may save yours as well. Maybe you don't want to ask someone in your own immigrant community to watch out for you. In that case, consider appealing to a neighbor or someone at work. She might see your situation differently from how people you are closest to view it.

Immigrant Communities Change

After living in the United States for years, many immigrants change. Members of your own community may have begun to realize how dangerous battering can be. It may seem to you that if you leave your partner no one will be on your side. People might say, "Divorce is not an option in our culture." Or "Battering does not happen" or "It is 'normal' in our culture." Not long ago almost everyone in the United States held very similar beliefs. Until about twenty years ago they said, "Battering doesn't happen to people like us." A couple of decades before that, divorce was generally frowned on.

People from many cultures gradually change as they become used to living in a new country. Some have learned that for women in danger, separation is the only way they can maintain their own safety or that of their children. And even though some denied it for years, many ethnic, religious, and national cultures now know there is battering within their communities. Such changes may be just one way they are becoming Americanized. They might not even realize themselves how much they are adapting to the U.S. culture. You might say with confidence that "the community" or "our people" follow certain customs or beliefs. But stop a minute and consider what evidence you have. Does everyone in your culture feel that way? For example, in East Indian communities marriages are arranged by families. But sometimes they are not. Or they are arranged in a variety of ways. The woman might not see the prospective groom before the wedding. Or she could meet him several times and approve the marriage. There are families in which the mother-in-law rules the roost and even abuses her daughter-in-law. In others she does not interfere with her son's family at all. A woman who divorces her abusive husband may be banished from her extended family. Yet another family may welcome her back.

Count the number of people who have actually expressed their opinions on the topic of battering. How many have told you what they think about men controlling their wives? About divorce? Maybe you can only be sure of what a small number of people believe. In general conversations with friends you can watch for opportunities to raise the topic of marital violence or divorce. Listen carefully to the responses to your questions. Some opinions might surprise you. Keep listening until you find someone who understands the problem in the same way you do.

Police Respond Differently

Police officers sometimes change, too. Sometimes the chief gives them new orders. There is a chance that since you called them, they have received more training about abuse. Maybe they have learned more about how to help immigrants or people who don't speak English. They have quite a bit of discretion, which means each officer might respond differently from another in a similar situation.

Your Situation Changes

Your circumstances might be different, too. Sometimes you have to change your life even though it isn't what you choose. Look at Tukata's story again; she had to make decisions she never thought she would face after her husband was ordered to keep away.

Tukata had not expected all that to happen. She was not ready to leave her husband. The house was owned jointly with him and it was paid off.

She was afraid that if she divorced she would have no place to live. Besides, in her community, as head of the household, the man makes all the important decisions, even if the woman earns money outside the home. She could not make such a big decision as initiating a divorce on her own.

Tukata's husband moved out of the house. Then two weeks later he filed for divorce. Tukata was shocked. During her ten years in the United States, she had maintained many Laotian traditions. Even though she had not initiated the divorce, she felt shamed in front of her Laotian community. Still, in her home country she would have been at home with the children. Or she might have worked in the fields all day with no money of her own. She would not have any knowledge of the economic world. She would have had no way to support herself. But in the United States she had a job as an assembler. Since her children were grown, she did not face serious financial problems. She was able to speak a little English, which was also an advantage.

LIFE IN THE UNITED STATES

Whether you stay with your husband or leave, life in the United States will be easier if you learn English. Maybe your husband has prevented you from doing that. It may seem an overwhelming task to persuade him it is a good idea or to attend a class secretly. To find a school you can afford and to learn English may seem impossible. But if your children are in school, you may be able to enlist their help. As mentioned earlier, a few important phrases, such as "Help!" and your name and address, "My husband hit me," and "I speak _____" can make a crucial difference, and may even save your life.

Battered Immigrant Women Adapt to New Lives

It can be hard to hold onto your own ethnic and cultural values while you also try to adapt to this new country. You might feel upset when your children take on the customs of schoolmates. Worry about their American habits can increase your fear of getting along on your own. Maybe you think you will never learn English, find your way around the city, or be able to get a job. So it is important to learn as much as you can about your options in this culture. Farhiya, an advocate, tells how one refugee woman I'll call Maryam used the services at Farhiya's agency to increase her options and change her life.

"Maryam had only been in the United States eight months and her husband was abusing her. She was 'countryside' and had never been to school. She lived in another state where she called 911, and her husband was put in jail. But she had five children, the youngest eight months. The other ones were under four and a half. Maryam's friends sent her money and told her to come here (to the agency). They showed her how to take a bus to this new place and she left her home state.

"She didn't know how to write even in her own language, so first she had to learn how to hold a pencil. She didn't know how to take the bus, or how to use a car. It was very hard. She didn't even know what food she could buy, because she couldn't read.

"But now Maryam is going by herself to the bus, taking her kids to school, has learned English, and has her own home. She knows how to get a money order and pay her bills. She can manage everything by herself. Before, with her husband, she could not do any of it."

Farhiya, the advocate, knows the struggles of women like Maryam because she came to the U.S. as a refugee herself when she spoke no English. She had to learn some of the same things as Maryam.

Here is another woman's story. Like many immigrant women, Maria was surprised to learn that U.S. laws and customs are different from those in her home country. She grew up in Mexico and was twenty years old when she gave birth to a baby boy. The father's family wanted him to have custody of the baby. Afraid that Mexican law and the father's family money would make it impossible for her to keep the baby, Maria escaped to the United States. She worked in the fields picking fruit for many years, married, and had four more children. She endured her second husband Jesus's cruelty and beatings because she loved him, and also because she didn't realize custody laws are different here.

"I thought he could take my children away. And when someone doesn't know about laws one person can say that in the U.S. they are exactly the way they are in Mexico. I saw a small ad in a newspaper: 'If you are a victim of domestic violence we have free lawyers to help.' It was for Las Amigas and I went there to a group. A prosecutor talked to us and that is when I started to be interested in learning more and I started training to help other women.

"So many women don't know the law. At Las Amigas we talk in the Hispanic community about the rights that females have. Sometimes the husbands kick them out of their houses and we find shelters for them. We have an office but our cars are really our offices because there are hardly any buses for women to come to us. We go to the community instead of waiting for them to come to us."

When Maria finally went to the police her husband followed her and tried to persuade them that *she* had beaten *him*. But they took one look at her injuries and believed her. After 23 years she was able to separate and to maintain custody of her two teenagers still at home. Now she is glad to help other women learn about the law and their rights to safety.

Like other abused women, what you have already been through has probably made you stronger than you realize. Most likely you are brave enough to stand on your own and create your own safe haven. But the great thing is that *you will not have to stand alone.* An entire movement against violence to women stands with you.

CHAPTER 26

RELIGIOUS CHALLENGES

"It's right here in the Bible, in black and white, Ephesians, 5:22-3: 'For the husband is the head of the wife as Christ is the head of the church, his body, and is himself its Savior.'"

"The Prophet Muhammad says men have rights over their wives. You have to do what I tell you."

"It's the obligation of a Jewish wife to create *Shalom Bayit*" (Peace in the Home).

If your husband makes a statement like one of those above, you might be intimidated into thinking he must be right. Honest believers can of course disagree about interpretations of religious texts. But an abusive man married to an observant woman will take words out of their context to distort their meaning deliberately. He will use whatever tools are available for his own benefit without regard for your desires or rights.

In addition to helping you decide if you are being emotionally or physically battered by your spouse, this chapter provides keys to deciding whether to consult the leader of your congregation or a domestic-violence advocate who is comfortable with your religious questions. I suggest ways to find the best person to guide you and how to evaluate him or her. You will also find brief descriptions of controversial issues for battered women, arising from changing interpretations and attitudes of religious leaders toward doctrines in the Bible, the Torah, and the Qur'an.

ARE YOU ABUSED?

If your religious beliefs are important to you, and you are involved with an abusive person, he will probably use those beliefs to try to undermine your confidence. He might do that whether or not his religious orientation is the same as yours. Your responses to the questions below will give you a good idea of whether he is using your religion as a form of abuse and control. As you read the rest of the chapter I hope you will come back to these questions from time to time. You can probably add to the list from your own experience. *Check* each item below that applies.

Activity 39 ⬦ Is Your Religion Used to Abuse You?

Does your husband or intimate partner:

1. tell you not to read religious texts because he is the only one who knows the correct interpretation? Does he strip phrases or words from their context to give them a different meaning? .... _____

2. interfere with your religious observance by "interpreting" what sources say about what you should wear or eat or when to fast?... _____

3. claim a religious source says you must obey your husband, no matter what?.. _____

4. say doctrine requires you alone to perform all household tasks? .... _____

5. claim that a particular text requires you to provide him with sexual gratification regardless of your own feeling? _____ Violate your understanding of religious proscriptions about purity? _____ Touch you in ways or circumstances that you believe are wrong?......... _____

6. say a peaceful family is exclusively your job and family conflict is your fault?... _____

7. keep you from spending time with people at your religious group or with certain people there? .... _____

8. move the family to a different congregation when community members realize he is abusing you?........................... _____

If you checked many of the questions above, you may wonder whether you have misunderstood your religious obligations. Many of the questions exemplify the promotion of the idea that a woman must comply with her husband's wishes. Obedience is a very close cousin of control. Control over your actions, speech, and even your thoughts is what an abusive husband wants. The easiest way to accomplish that is by manipulating your thoughts and feelings. After a while you may begin to believe his interpretations are correct and that they indicate you are not a good, devout wife.

Your spouse may be supported by a religious congregation that claims "abuse does not happen in *our* community." Insisting "it can't happen here" is only one of the ways people deny that battering exists in their religion or their particular congregation. Farhiya Mohamed is a domestic-violence advocate. She says that in some Muslim communities, if a woman complains of abuse others will not admit it is important. "They say, 'Oh, your husband is facing so many problems, he has to learn English, he has to work, he is educated but can't get a job he is qualified for.' Or they say, 'It's just because he loves you.'" Some groups admit that abusive control and even physical abuse exist. But they say it happens only because of the wife's faults. Therefore the problem of *battering* does not exist. The *wife* is the problem.

POLITICS AND CULTURE: RELIGIOUS INTERPRETATIONS

If you don't know whether you should trust your own interpretations of doctrine or your religious leader's or your husband's, that is hardly surprising. For centuries religious leaders have argued about the correct interpretation of certain verses or chapters in holy books, and many have been certain their understanding was the only one possible. Yet through time many of those same Jewish, Christian, and Islamic scholars did modify their judgments. Rabbi Elliot N. Dorff asks people to "remember that the Jewish tradition, after all, has spanned many centuries.

"During that time, it has not remained the same. Sometimes its development has been an internal unfolding of its inherent commitments in thought and in practice, and sometimes the example of other peoples among whom Jews lived produced changes within Judaism. . . . These changes have sometimes occurred through conscious, judicial decisions and sometimes through the changing customs and ideas of Jews in many times and climes."[1]

Religious doctrines and the interpretations of them differ from one generation to the next and from one culture or national group to another. What you wear or eat, whom you marry, or whether you may divorce can be more accurately called a cultural habit than a religious mandate.

"Islamic" views in Egypt differ radically from ideology in Saudi Arabia or Iran on whether women have the right to drive, to dress as they choose, work outside the home, or divorce their husbands. For instance, says Imam Mohamad Joban, "in Saudi Arabia women cannot drive. But Muhammad's wife rode a camel and today she would probably drive a Toyota."[2]

Mexican, Irish, and American Catholics hold different beliefs about marriage vows, abortion, birth control, and the roles of women and men. In Israel, a Jewish man who refuses his wife's request for a divorce may be jailed. Some orthodox Jewish communities shun the man or even have him beaten up by other men. That would not happen in the United States. Both religious and lay authorities call on selected articles of faith to reinforce customs, insisting their interpretations are true to the ancient texts.

When politics and religion become enmeshed, people can't tell where one ends and the other begins. Religious and government leaders merge their own religious beliefs with the politics of gender relationships, which claim dominance over women. But since in modern times women have become religious scholars, rabbis and ministers reap the benefit of their fresh interpretations.

Religious Leaders Change

Nations, cultures, individuals—and religions—change at dizzying rates. That can be unsettling if you rely on the stability of religious beliefs and traditional family and cultural practices to guide you along a predictable path. Now many religious leaders recognize that the incidence of battering among congregants is pretty much the same as in the rest of society. They are inclined to believe women who say their husbands abuse them. They interpret texts that illustrate doctrinal prohibitions of abuse. Some evidence shows that an increasing number of abuse victims and perpetrators seek help from religious leaders. So long as those religious leaders encourage women to seek expert advice from domestic-violence shelter and crisis-line advocates and so long as they hold perpetrators accountable, they will make important contributions to the safety of battered women.

Many religious leaders realize that change is inevitable. The important decision for them is whether to lead their congregations, or to be led by them. For Christian pastor Nathaniel J. Mullen, the understanding that he must lead came to him in one dramatic moment. In *God's Reconciling Love* he relates how "on one perfect spring day" in the midst of a Mother's Day service he was stunned into awareness:

"I called those who wanted to leave behind a lifestyle of worldliness and bondage to join the ranks of the redeemed to accept the embrace of a loving savior. A tall, attractive woman stepped forward, tugging at the diamond-studded gold band on her finger. She balled her fist up into the hand signal of a people's revolt and thrust the ring at her husband's feet, declaring that she wanted to be free from his ongoing abuse. Without a thought, the husband struck her with such force that the impact cracked the oak pew where she fell. The deacons of the church subdued this man, and the police were called. The shock of this event changed me forever."[3]

Pastor Mullen and his wife now provide education to victims of violence in his congregation, advocate for them, and refer them to sources of safety and healing.

Most religious leaders awaken more gradually to the issue of battering but more and more of them realize that their positions of authority oblige them to take action. Imam Mohamad Joban quotes the Qur'an: " 'And among His signs is this, that He created for you wives from among yourselves, that you may find peace and tranquility in them, and He has put between you affection and mercy (30:21).' "

Joban emphasizes that, "No spouse at any time or under any circumstances should behave in a way that compromises the security and safety of the other spouse. Safety and security is one of Allah's favors on human beings. Allah SWT says, 'Let them worship the Lord of This House Who fed them against hunger and secured them against fear.' "[4]

Imams, rabbis, priests, and ministers now speak out against marital violence from their podiums. Many understand that the abuse is not the woman's fault. They realize the perpetrator must be held accountable, and they try to help him change. As a result, many women no longer feel that they must choose between their religion and their safety. At least a quarter of the battered women interviewed in one study said religion gave them courage, hope, and support and increased their self-esteem—all factors that can lead to action enhancing their security.[5]

Carolyn Heggen describes a 1988 survey she and a colleague conducted. They found that many clergy in conservative Christian churches described a spiritually healthy woman as "submissive at home," "gentle and soft-spoken," "lets spouse make decisions," "dependent," "passive," "finds identity through spouse," and "withholds criticism." Those were not the qualities the respondents used to describe a spiritually healthy man. "Nor are they the qualities," Heggen notes, "that are likely to empower a woman to protect herself and her children from an abusive man."[6]

The Heggen study almost mirrors a 1970 survey asking similar questions of psychotherapists. The therapists said mature healthy females had characteristics very similar to Heggen's "spiritually healthy women," and mature healthy males were the opposite. But the "male" traits were the same as those of healthy *person.* So it was possible to be a "healthy woman" *or* a "healthy person," but not both. Heggen's study of clergy's attitudes brought to the surface their puzzling assumption that a spiritually healthy *woman* could not also be a spiritually healthy *person.* If she were a spiritually healthy *person* she could not be a spiritually healthy *woman.* If that seems confusing, it *is.* Its importance lies in the implication that only a man can understand spiritual ideas. If a woman claimed that right she would be a spiritually defective woman. It naturally follows that only the male can interpret scripture. Thus, he is the sole judge of what is correct behavior for his wife.

But there is good news. The belief that only men can be mentally healthy humans has largely disappeared among therapists. Claims of exclusively male rights to spiritual health are fading among clergy. Heggen criticized the ministers' assumptions found in her study and emphasized their negative impact on battered women parishioners. More good news arrived in 1996 when those ideas were accepted as a chapter of a book published by evangelical Christians. One religious community after another has opened a door one small crack at a time to shed light on abuse of women. Moving at their own rates, religious leaders of many faiths have gradually faced reality: Marital violence is prevalent in their own congregations and in the communities under their leadership. For many that has required a reinterpretation of religious sources and a willingness to change long-held beliefs.

Changing Interpretations of Obedience

At the beginning of this chapter a speaker quotes the Ephesians 5:22-3 biblical verse to support his insistence that a wife must submit to her husband ("the head of the wife"). While the quotation is accurate, it overlooks the preceding verse (5:21): "Be subject to *one another* out of reverence for Christ" (italics added).

In her book *Keeping the Faith*, Christian minister Marie Fortune explains that the statement that the husband is "the head of the wife" does not imply unquestioned authority of the husband over the wife. "What is described here," Fortune says, "is a model based on Christ's relationship to the church: Jesus was the *servant* of all who followed him and he gave himself up for them. Never did he order people around, threaten, hit, or frighten them."[7]

Imam Mohamad Joban says, "It is not true that a wife has to obey her husband. A Muslim woman is not obliged to obey at all except for what is in the Qur'an or Sunnah."[8] If her husband asks her to act contrary to what is mandated in those verses, Imam Joban says, she must *not* do that. On the contrary, she is obliged in that case to be disobedient to her husband. "In Islam," he says, "a man is responsible to provide shelter and food, and to work hard. In return, when he comes home, he asks his wife to cook. They have mutual rights and duties. If the woman works outside the home at a paid job, her husband would be expected to do his share of the cooking and cleaning. Muhammad said, 'The best man is the one who is the best to his wife.'"[9]

Muslim leader and scholar Sharifa Alkhateeb notes that an abusive husband will invariably cite the *only* verse that speaks of a husband's duty to his wife without mentioning the parallel obligations of husbands and wives stated in all other verses on the topic. " 'You have rights over your wives,'" Prophet of Islam Muhammad said, " 'and they have rights over you.'" Furthermore, Alkhateeb says, a proper translation of the passage emphasizes that the woman must be obedient to *Allah's (God's)* desires, and *not* to those of another human being. It describes "a caring, protective relationship, not a controlling and tyrannical one."[10]

Questioning Authority

Rabbi Cindy Enger emphasizes that Judaism does not usually present a monolithic view of the world or scripture. The tradition, she says, is very intentional about preserving minority viewpoints "with the awareness that what is the majority opinion at a given time may not be the majority opinion at a later time." For many Jewish women the important concept of *Shalom Bayit* or Peace in the Home represents a major value. A Jewish man who batters is very likely to take that idea and twist it, as other men twist scripture, to mean that it is the wife's responsibility—and never the husband's—to ensure peace in the home. But Orthodox Rabbi Mark Dratch says, "*Shalom Bayit* is everyone's responsibility."[11]

In contemporary times a group of Jewish women created a Haggadah, a text for a Passover ceremony, to guide them through the seder, or ritual journey. Its purpose is to illuminate parallels between "the ancient story of Jewish liberation from Egypt and the stories of courageous Jewish women who have experienced domestic violence." Part of this new ritual asserts the right to question authority:

"Now we affirm the right to our own questions.
Now we affirm the right to our own answers."[12]

"The act of wrestling with meaning is a religious act," says Rabbi Enger. "We look at Jacob wrestling with himself and the angel and look at Abraham arguing with God over the destruction of Sodom and Gomorrah. Everyone gets to argue with God, that's part of the tradition."

Sharifa Alkhateeb emphatically declares that "Muslim women need to improve their knowledge of their own faith, and then reclaim their right to define themselves in the light of the Qur'an and the *Sunnah* (practice of Prophet Muhammad)." Every woman has an obligation, not just a right, to read and question the Qur'an herself. Of special importance, she points out, are "those verses that give women the right to self-supervision, self-fulfillment, and the right to be God's representative on earth *(khalifatul-lah)*."[13]

In her book *Keeping the Faith*, Christian minister Marie Fortune says,

"If you have not yet talked with your pastor or priest about the abuse you have experienced, there is probably a good reason. You probably intuitively sense that he or she will not be helpful to you. . . . Trust your feelings about this. Do not go to this person unless you feel safe and assured that your clergyperson will listen, understand, and believe you. . . . Do not feel guilty about choosing not to discuss your abuse further with your minister at this time."[14]

After a time in a relationship with an abusive, controlling man, you may become confused about your beliefs and want to seek guidance from a religious leader you respect. That doesn't mean substituting another's judgment for yours. Consulting an authority gives you an opportunity to integrate new learning into your value system. That will probably increase your confidence about your beliefs. Then, when your husband mocks or contradicts your understanding of religious verses, you can be more confident and clear about what you believe.

CONSULTATIONS: RELIGIOUS AND DOMESTIC-VIOLENCE AUTHORITIES

Perhaps you have never heard your priest, rabbi, imam, or minister speak about wife abuse. That could indicate an assumption that the topic is not important, or that "it doesn't happen in *this* community." Unless you can find more reassuring information from someone who knows the leader's views, you will be safer consulting a different person, such as a professional counselor or domestic-violence advocate through a battered women's hot line. If you are not ready to make that decision yet, and you would rather consult with your religious leader, here are some questions and options to consider.

Questions to Ask Your Religious Counselor

Consider first asking a friend to telephone for you. Ask her to request, without identifying you, an appointment for "a woman who is abused by her husband." Ask your friend to report back to you on the reaction. Or, with permission, listen in.

Does your potential consultant question whether "the woman" is telling the truth about being abused? Or raise the possibility that she did something to provoke the violence or has exaggerated her danger? Does he suggest that to prevent future mistreatment, the woman should become a better wife? Consulting an authority skeptical about whether you are telling the truth or have "brought the abuse on yourself" may undermine your confidence. The experience could increase any self-blame you already experience. You will not be emotionally safe or comfortable with that person as your spiritual counselor.

But maybe you can't tell from your friend's telephone conversation whether you can trust the religious leader to be sympathetic to your situation. If you aren't sure, you might want to set up one consultation. Consider asking a friend to go with you, and before you keep that appointment make a list of topics to discuss. They might include your marriage, children's reactions to emotional or physical abuse, and interpretations of religious dogma on marital obligations. Maybe you want an expert opinion on religious doctrine on obedience, violence, sex, or separation and divorce. If it is safe to carry your list with you, take it to the appointment. If not, memorize it as well as possible and then destroy it. Take a pad of paper and a pen with you to note references to religious sources. The religious leader is probably not trained as a therapist, but some of the questions for interviewing a therapist in Chapter 9 may be useful in this situation as well.

Once the conversation begins, proceed carefully. Start by saying something general about wanting to discuss your marital relationship. Ask if you can be sure your husband won't be told about the conversation. Listen carefully to the answer to be sure you have a commitment of confidentiality. Then, if you are afraid of your husband, say so. Pause after each important statement, allowing plenty of time for a response. Pay attention to how you feel. If at any time your stomach begins to feel queasy or your breathing speeds up, maybe you have said enough for this visit.

If the leader quotes passages from religious texts it will be helpful to make a note of them. If that feels awkward, mention that distress about your relationship makes it hard to concentrate or remember. Explain that you don't want to forget which verses were referred to. You might also say that when you get home you want to read passages quoted by your husband to see whether they contradict or support what he has been telling you. You could also ask whether verses quoted by your consultant are contradicted by other verses in the same text. Your husband may have quoted a passage correctly but failed to tell you that others on the same topic can be interpreted in an opposite way.

Once you've returned home, it will be helpful to review the passages mentioned. Find time to be alone to evaluate the interaction. The experience of revealing personal information about your relationship may cause a physical reaction such as nausea or anxiety. But those feelings may also be a result of not trusting the responses you were getting. Evaluate the interview by answering the questions below; *write* "Yes" or "No" after each one.

Activity 40 ⊰ Evaluating the Religious Counselor

Did he or she:

1. really listen closely to what I was saying? How do I know that? _____
2. believe me? How do I know that?. . . . . _____
3. suggest I call a crisis line?. . . . . _____
4. tell me about doctrines that are against violence? Say my religion does not require a wife to obey her husband?. . . . . _____
5. take seriously that I am in physical pain or in danger (if that is true)?. . . . . _____
6. take seriously that my emotional or mental health is deteriorating because of chronic humiliation?. . . . . _____
7. indicate concern for children in the household? . . . . _____
8. demonstrate willingness to answer my questions without defensiveness?. . . . . _____
9. lecture me about what I should do to be a better wife?. . . . _____
10. quote religious authorities to "prove" me wrong?. . . . . _____
11. tell me to solve the problem by praying or reading psalms? _____

If you have all or nearly all "Yes" answers to the first eight questions, and "No" answers for the last three, you will probably find solace and help in continuing with more sessions. Your consultant will be able to help you identify and understand the religious beliefs that are important to you. Then you will be more confident in evaluating your husband's interpretations of doctrines and your religious duties.

When the most important person in your life has mistreated you, it is hard to know whom to trust. But the more crucial questions are *when* to rely on what he says and when to believe the word of an authority. You might have a tendency to go back and forth between extremes, first trusting everyone, then after a disappointment, no one. When you find a rabbi, imam, priest, or minister you feel safe in confiding in, don't celebrate right away. Give the relationship time to develop before you place too much faith in his or her judgment.

If you have left the man who abused you and you're living in a secret place, you may be tempted to reveal information about where you are staying. But even a religious leader who empathizes with your situation might feel a duty to help your family stay together. He or she might, with the best of intentions, do you irreparable harm by telling your husband where he can find you. So keep that information to yourself until the religious leader has had plenty of time to *earn* your trust.

If your answers to the first eight questions in Activity 40 above were mostly "No" and to the last three were "Yes," you may have left the interview wondering if you are the one at fault. If you felt as if you were neither heard nor believed nor taken seriously you may feel more helpless, guilty, or spiritually in the wrong than you did before. If you had a negative reaction to the interview, don't repeat the experience. You already have one person telling you that you don't know what you're talking about. You don't need another, even one backed by authority and years of study. You can find another equally learned spiritual counselor or religious scholar who takes a humane view of relationships and who has a compassionate understanding of your situation. If necessary you might find someone from another congregation or even in a distant city to consult with you by telephone.

Consulting a Domestic-Violence Advocate

When you are suffering from battering or emotional abuse, you can use several kinds of support and advice. While you look for the best religious authority, you can also consult with advisers who are experts in domestic violence and safety planning. You can tell your story without being judged for wanting to stay with your partner. Nor will you be criticized for planning to leave him or for your religious beliefs. You can get practical advice from an advocate without even mentioning religion if that's your preference.

The agency you contact may know of people who are authorities in your faith and who also understand abuse. They may refer you to a knowledgeable religious or spiritual leader who can help you refine your understanding of what you believe and why, without telling you what is right or wrong. Before you call, check out the questions for a therapist in Chapter 9. Advocates are not therapists, but you still might want to ask whichever questions seem useful for this situation. As you speak with a domestic abuse counselor, keep these questions in mind:

- Does the advocate accept what you say about your religion's doctrines about a wife's obedience?
- Does she respect your religion's position on divorce?
- Does she understand how big the risk may be of losing your religious community if they find out what has happened? Or if you leave your husband?

If your answers to the questions above are negative the advocate will not be helpful to you. But that is unlikely. Domestic-violence advocates are usually well trained and experienced at listening to women from all kinds of backgrounds. Still, you may want more from a counselor than to be believed about the abuse. So if religion is a core part of your life, do keep looking until you find a person you can trust to understand both domestic abuse and your spiritual concerns.

Crisis-line workers and psychotherapists worry most about your physical and emotional safety. Religious figures are concerned about your spiritual well-being, lawyers about your legal standing, and doctors about your physical health. Not every "expert" will understand each aspect of your life, and the process of searching for guidance may take a long time. As you talk to people about your life and feelings and beliefs you will probably become more comfortable with the process. Your thoughts and choices will become more clear.

SEX ABUSE

For many battered women, rape or other forms of sex abuse may be the worst of many horrors endured. Rape includes forcing you to perform particular *kinds* of unwanted sex. When you are sexually assaulted by your husband, you are physically at his mercy and possibly physically hurt. In addition you know he is trying to humiliate you and shame you. That is terrible to endure. You expect sex with your spouse to be one of the most intimate interactions you can have with him. Yet rape is alienating, not intimate. Because of its special qualities sex is difficult for most people to talk about. To relate the details or even the fact of a rape to a religious leader can be excruciating. It can bring to the surface all over again a sense of shame you may have felt during the rape.

But sexual abuse is not really about sex and not really about the victim. It is about violence. It is about what the *perpetrator* has done and the lengths he will go to in order to dominate. Nevertheless, if your spouse twists the meaning of such a fundamental and private part of life as sex into something repugnant or violent you are likely to feel in the wrong. Many religions place severe constrictions on sexual behavior and expect women to be the ones to enforce them. Cultures distort those meanings and men who batter often further corrupt the original meanings. Those forces often become entwined with society's mixed messages about sex being both shameful and alluring. You can easily become confused and conflicted about your purity as well as your sexual confidence.

In that type of circumstance you might become vulnerable and likely to accept the responsibility for your husband's verbal or physical sexual abuse. A batterer might tell you that you are "unclean" or that going unveiled in public is evidence of looking for a man or that you are a "slut." When the most private aspects of your being are violated it is impossible to speak of the unspeakable. Your husband undoubtedly knows you will feel that way and has chosen that form of abuse because you would feel too humiliated to report it to either the law or a religious authority. In any case, he is confident that no one would criticize him for exercising his right to sex. After all, the woman is his wife.

Only a few decades ago, nearly everyone greeted with derision the idea that rape within marriage is a crime. It was commonly assumed that a man has a right to sex with his wife when he wants it simply by virtue of being married to her. Yet today leaders in virtually all religions recognize that women are not the property of men, and that marital sex should be mutually desired.

Psychiatrist and Rabbi Abraham Twerski says the phrase "a kosher woman is one who does the wishes of her husband" is valid "only when the wishes of the husband are compatible with Torah teachings." He points out that "sexual abuse is clearly antithetical to Torah."[15]

In the book *Women, Abuse and the Bible,* published by evangelical Christians, Craig S. Keener says, "The New Testament teaches that the penalty God has decreed for those who exploit others sexually is eternal damnation."[16]

Imam Joban says, "The sexual relationship between spouses is a very important matter which has a great impact on the health of the marital relationship. Neglecting this aspect of the marital life or practicing it in an incorrect way can lead to drastic results and serious consequences."[17]

DIVORCE

More and more Jewish, Muslim, and Christian religious leaders realize that in some instances divorce is necessary to save a life. In those cases it may even be mandated by religious law and scripture. Sharifa Alkhateeb tells about a woman named Maria who was beaten by her husband and left him. When she consulted with her imam about what to do, he pointed out that "Islamically she should stay away from her ex-husband."[18] Naomi Graetz, author of *Silence Is Deadly: Judaism Confronts Wifebeating,* decries the fact that in Jewish law the husband still has the sole power to end the marriage. But she and others have offered a variety of proposals to change the situation.[19]

In 2002 U.S. Catholic bishops announced that "women who are victims of domestic violence should not stay in abusive marriages." It was reported in the *Catholic News:* "Condemning the ways religion has aided abusers and frightened wives into submission, the bishops overwhelmingly approved a church policy statement instructing clergy and lay ministers to put the safety of abuse victims ahead of efforts to restore the marriage."[20] The resolution was approved by a vote of 249 to 2.

Divorce may save a life, or several lives when children are involved with a violent parent. U.S. laws related to divorce, child custody, and property have made it possible for women to escape, though often with great difficulty. Remaining stigmas as well as a lack of court social workers' and judges' understanding of domestic violence create impossible dilemmas for some women. (See Chapter 28, Nurturing Your Children: Safety and Resilience.) Religions have played an important role in shoring up biases against divorce under any circumstances. As religious leaders become aware of the problem of abuse and of women's rights to dignity, they bring hope to women.

THE URGE TO FORGIVE

Many women who are serious about their religious faith believe they should forgive the men who battered them. (This urge is not peculiar to religious women, but they may feel it more strongly than some others.) In *Keeping the Faith,* Christian minister Marie Fortune says, "Forgiveness is a process. . . . It also does not happen just because your pastor has urged you to forgive. If you are not ready, you will not really be forgiving." She links forgiveness with repentance. "To repent, in both the Old and New Testaments, means to turn away from, to change, never to repeat again." Forgiveness, when it comes, should *follow* repentance, and repentance is action. It is changing, "never to repeat again."[21]

In her "Sermon on Domestic Violence," Rabbi Cindy Enger says, "We fail both victims and abusers when we encourage premature requests or grants of forgiveness." Healing is possible, she says, and "Our tradition teaches that the gates of repentance are always open (Deuteronomy Rabbah 2:12). With courage, commitment and appropriate treatment, an abuser may be able to change his behavior. . . . Real repentance is so complete that a new person emerges from this process of transformation."[22] It is at that point that forgiveness occurs.

In a training packet that is part of a Peaceful Families workshop for Muslim communities, Sharifa Alkhateeb says, "To be forgiven by God, a person has to make *Tawbah* (repentance) by first recognizing wrong in oneself, regretting the wrong, intending to desist from committing the wrong, righting the wrong, asking forgiveness of the victim(s) of the wrong, and making attempts at reconciliation. . . . A person who commits the same or similar sin again and again, like a game, will not be forgiven. . . . The victim is not obligated to forgive the perpetrator."[23]

COMMUNITIES PROTECT VICTIMS AND HOLD OFFENDERS RESPONSIBLE

A convergence of beliefs is growing among some religious figures from nearly all religious communities about the obligation of religious communities to protect victims and hold perpetrators accountable. Orthodox Rabbi Dovid Weinberger is serious about accepting the obligations to protect all lives in a congregation. He organized a conference and the Shalom Task Force for 200 New York rabbis to look seriously at what could be done about battering in Jewish communities. Out of the conference came a call for action. It includes a commitment to admit the problem exists, to hear and believe survivors, and to confront, combat, and prevent abuse—as a community. Plans developed at the conference have been put into action. They include training religious leaders in how to help victims of domestic violence, teaching young people about healthy relationships, and rallying men around the problem. Perhaps most important, the project pledges to hold abusers accountable.

Meira Shupack, advocate for the Project Dvora Orthodox Program at Seattle's Jewish Family Services, says that in the past many communities held *the woman* responsible for abuse, but that is shifting. Rabbi Weinberger's actions, she says, are important because they are all about "taking strong sanctions against abuse in the community. So when abuse does happen, the community responds instantly—to the woman."[24]

Sharifa Alkhateeb believes that the Qur'an mandates Muslims to protect the lives of people in danger, and her work throughout the country in teaching Peaceful Families workshops based on the teachings of Muhammad is another sign of a changing world. "In our Islamic law," she says, "saving lives is the highest level of priority, beyond all other considerations. For any Islamic judge or Islamic imam anywhere in the world the primary consideration before anything else is 'Where is the justice in it?' and 'How can we save lives?'"[25]

Baptist minister Dr. Randy J. Bridges, president of Puget Sound Christian College, came to his understanding of battering after failing to resolve parishioners' problems through pastoral couples' counseling. In retrospect he says he "wanted to believe that a 'good Christian man' would not be capable of further harm" to his wife. "Pastoral counseling does not substitute for a formal treatment/accountability program."

In a church resolution he made these points: "The Bible specifically condemns murder, enslavement, rape, incest, physical assault, mutilation, verbal and emotional abuse, threats and intimidation. God's Word provides absolutely no warrant for the violation or oppression of women. Neither should culture or tradition be allowed to contradict scripture." The church is called, he says, to denounce publicly those evils, to protect and provide for those in need of safety, and to offer healing to the wounded and admonish offenders.[26]

For women who are battered, a vision of transition into single life is offered by "A Journey Towards Freedom: A Haggadah for Women Who Have Experienced Domestic Violence."[27] Your journey may feel like this one excerpted from a modern Haggadah:

> *"The desert is a challenge . . . dust and sand . . . drought. . . . Then time passes. There are small life sustaining plants. . . . When one cannot go on any further, community and friends say one cannot stay behind and you must go on. As you go forward the desert offers its own lushness, blooms in the desert, wildlife, the rare rain or morning dew."*

The world is changing. Religious leaders are changing. There is hope.

STOPPING THE CYCLE OF ABUSE

CHAPTER 27

MEN WHO BATTER: CAN THEY CHANGE?

Twenty or thirty years ago, most people skipped right over the questions, "Why do men batter their wives?" and "Why do they stay with women they beat and disdain?" Instead, they went directly to implicating the victim: "Why do women stay?" Eventually therapists and researchers began to look at why men physically abuse the women they say they love. Studies focused on male anger and violence and suggested a variety of causes—stress, poor anger control, alcoholism, mental illness. They suggested the possibility that the batterer was himself abused as a child. From these attempts to understand domestic violence came the first programs to help male batterers change. But through the years, as the programs proliferated, it became clear that those possible causes were present in only a small minority of men who batter. Domestic-violence advocates had long made the claim that violence is an important power tactic *in conjunction with* threats and psychological, verbal, and economic methods to control a partner.

Because about 90 percent of intimate partner battering consists of men's violence against women, that is the subject of most research and programs to stop battering. This chapter relies on that research and is addressed to women abused by men. Nevertheless, many of the same principles discussed here apply to lesbians and gay men. Information on groups for lesbians and bisexual women is available at Emerge, the oldest organization running groups for batterers (visit its website at www.emerge.org).[1] Chapter 24 discusses lesbian battering.

Eventually researchers and therapists enlarged their focus beyond violence, including at least some attention to control tactics as part of a pattern of abuse. Still, if you are abused, you have probably asked yourself what causes your partner to behave the way he does. You may have also heard excuses from him, his family and friends, or even counselors. It's worthwhile to address some of the most common assumptions about why men batter before we go on to the real questions of what individuals and society can do about it.

WHY DOES HE DO IT?

Is it drugs or alcohol addiction? The assumption that drug and alcohol addiction cause battering neglects quite a few facts: Many people who are addicted do not physically abuse their spouses; of men who assault spouses, many are not substance abusers; some alcoholics get drunk with other people and don't become violent toward them, but push or attack only their spouses. Some studies find a statistical overlap or association of drinking with battering. But that doesn't mean one causes the other. Some men admit that they drink so they will be able to beat their wives. A good deal of evidence shows that drunken behavior is less a result of the alcohol than a consequence of what the drinker expects of himself when he gets drunk. Some drinkers believe liquor will "cause" them to laugh at a lot at silly things, others expect to break up football goalposts, and still others anticipate falling asleep. Not surprisingly, that's often exactly what happens. Men who batter may set themselves up by expecting that if they get drunk they will assault their partners.

Is he sick? Mental illness is another "explanation" offered for abusers' behavior, and a small percentage of batterers do fit into diagnostic categories but there is no persuasive evidence that their actions are caused by mental illness. A small number of batterers are classified as sociopaths, psychopaths, antisocial personalities, or narcissistic personalities. That says more about their attitudes toward right and wrong than about their psychology. In many areas of their lives, including family relationships, they are concerned only with their own desires and do not have much sense of right and wrong. Other men who batter may be conscientious in other aspects of life but at home they too tend to be interested only in what they believe will gratify their own desires.

Is it that he was abused as a child? Results are mixed from studies based on a "social learning" perspective. The theory is that batterers learn abusive behavior as children by observing or directly experiencing it. But among children who endure abuse, some grow up to be nonabusive while others choose to control and batter their partners. Others become perpetrators even though they have not been exposed to abuse as children. Childhood experiences may *contribute to* abuse but no definitive causal connection has been uncovered yet.

Is it my fault? Is it stress? Is it anger? For a number of years professionals and the general public thought it was the woman who caused her own abuse. "There must be something wrong with *her*, or he wouldn't treat her that way." Many women still look to themselves for an explanation. But the movement against battering helped expose how wrong that theory is.

Some psychotherapists and researchers began to think that spouse abuse resulted from both partners' dysfunctional interactions. The two of them were assumed to be equally at fault. The goal was not to stop the abuser's behavior, but rather to untangle how each of them interacted with the other. That, in turn, would lead to less abuse. Couple counseling (or marital or pastoral counseling) can be dangerous for abused women, because therapists tend to encourage them to speak up. Some counselors still don't realize how dangerous battering can be. But if a woman does tell the therapist what is being done to her, she may be beaten for it after the session. On the other hand, if her fear prevents her from telling the truth, her silence may be read by the therapist as passivity or being uncooperative. When the problem remains hidden there is no possibility of finding the cause.

Persuaded that couple counseling does not stop abuse, some therapists theorized that men batter because they do not know how to control their anger. Or they attributed abuse to stress from jobs or the lack of them or money worries. They tried to help by conducting anger-management groups or teaching stress management. Those techniques may have been useful to some clients, but they did not stop them from abusively controlling their partners. Some batterers do have difficulty handling angry feelings. But most of them are able to repress the emotion or express it in socially acceptable ways when interacting with a boss, a police officer, or a neighbor. Managing feelings of anger and stress may be difficult. But the ways they are expressed are a matter of choice. Eventually it became obvious that abusers experience no more stress than others who do not batter and that they are not out of control. On the contrary, people who batter try to be *in control* of everyone in their families and often they succeed. Women whose partners complete anger-management courses are often disappointed in the results. One disillusioned spouse said, "He went through court-ordered anger management six times and stress management four times and there was never any change."

It's a matter of choice. For quite a few years, researchers, therapists, and women involved with violent controlling partners were all looking in the wrong place for solutions to the problem. We were like the man who searched on the walk under the lamppost for the keys he dropped on the grass. When asked why he looked there, he said, "The light is better." The light was better for all of us in the place where we could hope to see a "cure" for an "out-of-control" or "provoked" problem. We didn't want to look at the possibility that the perpetrator uses his power tactics to control his partner *because he wants to control her.* Some activists had been saying that for a very long time, but the idea was often dismissed. It was easier to assume "he can't help it." The possibility that a man *chose* violence or emotional abuse as a conscious tactic made some people fear that nothing could stop the violence. It has taken quite a few years for new research and practice to provide a more constructive analysis and approach to the problem.

ENTITLEMENT AND CONTROL

Joan Zegree is a coleader of groups for men who batter. She says they are conservative and "tend to use the method of lowest impact to get what they want." The phrase *get what they want* is key. They *choose* their behavior. Power over a partner can be exercised by threats of violence without actually using it. When you believe that at any minute an "out-of-his-control" assault may erupt from your partner, you are likely to give him what he wants. Your own partner may have tried to control what you spend, where you go, and what friends you make. He most likely ridicules or insults you, treats you like a child, and threatens you if you refuse to comply. Many women say those tactics are more difficult to deal with and more damaging than physical abuse.

Researchers still have a lot to learn about violence to intimate partners, and as they continue to study the topic they will surely discover more subtle and complex theories about the roots of battering. Meanwhile, the most useful—and surprisingly most obvious—explanation is spelled out by Lundy Bancroft and Jay Silverman in their book *The Batterer As Parent.* They say, "The overarching *behavioral* characteristic of the batterer is the imposition of a pattern of control over his partner . . . [and] it is carried out through a mixture of criticism, verbal abuse, economic control, isolation, cruelty, and an array of other tactics." Those are essentially the actions listed on the Power and Control Wheel and on the Biderman Chart of Coercion shown in Chapter 22, Emotional Abuse.

Bancroft and Silverman say, "The overarching *attitudinal* characteristic of batterers is entitlement." (See references to their important book in Chapter 28, Nurturing Your Children: Safety and Resilience, and in the Resources section.) Some theorists suggest that batterers' behavior is more complicated than that. Their ecological model includes interactions of cultural norms and expectations, and personal experiences in childhood, to explain battering. That theory is compatible with the entitlement idea. The ecological explanation allows for the fact that some cultures encourage a man's right to control his family and for batterers' tendencies to interpret individual experiences as proof of that right. Seen through either of those theoretical lenses, a man who batters typically expects family members to meet his needs. He is self-centered and selfish. He sees his partner as inferior to himself and as "an owned object." He tends to be highly manipulative and to deny responsibility for his behavior.

IS CHANGE POSSIBLE?

The big questions for you may be these: "Is there reason to hope?" "*Can* batterers change?" "*Will* he change?" You might be thinking that if there is no hope then maybe you can walk away. If he is not serious about trying to change, then you can leave without remorse. But that statement brings up additional questions: What do we mean by "try" and "seriously" and even "change"?

Let's start with the last one. To "change" does not mean to "get better" or to become "less" violent—or even to stop the violence if that is all that happens. To fundamentally change in a way that promotes independence, safety, and dignity for you and any children in the picture, the abuser must give up his attitude of entitlement. No more "I'm the boss here, and everyone will do what I decide is to be done." No more assuming "It's up to all of you to take care of the house and listen to my needs, because I am *entitled* to all that." Your partner may not use those words, but you still get that message loud and clear.

He will need to give up his narrow focus on indulging his desires and his sense of entitlement. He will have to stop controlling you and other members of the family. That means he will stop minimizing the violence, denying his control, and manipulating everyone around him. Even if he sincerely intends to make all those changes, he almost certainly cannot do it without professional help. He will have to enroll in a group designed for men who abuse intimate partners. For him to be successful he will need high motivation that, ideally, is reinforced by a court order to attend a group. The program must be directed by professionals specifically trained in how to work on the problem. Even though more research is needed, a great deal has been learned about how to institute programs in the justice system as well as the most effective ways to run groups.

Programs for Batterers

Batterers' programs ideally include court monitoring of the offender, who is assigned to a group especially designed for abusive men. The group may be held out as a "carrot" to avoid the "stick" of jail time. I use the words "program" and "group" rather than "therapy" because therapy is designed for people who are mentally ill. As we have seen, battering is not caused by illness, but by a desire to control. A small number of volunteers do attend groups for abusers. But if they volunteer to participate without the pressure of court monitoring and possible censure, they are more likely to drop out early. When a judge sentences a batterer to a program that includes attendance at a group, there can be different results. *If the system works as it should,*there will be consequences for not showing up for a session. Unless he has an awfully good reason for his absence, the abuser will be back in court and possibly in jail. If he reoffends, that too will get him back into the court system. In many programs, a third of participants do not complete the sessions, and those dropouts should all be sent back to court. But that does not necessarily happen. In many jurisdictions, even when a system is in place, judges and probation officers fail to follow through.

Groups for men who batter should be state-certified and in compliance with statutes that spell out minimum requirements. But it is important to keep in mind that the standards are likely to be truly minimal. Some states mandate only a few months of group attendance. Others require the groups to meet for a year. Many domestic-violence specialists believe that, legally mandated or not, it takes at least that long to make significant attitude changes. Anyone who has "tried" to stop eating chocolate, being sarcastic, smoking, or cussing can tell you that. Even when you know it's bad for you or for a relationship, it is hard to resist a habit that brings immediate gratification. Someone used to getting what he wants in the short term will not easily or quickly change.

If there is only one group available in your community, standards may not be rigorously maintained and you will have no control over that. Your local shelter or hot-line advocate can tell you whether your state has mandatory standards, what they are, and whether they are followed by group leaders. That information is one small tool to evaluate whether there is any reason for optimism about the possibility of your partner's stopping his abuse. If he wants to change, either because he is afraid of losing you or his kids, or to avoid jail at all costs, then he may have a chance of doing it.

Ideally there will be a man and a woman group leader but often there is only one. You have a right to ask leaders plenty of questions about goals and methods and what kinds of contact you can expect to have with them.

Information from the Group Leader

Leaders are obliged to respond to your questions and you in turn can report your partner's infractions to them. They may otherwise not know about continued abuse. But what you say can be dangerous in the hands of someone who is an amateur in dealing with abusers. As you probably know, many abusive men are also charming and manipulative. Like other people, group leaders who are not well trained and experienced may be conned into believing a participant is trying hard to change and is not really dangerous. Before you tell a group leader that your partner has continued or restarted his controlling or violent behavior, *get a solid guarantee that he or she will not let your partner know what you have said.* Leaders should give you a written consent form to sign that spells out details of what can and what must not be repeated to anyone. Discuss with the leaders how they will use information you give them without exposing you to danger. Read the consent form carefully before you sign it.

Ask for an appointment with a group leader or someone from the same agency who knows about the program. You can get answers to your questions by telephone too. However, a face to face interview might better enable you to determine whether the leader is likely to take your concerns seriously and to keep you informed. Here are some questions you may want to ask. Some of them may not apply to you at all, and others may seem less important, so choose the ones that seem most vital to ask first. Then if you run out of time you can ask the others at a later meeting. The first four questions are essential for your safety so let the leader know that you will need enough time at this session to get those answers at least.

On the lines below *write* short versions of the answers, and when you get home fill in more about what you have learned. Make a note of any other questions you have, and don't hesitate to make another appointment to ask them. You can also repeat some of the same questions if the leader's responses weren't clear, or you have forgotten part of them.

Activity 41 ॐ Interviewing the Group Leader

1. What ideas do you have about how I can keep myself safe?

_____

_____

_____

2. What will you do if you think my husband is likely to become violent? (Warn me? Call his probation officer, etc.?)

_____

_____

_____

3. What kind of contact will I have with you? Will you call me regularly? Will you expect me to call you when my partner is verbally abusive or controlling or violent?

_____

_____

_____

4. How can I be sure that if I do tell you about his abuse, he won't find out I have told you? Do you have a consent form for me to sign?

_____

_____

_____

5. Please tell me about the group: what you expect of the men during the time they are in the group and afterward, how many sessions, and what topics they include. What changes will you expect in the men's relationships?

_____

_____

_____

6. Will the group include instruction on nonabusive parenting? If not, will you refer my partner to such a class or group?

_____

_____

_____

7. How will you handle his abuse of drugs or alcohol? Will you refer him to a program for alcoholics or other drug addicts?

_____

_____

_____

8. What consequences will there be for my husband if he misses a group meeting or continues to abuse me?

_____

_____

_____

9. How will you evaluate whether a participant in the group has succeeded in reaching the goals? How often do you evaluate progress? How will I know whether he is complying with the program or whether he seems likely to succeed in stopping violence and the use of power and control tactics? What will happen if he does not succeed? (Return to court, jail, etc.?)

_____

_____

_____

If leaders are not willing to tell you about the group, if they seem impatient with your questions, or stall when you ask for information, that probably indicates that your safety does not come first for them. If they don't return calls, that is a red flag that they don't understand how dangerous battering and abuse can be for you. In that case, you shouldn't count on your partner's changing his behavior and attitudes as a result of participation in the group.

If you have reason to hope the group will help your partner change, be sure to keep in touch with the leaders. Let them know if he continues to threaten or insult you or if he continues to try to control you. If he abuses drugs, leaders should either include work on that problem in their group sessions or refer him to a special program for substance abusers and work closely with them to monitor his compliance.

Groups for Men of Color

Ricardo Carillo and Jerry Tello's book _Family Violence and Men of Color_ shows how groups for men of color can differ from other programs. Each chapter and apparently each group session begins with a poem, a ritual, a story, or a song. Opening themes exemplify basic aspects of the cultural tradition of the men in the group, which are carried out through group activities. Some advocates for battered women are suspicious of those themes, fearing the focus will be on the oppression of the participants as men of color in a white-dominated society.

But the authors insist that the ethnic or cultural content and references to racial oppression set the stage for deeper understanding of their oppression of the women with whom they are involved. "It is necessary," says Jerry Tello, "for the person to dream, reflect, and rediscover the life-enhancing values and gifts of his own indigenous culture. It is necessary to know and understand his history in order to understand the process that created his present situation." Joan Zegree coleads groups that sometimes include men of color and sometimes don't. But she believes it is important in all groups to introduce content on all kinds of oppression. The group discusses the dominant society's power and control over people of color, poor people, and other marginalized populations. Understanding the prevalence of oppression helps all participants realize the effects of their own oppressive behavior.

The dropout rate is key to evaluations of all groups, and some leaders of groups for men of color believe more black, Latino, American Indian, and Asian men consistently attend a group and complete the course when they are with men of their own ethnic or racial group. In the Carillo and Tello book, Oliver Williams says, "Men of color, as a group, drop out of treatment sooner and complete treatment at lower rates than their White counterparts." He believes that is less likely to happen when they are in culturally defined groups. Edward Gondolf found in the groups he studied that more African Americans and Latinos than Anglos dropped out after three months. Yet at the four-year follow-up they "did as well as the Anglo men in terms of decreased re-assault and women's perceptions of safety."

This is just one example of the differences researchers find in how well groups work. Ultimately you have to go on what your partner's group leader tells you, combined with your own gut feeling about how safe and how free you feel to choose your own friends, go where you want, and do what you want. Your feelings about your safety when you are with your partner may be as important as group leaders' evaluations. They are far more significant than researchers' conclusions about large groups of batterers.

Groups for Religiously Observant Men

Some victim advocates distrust programs for men run by religious organizations because traditional religious organizations have been slow to recognize that battering can be lethal. Years of religious training may have included an emphasis on helping families stay together at any cost. Advice that it is God's will that a victimized woman practice forbearance and forgiveness toward a batterer may put her life in danger. Even with the best of intentions, devout religiously observant leaders may find it hard to overcome those traditions. When a group leader believes a wife should obey her husband, he may not see control and misuse of power as dangerous. But some religious leaders and congregations are changing. As they become more aware of dangers to women from their spouses, some preachers speak publicly against battering. See Chapter 26 on Religious Challenges. Some evidence suggests that more men who are referred to groups through religious institutions complete the program than do other men. If your partner signs up for such a program, you should be sure to ask all the same questions suggested above. Ask also about what references to religious texts and beliefs are threaded into group's exercises.

How Men Manipulate Batterers' Groups: Anita's Story

Your husband's seeming acceptance of group intervention might only mask a cynical intention to go through the motions and be pronounced a "graduate." His participation in the group may be just another way to get what he wants without changing how he treats you. He might attend a few times or even for a few months but still not modify his attitudes or beliefs about his right to run the show regardless of your rights and desires. Or he might stop the physical assaults but continue controlling you by other means. Your memory of previous violence might be so strong that even small gestures of your partner can give you a message to obey and can keep you from asserting your rights. To be serious about change means working at it all the time, and working at it for a long time. Some people think it requires a lifetime. Against the odds, Anita was reluctant to give up hope.

"I lived with my husband when he attended anger management, and then for an entire year while he attended a perpetrator's group. After a few months, I had doubts about whether he would change, but when I asked the group leader about it he said it was too soon to tell. By the nine-month marker, my husband told me he was passing and that I should be proud of him because he was doing so well he was getting to the last phase of treatment. But then the group leader told me he was sure he would not complete the program successfully, because he was not serious. He stayed for the entire year, but failed the course."

Anita's husband apparently thought he could go through the motions of changing for a year and be automatically "graduated." A program that does not have strict standards and that is not backed by a cooperative legal system can wind up effectively colluding with a participant who is not serious. Fortunately for Anita, her husband's group leader was not fooled by his manipulations and the leader's straightforward appraisal offered Anita a way to evaluate whether to leave her husband. Not long afterward she did exactly that.

DO PROGRAMS WORK?

Studies in which men are followed up for a number of years after completing well-designed programs with experienced leaders have found wide-ranging results. Follow-up studies found that among men who *completed* them, between 45 percent and as high as 90 percent stopped their violence for at least a year. Cooperation with judges, prosecutors, and other court personnel who understand the problem of abuse is an essential component of a successful program. So is their willingness and ability to follow through on monitoring guidelines. Success also depends on the principles and practices of the program and the experience and the training and professionalism of the leaders. When each of those factors operates well and the participant is willing to do the hard work, significant change can result. If *your* partner is willing, he just might succeed. The following traits make the odds more favorable:

- The abuser is accountable for his behavior: "I am the one who did it, and it was wrong."
- The batterer wants to stop abusive controlling behavior.
- If he has a substance-abuse problem he participates in a program to deal with that.
- The batterer has no severe psychiatric diagnosis.
- He has either no prior domestic-violence history or little of it.

If you hear about impressive success rates for batterers' groups, that may persuade you that your partner can participate in a group and will change so you can feel safe with him. But there are serious barriers to men's *successfully* completing intervention programs. If the leaders are not thoroughly experienced in the arena of battering, they may not define "success" clearly or completely. For a man to succeed in changing, his partner needs to be and feel safe. For that to happen, the man must cease violence *and* give up using control and power tactics directed toward his partner and children.

A large study by Edward Gondolf of four groups with a four-year follow-up of program "completers" found that most of their violence took place during the first six to nine months after entering a group. At nearly three years after the study began, violent incidents had tapered off, and four years after the groups began, 90 percent of participants had not been violent for the previous year. That is the good news. However, *those first months of the program were especially dangerous for the women, and the incidents during that period were also among the most severe.* That pattern has not been evident in other studies, so it is impossible to know whether it will be found in the group your man attends.

The main thing to remember is that *just because he has joined a group does not mean the perpetrator will never assault you again.* There is no telling how participation in a group will affect him, and if he finds it confining or embarrassing he may blame you. His violence could increase. Even if he stops his violence, he might still insist on controlling your every move, insulting or humiliating you, or mistreating the children, and you will be only slightly better off than you were before he joined the group.

HOW TO TELL IF THE PROGRAM IS WORKING FOR YOUR PARTNER

Skepticism about batterers' intervention groups in general does not necessarily mean your partner is beyond hope. Nor does it imply that a program will necessarily work for him. Until he begins a group you won't know whether he intends to stop abusing you. If your partner continues to be controlling, you won't know how well the court monitors him until you learn whether group leaders have reported him. Until he *completes* a group you won't know how serious he has been. Until you talk to the group leader you will not know whether it is reasonable to hope he won't revert to old behavior and attitudes. Even then, if you are honest with yourself, your own sense of safety and feeling of freedom may be your best guides to what to expect.

If the feedback you get from the leader is optimistic, and it matches your own experience with your partner, it still may take a year or even much more for him to make his changes stick. Not all state standards mandate a year of intervention, so if after four months he has completed the program and stopped the violence, leaders may not focus on whether he has stopped using power and control tactics. They may be too eager to have "successful graduates" and to let him off the hook. "Unless they have made an attitude change," says Joan Zegree, "they bring the same controlling attitude to the relationship. They just have more finesse." That can spell increased danger to partners and Zegree says it takes time for abusers to change their attitudes toward relationships.

Before your partner is assigned to a group and even before a situation arises that forces you to call police, contact a domestic-violence crisis line or shelter advocate. Ask for information about what to expect from the justice system. Do police consistently write accurate reports as they are supposed to? Is there even a program for men who batter? Do judges send batterers to them? Are they monitored by court personnel? Get all the information you can about how reliably the system works. Find out how long it takes for a court-ordered abuser to begin a group. Every town is different, and advocates will have the best and most recent information about the local scene. If the "best" treatment offered is couples counseling or anger management, keep in mind that either one could be worse than nothing. Either one could cause you to let down your guard, so that either one could be more dangerous than nothing.

If your partner shoves, hits, or threatens you or continues emotional abuse of you or your children while he is enrolled in a group, do call the leaders. That may be a hard thing to do, and you will need to proceed carefully. Leaders should use the information in ways that don't expose where it came from. Even though group leaders may have told your partner they will check with you, if he knows you are telling them what he has done he may punish you for being a "traitor." But if he does, he will be in violation of the goals and standard of the group, and the leaders should know that.

The purpose of participation in a group is for the batterer to learn to behave in ways that do not risk your safety or violate your dignity or independence. The goal is to be able and willing to set the stage for a relationship of mutual respect. Although many experienced professional group leaders are good at figuring out when a perpetrator is lying, they can't always tell what he is doing outside of the group. A key to your safety is for you to be honest and informative to the group leader. If you don't feel safe doing that, then you aren't safe being with your partner.

Your partner, like Anita's partner, may lie about how hard he is working and how seriously he is taking the group. As a check against that, in addition to talking to the group leader, you can question yourself on a regular basis. Go through each one of the questions below, and *put a check mark* in front of any "yes" answers. You may be tempted to slide over some of the items that seem minor compared to being beaten, but any one of them can be a sign that your partner is not committed to treating you with respect and that he still feels entitled to do as he pleases. Be as honest as you can be, and if you are sure it is safe, let the group leader know how your partner is behaving.

Activity 42 ❧ Warning Signs Your Partner Is Not Changing[3]

Put a check mark in front of "yes" answers, and a zero in front of "no" answers.

Does he:

1. use group information or sessions against you? . . . . _____
2. tell you that you are the one who is abusive? . . . . _____
3. pressure you to go to therapy for yourself or to couples counseling? . . . . _____
4. minimize the abuse when he talks in the group (according to the group leader)? . . . . _____
5. demand a second chance, if you have left him? . . . . _____
6. say that he cannot change without your support? . . . . _____
7. try to get sympathy from you or the children? . . . . _____
8. fail to attend group meetings unless you keep after him? . . . _____
9. expect something in return from you for attending group? . _____
10. tell you if you don't do as he says it might start him drinking again? . . . . _____
11. pressure you to make up your mind about the relationship or moving back together? . . . . _____
12. pressure you not to cooperate with the justice department on criminal charges or to get a restraining order? . . . . _____

Check marks above indicate that your partner continues to try to control you by making you seem responsible for his participation in his program. He shows a lack of seriousness about stopping the abuse. Each zero suggests that he may be working to make changes.

Activity 43 ❧ Signs He May Be Changing[4]

Put a check mark in front of "yes" answers, and a zero in front of "no" answers.

1. Has your partner completely stopped saying and doing things that frighten you? . . . . _____
2. Can you express anger without being punished for it? . . . . . . _____
3. Does it feel safe to bring up topics that you know your partner disagrees with? . . . . _____
4. Can your partner listen to your opinion and respect it, even when disagreeing with you? . . . . _____
5. Does your partner argue without being abusive or having to be

right? . . . . _____

6. Does your partner respect your wishes about sex and physical contact? . . . . _____

7. Has your partner stopped expecting you to do things that you may not want to do? . . . . _____

8. Can you spend time with friends or family without being afraid that your partner will retaliate? Can you do other things that are important to you, such as go to school or get a job? . . . . _____

9. Are you comfortable with the way your partner interacts with the children? . . . . _____

10. Do you feel safe leaving the children with your partner? . . . . _____

11. Does your partner support you and give compliments? . . . _____

12. Does your partner listen to what you have to say? . . . . _____

13. Does your partner do enough housework and childcare? . . . _____

If there are more than a few zeros, he may not be taking seriously the need to change. It might be that you have been mistreated for so long that this list of positive behavior seems too good to even hope for. But each one of the "yes" answers indicates that your spouse views you as an equal partner to be respected and cared for. That should be your partner's goal. You might want to talk about your answers to these questions with your partner, but you feel wary of rocking the boat. If you are still afraid to bring up certain subjects with him, that is probably a sign that he is not changing.

Using the Information to Increase Your Safety

Progress made by researchers, group leaders, and court programs is promising. They provide hope for change for some families in the future, but they do not tell you what to do. I started out this chapter suggesting that the hope your partner will change might have nudged you in the direction of staying with him. You might have decided to stay long enough to see whether he would participate in a group and do the work to change himself. If he has done that and if you decide to stay, re-evaluate that decision on a regular basis, say every month. Use the Power and Control Wheel, the Danger Assessment list, and the Activities in this chapter as guides. Give yourself permission to make a new decision if your partner's behavior or attitudes revert to dangerous and damaging patterns. Be sure to keep your safety plan updated in case you are threatened in such a way that you have to get away from your partner immediately.

Maybe reading this book has persuaded you that your partner is not going to change. You may decide to leave. But that doesn't necessarily mean you should walk out the door right now. See other chapters in this book on making the decision, safety plans, and what you can expect after you leave. Your plan for leaving should include safety measures that are thought out in detail. Timing is crucial. For advice on leaving with the best degree of safety you can manage, consult with a domestic-violence advocate. If you decide to separate, alert group leaders to your plan and caution them not to tell your partner anything you don't want him to know until you are in a safe and secret place.

Most likely the safest path in the long term is to separate when your partner is assigned to a group and to continue that arrangement until the group leader lets you know that he has successfully completed the program. Ask the leader whether he is confident that your partner is committed to not being violent and to not being emotionally abusive or controlling. Combine that information with your own observations. If your conclusions are positive, it might be safe for you to return. But go slowly. Spend time together before you move in with him. If you have been separated for several months or a year, the very fact of your moving back may reactivate your partner's old patterns of control. And even if he has changed you may still not trust him. The pertinent question might be whether, even if he has stopped the abuse, you are willing to live out the rest of your life at a caution light.

CHAPTER 28

NURTURING YOUR CHILDREN: SAFETY AND RESILIENCE

If you have children and you have stayed with their abusive father or another man, you might struggle with conflict between what you want for yourself and what might be best for your kids. Or maybe it is hard to know just what is the best choice for any of you. Once you are involved with an abusive partner, all your choices carry some amount of risk. Maybe relatives or friends or a child-protection worker has told you that you must get out for the sake of the children. That can make you feel guilty, which in turn might lead to helplessness. To reduce your guilt feelings, you might tell yourself that the children aren't injured and maybe even that they don't know what is happening. Maybe you're afraid that if you did look at the harm, you would feel even worse because there is no way you can protect them.

This chapter suggests practical ways of helping your children become safe and resilient. Recent research makes it clear that children do know what is happening when one parent abuses another. They hear it, they see it, and they can sense it from the way their parents behave. Even if they are not directly abused themselves, and "only" observe the violence, they can suffer serious harm. That does not mean you can't do anything to help.

You first have to understand how abuse—experienced directly or observed—affects the children. Then, whether you stay with the abusive partner or leave him, you can significantly reduce the harm. "Help" means first increasing their physical safety, and then finding ways to diminish the development of long-term emotional harm to them by showing them how to be competent, useful—"resilient"—people who can take care of themselves, and by showing them how to appreciate their own abilities. This chapter gives you ideas about how to do that.

SAFETY WHETHER YOU LEAVE OR STAY

Section I of this book includes many exercises to help you weigh the decision of whether to leave or stay. The decision is far more complex than it looks. Lawyers, therapists, court social workers, and child-protection workers may mean well when they say that for the sake of the children you have to leave a violent partner immediately. But if they think the decision is simple and that leaving is free of risk, you may need to give them a few facts.

Women who have separated are 25 times more likely than married women to be victims of violence by an intimate partner and three times more likely to be assaulted than divorced women.[1] Fathers who batter mothers are twice as likely to seek sole custody of their children. Some of them use the system to continue abuse by retaliatory legal actions. During visitations with the children some threaten to kill the mother (5 percent), to kidnap their children (34 percent), or to hurt the children (25 percent).[2] A study of more than 2,100 disputed custody cases found that "fathers win sole custody more than three times as often as do mothers" and they win at least joint custody in more than 70 percent of such cases.[3]

These frightening facts are not an argument for staying with the abuser. They do make it clear that if you leave, it is of great importance to plan carefully how you will do it. Nearly half of domestic-violence homicides occur a month or more after the couple has separated. That first thirty days after you separate can be stressful for many reasons and fear of increased violence can exacerbate it. Of homicides by ex-partners, 90 percent occur during that first year of separation. Nothing is magical or definitive about the one-month or the one-year markers. But they do suggest two things: You may want to consider staying at a battered women's shelter for a month, and you can take comfort in knowing that after that first year you may be able to relax a little. The challenge if you leave will be to maintain hope for your safety while staying alert to the possibility of danger.

A continuing state of uneasiness might make it hard to focus on your children's needs. But studies have found that by six months after leaving an abusive partner, most mothers' parenting skills improve dramatically. Though it may seem unlikely now, you can be one of those mothers, especially if you start concentrating now on what you can do for them. The first thing you have to do is protect the lives and safety of your kids and yourself.

In some instances, a person who says to you, "Get out right now," could be right. Staying with a violent partner could put your life and those of your children at risk and your only choice might be to grab your children and run. It is essential that you think through what actions you will take if such an emergency comes up. Decide ahead of time how you will get out of the house, how you will protect your children, where you will go, and how you will get there. The frightening statistics mean it is essential to recognize the dangers of staying and the dangers of leaving, and in either case to plan what you will do in case of an increase in violence.

Safety Plan if You Leave

In the *long run* it is almost certain that you and your children will be safer if you leave, but timing is important. *When you tell your partner you are going to leave, or when you have just moved out, or in some other way he realizes that this time he may lose you, that is the time when you are in most danger.* Studies of women who were killed after leaving a batterer don't tell us whether she planned carefully for her safety before she left. Many probably hoped for the best and when they found themselves in danger left suddenly without a plan at all. Others might have had plans but did not carry them out.

If you are able to completely separate from the batterer with no contact between him and your children, you have a good chance of maintaining safety. But if he has a legal right to visit them, you need to take extra precautions for them and yourself. You won't be able to let down your guard for at least a year and you'll need to be constantly on the alert during the early period after separating. Risk is also high any time you get a court order to keep the batterer away or to limit his interactions with the children.

While you are considering the issue of your security, this is a good time to look at the Danger Assessment list at the beginning of this book, and read about how to use it to evaluate your situation. Turn to the list in Who This Book Is For and How to Use It and follow the accompanying instructions.

You don't have to wait until you have left an abusive partner to start increasing your children's security. You can start right now by including them in your safety plans and helping them make plans of their own. Tell them about how you have arranged for security at work. As they see you doing everything you can to protect yourself, your kids will learn that they too need not put themselves in danger or stand helplessly by doing nothing. You can use the ideas on the following page and the Safety Plan at the beginning of this book to create a personal plan that suits your way of life. (You'll find the Safety Plan for You and Your Family, in Who This Book Is For and How to Use It; it is repeated in the Resources section at the back of the book.) Some of the safeguards apply to life without the batterer; others are for emergencies while you are living together. You might want to introduce the topic by relating it to what your children have learned at school about fire-safety programs. Allow them plenty of time to come up with their own ideas about the most practical and useful precautions they can take.

Activity 44 ⁊ Steps for Safety Planning at Home

1. Ask the children to identify someone who might help them in a dangerous situation.
2. Find out whether they would ask that person for help and if not, talk about the reasons. Consider talking with that person together as you plan.
3. Children should know that the plan may not always work. Be sure they understand that if it doesn't work it is not their fault.
4. Identify warning signs. First, think about what are the warning signs (if any) that you have when your partner is about to become abusive. Here are some examples:
   • Mom and Dad are arguing.
   • Dad is raising his voice.
   • Dad or Mom is drunk or high.
   • Dad is name-calling or threatening.
   • Dad is slamming doors, stomping around.
   In talking to your child about his or her father, always stay focused on behavior. You could say something such as, "Sometimes your Dad acts in ways that are scary and when he does we need to do things to try to stay safe." Then discuss with them specific actions they can and should take to stay safe.
5. Determine what children can do to stay safe. For example, if they observe that abusive behavior is imminent, they can:
   • Go to their rooms.
   • Leave the house for somewhere safe: a neighbor's or relative's house, or outside—if the neighborhood is safe.
   • Stay out of the way.
   • Try to get to a room where there is a phone.
   • Know how to dial 911 if there is a phone where the father can't hear them.
   • Stay away from the kitchen and bathroom.
   • Do not try to stop the violence.[4]

CHILDREN'S VISITS WITH THEIR FATHER

Making the Most of an Interview with a Social Worker

Before you get to the point of organizing your children's visits with their father, you may have to talk to a social worker in the judicial system. It might be obvious to you that their father is a danger to the children. But your family court evaluator or child-protection worker may view him as charming, reasonable, and incapable of violence or abuse. That shouldn't surprise you because you've probably thought that yourself in the past. He might have told the worker that you are the one who is crazy, violent, or negligent toward the children. As unfair as it is, you may have to persuade the social worker that you are not.

Planning carefully for custody interviews might enable you to get the social worker on your side. You are each concerned about the welfare of the children, so *you are on the same side.* As in dealing with other difficult situations, ask a domestic-violence advocate for specific advice about handling workers at the local court or state agency. Maybe an advocate will be able to go with you. The more prepared you are the more likely you are to get what you want.

Make a list of your husband's violent acts toward you and your children. If you don't already have them get copies of police reports. In the most clear and objective language you can muster, and based on your experience, list the dangers you foresee for your kids if their father is allowed unsupervised visits. Take the list with you.

When you meet with the social worker, your task will be to help her realize that your main goal is to create a safe environment for your kids. That might be hard to do if you are so frightened of losing custody that you feel on the edge of hysteria. Or your fear might turn into anger and you want to scream in frustration. But even if it is the last thing in the world you feel like doing, make the effort to seem reasonable and calm. Put out of your mind any horror stories you have heard about child-protective or court social workers. The social worker does have some power over your life, and some of those stories may be true. But dwelling on all that won't reduce your fear or anger. It can prevent you from being your best self. It can prevent you from getting what you want.

If you have stayed with the abusive man for a long time, the social worker might blame you for putting your child in danger. You will have to help her understand that one reason you stayed was to protect them.

Explain—if it is true—that you were afraid they would be in even more danger if you had left. If you have now separated, explain what has changed. Help her understand that you will do what is necessary to keep your kids safe: "My goal is to cooperate in protecting my kids from my husband's violence (or insults/humiliations). I'd be glad to explain how I've tried to do that. I would like to hear your ideas about other things I can do to keep them safe."

You may have to educate social workers about the special situation of mothers who are battered and the potential hazards to children of unsupervised visitation by a man who batters. You can tactfully suggest they read Lundy Bancroft and Jay Silverman's book, *The Batterer As Parent,* listed in the Resources section at the end of *Getting Free.* Or to make it easy for the social workers, download copies of excellent articles by Bancroft from his website at www.lundybancroft.com. But be sure you don't imply they don't know their jobs. Assume they are as interested in protecting your children as you are.

When Your Children's Father Has Unsupervised Visitation

If you are not awarded full custody, try to have the judge order your husband's visits to be supervised. Ask a legal advocate at a domestic-violence program to help you plan for that. This is another situation in which Bancroft's work (noted in the paragraph above) can be exceptionally useful. If you have a lawyer, make it easy for him or her to understand your situation by making Bancroft's short articles available. Unfortunately, the opinions of an experienced professional researcher and group worker will probably carry more weight with a lawyer or judge than what you have learned from your own experience.

For your own safety and the well-being of your children, limit contacts with your ex-partner to only those that are necessary. If he has visitation rights, arrange to have the children picked up and returned to you in the presence of someone who understands your situation. Resist the temptation to get into arguments with the father. If he is hostile toward you, do not respond. Have the visitation rules clearly written in the legal documents and scrupulously follow them yourself. They should include very specific details about location, time, days, and arrangements for the safe transfer of the child or children. If necessary, educate your lawyer or CPS worker about safety measures.

- Be consistent with your visitation-parenting plan. Don't be manipulated or threatened into changing it.

- Don't get into arguments with your child's father about visitation. If he wants to argue about it with you, hang up the phone or leave the situation.
- Try to make your child's experience as positive as possible, even though this can be extremely difficult.

These guidelines are adapted from the Crager and Anderson curriculum.[5]

HOW VIOLENCE AFFECTS CHILDREN

Some children survive life in a family war zone with few wounds and no visible permanent scars. They are like the rubber clown that keeps getting knocked down, yet again and again miraculously bounces back. Researchers are still learning about how abused children manage to keep getting up after each blow. We do know that even those who do that can use a lot of help. The children who aren't able to keep recovering may be the ones who don't have one adult they can count on to appreciate them and care for them. Maybe their mothers are so beaten down they can't make themselves take good care of their children. But if you keep your eye on your next step in caring for *your* kids, you can help them feel competent and secure.

This chapter contains several closely related messages and it will be useful to couple the negative ones with the positive: Whether your children observe you being abused or endure direct emotional, sexual, and physical abuse, they can benefit from hearing you admit to what has happened rather than denying it, and by being reminded that they are not the ones at fault. Without help and support they could suffer from long-lasting harm, as many children do, that results from *observing* those assaults. But they can also be helped to recognize that they don't have to act like little adults taking care of their father or you. You can let them know every day that they can count on you to care for them. When they feel helpless or angry about what is happening in the household, encourage them to talk about those feelings. It is pretty clear from research that many of the children who recover from observing abuse or experiencing it directly have one adult in their lives they can count on. You can be that one person. You can help them bounce back.

Let's look first at the harm done directly to children. Until fairly recently it has not been generally recognized how many men who batter partners also emotionally, physically, or sexually abuse children. In homes where women are physically abused by partners, the rate of physical abuse and neglect of children is fifteen times the national average. One in every eight men who murder intimate partners or ex-partners kills at least one child as well. Battered women are frequently assaulted while pregnant and many of those attacks deliberately target the woman's stomach. Some evidence shows that battering of pregnant women contributes to premature labor, "fetal stress," and low birth weight.[6]

Not surprisingly, men who assault intimate partners use abusive "power parenting" tactics against children.[7] One of the least noticed and most damaging of a batterer's control tactics is the undermining of normal family relationships. He manipulates everyone, setting child against child and children against their mother. As family relationships get turned upside down, kids become confused about who can be trusted and who is the responsible adult.

In Janeese's case, her partner treated her like one of the children. She says that when she left him, "It was hard to take on the role of a parent, because I had never learned to do that. My oldest son was thirteen and wanted to take on that role of the man of the house." Janeese kept assuring him it was "okay to be a kid," but he didn't want to go out for sports or play with friends. She enrolled in parenting classes and the children in therapy, and finally, after a couple of years of hard work, her son has decided he wants to play football. He is learning it's okay to "be a kid" and Janeese is becoming comfortable in the role of responsible parent.

The Children Who "Only" Observe Battering

"They're asleep; they never hear it," you say.

"They're too young to understand; they don't know it's happening," he says.

About half of mothers abused by intimate partners cling to the hope that the children don't know they have been assaulted. But most children interviewed after their mothers were hit say they saw and heard and understood much more than their parents thought they did. The surprising part is that until recent years, experts also believed children weren't aware of violence in their homes. It has taken even longer for researchers to discover how much damage is done to a child from observing a mother being assaulted.

Some studies have found that observing the assault of his or her mother is even more harmful to a child than direct abuse and can cause sleeplessness, anxiety, and depression. One study compared reactions of children who observed battering to those of child survivors of war. "Both groups of children told of persistent feelings of loneliness, eating and sleeping difficulties, recurrent headaches, and intrusive thoughts and fears. Some recounted feeling immobilized and depressed."[8] Some children who observe violence against their mothers identify with the powerful batterer, become aggressively angry, and bully other children—or bully their mothers.

Promoting Resiliency in the Midst of Chaos

Despite the harm from observing abuse, and even without special focused help, and about 50 percent of such children turn out to be resilient. That is, they develop ways to cope and they recover. *With your help, there is every reason to believe your children can be protected against permanent damage from the abuse they experience or observe.* Don't assume that because you have stayed with their father for a long time your children are "ruined forever" or that it's too late to help them. One important contributor to children's coping well is the knowledge that there is one adult they can trust. You *will* affect their lives. The only question is whether that will be for better or worse.

With thoughtful planning, probably professional help, and a whole lot of patience you can become a positive influence on your children. You can do that regardless of what your husband or ex does to make that task excruciatingly difficult. Anita found that she could keep her son from being beaten by putting herself between him and his father. Rachel struggled successfully with her son's school administrator to be sure he could stay in a classroom where he received the kind of care he needed to help him recover from abuse. Each action of their mothers to protect the children gave a message that they were loved and their safety was important.

As you learn about how damaging abuse can be to your children, you might blame yourself for staying in a marriage steeped in violence and turmoil. Maybe any hint that you are falling short of your goals as a parent causes so much anxiety or guilt that you don't want to think about it. If it seems as if you've tried everything and nothing works to make your children's lives better, maybe depression or a sense of hopelessness makes you unable to see that you have had some successes. Try to form a habit of focusing on the positive—yes, even among the many difficult aspects of your life. If you have practiced the exercises in Chapters 10 and 11 you're already beginning to do that.

If you have teen- or preteen-aged children, consider including them in working through some of those same exercises. Help them learn to pay attention to the negative comments they make about themselves and each other, and let them know you're working at changing your own negative thought patterns. That is not an argument for encouraging the kids to deny what has happened, or the anger or fear or sadness they feel about it. You probably have lots of good ideas yourself about how to help your kids deal with the problems they live with. Here are some more.

HELPING CHILDREN WHO HAVE WITNESSED VIOLENCE

Children who have seen or experienced violence need a lot of attention from you if they are to heal. These are suggestions for focusing your attention in ways that will be helpful to them.

- When they are ready, talk with them about the violence.
- Accept that they may not be willing or able to talk about it right away.
- Listen to them.
- Encourage them to talk about their feelings and to express them in appropriate ways.
- Show understanding.
- Let them know it's not their fault.
- Let them know you love them.
- Let them know, by words and actions, that you will try to keep them safe.
- Let them know you will help them act in ways that are safe.
- Let them know violence is not okay.
- Acknowledge it's hard and scary to live through violence.
- Always act in a way that is non-threatening and nonviolent.
- Take them to counseling if they need it.
- Set limits respectfully when your child acts in aggressive, abusive, or violent ways.
- Give your child plenty of time to adapt to the new nonviolent atmosphere you're creating.[98]

With those goals for helping your children in mind, focus on one problem. Take one step at a time toward one goal that is doable. Let's start with a relatively easy situation in which you have a chance to be alone with your child a fair amount of the time. Suppose the batterer is at his job or that you have already left him. Either way, you have a big chunk of the day to create an environment for your children that he can't destroy.

Maria: An Anxious and Clinging Child

Let's say five-year-old Maria is very timid and does not want to play with other children. Whenever she is not in kindergarten she clings to you, whining about what she wants. If anxiety keeps her wakeful at night, it's natural for her to feel irritable and to be unable to focus on schoolwork or other tasks. Those problems might increase her conviction that she can't control any part of her environment or even predict what will happen next. If she has heard you or your husband threaten to leave home, that probably has added to her fear. But all that is much too complicated for her to figure out. All she can think of is that you should fix it. If you are still living with the abusive man, you might feel exhausted and in pain from having been harassed or assaulted. Maria's whining cuts right through you like the squeal of chalk on a blackboard. You want to scream. Sometimes you do scream.

"Maria, just *be quiet*. Just leave me alone. Can't you see I'm worn out?"

The trouble is, Maria can't see much beyond her own worries about what will happen next. *Will you be hurt? Will she be assaulted? Is it her fault that her father beats you up?* But she is afraid you don't want to talk about those things, and she might be right. Maria's whining might be her way of saying, "Please pay attention. I'm scared."

Maybe you're scared too. Or furiously angry. Or depressed or sad. You tell yourself you don't have what it takes to care for anyone, not even your own child. If you are in pain, even a half hour devoted to Maria might seem impossibly long. But somehow you have to find the energy for it. Start with what you can tolerate, even if it is only five or ten minutes. Consider turning the activity into a ritual you do together once an hour or twice a day. When you are with your child, be truly *with* her. Don't answer the phone or watch the television out of the corner of your eye.

Notice what she does well in the game you play with her or in listening to a story you read aloud. Your undivided attention tells her you care about her. Complimenting her on what she does well helps her feel confident. Try to think of activities to do together that give her a chance to practice listening, follow rules, or stretch her imagination. That will strengthen her competency and reduce her sense of helplessness. If you gradually increase the time you spend with her, and take half an hour to help her learn to ride her bike, bake cookies, or plant something in the garden, you are letting her know you have confidence that she can learn and accomplish things. She will see that some of her life is coming under control and can be predicted. She will have a chance of becoming a resilient child. Meanwhile, she just might whine a whole lot less than she does now.

Tyree: He Wants to Be the Boss

Suppose Maria's older brother, twelve-year-old Tyree, has begun to act like your husband. He insults you, hits his sister, and even orders you around. You yell at him, "Just cut it out." Maybe you add that he is just like his father, letting him know there are few things worse than that. Because he acts tough, "externalizing" his feelings, it is easy to forget he is suffering from feelings similar to yours and your daughter's. If you leave your partner, he may want to take over the role of "man of the house." Your job is to let him know *you* are the parent and when you discipline him, you mean what you say. But let him see that you know he hurts and you will help him feel confident in constructive ways appropriate to his age.

Tyree may not want to admit it, but he needs your attention and access to your nurturing. If he has emotionally pulled away from you, go slowly in letting him know he can let down his guard. Begin with something non-threatening such as watching a television show with him. It doesn't have to be something you enjoy. Just sit with him and watch it and during a commercial ask what he likes best about the program or what he thinks will happen next. If he follows football moves that are a confusing blur to you, ask him to explain. Then let him know you are impressed with his ability to understand the game. The principles are the same as those you follow for helping Maria. Give him your time and attention without any criticism and whenever you notice a skill he has developed, let him know about it. Then encourage him in activities where he can experience learning new skills.

A sense of predictability will help your children feel secure. It will be much easier to establish regular routines if you have left your abusive partner, and you will be able to establish rules and rituals related to meals and bedtime that the children know they can count on. For example, after Sachiko escaped a violent husband, her three-year-old daughter lay awake for long hours at night and was tearful in the morning. But with a counselor's help, Sachiko created a consistent reliable environment for her daughter. Each night, she said to her, "Before 8:30 we can read two books. Before 9:00 we can read one book. And after 9:30, zero."

"If she spent a long time in the bath she would have zero. And," Sachiko told me proudly, "I would do what I said every time." Knowing what she could count on made her daughter feel secure and helped her sleep.

When the Abuser Dominates the Household

If you are living with an abuser, chaos may threaten at almost any time that he is home. But you can set up regularly scheduled activities to do while he is out of the house. When the children first come home from school, resist the urge to have them do homework right away or to let them watch television. Instead involve them in planning and fixing a special snack that you can all enjoy. Listen to them talk about their day or about what they want to do during the rest of the afternoon. This is not a time to check up on school behavior or grades. You can think of other ways to make at least some parts of their lives predictable. Ask the children to think of activities you can do together once every day or once a week.

If you and your husband get home from work about the same time, you might have trouble engaging the children, because he may claim he is being left out and make the whole project backfire. But maybe you and the kids can get away together to the store, where you can enjoy yourselves and accomplish something at the same time. You could use the opportunity to teach the children how to solve the problem of getting the most nutritious food for the least money. But try to make it fun, too. Encourage them to figure out what kind of tasty snack they can also fit into the budget. The ability to solve problems builds confidence, which leads to a sense of being in control of what happens. That leads the way to resilience.

"Mistakes Are Teachable Moments"

Many books on parenting assume two parents live together in a comfortable house with one boy and one girl in a safe suburban neighborhood. They have only minor problems to resolve. But you and *your* boy and girl—or five children—may live in a poor, unsafe, rundown neighborhood and feel overwhelmed much of the time. If you are on your own, you fret about how to pay bills and fear your ex-partner's actions. You worry about your children's ability to recover from their own fears. Still, you can learn from some of those guidebooks. *Raising Resilient Children* by Robert Brooks and Sam Goldstein offers good tips on being the best parent you can be. The authors suggest that both you and your children can learn that "mistakes are teachable moments."

If you've watched a one-year-old learning to walk, you'll know that miracles of courage and determination happen every day in a child's life. Down she goes. Boom. And she might cry. But up she goes again, and gingerly hanging onto the coffee table, she takes off on foot to explore life's adventures. Just as mistakes cause a toddler to fall—and learn—mistakes can also give you and your kids a chance to figure out what you can do better next time. You have probably tried many ways to protect them from violence and other forms of abuse. Maybe some worked for a while and then didn't the next time. So then the challenge is to bounce back and try something else.

The more you can provide your children with experiences that counteract the horrors of abuse, the more likely they are to become resilient adults. The goal is not to create a problem-free environment. After all, life is full of dilemmas and obstacles. But you can encourage an attitude of "I can solve this problem. If this doesn't work, I can try something else."

Turn to the Equality Wheel in the back of this book. Have it enlarged and mount the copy on a bulletin board in the kitchen where you and your kids will notice it several times a day. Remind each other regularly that you are striving to put equality and nonviolence into practice. Each time someone in the family overcomes an urge to use power unfairly, encourage her or him to take credit for it. Take every opportunity to notice the changes your family is making. You are working to create a family that is not just free of abuse and power and control tactics. Most important, it is a home that fosters nonviolence and equal treatment of everyone.

CHAPTER 29

MOVING FORWARD: WHAT COMMUNITIES CAN DO

Maybe, as for many other abused women, one of the most frightening aspects of what has been done to you is the feeling that you are all alone. That is an important reason to keep in touch with domestic-violence hot line and shelter advocates. All over this country—all over this world— hundreds of thousands of women are struggling for their freedom. Advocates and researchers also work to understand and change institutions that indirectly support abuse. Even though research is often slow to reach the general public or professionals, it does gradually advance understanding of social problems and it can contribute to your freedom. Knowing about studies on domestic violence can help you understand and change your situation. Social scientists' findings offer us important information about causes of abuse and suggest ways to minimize it. Statistics that reflect horrifying realities sometimes focus the attention of influential people on how to help battered women and their children. Below are reminders of important facts. They can scare you even more than you may be already. But they can also give you a broader perspective on your situation. You might even want to pass on this information to your doctor or therapist or boss.

DANGER IF YOU STAY, DANGER IF YOU LEAVE: THE STATISTICS

These are some of the data that show how dangerous battering really is:
- According to a 1989 U.S. Surgeon General report, battering may be the single most important context for female alcoholism, attempted suicide by women, rape and child abuse, homelessness for women and children and a major contributor to a range of mental health problems.[1]
- The American Medical Association reports that one out of every four women will be a victim of violence by a husband or boyfriend at some point in her life.[2]
- By conservative estimates, at least two million women are assaulted

by partners every year in the United States.[3]

- Women who obtain a permanent civil protection order experience an 80 percent reduction in the risk of police-reported physical violence. But only 20 percent of those raped, physically abused, or stalked by partners obtained such orders.[4]

Those figures cause some people to believe the safest thing a battered woman can do is to leave her partner right away. They might reach a different conclusion if they knew about another set of facts:

- Nearly half of domestic-violence homicides occur a month or more *after* the couple has separated.[5]
- "Preexisting problems in the parenting behavior of a particular batterer tend to intensify *after* separation . . . including retaliatory tendencies common in batterers."[6]
- "Numerous studies have found that mistreatment of women by abusers tends to continue for a substantial period *after* separation and commonly escalates to levels worse than those when the couple was together." Rape or other forms of sexual assault are particularly common.[7]

When this book was first written, few people in positions of power and responsibility knew that abused women often face continued danger after they leave a partner and even after legal ties are severed. They didn't realize that a woman is more likely to be killed after she leaves a perpetrator than while she lives with him. In contrast, many battered women intuitively understood those hazards long before statistics were gathered. They didn't need studies to prove their fears were justified. But the public did.

Thanks in part to research, more people are beginning to understand that if your partner is violent and controlling, your greatest risk of dangerous assault or even murder occurs when he realizes you are serious about separating from him. As mentioned in Who This Book Is For And How to Use It, we do not know how many women who were killed by partners had carefully followed safety plans when they left. Some probably thought they would never have to try to get away. When they learned they were mistaken, they had to leave suddenly without having thought through where they would go, how they would get there, and how they would stay safe. Perhaps they told themselves, "It can't happen to me," and never let themselves consider the possibility of homicide.

Now we know that once a woman becomes involved with a violent partner, any decision she makes—including one to do nothing—might be high-risk. To "do nothing" is as much of a decision as calling police, leaving, or hitting back. Not coming to a decision about what action to take might be a bigger risk than using information from the Danger

Assessment list and the Safety Plan for You and Your Family, to get to a secure place. Using information from the list and the safety plan (both located at the back of this book) may even save your life.

BAD NEWS GIVES BIRTH TO A MOVEMENT AGAINST BATTERING

The facts about assault and murder may frighten you. But other heartening signs tell us that attitudes and policies have changed for the better. A brief look backward will help us gain perspective on this trend. In the mid-seventies groups of women scattered throughout the country began to realize that hundreds of women in every city needed safe places to stay for a night or two to escape dangerous partners. Wherever women gathered to address the problems of battered women, they found pretty much the same story—no one was taking care of women's and children's needs.

For a New York City population of eight million, for instance, there were 1,000 beds for homeless men and 45 for homeless women. In Los Angeles there were 4,000 beds for men and 30 for women and children. But not one of those 30 beds would accept mothers with boys older than four.[8] That was certainly disturbing news. But when connected to other information about the plight of abused women, it helped galvanize women into action. Collective action became the movement against battering. Since that time our efforts have advanced women's safety, including the increase in availability of emergency shelter.

As Susan Schechter said in her history of the early years of the movement, "To start 500 shelters, win legal and social services reforms in hundreds of localities, form almost 50 state coalitions, and capture the imagination of a nation in approximately 8 years are extraordinary achievements."[9]

Continuing those trends, we have contributed extensively to changing police, medical, and mental health protocols and continually expanded services to a broad range of women who have been abused as well as to their children. In addition to countless hot lines and other services, there are now more than 3,000 shelters for women abused by intimate partners.[10]

Statistics on rates of intimate-partner violence against women differ depending upon who gathers the data. The National Crime Victimization Survey reported that intimate-partner violence decreased 21 percent from 1993 to 1998, from about 1.1 million incidents in 1993 to about 900,000 in 1998. It found that from 1996 through 1998, intimate partners committed fewer murders than in any other year since

1976, down from 3,000 in 1976 to about 1,830 in 1998.[11]

Because violent crime in general decreased during the nineties, there is no way to know how much of the apparently significant drop in crimes against women by intimate partners is caused by the same forces as the broader trend in crime reduction. Study conclusions vary on whether arrests and protection orders stop violence. But it is reasonable to assume that women's increased calls to police and use of emergency shelters and of court orders for protection have saved lives.

Public Perceptions of Abuse Shift

In the mid-nineties a well-planned national public-awareness campaign about domestic violence helped shift public attitudes.[12] During the same period O. J. Simpson's trial for murder captured the public's attention for many months. That sad, terrible event contributed to raising the public's awareness of the horrors of battering.

Many people now understand that when a batterer inflicts injuries severe enough for medical attention, outside intervention is necessary. The next step for our movement has been to increase understanding of the connection between acts of violence and the devastating effects of power and control tactics. Many people continue to resist the idea that *batterers batter because they want to control their partners.*[13] As recently as 1995, almost half of women and men surveyed believed that men sometimes physically abuse women because they are stressed out or drunk.[14] That kind of thinking lets a perpetrator off the hook on the false claim that "he can't help himself." See Chapter 27, Men Who Batter: Can They Change? To stop battering, professionals and religious, legal, neighborhood, and other communities must work together to hold batterers accountable for using abusive control tactics in addition to violence.

That community task is especially difficult because those power tactics are often invisible, as are their effects. We will have to intensify campaigns to increase public concern and pressure institutions and government agencies to take on their shares of the responsibility for holding batterers accountable. Society's institutions either make that behavior attractive and rewarding or they make it unacceptable. We will have to challenge institutions to confront their lack of commitment to peaceful and respectful communities. In the past two or three decades we have learned a great deal about how to change the judicial system and about how deeply the acceptance of violence against women permeates our institutions. Change depends partly on passing our information to the general public.

So far the public has been exposed to little information about the dollar costs of battering. That makes it easy for those who would rather not know the truth to believe domestic abuse does not affect them. Some don't want to know, for instance, about the figures below, which may be unwelcome news to you as well. But the facts illustrate that the problem does not belong to only a few of us. They suggest how communities can help the individuals most immediately affected—women, perhaps, like you. Your increasing awareness of potential solutions can remind you that you are not alone.

MEDICAL COSTS

The costs of abuse to society are astounding:
* Medical expenses resulting from domestic violence are estimated to cost American business at least $3 billion to $5 billion per year.[15]
* One in five battered women treated in a hospital had been to the emergency department at least eleven times with trauma.[16]
* One-fifth of women with a history of violence or abuse reported having a disability or illness that limits the ability to work or carry out daily activities, compared with 15 percent of women without a history of violence.[17]
* Each year, battering of women results in 40,000 doctor visits, 30,000 hospital emergency room visits, and 100,000 total days of hospitalization.[18]
* "Thirty percent of women presenting with injuries in an Emergency Department are battered "(American Journal of Public Health).[19]
* A Seattle study found that families that experience domestic violence go to emergency rooms six times more often than other families, see physicians eight times more often, and use prescription drugs six times more often than those without violence.[20]

CHILD-PROTECTION COSTS

In a national survey of more than 6,000 American families, 50 percent of the men who frequently assaulted their wives also frequently abused their children.[21]
* Total direct costs of child abuse and neglect in the United States are estimated to be $24,384,347,302 annually. At least half may be directly or indirectly caused by batterers. The child-welfare system alone is estimated to pay more than $14 billion per year for care resulting from child abuse and neglect, with hospitalization estimated at more than $6 million and chronic health problems just short of

$3 billion. Estimated indirect costs come to about $94 billion.[22]

- Between one-third and half of mothers in child-protection service caseloads have been battered.[23] Many social workers are not aware of that and do not probe for that information. Afraid of not receiving support, women who are abused may be afraid to say so. So the social worker focuses on the mother as the assumed perpetrator or the one who has failed to protect the children. Meanwhile, the most likely perpetrator, the father or the mother's boyfriend, is not even questioned. Even when they do know a client is abused, few social workers understand the complex, multiple effects on family relationships. Funds spent on addressing the actions or failure to act of the wrong people in the wrong way unnecessarily raise government and other costs from battering.[24]

COSTS TO BUSINESS

Costs to business are also staggering:

- Estimates are that the cost of violence in the home to American companies ranges between $3 billion and $5 billion annually, including $100,000 in lost wages.[25]
- Seventy-five percent of domestic-violence victims deal with harassment at work.[26]
- When 100 senior executives were asked about domestic violence, close to half said battering causes major problems on the job, including decreased productivity, increased health-care costs, absenteeism, errors, turnover time spent coping with problems, and acts of physical violence in the workplace.[27]

Employers Take Action

Major corporations such as Polaroid, Liz Claiborne, Marshall's, and the Body Shop have already taken a stand against domestic violence by developing public-service campaigns that suggest how employers can be of significant help to women who are abused.[28] Some companies have installed safety precautions, including flexible work hours that make it difficult for a stalker or batterer to track a victim. Others provide cell phones for women at risk and escorts to well-lit company parking lots. Still others have arranged for temporary transfers to different offices and put emergency procedures in place by making work phone numbers secure.

Companies can take a clear stand to prevent domestic violence. They can pay attention to warning signs, offer support to abused employees, and refer those who want it to counseling. They can create an environment that encourages employees to come forward with concerns because they know their situations will be treated seriously. As more business owners and managers learn that safety measures can save them money in the long run, more may adopt safety measures. If you are in a work environment that is not secure, consider talking to your boss about what can be done to increase your safety. Better yet, gather with coworkers and draw up a plan that the boss might put into place throughout the company. Show managers the statistics above and examples of what has been done by other companies.[29]

MOVING FORWARD

The costs of battering are not all in dollars, of course. But it is dollars, often, that translate into stopping violence and abuse. Dollars are important in enabling victimized people to heal. When wisely spent, they can prevent long-term direct or indirect pain and suffering. Dollars spent in the short run can save money in the long term. A dollar spent on child welfare to prevent neglect and abuse can translate into many, many thousands saved in criminal-justice expenses and medical care. We have models for change of judicial, medical, and corporate systems as well as of schools and universities, media, religious groups, psychological counselors, and corporations. Most require spending public money, but in the long run the savings would be significant.

Why Battered Women Need Financial Help to Be Safe

The costs of battering to corporations and other organizations are proportionately minuscule compared to the price paid by individual women, the people who can least afford it. Women's wages are still at about 75 percent of men's pay, down from 77 percent in 1993.[30] Battering cuts across all classes. About 25 percent of women with incomes above $50,000 are abused at least once in their lifetimes by intimate partners. That contrasts with 37 percent of women who earn $16,000 or less who are similarly abused.[31] A woman who is battered may start out poor, or the abuse may drive her into poverty. A woman with children who leaves home has a 50 percent chance that her standard of living will drop below the poverty level.[32] An estimated 24 percent to 30 percent of abused working women lose their jobs because of their domestic-violence situations.[33]

As mentioned above, one-fifth of women who are domestic-violence victims reported having a disability or illness that limits their ability to work or carry out daily activities, compared with 15 percent of women without a history of violence who report such disability or illness.[34] Rural women are especially at risk because of shortages of domestic-violence services, poor job prospects, lack of transportation systems, availability of weapons common in rural households, poverty, and the probability that a health provider is acquainted with the abuser.[35] Lesbians may fear being "outed" by abusive partners and even in this relatively liberal age may face discrimination in housing or employment. Immigrant women face language, cultural, and job-skill barriers in addition to fears of being deported. Women of color are disproportionately abused, disproportionately poor, and may face housing and job discrimination, which adds to financial and emotional stress.

The young are especially vulnerable, and few have access to enough money to establish independent households. Women between the ages of sixteen and twenty-four in dating relationships experience the highest rate of domestic violence and sexual assault.[36] An average of 28 percent of high school and college students experience dating violence at some point, while 26 percent of pregnant teens reported being physically abused by boyfriends.[37]

Financial vulnerability because of age, immigrant status, sexual orientation, lack of job skills, or disability puts a woman at risk and is exacerbated by battering and efforts to change the situation. Underlying each of her disadvantages is the accompanying factor of poverty. For her safety a woman leaving an abuser may have to change her job and where she lives. Affordable housing, if she can find it at all, may be available only in a building or neighborhood that lacks security. She runs the risk of becoming one of America's Internally Displaced Persons. In a Pennsylvania study, one of three homeless households identified domestic violence as the cause of their homelessness.[38] That is one more situation that is both cause and effect.[39]

Safety has additional costs, including doctor bills and the loss of health insurance at a new job. If her husband uses court proceedings and custody or property disputes to harass her, a woman may have to choose between a lawyer and a decent place to live. Or she may not have the money for either one of them. She may need to find counseling for her children and herself. She may need childcare. All of these expenses can be daunting and are often overlooked or minimized by people in positions to institute necessary changes. The remarkable thing is that thousands of women overcome economic trials and create stable, safe households.

How Corporations and Government Can Help

In addition to enhanced security and support on the job, businesses can decline to pay batterers' court costs, as some now do. If they give them time off for court appearances, they can require that they make up the time as a way of holding them accountable. They can let employees who batter know that their jobs are contingent on their participating in a program for batterers and a drug or alcohol program if appropriate.

Even our brief lists of the costs of battering tell us something about who can take action to stop battering. The moment a woman trying to escape violence steps outside her door, she is confronted with the question of where she can find a safe, affordable place to live. Real-estate developers could help enormously by making low-rent housing available. Significant increases in government-sponsored housing that is safe and affordable could save lives.[40] The second question the woman is likely to ask is where she can find a job that supports a decent life for herself and her children. Legislators can answer her by sponsoring bills to raise the minimum wage and to provide training for jobs that pay a living wage to single mothers.

Corporations can take seriously the figures that show the costs to them of battering and insecure work environments. They can raise wages high enough to support an adult and two children. They can provide childcare at the job site. Along with the other security improvements mentioned above, these are investments that increase employees' security. Changes might translate into lowered rates of absenteeism and better concentration. Those improvements could lead to higher productivity.

By working together, unions and activists can pressure Congress to raise the minimum wage and establish universal health care.[41] Several decades ago women organized a campaign for equal pay for work of equal value. It is time to put it on our agenda again. Access to a truly living wage and decent housing, medical and mental health services, and childcare will not stop battering. But it could enable women who want to leave abusive partners to live in safety.

When hospital administrators and medical personnel realize the enormous long-term medical costs to battered women, they might decide to supplement their usual budgets to allow for protocols and extra personnel to help battered women and children. Staff training in how to find safe shelter and how to work closely with domestic-violence advocates can result in patients feeling safe enough to tell what has been done to them. Working together, some hospital staffs and advocates have learned to trust each other, which has been crucial in helping mothers of children who have been abused. The result is increased safety for mothers and a higher proportion of children remaining safely with their mothers.[42] The program has been adopted in a number of hospitals, and if it were established in all children's hospitals, it would probably result in a great deal less family pain and suffering. It might also significantly reduce long-run costs to hospitals from repeat visits to emergency rooms. Similar reforms can be initiated in child-protection agencies and family courts.

Much remains to be done. But because of the movement's work during past decades, most people now agree that battering is wrong and that it must be stopped. For the first time in history, international organizations and governmental bodies have made declarations against the battering of women by intimate partners. Such statements have been made by Human Rights Watch, attorneys general, Amnesty International, several U.S. surgeon generals, priests, imams, rabbis and ministers, bishops, the U.S. Bar Association, the United Nations, and ethnic and immigrant organizations.

Most of this book suggests what you as an individual can do to make your life safer, more peaceful, and more satisfying. But the public has begun to understand that you should not be expected to do it alone. As you work at changing your life, I hope you will envision yourself accompanied by a great number of people devoted to enacting change. Think of us—advocates, international human-rights workers, and the best of religious leaders, corporate leaders, and researchers—as part of your team. Some of us are coming late to this race for freedom. But women and men of all ages, lifestyles, ethnicities, and religions are running alongside you.

RESOURCES

NOTES

Who This Book Is For and How to Use It

1 See http://ncdv.org/Risk_Being_Murdered.html for the Reuters story. Or read a more academic article on the study in the October 2003 issue of *Journal of General Internal Medicine.*

2 "Domestic Violence Facts," on the National Coalition Against Domestic Violence website www.ncadv.org (2003); source: Victoria Holt, Ph.D., MPH et al., "Do Protection Orders Affect the Likelihood of Future Partner Violence and Injury?" *American Journal of Preventative Medicine,* 24, 1, pp. 16, 20. Task Force on Domestic and Sexual Violence, Florida Mortality Review Project (1997).

3 Ibid.

SECTION I MAKING THE DECISION TO LEAVE OR STAY

Chapter 1 Social and Political Aspects of Abuse

1 Inge K. Broverman, et al., "Sex-Role Stereotypes and Clinical Judgments of Mental Health," *Journal of Consulting and Clinical Psychology,* 34:i (1970), pp. 1–7.

2 Suzanne Steinmetz and Murray Straus, eds., *Violence in the Family* (New York: Harper and Row, 1974), p. 80.

3 R. Emerson Dobash and Russell Dobash, *Violence Against Wives: A Case Against Patriarchy* (New York: The Free Press, 1979), p. 154.

Chapter 5 "But I Still Love Him"

1 Morton Hunt, *The Natural History of Love* (New York: Knopf, 1959), p. 341.

2 Ibid., p. 342.

3 Stanton Peele with Archie Brodsky, *Love and Addiction* (New York: New American Library, 1976).

SECTION II GETTING PROFESSIONAL HELP

Chapter 7 Emergency Help from Doctors, Police, and Prosecutors

1 From "Legal Issues in Domestic Violence," Washington State Department of Social and Health Services.

2 Jennifer Baker Fleming, *Stopping Wife Abuse* (New York: Anchor Books/Doubleday, 1979), pp. 198–99, 200.

SECTION III HELPING YOURSELF TO SURVIVAL

Chapter 10 You Can Be Your Own Counselor

1 Adapted from Sharon Berlin's work on self-criticism reduction in *Behavioral Methods in Social Work,* Steven Paul Schinke, ed. (New York: Aldine Publishing Company, 1981). pp. 135–136.

SECTION IV AFTER YOU LEAVE

Chapter 18 Sexuality

1 Shere Hite, *The Hite Report* (New York: Dell, 1979), p. 612.

2 Ibid., p. 297.

3 These vaginal orgasms originate from an area on the upper wall of the vagina called the Grafenberg spot. The size varies from about the size of a dime to that of a half dollar. It's extremely sensitive and when stroked it produces a strong desire to urinate at first, quickly followed by intense sexual excitement and orgasm. A woman may at the same time expel fluid that originates in the same spot. The existence of this fluid, expelled at orgasm by some women, has been denied and explained away as merely urine during most of our history, though it has also been recognized at various historical periods. Masters and Johnson reported that there is no such phenomenon in women.

4 Hite, *The Hite Report,* pp. 423–25.

SECTION VI NEW DIRECTIONS

Chapter 23 Teen Abuse

1 Maria Roy, ed., *The Battered Woman* (New York: Van Nostrand Reinhold, 1977).

2 Mildred Pagelow, *Family Violence* (New York: Praeger, 1984), p. 292, citing a study by Henton et al.

3 Karen Susan Brockopp, et al., *A Descriptive Study Surveying the Frequency and Severity of Intra-Couple Dating Violence at the High School Level,* doctoral dissertation.

4 Pagelow, op. cit., p. 68, citing Murray Straus, Richard Gelles, and Suzanne Steinmetz, *Behind Closed Doors.*

5 Pagelow, op. cit., p. 292, citing Parcell and Kanin.

6 Pagelow, ibid.

7 Pagelow, op. cit., p. 293, citing works by Laner and by Makepeace.

8 Pagelow, op. cit., p. 286, citing Dobash and Dobash and a study by Bowker.

9 Brockopp, op. cit.

Chapter 24 Lesbian Abuse

1 One step in that direction was the lesbian battering anthology initiated by the coalition: Kerry Lobel, *Naming the Violence: Speaking Out about Lesbian Battering*, (Seattle: Seal Press, 1986).

2 Though there are still relatively few studies, by 2004 enough had been conducted to indicate strongly that the prevalence of lesbian (and gay) battering is about the same as in heterosexual relationships. See Lori B. Girshick, *Woman-To-Woman Sexual Violence: Does She Call It Rape?* (Boston: Northeastern University Press, 2002). Girshick discusses the results of the few studies that exist; the dearth of information about rape in lesbian relationships; the myth of butch/femme roles being responsible for battering; and theories about lesbian battering in the context of feminist theories. She provides many other sources for further investigation of these questions. See also the Resources section for further reading.

Chapter 25 Immigrant Women: Challenges and Solutions

1 Gloria González, "Barriers and Consequences for Battered Immigrant Latinas," faculty mentor Troy Duster, on the website www.aad.berkeley.edu/96journal/gloriagonzalez.html; source: Chris Hogeland and Karen Rosen, *Dreams Lost, Dreams Found: Undocumented Women in the Land of Opportunity: A Survey Research Project of Chinese, Filipina, and Latina Undocumented Women* (San Francisco: Coalition for Immigrant and Refugee Rights and Services, Winter 1991).

Chapter 26 Religious Challenges

1 Rabbi Elliot N. Dorff, "Aspects of Judaism and Family Violence," *Healing and Wholeness: A Resource Guide on Domestic Abuse in the Jewish Community*, ed. Diane Gardsbane (Washington, D.C.: Jewish Women International, 2002), pp. 43–44.

2 Interview.

3 Rev. Nathaniel J. Mullen, "A Pastor's Experience," in Nancy A.

Murphy, M.A., *God's Reconciling Love* (Seattle: Faith Trust Institute, 2003; www.faithtrustinstitute.org), p. 24.

4 From an unpublished article, "Importance of Peaceful Families for Our Community," part of a Peaceful Families Workshop packet prepared by Sharifa Alkhateeb. (Note: According to the Muslim Students Association of the University of Southern California, *Subhanahu wa ta'ala* [SWT] "is an expression that Muslims use whenever the name of Allah is pronounced or written." It is a term of glorification; see www.usc.edu/dept/MSA/reference/glossary/term.SUBHANA.html.)

5 Anne L. Horton, Melany M. Wilkins, and Wendy Wright, "Women Who Ended Abuse: What Religious Leaders and Religion Did for These Victims," in *Abuse and Religion: When Praying Isn't Enough*, eds. Anne L. Horton and Judith A. Williamson (Lexington, Mass: Lexington Books/D.C. Heath and Company, 1988), p. 243.

6 Carolyn Holderread Heggen, "Religious Beliefs and Abuse," in *Women, Abuse, and the Bible*, eds. Catherine Clark Kroeger and James R. Beck (Grand Rapids, Mich.: Baker Books, 1996) pp. 15–27.

7 Marie Fortune, *Keeping the Faith* (San Francisco: Harper, 1995) p. 15.

8 Interview.

9 Interview.

10 Lecture at Peaceful Families workshop sponsored by Chaya, Seattle, 2003.

11 *To Save a Life: Ending Domestic Violence in Jewish Families* [videotape] (Faith Trust Institute, 1997), op. cit.

12 "A Journey Towards Freedom: A Haggadah for Women Who Have Experienced Domestic Violence," eds. Alison Iser, Michelle Lifton, Rabbi Lisa B. Gelber, Rabbi Cindy G. Enger, Irit Eliav, M.S.W., and Leigh Nachman Hofheimer (Faith Trust Institute, 2003), op. cit. p. 10.

13 Sharifa Alkhateeb, Peaceful Families workshop, op. cit.

14 Fortune, op. cit. pp. 87–88.

15 Rabbi Abraham J. Twerski, M.D., *The Shame Borne in Silence: Spouse Abuse in the Jewish Community* (Pittsburgh: Mirkov Publications, 1996; 800/851-8303), p. 72.

16 Craig S. Keener, "Some Biblical Reflections on Justice, Rape, and an Insensitive Society," *Women, Abuse, and the Bible*, op. cit., p.129.

17 Imam Mohamed Joban, "Importance of Peaceful Families for Our Community," op. cit.

18 Sharifa Alkhateeb, "Ending Domestic Violence in Muslim Families," *Sisters: The Magazine of Dialogue among Muslim Women*, Vol. 1, No. 4, pp. 1–2.

19 Cited in "The *Get* as a Tool of Abuse," *Healing and Wholeness,* ed. Diane Gardsbane, op. cit., pp. 33–37.

20 "US Bishops Tell Battered Women Not to Stay in Abusive Marriages," on the website www.cathnews.com/news/211/79.php.

21 Marie Fortune, op. cit., pp. 52-53.

22 Rabbi Cindy Enger, Faith Trust Institute, p. 6, on the website www.faithtrustinstitute.org.

23 Interview.

24 Interview.

25 Peaceful Families workshop.

26 Rev. Dr. Randy J. Bridges, "One Couple's Story," *God's Reconciling Love,* op. cit., p. 43.

27 Iser et al., op. cit.

SECTION VII STOPPING THE CYCLE OF ABUSE

Chapter 27 Men Who Batter: Can They Change?

1 You can order numerous articles on battering, including lesbian battering. See the Resources section.

2 Lundy Bancroft and Jay G. Silverman, *The Batterer As Parent* (Thousand Oaks, Calif.: Sage Publications, 2002), p. 5.

3 These questions were adapted from "Signs an Abuser Is NOT Changing" on the Emerge website at www.emergedv.com/signs_the_abuser_is_not_changing.html.

4 "Signs an Abuser May Be Changing" appears on the Emerge website at www.emergedv.com/signs_the_abuser_is_changing.html.

Chapter 28 Nurturing Your Children: Safety and Resilience

1 "Domestic Violence Facts," a fact sheet from the National Coalition Against Domestic Violence; source: Ronet B. Achman and Linda Salzman, Bureau of Justice Statistics, *Violence Against Women: Estimates from the Redesigned Survey* (January 2000).

2 "The Effects of Domestic Violence on Children" fact sheet, op. cit.; source: American Psychological Association, *Violence and the Family: Report of the APA Presidential Task Force on Violence and the Family* (1996), p. 40.

3 Lundy Bancroft and Jay G. Silverman, *The Batterer As Parent* (Thousand Oaks, Calif.: Sage Publications, 2002), p. 121. Reference

is to the Gender Bias Study Committee of 1990, commissioned by the Supreme Court of Massachusetts.

4 Adapted from Meg Crager and Lily Anderson, "Safety Planning When Violence Takes Place at Home" section of *Helping Children Who Witness Domestic Violence: A Guide for Parents* on the website of the Minnesota Center Against Violence and Abuse at www.mincava.umn.edu/documents/materials/study.doc.

5 Adapted from Meg Crager and Lily Anderson, "Safety Planning for Yourself When Your Children Visit Their Dad" op. cit.

6 Lundy Bancroft and Jay G. Silverman, *The Batterer As Parent* (Thousand Oaks, Calif.: Sage Publications, 2002), p. 44.

7 Bancroft and Silverman, op. cit., p. 29.

8 Helen Berman, "The Relevance of Narrative Research with Children Who Witness War and Children Who Witness Woman Abuse," eds. Robert A. Geffner, Ph.D., Peter G. Jaffe, Ph.D., and Marlies Sudermann, Ph.D., *Children Exposed to Domestic Violence: Current Issues in Research, Intervention, Prevention, and Policy Development* (Binghamton, New York: The Haworth Press, 2000), pp. 107–125.

9 Adapted from Meg Crager and Lily Anderson, *Helping Children Who Witness Domestic Violence: A Guide for Parents,* on the website of the Minnesota Center Against Violence and Abuse at www.mincava.umn.edu/documents/materials/study.doc.

Chapter 29 Moving Forward: What Communities Can Do

1 U.S. Surgeon General, "Domestic Violence Statistics" (1989), on the website http://home.gwi.Net/~sanpd/domest8.html.

2 "The American Medical Association Treatment Guidelines" on the website www.s-t.com/projects/DomVio/amatreatment.html.

3 Richard J. Gelles, "Domestic Violence Factoids" (1995), on the website www.mincava.umn.edu/documents/factoid/factoid.html.

4 "Domestic Violence Facts" on the National Coalition Against Domestic Violence website www.ncadv.org.

5 Lundy Bancroft and Jay G. Silverman, *The Batterer As Parent* (Thousand Oaks, Calif.: Sage Publications, 2002), p. 153.

6 Lundy Bancroft and Jay G. Silverman, op. cit., p. 76.

7 Lundy Bancroft, *Why Does He DO That?* (New York: G. P. Putnam's Sons, 2002), p. 218.

8 Susan Schechter, *Women and Male Violence* (Boston: South End Press, 1982).

9 Ibid., p. 320.

10 Public Policy office, National Coalition Against Domestic Violence (Washington, D.C.)

11 "Trends in Violence Against Intimates," *National Crime Victimization Survey 1992–96; Supplementary Homicide Reports, 1976–96.*

12 Ethel Klein, Jacquelyn Campbell, Esta Soler, Marissa Ghez, *Ending Domestic Violence: Changing Public Perceptions/Halting the Epidemic* (Thousand Oaks, Calif.: Sage Publications, 1997).

13 Some professionals rely on an ecological model, which takes into consideration social norms, community factors including poverty, relationship factors, and individual characteristics such as being abused as a child or witnessing it. Ultimately though, those societal, community, relationship, and individual situations feed a batterer's feelings of entitlement and his choice to control his partner through power tactics—because he wants to.

14 Ethel Klein et al., op. cit., p. 89.

15 "Facts and Statistics: Workplace Statistics," p. 5, on the Corporate Alliance to End Partner Violence website at www.caepv.org/membercenter/fact_display.asp.

16 "National Statistics," on the National Domestic Violence Hotline website www.ndvh.org/Info.html.

17 "Domestic Violence and the Health Care Profession," on the National Domestic Violence Hotline website www.ndvh.org/Info.html.

18 "Battered Women," on the Benton County, Arkansas, Battered Women, Domestic Violence, and Rape website www.co.benton.ar.us/DomViolence/battered.htm.

19 "Fast Facts," on the website www.akhopecenter.org/facts.htm.

20 "Engaging Employers in Domestic Violence: Background Information" (2001) on the Partnership for Prevention website www.prevent.org.

21 "Get the Facts," Family Violence Prevention Fund, on the website http://endabuse.org/programs/printable/display.php.

22 Prevent Child Abuse America (2001), website www.preventchild-abuse.org/learn_more/research.html.

23 Linda Spears, "Building Bridges Between Violence Organizations and Child Protective Services" (rev. 2000).

24 For one example of communities working together, see V. Pualani Enos, principal investigator and project director, *Learning from the*

Experiences of Battered Immigrant, Refugee and Indigenous Women Involved with Child Protective Services to Inform a Dialogue among Domestic Violence Activists and Advocates, (2003); Family Violence Prevention Fund, www.endabuse.org; Asian & Pacific Islander Institute on Domestic Violence, www.apiahf.org/apidvinstitute; and Institute on Race and Justice, Northeastern University, www.irj.neu.edu. The result of a survey, focus groups, and interviews of domestic-violence survivors, plus advocates, CPS workers, and stakeholders working together, the report offers recommendations to families, CPS, domestic-violence advocates, and funding and monitoring agencies.

25 "Facts and Statistics: Workplace Statistics," on the Corporate Alliance to End Partner Violence website at www.caepv.org/membercenter/fact_display.asp.

26 "Engaging Employers in Domestic Violence Background Information," op. cit., p. 2.

27 "Facts and Statistics," op. cit., p. 1.

28 See "Facts and Statistics: Workplace Statistics," op. cit.; "Engaging Employers in Domestic Violence: Background Information" (2001) on the website www.prevent.org; and "When Domestic Violence Comes to Work" (2000) on the website www.intermedia-inc.com/WHO2.htm.

29 Ibid.

30 Monica Moorehead, "What's Behind Falling Women's Wages?" *Workers World,* September 25, 1997; website www.workers.org/ww/women0925.html.

31 "National Statistics," p. 13, on the National Domestic Violence Hotline website www.ndvh.org/dvInfo.html.

32 See the website www.akhopecenter.org/facts.htm.

33 The Taylor Institute, "Facts and Statistics: Prisoners of Abuse," on the Corporate Alliance to End Partner Violence website at www.caepv.org/membercenter/fact_display.asp.

34 "Health Care Statistics," p. 13, National Domestic Violence Hotline, op. cit.

35 "Violence Against Rural Women—What Is Different" on the website www.ruralwomyn.net/rural_violence_difference.html.

36 Family Violence Statistics.

37 Ibid. S. Brustin, "Legal Response to Teen Dating Violence," *Family Law Quarterly,* Vol. 29, 2, pp. 333–334.

38 Fast Facts, op. cit.

39 A wide variety of circumstances cause people to be temporarily or permanently homeless. See "Coalition on Homelessness and Housing in Ohio," a survey based on research throughout the nation, not just in Ohio. http://www.cohhio.org/resources/fact-sheets/whofactsheet.html.

40 The Housing Assistance Council is one of several organizations and coalitions that promotes government action to increase affordable housing. See "Why Housing Matters: HAC's 2000 Report on the State of the Nation's Rural Housing." It includes information on the effects of housing on quality of life, costs, who gets loans, and much more. http://www.ruralhome.org.

Corporation for Supportive Housing, "Ending Long-term Homelessness Services Initiative," proposal for a new federal initiative including specific strategies: http://www.csh.org/index.cfm?fuseaction=Page.viewPage&PageId=452

The National Housing Trust Fund Campaign boasts more than 5,000 endorsing organizations for legislation to establish a trust fund "to build and preserve 1.5 million units of rental housing for the lowest income families over the next 10 years." http://www.hntf.org.

41 "Domestic Violence: What Unions Can Do" views domestic violence as a workplace issue and recommends not only training for union stewards and safety plans and support for workers who are victims of battering, but offers sample union contract language to ensure employer responsibility for employees' safety. http://end-abuse.org.

42 See Janet Carter and Susan Schechter, "Child Abuse and Domestic Violence: Creating Community Partnerships for Safe Families" (Family Violence Prevention Fund, 1997), on the website www.mincava.umn.edu/link; and Susan Schechter, "Expanding Solutions for Domestic Violence and Poverty," on the website www.vaw.umn.edu.

SUGGESTED READING

Inspiration: Guides on How to Survive and Stories of Women Who Have Been Abused and Their Children

Numerous books tell stories of women who have gotten free of abusive partners. You can find many of them at your library in section 162.8292. Here are a few:

Cleghorn, Andrea. *Rosie's Place.* Acton, Mass.: VanderWyk & Burnham, 1997. In this short, friendly book you meet residents, mostly women of color, staff, and volunteers involved with this unusual, inspiring shelter in Boston.

Doane, Sharon, M.S.W. *New Beginnings: A Creative Writing Guide for Women Who Have Left Abusive Partners.* Seattle: Seal Press, 1996.

Goldstein, Barry. *Scared to Leave, Afraid to Stay: Paths from Family Violence to Safety.* San Francisco: Robert D. Reed Publishers, 2002. Written by a lawyer, the ten stories of women who had to struggle against both the judicial system and their abusers are sometimes disheartening, but ultimately fulfilling.

Jones, Ann, and Susan Schechter. *When Love Goes Wrong: What to Do When You Can't Do Anything Right: Strategies for Women with Controlling Partners.* New York: Harper Collins Publishers, 1992. Just because you are not physically assaulted does not mean you don't hurt.

NiCarthy, Ginny, and Sue Davidson. *You Can Be Free: An Easy-to-Read Handbook for Abused Women.* Seattle: Seal Press, 1989. An easy-to-read version of *Getting Free.*

Raphael, Jody. *Saving Bernice: Battered Women, Welfare, and Poverty.* Boston: Northeastern University Press, 2000. Bernice's story illustrates the intersection of battering, poverty, and periodic reliance on public assistance. The drama of her struggle is threaded together with references to findings of academic studies.

Schwartz, Diane. *Whose Face Is in the Mirror? The Story of One Woman's*

Journey from the Nightmare of Domestic Abuse to True Healing. Carlsbad, Calif.: Hay House, 2000. Schwartz gradually claims her freedom from her husband and then from her father's domination and lets the reader in on the lessons she learns as she takes one step backward, and then two steps forward.

Weitzman, Susan, Ph.D. *Not to People Like Us: Hidden Abuse in Upscale Marriages.* New York: Basic Books, 2000. The experiences of battered educated career women married to men in prestigious occupations and considered "pillars of the community" are rarely reported to authorities and their stories are rarely told. Wietzman goes a long way toward making up for that gap in our understanding.

Books for Children and Teens

For Young Children
Bernstein, Sharon Chesler, and Karen Ritz, illustrator. *A Family That Fights.* Morton Grove, Ill.: Albert Whitman & Company, 1992.

Davis, Diane, and Marina Mengale, illustrator. *Something Is Wrong at My House.* Seattle: Seal Press, 1986.

Paris, Susan, and Gail Labinski. *Mommy and Daddy Are Fighting.* Seattle: Seal Press, 1999.

For Teens
Levy, Barrie, ed. *Dating Violence: Young Women in Danger.* Seattle: Seal Press, 1991.

Levy, Barrie. *In Love and in Danger: A Teen's Guide to Breaking Free of Abusive Relationships.* Seattle: Seal Press, 1998.

Books for Lesbians, Gays, Bisexuals, and Transgendered People

Clunis, Merilee D., and Dorsey Green. *Lesbian Couples: A Guide to Creating Healthy Relationships.* Seattle: Seal Press, 2000.

Girshick, Lori B. *Woman-to-Woman Sexual Violence: Does She Call It Rape?* Boston: Northeastern University Press, 2002. Girshick combines theory, references to studies, and the personal stories of seventy women who have experienced sexual violence from lesbian partners. The topic is slowly emerging from yet another closet and this book opens the door to the light.

Kaschak, Ellyn. *Intimate Betrayal: Domestic Violence in Lesbian Relationships.* New York: Haworth Press, 2002. Kaschak applies "new lenses" to lesbian battering, says one reviewer. According to the publisher's blurb, the author explains lesbian battering in terms of social forces such as homophobia and stress rather than as a result of the desire to control.

Lobel, Kerry, ed. *Naming the Violence: Speaking Out about Lesbian Battering.* Seattle: Seal Press, 1986. The first book on lesbian battering, *Naming the Violence* is still one of few available. The bulk of it consists of first-person stories, but it includes a short history of the painful coming out of the "second closet," theories about lesbian battering and suggestions about community responsibility.

Lundy, Sandra, and Beth Leventhal. *Same Sex Domestic Violence: Strategies for Change.* Thousand Oaks, Calif.: Sage Publications, 1999. Even after many battered lesbians had come out of this second closet, it was a long time before justice-system personnel and professionals would take the topic seriously. This book explores legal aspects of the problem, how to help battered lesbians, and how coalitions and communities can organize to stop the violence.

Renzetti, Claire, and Charlie Miley, eds. *Violence in Gay and Lesbian Domestic Partnerships.* New York: Haworth Press, 1996. A variety of topics are covered in this book, including lesbian and gay battered people of color, HIV/AIDS, interventions, and theoretical questions about same-sex violence.

Books about Battered Women of Color and Immigrant Women

Abraham, Margaret. *Speaking the Unspeakable: Marital Violence among South Asian Immigrants in the United States.* Piscataway, N.J.: Rutgers University Press, 2000. The book is the result of interviews in an academic study and the stories are threaded throughout the work. The stories and analysis are very accessible.

Agtuca, Jacqueline, in collaboration with The Asian Women's Shelter. *A Community Secret: For the Filipina in an Abusive Relationship.* Seattle: Seal Press, 1994.

West, Carolyn M., ed. *Violence in the Lives of Black Women: Battered, Black, and Blue.* New York: Haworth Press, 2002. Chapters on breaking the silence, strategies for leaving abusive partners, black lesbian battered women, research, and more.

White, Evelyn C. *Chain Chain Change: For Black Women in Abusive Relationships.* Seattle: Seal Press, 1985.

Zambrano, Myrna M. *Mejor Sola Que Mal Acompañada: Para la Mujer Gopeada/For the Latina in an Abusive Relationship.* Seattle: Seal Press, 1985.

Zambrano, Myrna M. *¡No Mas!: Guía Para La Mujer Golpeada.* Seattle: Seal Press, 1994.

Religion

Engineer, Ashgar Ali. *The Rights of Women in Islam.* New York: Saint Martin's Press, 1996. A *Book News* review says, "Theologian Engineer, director of the Institute of Muslim Studies in Bombay, refutes Islamic fundamentalist views that men are superior to women. He returns to the Quran, and to the context in which it was written, to argue that Islamic law calls for equality between the sexes in personal, democratic and human rights."

Fortune, Marie M. *Keeping the Faith: Guidance for Christian Women Facing Abuse.* San Francisco: HarperSanFrancisco, 1987. At 103 pages, this book will fit into your pocket. Reverend Fortune discusses various interpretations of the Bible that are pertinent to women who are battered.

Gardsbane, Diane, ed. *Embracing Justice: A Resource Guide for Rabbis on Domestic Abuse.* Washington, D.C.: Jewish Women International, 2002; and Gardsbane, Diane, ed. *Healing and Wholeness: A Resource Guide on Domestic Abuse in the Jewish Community.* Washington, D.C.: Jewish Women International, 2002. The topics overlap considerably, but the content is varied to suit the two different audiences. Both volumes include testimony by Orthodox and other rabbis, an extensive list of power and control tactics, detailed references from religious texts with discussions of their meanings, and advice for anyone in touch with a religiously observant Jewish woman who is battered.

Iser, Alison, Michelle Lifton, Rabbi Lisa B. Gelber, Rabbi Cindy G. Enger, Irit Eliav, M.S.W., and Leigh Nachman Hofheimer. "A Journey Towards Freedom: A Haggadah for Women Who Have Experienced Domestic Violence." Seattle: Faith Trust Institute, 2003.

Kroeger, Catherine Clark, and James R. Beck, eds. *Women, Abuse, and the Bible: How Scripture Can Be Used to Hurt or Heal.* Grand Rapids, Mich.: Baker Books, 1996.

Kroeger, Catherine Clark, and Nancy Nason-Clark. *No Place for Abuse: Biblical Resources to Counteract Domestic Violence.* Downers Grove, Ill.: InterVarsity Press, 2001.

Murphy, Nancy A., M.A. *God's Reconciling Love: A Pastor's Handbook on Domestic Violence.* Seattle: Faith Trust Institute, 2003. The Faith Trust Institute sells other books, some for clergy, some for the general public or battered women. Some are translated into several languages. The institute has produced videotapes featuring religious leaders and battered women in Christian parishes and Jewish communities, available for rent or purchase. Its catalog is on-line at www.faithtrustinstitute.org.

Tate, Sonsyrea. *Little X: Growing Up in the Nation of Islam.* San Francisco: HarperSanFrancisco, 1997. From the blurb on the book: "Now, Sonsyrea Tate draws back the curtains to reveal the mysterious Nation *behind* its controversial leaders, by sharing her experience as a girl growing up inside the Nation of Islam." Tate's ambivalence about her family, gender roles, and religion creates tension and makes for a good read.

Twerski, Rabbi Abraham J., M.D. *The Shame Borne in Silence: Spouse Abuse in the Jewish Community.* Pittsburgh: Mirkov Publications, 1996. Psychiatrist and Orthodox Rabbi Twerski is a compassionate, wise, and sensitive writer who passes on his knowledge about Judaism and women's rights in an accessible style. The book can be ordered from the publisher, P.O. Box 81971, Pittsburgh, PA 15217, tel. 800/851-8303.

Volcano Press. *Family Violence and Religion: An Interfaith Resource Guide.* San Francisco: Volcano Press, 1995. This provocative patchwork quilt of a book written by the staff of Volcano Press includes chapters on abuse in Hispanic-American, African-American, Asian-American, rural, and religious communities.

Men Who Batter

Bancroft, Lundy. *Why Does He DO That? Inside the Minds of Angry and Controlling Men.* New York: G. P. Putnam's Sons, 2002. Bancroft explores the reasons that men batter, especially focusing on their characteristic trait of entitlement.

Carrillo, Ricardo, and Jerry Tello, eds. *Family Violence and Men of Color: Healing the Wounded Male Spirit.* New York: Springer Publishing, 1998. The book describes how leaders and participants in groups for men who batter weave their particular ethnic history and lore into the work of ending their violence to partners. African-American, Asian, Latino, and American-Indian myths, songs, and stories become part of the process of accountability.

Dutton, Donald G., Ph.D., with Susan K. Golant. *The Batterer: A Psychological Profile.* New York: Basic Books, 1995. Using a complex analysis, Dutton answers the question of who batterers are and why they do what they do.

Gondolf, Edward. *Batterer Intervention Systems: Issues, Outcomes, and Recommendations.* Thousand Oaks, Calif.: Sage Publications, 2002. Gondolf reports his four-year findings on four groups of men who batter and discusses the meaning of results in the context of other research. A highly academic book and his findings are controversial.

Nurturing Your Children

Bancroft, Lundy. *When Dad Hurts Mom: Helping Your Children Heal the Wounds of Witnessing Abuse.* New York: G. P. Putnam's Sons, 2004. Based on his experience in working with men who batter and their partners and as a guardian ad litem for children in court, Bancroft offers practical advice about how women can protect their children and help them heal from abuse.

Bancroft, Lundy, and Jay G. Silverman. *The Batterer As Parent: Addressing the Impact of Domestic Violence on Family Dynamics.* Thousand Oaks, Calif.: Sage Publications, 2002. Calling on experience as group leaders for men who batter, the authors show how perpetrators of violence against women use similar tactics to control children. They describe problems that arise in court custody disputes and offer advice on how to handle professionals who may be unaware of the consequences of abuse.

Brooks, Robert, Ph.D., and Sam Goldstein, Ph.D. *Raising Resilient Children: Fostering Strength, Hope, and Optimism in Your Child.* Chicago: Contemporary Books, 2001. The book offers sound advice on most parenting issues—from listening to loving to disciplining and using the mistakes you make to do better next time.

Levy, Barrie, and Patricia Occhiuzzo Giggans. *What Parents Need to Know about Dating Violence: Learning the Facts and Helping Your Teen.* Seattle: Seal Press, 1995.

Rubin, Lillian. *The Transcendent Child: Tales of Triumph over the Past.* New York: Basic Books, 1996. A "transcendent" child herself, Rubin weaves her own story into those of eight women and men who rose above childhood abuse, poverty, and other painful experiences. To answer her question, "What makes such transcendence possible?," Rubin relies on the lives of her subjects and findings from research.

What the Community Can Do

Brewster, Susan, M.S.W. *To Be an Anchor in the Storm: A Guide for Families and Friends of Abused Women.* New York: Ballantine Books, 1997.

Holloway, Susan D., Bruce Fuller, Marylee F. Rambaud, and Costanza Eggers-Pierola. *Through My Own Eyes: Single Mothers and the Cultures of Poverty.* Cambridge, Mass.: Harvard University Press, 1997. Fourteen poor women—fourteen rich lives—are seen through their stories and their struggles and triumphs understood in the light of social policy. Many of the women have been battered. The authors make recommendations for easing the lives of poor women and their children.

INTERNET RESOURCES

This first group of websites provides general information on domestic violence: what it is, how to get help, and links to just about any aspect of abuse you might look for. Several have safety plans, lists of state coalitions, links to Power and Control Wheels, and extensive lists of books and articles. Most include information for and about battered lesbians, women of color, immigrants, and other women who are challenged in special ways.

National Domestic Violence Hotline
tel. 800/799-7233 (800/799-SAFE), TTY 800/787-3224
www.ndvh.org

National Coalition Against Domestic Violence
www.ncadv.org/resources/resources.htm

National Coalition Against Domestic and Sexual Violence
www.ncdsv.org/publications_wheel.html

Minnesota Program Development
www.duluth-model.org

Violence Against Women Online Resources
www.vaw.umn.edu

Minnesota Center Against Violence and Abuse
www.mincava.umn.edu/library/articles

Asian and Pacific Islander Institute on Domestic Violence
www.apiahf.org/apidvinstitute/CriticalIssues/culture.htm
>   Not for Asians and Pacific Islanders only (see Women of Color and Immigrant Women for more information).

Liznotes
www.gate.net/~liz/liz/013.htm

Precious Heart
www.preciousheart.net/Main_Archives/Links_Folder/SUPER_List_Domestic
_Violence.htm

Getting Away

Cybergrrl
www.cybergrrl.com/fs.jhtml?/views/dv/books.shtml
>   Short bibliography of mostly survivor stories.

TECHNOLOGY SAFETY PLANNING WITH SURVIVORS

Tips to discuss if someone you know is in danger

Technology can be very helpful to victims of domestic violence, sexual violence, and stalking; however, it is important to also consider how technology might be misused.

1. Trust your instincts. If you suspect the abusive person knows too much, it is possible that your phone, computer, email, or other activities are being monitored. Abusers and stalkers can act in incredibly persistent and creative ways to maintain power and control.

2. Plan for safety. Navigating violence, abuse, and stalking is very difficult and dangerous. Advocates at the National Domestic Violence Hotline have been trained on technology issues and can discuss options and help you in your safety planning. Local hot-line advocates can also help you plan for safety.

(National DV Hotline: 800/799-7233 or TTY 800/787-3224)

3. Take precautions if you have a "techy" abuser. If computers and technology are a profession or a hobby for the abuser/stalker, trust your instincts. If you think he/she may be monitoring or tracking you, talk to a hot-line advocate or the police.

4. Use a safer computer. If anyone abusive has access to your computer, he/she might be monitoring your computer activities. Try to use a safer computer when you look for help, a new place to live, etc. It may be safest to use a computer at a public library, community center, or Internet café.

5. Create a new email account. If you suspect that anyone abusive can access your email, consider creating an additional email account on a safer computer. Do not create or check this new email from a computer your abuser could access, in case it is monitored. Use an anonymous name and account: (example: bluecat@email.com, not YourRealName@email.com). Look for free web-based email accounts, and do not provide detailed information about yourself.

6. Check your cell phone settings. If you are using a cell phone provided by the abusive person, consider turning it off when not in use. Also, many phones let you "lock" the keys so a phone won't automatically answer or call if it is bumped. When it is on, check the phone settings; if your phone has an optional location service, you may want to switch the location feature off/on via phone settings or by turning your phone on and off.

7. Change passwords and pin numbers. Some abusers use the victim's email and other accounts to impersonate and cause harm. If anyone abusive knows or could guess your passwords, change them quickly and frequently. Think about any password-protected accounts—online banking, voice mail, etc.

8. Minimize use of cordless phones or baby monitors. If you don't want others to overhear your conversations, turn baby monitors off when not in use and use a traditional corded phone for sensitive conversations.

9. Use a donated or new cell phone. When making or receiving private calls or arranging escape plans, try not to use a shared or family cell phone because cell phone billing records and phone logs might reveal your plans to an abuser. Contact your local hot-line program to learn about donation programs that provide new cell phones and/or prepaid phone cards to victims of abuse and stalking.

10. Ask about your records and data. Many court systems and government agencies are publishing records to the Internet. Ask agencies how they protect or publish your records and request that court, government, post office, and others seal or restrict access to your files to protect your safety.

11. Get a private mailbox and don't give out your real address. When asked by businesses, doctors, and others for your address, have a private mailbox address or a safer address to give them. Try to keep your true residential address out of national databases.

12. Search for your name on the Internet. Major search engines such as Google or Yahoo may have links to your contact information. Search for your name in quotation marks: "Full Name". Check phone directory pages because unlisted numbers might be listed if you have given the number to anyone.

For more safety information, call the National Domestic Violence Hotline at 800/799-SAFE (800/799-7233) or TTY 800/787-3224.

Created June 2003, revised May 2004 by Cindy Southworth, Shawndell Dawson, and Cynthia Fraser of the Safety Net Project at the National Network to End Domestic Violence, www.nnedv.org.

Safe Horizon Virtual Domestic Violence Shelter Tour and
Information Site
www.dvsheltertour.org

> This site will take you on a virtual tour of a domestic-violence shelter and answer your questions about shelters.

National Electronic Network on Violence Against Women
www.VAWnet.org

> A resource for advocates working with abused women, with information on all forms of oppression and their intersection with intimate partner violence, among other resources.

Women in Special Circumstances

Teens

Family Violence Prevention Fund Fact Sheet on Teens
http://endabuse.org/resources/facts/Teenagers.pdf

Center for Domestic Violence Prevention
www.cdvp.org/community/teens
www.teenrelationships.org

> Support line for teens and link to Teen Relationships website

Lesbians

National Violence Against Women Prevention Research Center
www.nvaw.org/index.html

> Article/fact sheet on basics of battering of lesbians includes bibliography of studies and academic articles.

National Coalition of Anti-Violence Programs
www.avp.org/ncavp.htm

> Studies and reports on battering in lesbian, gay, bisexual, and transgender communities. This is a coalition of more than 20 programs in many states.

Gay and Lesbian Domestic Violence Bibliography
www.xq.com/cuav/dvbibl.htm

> A few books and articles.

Women with Disabilities

Minnesota Center Against Violence and Abuse: Disability
www.mincava.umn.edu

> Bibliographies and other on-line resources can be sorted in several ways.

Washington State Coalition Against Domestic Violence (WSCADV)
www.wscadv.org/projects/disability_protocol.pdf

Cathy Hoog's "Model Protocol for Safety Planning for Domestic Violence Victims with Disabilities," published on-line by WSCADV, is a nineteen-page publication written for advocates and others who work with people who are disabled, but it can be a useful guide in making a safety plan for yourself. If you go to a shelter that may not be knowledgeable about how to help a person who is disabled, take a copy of the article to let the staff know what you need.

www.wscadv.org/Resources/screening_protocol.pdf

Also by Cathy Hoog, this WSCADV document explains how to screen women to enable people with disabilities to make the best use of services. The paper is designed for advocates, but if you scroll to the suggested questions that advocates or social workers should ask you, the items will probably trigger your own ideas about questions you might ask advocates about their services that relate to your disability.

Overview of Literature on Domestic Violence and Disabilities
www.wwda.org.au/keran.htm

Read Karen Howe's "Violence Against Women with Disabilities: An Overview of the Literature."

Coalition for Research on Women with Disabilities
crowd@bcm.tmc.edu

Studies and policy on many aspects of the lives of women with disabilities, including sexual and domestic abuse, and how to help. It includes one woman's personal story of domestic abuse.

Rural and Native American Women

Rural Women's Advocacy Programs
www.letswrap.com/index02.htm

Information for rural battered women, links, and personal stories of survival.

www.letswrap.com/nadvinfo

Native American women often suffer the same disadvantages as other rural women in addition to challenges specific to being Indian Americans.

The Rural Womyn Zone
www.ruralwomyn.net/domvio.html

News about rural-woman abuse and Native-American abuse; links to national rural women's task force on abuse and resources.

Indian Child Welfare Act
www.ilcadv.org/legal/special_NA.htm

Information on the Indian Child Welfare Act and other legal questions related to status as an American Indian.

Native American Women: Barriers to Living Free
www.actabuse.com/NativeAmerican.html

Short informative article on historical context, spirituality, and more.

Women of Color and Immigrant Women

Multicultural Perspectives on Domestic Violence in the U.S.
www.lib.jjay.cuny.edu/research/DomesticViolence/ii.html

Extensive bibliography of mostly academic articles and books on Asians, South Asians, Latin Americans, Native Americans, and African Americans listed by author, country, and tribe (for specific websites on Native American women, see Rural Women above under Women in Special Circumstances).

Race, Health Care, and the Law
http://academic.udayton.edu/health/01status/violence04.htm

Text in English, Spanish, and Portuguese, with links and bibliography including videotapes. It aims to improve the health status of people "who are discriminated against based on race and/or ethnicity." It's specifically concerned with African Americans, Asian Americans, Latino and Latina Americans, Native Americans, and Pacific Islanders. Links include articles such as "The Plight of Black Battered Women," on the mistreatment of battered black women by the law, and "The Effect of Racism on Domestic Violence Resources," on implications of race for women, men, the family, and the justice system.

Hot Peach Pages
www.hotpeachpages.org

Domestic-violence information in seventy languages.

Family Violence Prevention Fund: The Facts on Immigrant Women and Domestic Violence
http://endabuse.org/resources/facts/Immigrant.pdf

Fact sheet on immigrant women.

Tapestri: Immigration and Refugee Coalition Challenging Gender Based Oppression
www.tapestri.org

Works on sexual assault, domestic violence, and trafficking in various ways.

African-American Women

Black Women's Health
www.blackwomenshealth.com/domestic_violence.htm

Everything an African-American woman would want to know about her health and information about domestic violence in the lives of African-American women.

Domestic Violence among African Americans
www.dvinstitute.org

The 2002 report "Community Insights on Domestic Violence among African Americans: Conversations about Domestic Violence and Other Issues Affecting Their Community" was prepared by Oliver J. Williams, Ph.D., and Carolyn Y. Tubbs, Ph.D., in San Francisco and Oakland. This report is based on interviews with African Americans about their perceptions of domestic violence in their communities. It includes recommendations and emphasizes the social context of battering in high-stress environments.

Domestic Violence by Specific Racial/Ethnic Group
www.lib.jjay.cuny.edu/research/DomesticViolence/ii.html#african

On the Multicultural Perspectives on Domestic Violence in the U.S. website, click on African American and scroll down to find an extensive bibliography.

Latina Women

National Latina Alliance
www.dvalianza.org/BiblioD.htm

Extensive bibliography.

Domestic Violence Resources: En Español/In Spanish
http://safenetwork/net/links/inspanish.htm#TOP

California's Department of Health Services maintains the SafeNetwork website offering numerous topics and links, all in Spanish.

Arte Sana; Healing Hearts Through the Arts
www.arte-sana.com/resources.htm

Links and bibliography including videotapes. Some sources are bilingual/trilingual.

Asian Women

South Asian Women's Network
www.umiacs.umd.edu/users/sawweb/sawnet

Resources on-line for battered South Asian women in the United States, Canada, United Kingdom, and India. Bibliography on domestic and sexual violence against South Asian women in the United States and India. Links to cultural topics, domestic violence, and much more in the United States and in India.

Indian Women and Violence
www.lib.virginia.edu/area-studies/SouthAsia/Ideas/womvio.html

Lengthy bibliography on women in India.

Project Aware (Asian Women Advocating Respect and Empowerment)

www.themodernreligion.com/women/dv-ending.htm

Asian scholars have produced important work, some of it available on-line. Project Aware examines the needs of abused Asian women, the barriers that stand in the way of adequate services, and it makes recommendations about how to provide what women need.

Asian Family Violence Report
www.atask.org

The Asian family violence report is "A Study of Cambodian, Chinese, Korean, South Asian and Vietnamese Communities in Massachusetts" by Marianne Yoshioka. The purpose of the report is to "help members of Asian communities start a dialogue about family violence."

Asian and Pacific Islander Institute on Domestic Violence
www.chnm.gmu.edu/dvrp/docs/aware.pdf

Articles on numerous topics specializing in but not limited to Asian and Pacific Islanders, trafficking, domestic violence, and the intersection of cultures.

Muslims

Islamic Society of North America
www.isna.net/dv/coercion.asp

Forum on domestic violence; articles on sexual and domestic assault, safety plans, children, and much more.

Islam: The Modern Religion
www.themodernreligion.index1.com/html

Numerous articles on many aspects of Islam and domestic violence.

www.themodernreligion.com/women/dv-ending.htm

Muslim scholar Sharifa Alkhateeb's article, "Ending Domestic Violence in Muslim Families," covers the basics on the topic, illustrating her points with Muslim women's experiences.

Crescent Life
www.crescentlife.com/articles/homelessness.htm

Article on homelessness of Muslim women; link to organizations that may help.

Men Who Batter

Emerge
www.emergedv.com

This is the oldest organization running groups for men who batter, both heterosexual and gay. Some materials designed to help victim/survivors be safe are available on-line. Other useful articles on a number of topics can be ordered.

Lundy Bancroft
www.lundybacncroft.com

Bancroft's website makes available on-line his articles on custody, groups for men who batter, and other topics, as well as a bibliography.

What Communities Can Do

Institute on Domestic Violence in the African American Community
www.dvinstitute.org/newsletter/ASSEMBLwinter.pdf

This is the institute's newsletter. African Americans speak out on abuse and what could have helped victims/survivors. Institute goals are to gather information about violence in African-American communities, produce policy papers, organize conferences, and more.

Battered Immigrant, Refugee, and Indigenous Women's Interactions with Child-Protective Services
www.apiahf.org/apidvinstitute/PDF/EnosReport.pdf

The report "Learning from the Experiences of Battered Immigrant, Refugee, and Indigenous Women Involved with Child Protective Services to Inform a Dialogue among Domestic Violence Activists and Advocates" is a study of Asian and Pacific Islanders and other indigenous and immigrant groups' interactions with CPS, along with recommendations.

Homelessness

www.cohhio.org/index.shtml
www.ruralhome.org/pubs/hsganalysis
www.ruralhome.org
www.nhtf.org

Who are the homeless? That is the question most of these websites begin with. They report on the topic in different ways, collectively providing a stunning amount of information on the people who have no homes and plans for what can be done about it.

National Housing Trust Fund
www.nhtf.org

Information about the campaign to urge government to provide low-income housing.

Corporation for Supportive Housing
www.csh.org/index.cfm?fuseaction=Page.viewPage&pageID=452

This describes the Ending Long-Term Homelessness Services Initiative, a proposal for a new federal program.

http://documents.csh.org/documents/pubs/LayingANewFoundation.pdf

The Corporation for Supportive Housing's "Laying a New Foundation: Changing the Systems that Create and Sustain Supportive Housing" (2003) provides several state case studies and

CSH publications illustrating approaches to solutions; 77 pages of practical strategies, step by step.

Family Violence Prevention Fund (FVPF)
http://endabuse.org/resources/facts/Housing.pdf
http://endabuse.org/resources/facts/Welfare.pdf

Fact sheets on housing/domestic violence and on welfare/domestic violence.

Work

Besides the websites listed here, see also the notes to Chapter 29, What Communities Can Do.

Family Violence Prevention Fund (FVPF)
http://endabuse.org/newsletter/spring2004.pdf

"Founding Fathers," a newsletter article, focuses on engaging men in the struggle against violence to women through a Founding Fathers workplace campaign, among other actions.

What Unions Can Do
www.afscme.org/wrkplace/domvio.htm

Step-by-step suggestions on action by unions to aid abused workers, plus union contract agreements that incorporate safety for abused workers and accountability and support for perpetrators.

TIPS AND WHEELS

See Who This Book Is For and How to Use It for more detailed explanations of how to use the tools in this section—the safety plan, the Danger Assessment, and the Power and Control Wheels.

How to Make a Safety Plan

Planning will give you a concrete way to keep yourself as safe as possible. Put a check mark next to each action on the Safety Plan for You and Your Family list that you have already taken. Circle the dot beside each one that you can do right away. Put a date next to each of the items that will take a little time as a reminder to take care of them—within the week if possible.

How to Assess Your Danger

Using the Danger Assessment questionnaire consists of two parts. First, on a calendar that shows the entire year, put an X on the date of each violent incident you experienced from among those listed here. Then add a number that corresponds to the degree of danger or the seriousness of the injuries: Number 1, slapping, for instance, without lasting pain or injuries, through Number 5, for wounds or use of a weapon. The Xs on your calendar and the numbers after them indicating severity will indicate trends, the subject of Question 1. Next put a check mark on the line next to each question to which your answer is "yes." The more items you check, the more likely you are to be in serious danger.

Understanding the Power and Control Wheels

The Power and Control Wheels provide an at-a-glance summary of what you face every day or every week. Intimidation, isolation, insults, economic and other types of control—the "spokes" of the wheel—can wear away your confidence, your sense of independence, and your will to resist. Emotional abuse or tactics of power and control can damage the strongest of people; you may have begun to believe there is something wrong with *you*. When you feel beaten down by "spokes" of insults, intimidation, and control of your life, you risk losing sight of the extreme physical danger hovering on the "rim."

SAFETY PLAN FOR YOU AND YOUR FAMILY

Make a safety plan before you are in immediate danger.

If you are being assaulted or are threatened with assault call 911.

If you need help drafting a safety plan, call the Domestic Violence Hotline at 800/799-SAFE (800/787-3224 TTY).

Think of a safe place you can go to in an emergency and plan how you would get there:

- Practice the route, whether it is running to a neighbor's, driving your car to a police station, or getting to a safe place that is open 24 hours and where you can use a phone and be picked up by a friend.

- Talk to a neighbor about what kind of signal you can give that will serve as an alert for help, such as turning a light on and off, yelling a particular word, or banging on a wall in a specific way. Ask the neighbor to call 911 if you use the signal.

- Pack a bag with important papers (protection order, extra checks, and other documents listed in "Safety Plan for Staying or Leaving" in Chapter 25 Immigrant Women: Challenges and Solutions), money or a credit card for a cab or motel, an extra set of clothing, favorite toys for your children, and any medications. Leave the bag with a reliable friend.

- If you plan to use your car to get away keep an extra key with you at all times. Keep an extra key to your house with you as well.

- Memorize telephone numbers of the national hotline and your local shelter or hotline.

AT HOME

- Go to a room that has a way to get out.

- Go to a room that has a phone and a door that can be locked if you cannot get to a room with a way out.

• Stay out of the kitchen and bathroom (where there are things that can be used as weapons).

• Use the plan you have made to escape the house and/or to get help from a neighbor.

• Teach your children how to use your safety plan.

AT WORK

• Let a trusted coworker know about any danger you are in. Let him or her know about any phone harassment on the job.

• If it seems safe, talk to your boss about your safety.

• If you are or might be harassed by phone at work, ask for help in making your phone secure. If there are security guards, let them know that you are in danger, especially if you are being stalked. Show the guards a picture of the person to look out for.

• If you drive to and from work, ask to be escorted to your car. If the parking lot is not well lighted, ask to have it made safer.

• Vary your route each day, in case you are being followed.

• If you walk to a bus stop, try to be accompanied by coworkers.

SAFETY FOR YOUR CHILDREN

• Teach your children how and when to dial 911.

• See the "Safety Plan if You Leave" in Chapter 28 Nurturing Your Children, and Chapter 15 Protecting Yourself and the Children ("Making the Decision; Planning for the Emergency").

The best plan will incorporate most of these suggestions, but will also take into account your particular situation. An advocate at the national hotline can help you make a plan that is best for you. She can also give you a number for a local shelter or hotline where you can get similar advice from someone who knows your community.

DANGER ASSESSMENT

Jacquelyn C. Campbell, Ph.D., R.N.
Copyright, 2003

Several risk factors have been associated with increased risk of homicides (murders) of women and men in violent relationships. We cannot predict what will happen in your case, but we would like you to be aware of the danger of homicide in situations of abuse and for you to see how many of the risk factors apply to your situation.

Using the calendar, please mark the approximate dates during the past year when you were abused by your partner or ex-partner. Write on that date how bad the incident was according to the following scale:

1. Slapping, pushing; no injuries and/or lasting pain
2. Punching, kicking; bruises, cuts, and/or continuing pain
3. "Beating up"; severe contusions, burns, broken bones
4. Threat to use weapon; head injury, internal injury, permanent injury
5. Use of weapon; wounds from weapon

(If any of the descriptions for the higher number apply, use the higher number.)

Mark Yes or No for each of the following. ("He" refers to your husband, partner, ex-husband, ex-partner, or whoever is currently physically hurting you.)

_____ 1. Has the physical violence increased in severity or frequency over the past year?

_____ 2. Does he own a gun?

_____ 3. Have you left him after living together during the past year?

   3a. (If you have never lived with him, check here. _____)

_____ 4. Is he unemployed?

_____ 5. Has he ever used a weapon against you or threatened you with a lethal weapon? (If yes, was the weapon a gun? _____)

_____ 6. Does he threaten to kill you?

_____ 7. Has he avoided being arrested for domestic violence?

_____ 8. Do you have a child who is not his?

_____ 9. Has he ever forced you to have sex when you did not wish to do so?

_____ 10. Does he ever try to choke you?

_____ 11. Does he use illegal drugs? By drugs, I mean "uppers" or amphetamines, speed, angel dust, cocaine, "crack," street drugs, or mixtures.

_____ 12. Is he an alcoholic or problem drinker?

_____ 13. Does he control most or all of your daily activities? For instance: Does he tell you who you can be friends with, when you can see your family, how much money you can use, or when you can take the car? (If he tries, but you do not let him, check here. _____)

_____ 14. Is he violently and constantly jealous of you? (For instance, does he say "If I can't have you, no one can."?)

_____ 15. Have you ever been beaten by him while you were pregnant? (If you have never been pregnant by him, check here. _____)

_____ 16. Have you ever threatened or tried to commit suicide?

_____ 17. Has he ever threatened or tried to commit suicide?

_____ 18. Does he threaten to harm your children?

_____ 19. Do you believe he is capable of killing you?

_____ 20. Does he follow or spy on you, leave threatening notes or messages on your answering machine, destroy your property, or call you when you don't want him to?

_____ Total "Yes" Answers

Thank you. Please talk to your nurse, advocate, or counselor about what the Danger Assessment means in terms of your situation.

VIOLENCE — physical — sexual

COERCION AND THREATS: Making and/or carrying out threats to do something to hurt her. Threatening to leave her, commit suicide, or report her to welfare. Making her drop charges. Making her do illegal things.

INTIMIDATION: Making her afraid by using looks, actions, and gestures. Smashing things. Destroying her property. Abusing pets. Displaying weapons.

MALE PRIVILEGE: Treating her like a servant: making all the big decisions, acting like the "master of the castle," being the one to define men's and women's roles.

EMOTIONAL ABUSE: Putting her down. Making her feel bad about herself. Calling her names. Making her think she's crazy. Playing mind games. Humiliating her. Making her feel guilty.

POWER AND CONTROL

ECONOMIC ABUSE: Preventing her from getting or keeping a job. Making her ask for money. Giving her an allowance. Taking her money. Not letting her know about or have access to family income.

ISOLATION: Controlling what she does, who she sees and talks to, what she reads, and where she goes. Limiting her outside involvement. Using jealousy to justify actions.

USING CHILDREN: Making her feel guilty about the children. Using the children to relay messages. Using visitation to harass her. Threatening to take the children away.

MINIMIZING, DENYING, AND BLAMING: Making light of the abuse and not taking her concerns about it seriously. Saying the abuse didn't happen. Shifting responsibility for abusive behavior. Saying she caused it.

VIOLENCE — physical — sexual

VIOLENCIA

física

sexual

AMENAZAS:
Asustarla con amenazas de hacerle mal. Amenazarla con dejarla, con el suicido, o con denunciarla falsamente a la autoridad. Obligarla a retirar los cargos presentados contra él. Obligarla a cometer actos ilegales.

INTIMIDACION:
Provocarle miedo a través de sus mirados, acciónes, y gestos. Destrozar objetos. Intimidarla rompiendole sus cosas personales, maltratando a los animales domésticos, mostrandole armas.

ABUSO EMOCIONAL:
Hacerla sentir inferior. Hacerla sentir mal. Insultarla con nombres ofensivos. Hacerla pensar que está loca. Confudirla a propósito. Humillarla. Hacerla sentir culpable.

PRIVILEGIO MASCULINO:
Tratarla como una sirvienta. No dejarla tomar decisiones importantes. Actuar como el rey de la casa. Definir los partes del hombre y de la mujer.

PODER
Y
CONTROL

ABUSO ECONOMICO:
No dejarla trabajar o impedirle que mantenga su empleo. Obligarla a que le pida dinero. Darle una mensualidad. Quitarle el dinero. No informarle acerca de los ingresos familiares o no permitirle disponer de los ingresos.

AISLAMIENTO:
Controlar lo que hace, a quien puede ver, con quien puede hablar, lo que puede leer, y donde va. Limitarle su vida social, utilizando los celos para justificar sus actos.

MANIPULACION DE LOS NIÑO(A)S:
Hacerla sentir culpable por el comportamiento de los niño(a)s como intermediarios y mantener así el control. Usar las visitas con los niño(a)s para molestarla o amenazarla. Amenazarla con quitarle los niño(a)s.

DESVALORIZAR, NEGAR, CULPAR:
No tomar seriamente la preocupación que ella tiene sobre el abuso. Negar que hubo abuso. Hacerla sentir responsable de la conducta abusiva. Decirle que ella lo provocó.

física

sexual

VIOLENCIA

Developed by the Domestic Abuse Intervention Project, Duluth, MN; downloaded from the web site (www.ncdsv.org) of the National Center on Domestic and Sexual Violence, Austin TX.

VIOLENCE

physical   *sexual*

PEER PRESSURE:
Threatening to expose someone's weakness or spread rumors. Telling malicious lies about an individual to peer group.

ANGER/EMOTIONAL ABUSE:
Putting her/him down. Making her/him feel bad about her or himself. Name calling. Making her/him think she/he's crazy. Playing mind games. Humiliating one another. Making her/him feel guilty.

ISOLATION/EXCLUSION:
Controlling what another does, who she/he sees and talks to, what she/he reads, where she/he goes. Limiting outside involvement. Using jealousy to justify actions

USING SOCIAL STATUS:
Treating her like a servant. Making all the decisions. Acting like the "master of the castle." Being the one to define men's and women's roles.

TEEN POWER AND CONTROL

SEXUAL COERCION:
Manipulating or making threats to get sex. Getting her pregnant. Threatening to take the children away. Getting someone drunk or drugged to get sex.

INTIMIDATION:
Making someone afraid by using looks, actions, gestures. Smashing things. Destroying property. Abusing pets. Displaying weapons.

THREATS:
Making and/or carrying out threats to do something to hurt another. Threatening to leave, to commit suicide, to report her/him to the police. Making her/him drop charges. Making her/him do illegal things.

MINIMIZE/DENY/ BLAME:
Making light of the abuse and not taking concerns about it seriously. Saying the abuse didn't happen. Shifting responsibility for abusive behavior. Saying she/he caused it.

physical   *sexual*

VIOLENCE

Adapted from the Power and Control Wheel, developed by the Domestic Abuse Intervention Project, Duluth, MN; downloaded from the web site (www.ncdsv.org) of the National Center on Domestic and Sexual Violence, Austin TX.

VIOLENCIA

física

sexual

HONESTIDAD:
Aceptan su propia responsabilidad. Tratan de saber si existió violencia en su pasado.

COMPORTAMIENTO SIN AMENAZAS:
Hablan y actúan de tal forma que se pareja se siente libre de expresarse. Promoten no usar amenazas para manipular sus acciones.

INDEPENDENCIA:
Reconocen y entienden la necesidad de independencia de cada uno. Aceptan separaciones individuales como las personas nocasadas. Fomentan identidades individuales.

JUSTICIA:
Tratan de encontrar soluciones a sus conflictos de una forma mutua y satisfactoria. Aceptan cambios. Se sienten dispuestos a cumplir compromisos positivos.

IGUALIDAD PARA LOS JOVENES

CONFIANZA Y APOYO:
Se apoyan mutuamente en sus metas. Respetan sus derechos, sentimientos, amistades, actividades, y opiniones. Evitan escenas de celos, envidia, y resentimiento.

COMUNICACIÓN:
Se comunican abierta y sinceramente. Son honestos consigo mismo y con los sentimientos de su pareja.

RESPETO:
Escuchan sin juzgar. Demuestran sus apoyo mocional, firme, y comprensivo. Valoran la opinión de su pareja.

COMPARTIR RESPONSABILIDADES:
Tienen mutuo acuerdo en como distribuyen sus obligaciones. Toman decisiones juntos. Comparten sus responsabilidades de padres si tienen hijos.

física

sexual

VIOLENCIA

Adapted from the Power and Control Wheel, developed by the Domestic Abuse Intervention Project, Duluth, MN; downloaded from the web site (www.ncdsv.org) of the National Center on Domestic and Sexual Violence, Austin TX.

NONVIOLENCE

NEGOTIATION AND FAIRNESS: Seeking mutually satisfying resolutions to conflict. Accepting changes. Being willing to compromise.

NON-THREATENING BEHAVIOR: Talking and acting so that she feels safe and comfortable expressing herself and doing things.

ECONOMIC PARTNERSHIP: Making money decisions together. Making sure both partners benefit from financial arrangements.

RESPECT: Listening to her non-judgmentally. Being emotionally affirming and understanding. Valuing her opinions.

EQUALITY

SHARED RESPONSIBILITY: Mutually agreeing on a fair distribution of work. Making family decisions together.

TRUST AND SUPPORT: Supporting her goals in life. Respecting her right to her own feelings, friends, activities, and opinions.

RESPONSIBLE PARENTING: Sharing parental responsibilities. Being a positive, nonviolent role model for the children.

HONESTY AND ACCOUNTABILITY: Accepting responsibility for self. Acknowledging past use of violence. Admitting being wrong. Communicating openly and truthfully.

NONVIOLENCE

Developed by the Domestic Abuse Intervention Project, Duluth, MN; downloaded from the web site (www.ncdsv.org) of the National Center on Domestic and Sexual Violence, Austin TX.

SIN VIOLENCIA

NEGOCIACION JUSTA:
Ante un conflicto, buscar soluciones convenientes para ambo partes. Aceptar cambios. Estar dispuesto a llegar a un acuerdo.

CONDUCTA NO AMENAZANTE:
Actuar y hablar de tal forma para que ella se sienta segura y cómoda al hacer sus cosas y al expresarse.

ECONOMIA COMPARTIDA:
Tomar juntos las decisiones económicos. Asegurar que los acuerdos económicos beneficien a los dos.

RESPETO:
Escucharla sin juzgarla. Apoyarla y comprenderla. Valorar sus opiniones.

IGUALIDAD

RESPONSABILIDAD COMPARTIDA:
Llegar a un acuerdo para una justa distribución de los tareas. Tomar juntos las decisiones familiares.

CONFIANZA Y APOYO:
Apoyarla en sus proyectos. Respetarle sus sentimientos, amigo(a)s, actividades. y opiniones.

ASUMIR LA RESPONSABILIDAD PATERNA:
Compartir las responsabilidades paternas. Ser un modelo de conducta para sus hijo(a)s, actuando positivamente y sin violencia.

HONESTIDAD Y RESPONSABILIDAD:
Aceptar responsabilidad por sus acciones. Reconocer y aceptar que actuó violentamente en el pasado. Reconocer que estaba equivocado. Comunicarse abiertamente y con la verdad.

SIN VIOLENCIA

Developed by the Domestic Abuse Intervention Project, Duluth, MN; downloaded from the web site (www.ncdsv.org) of the National Center on Domestic and Sexual Violence, Austin TX.

HETEROSEXISM

PHYSICAL VIOLENCE SEXUAL

EXTERNAL HOMOPHOBIA

slapping · pulling hair · choking · grabbing · punching · kicking · biting · twisting arms · tripping · hitting · shoving · pushing

USING COERCION & THREATS: Making and/or carrying out threats to do something to harm you. Threatening to leave or commit suicide. Driving recklessly to frighten you. Threatening to "out" you. Threatening others who are important to you. Stalking.

USING INTIMIDATION: Making you afraid by using looks, gestures, actions. Abusing pets. Displaying weapons. Using looks, actions, gestures to reinforce homophobic control.

USING ECONOMIC ABUSE: Preventing you from getting or keeping a job. Making you ask for money. Interfering with work or education. Using your credit cards without permission. Not working and requiring you to support her/him. Putting assets in partner's name only.

USING EMOTIONAL ABUSE: Putting you down. Making you feel bad about yourself. Calling you names. Playing mind games. Making you feel guilty. Humiliating you. Questioning if you are a "real" lesbian. Reinforcing internalized homophobia.

USING PRIVILEGE: Treating you like a servant. Making all the big decisions. Acting like the "lord of the castle." Being the one to define each partner's place or duties in the relationship.

USING ISOLATION: Controlling what you do, who you see or talk to. Limiting your outside activities. Using jealousy to control you. Making you account for your whereabouts. Saying no one will believe you because you're lesbian or gay

USING CHILDREN: Making you feel guilty about the children. Using children to relay messages. Threatening to take the children. Threatening to tell your ex-spouse or authorities that you are lesbian or gay so they will take the children.

MINIMIZING, DENYING, & BLAMING: Making light of the abuse. Saying it didn't happen. Shifting responsibility for abusive behavior. Saying it's your fault, you deserved it. Accusing you of "mutual abuse." Saying women can't abuse women.

INTERNALIZED HOMOPHOBIA

Power and Control

victim & abuser

PHYSICAL VIOLENCE SEXUAL

HETEROSEXISM

EXTERNAL HOMOPHOBIA

Developed by Roe and Jagodinsky, insipred and adapted from the Domestic Abuse Intervention Project, Duluth, MN; downloaded from the web site (www.ncdsv.org) of the National Center on Domestic and Sexual Violence, Austin TX.

INDEX

ACKNOWLEDGMENTS

In writing the new chapters for this edition of *Getting Free* I relied on the expertise and experience of dozens of people: women who have been abused, the advocates who work with them, public policy wonks, grass-roots organizers, attorneys, and others. Some, including women who have suffered abuse themselves, gave time for interviews, others critiqued early versions of specific chapters, and still others talked with me at length about particularly knotty questions. All of the contributors were pressured to do more work than seems possible in a twenty-four-hour day or seven-day week. Yet each made time to let me pick their brains and learn from their organizations' work. My good friends encouraged me when the volume of material I collected seemed unmanageable, and the time available too short.

I have listed some informants only by first names, to preserve their safety; any errors, misjudgments, or omissions present are my oversight. The following people shared their life stories and made this new edition of *Getting Free* possible: Women have been named Anita, Anju, Asha, Beth, Janeese, Maryam, Rachel, Sachiko Tukata; children of battered women have been named Carol, Karen, Michelle, and Patsy.

Thanks also to David Adams, Sharifa Al-khateeb, Karen Bosley, Evelyn Brom, Jacquelyn Campbell, Merril Cousin, Meg Crager, Sue Davidson, Don Dutton, Rabbi Cindy Enger, Elida Espinoza, Kay Frank, Bob Free, Ed Gondolf, Ruth Goodman, Sandra Gresl, Barbara Hart, Marie Hoddevik, Leigh Hofheimer, Imam Mohamad Joban, Andy Klein, Michele Lipton, Lois Loontjens, Vicky Miellie, Farhiya Mohamed, Nancy Murphy, Andrea Parra, Lupita Patterson, Teryn Peroff, Anita Prasad, Sarah Rizvi, Ruby Romero, Liz Schott, Meira Shupack, Rita Smith, Carlin Tsai, Maria Verdin, Amber Vora, Ginny Ware, June Wiley, Louise Wisechild, Rebecca Wisotsky, and Joan Zegree.

Some agencies have generously shared specific resources. Others have indirectly informed and supported my work on these chapters. The following agencies have made the task significantly easier: Chaya; Emerge; Faith Trust Institute; Jewish Women International; King County Coalition Against Domestic Violence; Las Amigas; New Beginnings for Battered Women and Their Children; Northwest Immigrant Rights Project; Northwest Network of Bisexual, Trans, Lesbian and Gay Survivors of Abuse; Project DVORA at Jewish Family Service; Refugee Women's Alliance (Re-Wa); Washington State Coalition Against

Domestic Violence; National Coalition Against Domestic Violence; and Washington Coalition Against Domestic Violence.

I appreciate Christina Henry de Tessan's dedication in the early stages of editing this work. I am grateful for Justin Marler's willingness and patience in tracking down copyrights and his care in designing their fit into the overall product. Avalon Publishing Group's willingness to put this new edition on the fast track illustrated a welcome faith in the project and an understanding of the need for information to get to women who need it as quickly as possible. Karen Bleske's fact-checking and attention to the all-important details of editing made a significant difference in our final product. Marisa Solís's multiple skills include excellent editorial judgment, a fine sense of organization, attention to detail, and the ability to keep the project on time and on track; her patience with my periodic expansions of the chapters was remarkable.

I am not at all sure I could have written these chapters without Barbara Sjoholm at the editor's helm. She presided at the birth of the first *Getting Free* when Seal Press took a gamble on the then new topic of battering that few publishers were ready to tackle. This time Barbara again unscrambled my overload of information and time and time again set me on the right path. Patience, clarity of thought, and good cheer are only a few of her valuable editorial virtues.

ABOUT THE AUTHOR

© ISKRA JOHNSON

Ginny NiCarthy has written and cowritten many books that have helped change the lives of thousands of women, including *You Don't Have to Take It!: A Woman's Guide to Confronting Emotional Abuse at Work; You Can Be Free: An Easy-to-Read Handbook for Abused Women; The Ones Who Got Away: Women Who Left Abusive Partners;* and *Talking It Out: A Guide to Groups for Abused Women*. Ginny began her work in the movement to end violence against women in 1972 as the founder and director of Rape Relief in Seattle. She later founded and directed the Abused Women's Network. For six years she wrote a newsletter on the international movement to end violence against women, and is a member of the board of directors of Chaya, which serves South Asian women, and of the King County Coalition Against Domestic Violence, where she edits a quarterly e-newsletter. She sees her work with individual battered women as closely intertwined with other community, national, and international campaigns to stop abuse of power and to promote peace and justice.

SELECT TITLES FROM SEAL PRESS

You Can Be Free: An Easy-to-Read Handbook for Abused Women by Ginny NiCarthy, M.S.W. and Sue Davidson. $10.95, 1-878067-06-0. A simplified version of *Getting Free, You Can Be Free* is written in an accessible style for the woman in crisis. It covers a range of topics designed to help women leave abusive relationships.

To Be an Anchor in the Storm: A Guide for Families and Friends of Abused Women by Susan Brewster, M.S.S.W. $12.95, 1-58005-037-9. Here is the first practical guide for those who want to assist a friend or loved one in her struggle to escape from an abusive relationship.

Mejor Sola Que Mal Acompanada: For the Latina in an Abusive Relationship by Myrna M. Zambrano. $12.95, 0-931188-26-1. This bilingual handbook in Spanish and English speaks directly to Latin American women who are preparing to leave abusive relationships.

Chain Chain Change by Evelyn C. White. $12.95, 1-878067-60-5. This invaluable guide for black women suffering from domestic violence offers words of advice and solace to victims of abuse.

In Love and In Danger: A Teen's Guide to Breaking Free of Abusive Relationships by Barrie Levy. $10.95, 1-58005-002-6. This clear and compassionate guide speaks directly to teens about what constitutes abusive relationships—emotional, physical, and sexual—and how to break free of them.

I Will Survive: The African-American Guide to Healing From Sexual Assault and Abuse by Lori S. Robinson. $15.95, 1-58005-080-8. This valuable resource for survivors—and their families, friends, and communities—walks readers through the processes of emotional, physical, sexual, and spiritual healing, and the particular difficulties African Americans face on their journey toward recovery.

Seal Press publishes a range of self-help, health, parenting, fiction, and nonfiction books by women writers. Please visit our website at www.sealpress.com.